DOWN-TO-EARTH JUDAISM

Down-to-Earth

JUDAISM

Food, Money, Sex, and the Rest of Life

ARTHUR WASKOW

Illustrated with Papercuts by Judith Hankin

WILLIAM MORROW AND COMPANY, INC.

New York

Illustrations copyright © 1995 by Judith Hankin

The first two excerpts of poems by Samuel Ha-Nagid on page 297 are reprinted by permission of Jerome Rothenberg from Jerome Rothenberg and Harris Lenowitz, eds., *Exiled in the Word: Poems and Other Visions of the Jews from Tribal Times to the Present* (Copper Canyon Press, 1989).

The excerpt from a poem by Samuel Ha-Nagid on page 298 is reprinted by permission of Norman Roth from his article "Deal Gently with the Young Man: Love of Boys in Medieval Hebrew Poetry of Spain," *Speculum* (January 1982), pp. 20–51.

The excerpts from poems by Moses ibn Ezra on page 299 are reprinted by permission of Raymond P. Scheindlin and the Jewish Publication Society from Raymond P. Scheindlin, *Wine, Women, and Death: Medieval Poems on the Good Life* (Jewish Publication Society, 1986).

The excerpt from Marge Piercy's poem "Nishmat" on page 140 is reprinted by permission of Marge Piercy and Alfred A. Knopf from Marge Piercy, *Available Light* (Alfred A. Knopf, 1988, copyright © 1988 by Middlemarsh, Inc.). Also published in the prayerbook *Or Chadash*, published by ALEPH: Alliance for Jewish Renewal, 7318 Germantown Ave., Philadelphia, PA 19119.

The passage from an article by Laurence Milder on page 224 is reprinted by permission of Rabbi Laurence Elis Milder.

It is the policy of William Morrow and Company, Inc., and its imprints and affiliates, recognizing the importance of preserving what has been written, to print the books we publish on acid-free paper, and we exert our best efforts to that end.

Library of Congress Cataloging-in-Publication Data

Waskow, Arthur I.
    Down-to-earth Judaism : food, money, sex, and the rest of life / Arthur Waskow.
      p.   cm.
    ISBN 0–688–11840–2
    1. Judaism—Essence, genius, nature. 2. Food—Religious aspects—Judaism. 3. Money—Religious aspects—Judaism. 4. Sex—Religious aspects—Judaism. 5. Rest—Religious aspects—Judaism. I. Title.
    BM565.W27 1995
    296.7'4—dc20
                                           94–47659
                                                CIP

Printed in the United States of America

First Edition

1 2 3 4 5 6 7 8 9 10

BOOK DESIGN BY JUDITH STAGNITTO-ABBATE

For Phyllis,
with whom I learn,
again and again and again,
how to live a Judaism
that is down-to-earth

And in memory of Ira Silverman and Ann Sara Weiss,
whose lives were blessings
of hard work for renewal of the Jewish people,
love for the earth and all its children,
courage,
and *mentshlichkeit*

CONTENTS

Why This Book? A Note to Readers   I

PART ONE—FOOD

I. In the Beginning, Food   15

II. These You May Eat   26

    Is Meat the Problem? Is Separation the Goal? Time Out for a Word on Time

III. Sacred Flow and Sacred Celebration   40

    Hallowing All Food; The Temple Offerings; The Public Rhythms; Individual Offerings

IV. Oral Torah for an Oral People   52

    The Rabbinic Transformation; Holy Food, Holy Fast; A Word of Blessing; "And You Are Satisfied"

V. The Kosher Kitchen   69

    Species and Specifics; In the Blood Is the Life; Food of Life, Food of Death; Fruits of the Earth

VI. Grinding Corn, Baking Bread   83

VII. Grown-ups or Blown-ups?   89

    The Fasts of Communal Self-restraint; The Trees You Shall Not Destroy

VIII. The Holy Sparks at Every Meal   97

IX. The End of the Matter   104

X. The Dinner Table Full of Choice   107

XI. What Is "Eco-Kosher"?   117

    The Postmodern Crisis; New World, New Paths; Beyond Food; The Eco-Kosher Project; Continuing the Work

XII. See God, and Eat   130

PART TWO—MONEY

XIII. The Land Is God's   147

    The Rhythm of Release

XIV. "Silver and Gold He Shall Not Multiply"   153
    Head by Head; Harvest by Harvest; If the Poor Are Still with You

XV. The Torah of Work   166
    How to Make a Living; The Work of Torah; The Moral Calculus of Work;
    Work and Women; Employers and Employees

XVI. Just Weights, Whole Measures   177

XVII. The Flow of Abundance   182
    Borrowing Is Business; Sharing Money; The Central Treasury

XVIII. From Runaway Slaves to Socialists   194
    Five Versions of Socialism; Grass-roots Communities of Money; Jews with
    Money; Meanwhile

XIX. Images on the Coin   212
    Is This a Jewish Issue? Does the Jewish People Have a Purpose? Tzedakah
    Collectives; Shailas *and* Tshuvas; *Ultimate Cases; Plans for Change; Women,*
    Men, and Money

XX. Holiness in Money   231

PART THREE — SEX

XXI. And He Shall Rule Over You   243
    The Rule of Men

XXII. Be Fruitful and Fill Up the Earth   255
    Pruning the Fruitful Tree; The Seed of David; The Seductive Foreigner; Issues of
    Life and Death; Eden Once Again

XXIII. Making Love to Torah   269
    Earthy Woman, Spiritual Man; Lovers of the Torah; The Song: An Allegory?

XXIV. Under the *Chuppah*   280
    After the Chuppah; *The Menstrual Taboo; Be Fruitful and Multiply; The*
    Process of Divorce

XXV. Beyond the *Chuppah*   295
    The Erotic Poets; The Ascetic Philosopher; Walking the Tightrope: Erotic / Ascetic
    Mystics; The Pilegesh *Tradition; The Beginnings of Modernity*

XXVI. Toward a New Jewish Sexual Ethic   310
    The Granddaughters of Miriam and B'ruriah; Eden for Grown-ups; Before the
    Chuppah; *The New Life Cycle; The Gay Possibilities; The Meaning of*
    Marriage; Your Bed Is Torah; The Meaning of Divorce; The House of Loving
    Counsel

XXVII. The Song of My Beloved   333
    Unlocking the Door; Opening the Door; Bedecking the Chamber; Inner Space;
    And Beyond; The Public Framework

PART FOUR—REST

XXVIII. The Rest of Our Days   353
Rhythms in Cosmos and Creation; Surrounding Sacred Space in Sacred Time; Rhythms of Freedom and Justice; Forty Labors Minus One; Shabbat and Shekhinah; Shabbat and All the Earth; Shabbat for Eve and Adam
XXIX. Rest, Reflect, Renew, Return   377

GO AND STUDY, GO AND DO   383
Index   393

WHY THIS BOOK? A NOTE TO READERS

Why this book?

I can answer this question in two ways:

why from my own head, heart, and *kishkes* I chose to

write it; and what my eyes and ears have told me that other people thirsted for, hungered for. People who might choose to read a book that recognized their thirst and hunger.

When I started this book, I thought it would be an "everyday" version of my handbook and spiritual guide to the cycle of the Jewish festival year, *Seasons of Our Joy*. I thought it would simply report what Jews have done about these questions at different times over the last three thousand years, and suggest new approaches that are beginning to emerge. *Genug* already—enough. *Dayenu*—surely enough.

Fairly simple to write, I thought.

I was wrong. This has been the hardest to write of all my fifteen books. It turned out to be the one of all my books that is most inside my own skin. Even more than the book I wrote with my brother about our rages, wrestles, and reconciliations, about "becoming brothers."

Why has this book been so hard to write? It turned out that my heart and *kishkes* had played a trick on my head. Turned out that I had carefully, though unconsciously, chosen the very issues that *were* inside my own skin. So writing each chapter scraped raw my own senses of food, money, sex, and rest.

(Oh, yes, you might as well know right away: The last part of the title of this book, the part that says "the rest of life," is a gentle irony, a joke. Besides food, sex, and money, the book does not address the entire rest of life. It addresses "rest." Resting. Releasing one's self from working and doing and making, into being. If this book were really about the whole "rest of life," neither I nor any reader would ever have gotten any rest.)

This book is about all my own issues:

- How to eat in moderation and enjoyment, rather than gobbling up the world
- How to make a reasonable livelihood at work I respect, rather than feel frightened that the wolf is at the door (ready to gobble me up)

- How to find pleasure and joy in a loving sexuality, neither frenzied nor prudish
- How to rest and reflect, rather than plunge always forward into another piece of work
- How to move beyond the fear that resting is just another way of dying.

When I met these issues face-to-face, refracted through three thousand years of Jewish experience and wisdom, I had trouble.

Stuck in the writing? Off to the refrigerator. Is food an issue? More like an addiction.

Stuck in the writing? Off to the TV set—me, who all my life had no interest in watching TV!—is this a way of resting? More like an addiction to a phony version of resting. Not even restful.

The more I realized these issues were *in here,* inside me, not just in scrolls of Torah or pages of Talmud, the more possible it became to write the book.

Why "Jewish," then? If these issues *are* inside me, what is the point of down-to-earth Judaism? Why not just report my own experience and be done with it?

Because in my own experience, there is wisdom in community. Wisdom in history. Wisdom in joining a three-thousand-year-old conversation.

Not that everything in Jewish tradition is wise. Not by a long shot. But the conversation is wise. The talking, questioning, advising, debating have gone on through times of military triumph and times of unspeakable torture, times of herding sheep on a mountainside and of owning great commercial banks, living in close-knit families and leaving on ten-thousand-mile migrations, chanting sweet verses and shouting sharp-tongued revolutionary slogans.

When I reach outside my own skin to lecture and to shmooze, to listen and be sung to, to cry at a friend's funeral and cry out at a public demonstration, I meet three different sorts of thirsting people, people thirsting to join this age-old conversation.

First of all, I meet many many people, some of them Jews and some of them not, who grew up with little or no sense of anything rich and nourishing in Jewish life—perhaps even with anger at what they remember of a childish Judaism that was stuffed down their throats—but who have as adults somehow caught a glimmer, a faint echo, a fleeting fragrant whiff of something that attracts them. And have as a result said, "Maybe... maybe..."

Why? Perhaps because they have realized that sheer individualism, their own absolute freedom and disconnectedness, leaves them bereft. Without a community that shares a culture, a language, some depth and intensity, they lack both a sense of loving connection and a sense of ethical wisdom to turn to.

Secondly, I meet people who are members of some Jewish institution, who take part in some of its gatherings and celebrate some of its rituals, but who are doing this far more out of respect for the past than out of any hope that their own lives could be nourished. They are startled to hear that what tastes dry and empty may be freeze-dried food—delicious, once some living juice, some heat, a pinch of spice are added.

Finally, I meet people who have already begun to take part in the process of Jewish renewal, the movement for Jewish renewal that is much less made up of specific institutions than it is a motion, a wave of energy. Who have discovered that there can be joy in improvising the missing tales of Torah in a dance, a play, a story; intensity in a prayer that is chanted over and over, each sound and letter caressed on lip and tongue. For whom the Passover Seder takes on new excitement when they say, "In *our* generation, we ourselves seek liberation from..." and tell the stories of their own rebirth. And who want to take the next step: What would a renewed Judaism bring not only to prayer and celebration, not only to the great moments of life-change, but to the everyday moments of eating, making money, making love, resting?

For all these sorts of people, as well as for myself, this book is written. To help all of us move out of our frozen postures, out of our various addictions, out of our thirst and hunger.

ॐ

So why is this book about "down-to-earth Judaism," about the everyday issues of food and money and sex and rest?

For many of us, the very notion of a "down-to-earth Judaism" does not make sense. For many of us, Judaism is not about daily life. It is about precisely those parts of our lives that are not "daily." The days and moments that come infrequently: Passover. Hanukkah. Rosh Hashanah. Yom Kippur. Remembering the Holocaust. Feeling joy or sadness in a news flash from Israel. A birth. A wedding. Entering adolescence. Dying. Moments of special passion, ecstasy, spiritual elation, grief. Once a year, once or twice a life.

Not down-to-earth, not regular, not every day.

True, some Jews keep kosher when they eat. But most Jews don't, whether in America, in Israel, in Russia or Ukraine. And some Jews keep Friday night, or Saturday, as a Jewishly defined time of rest and quiet. But very few Jews think that how to deal with money has anything to do with being Jewish except perhaps as a wry—and probably anti-Semitic—joke. And the same with sex.

For what is "down-to-earth," for food and money and sex and rest, we turn... to what, exactly?

Mostly to this year's, this decade's conventional wisdom. Maybe a best-selling how-to book. A therapist. A doctor. Maybe our closest friends. Rarely any wisdom from more than fifty years ago—at most.

And whatever counsel we consult, we rarely imagine that it might have any wisdom for our children or our children's children. Fifty years from now? We are tongue-tied.

And yet, and yet—there are moments when we are hungry, thirsty, for an older wisdom, a deeper perspective, and a closer community. Not necessarily for the whole three-thousand-year-old package, but for a spark here, a pattern there. A single spark that we can lift from its old place and breathe into a brighter glow in some new context. Or an older, broader, overall pattern into which we can weave some newer threads.

Something we can feel grateful for having been given by our forebears, something we can feel joyful to pass on to our descendants.

Perhaps a "makeable community"—not one that comes already fully made, but as well not one that must be made from scratch. One that has a language and a set of symbols and an interesting assortment of members—even members who are tentative about the depth of their commitment.

I do not myself believe that *all* the ancient teachings are sparks of wisdom. I do not believe that we can simply replicate the paths of life that worked—if they did work—for Jews who were shepherds, farmers, nomads, warriors, milkmaids, moneylenders, spice merchants, matchmakers, butchers, peddlers, seamstresses.

There are a number of reasons for my caution. One major one is that the wisdom we have had encoded for us is the wisdom of only half the Jewish people: the men.

Women are not totally absent from the story, and there are even fragments of the story that may have been written or edited by women. But until very recently, what was chosen to be preserved, celebrated, canonized was what seemed wise to men. And the life experience of women and men during that same history was different enough that we cannot pretend that we have the full wisdom of the whole people.

Even when women appear in the story, rarely do they speak in their own voices. Even more rarely do we have a sense that the texts in which they appear were in their own hands to write or that the societies in which they lived their lives were in their own hands to shape. Women and men are described as living in different roles and life-paths—but it is men who are doing the describing. Sometimes the lives of women are blank—as if the men did not know their paths or did not care to write about them.

As we try to understand the past, it is hard to know how women themselves experienced the sacredness of food, money, sex, work, or rest. So whenever we find texts that women seem to have written or edited, or in which women's experience seems to be reported with little distortion, we should pay special attention.

As we shape the future, we can choose from a range of possible approaches:

Some of us may decide that holiness can emerge from preserving at least some different roles for women and men.

Some of us may decide that we can learn from the old differentiations how to affirm different individual life-paths, without saying that one such path is for men and another for women.

Some of us may decide that a whole new model for Jewish culture and life must be created by women and men working together to shape it, and that all the old materials from a male-dominated society must be weighed with great caution before being used in the new model.

We might easily think that the limitations on women's power to shape Jewish life had their chief effect on issues, like sexuality, that explicitly involve the relationships of women and men. But the issues may go much deeper. Just to cite one specific possibility: Much of the Jewish past that we will examine in this book is a system of strong separations and distinctions—between what can be eaten and what cannot; between how money is to be shared with other Jews and how with people from other communities; under what conditions two people can have sex together and under what conditions not; what is work and what is rest, and when to do each. Rabbi Nina Beth Cardin has suggested that in this system of tough boundaries, shaped almost entirely by men, women came to symbolize soft boundaries, thresholds, and connections. They themselves were seen as marginal, "fringe" people, anomalous. This very way of seeing them may have strengthened the "official" (male) Jewish focus on strong separations.

So if today women are moving away from the edges toward sharing the center of Jewish life, Cardin asks, may the emphasis on distinctions and separations be softened? May the crossing of thresholds become a cherished aspect of a new Judaism in which categories remain important and the connecting of categories becomes important?

Whatever the future, we can see how this speculation gives a new framework to our understanding of the past.

Of course, the marginality of women is not the only reason to be cautious about what we can learn from age-old texts and an age-old culture. In one epoch of our history, most of us were shepherds or farmers in a world where most human beings were shepherds or farmers. Now we live so differently that we must use great care in drawing on the wisdom of those past ages.

Yet I believe that we have much to learn from life-paths that go back before the Modern Age—*precisely because* they go back before the modern era.

In a generation when we have once again discovered that the earth must be treated as shepherds and farmers at their wisest treated her, it makes sense to reexamine the ancient wisdom of Israelite shepherds and farmers. We can learn from their life-paths just as we have begun to learn from those of the indigenous peoples of the Americas, Asia, and Africa:

Jewish life-paths that treated the earth not as a dead object to be used and thrown away, but as a living organism of which human beings were a part

Jewish life-paths that looked many generations into the past and future in order to walk with care into the present

Jewish life-paths that infused what was down-to-earth and day-to-day with a sense of sacredness and holiness.

Though I think we have much to learn from the premodern past, I do not mean to throw out the Modern Age. I agree with those who date Modernity from 1492, from the moment when the European world began with compass and gunpowder to subjugate the continents that came to be called the Americas, the moment when the human race began an unchecked, unreflective scramble to abolish Mystery and control every aspect of its own life and all life upon the planet. Perhaps the Modern Age, defined that way, came to an end in 1945 with Auschwitz and Hiroshima. Or perhaps the human race is still deciding. But even if we think Modernity was problematic, even if we think it was limited in time and in the way it reflected only one aspect of humanness, then we may need to learn from it all the more.

We have much to learn from the Modern Age of how Jews adapted Jewish pathways in order to absorb modern science, democracy, individual growth and freedom, the teachings of women, the presence and worth of other peoples.

Down-to-Earth Judaism is rooted in the sense that the Jewish people has, generation after generation, epoch after epoch, drawn on its own past in order to reshape the way it lived, and that we are in the midst of doing this today. I intend this book to be a resource in that process, rather than a set of prescriptions: what could be done, not what must be done.

For some of us, this may seem a natural extension of what we have already been doing with our lives: drawing on Jewish wisdom to shape our daily life-paths. For even during the upheavals of Modernity, some Jews kept finding in Judaism a path of joyful songs and haunting melodies, supportive neighborhoods and committed teachers, a noble history pointing toward a noble future.

Yet some Jews who grew up in these satisfying pathways have been profoundly shaken by trying to walk them in a world that is shaking underfoot: where women and men are equal, the ghetto walls are gone, and even great national boundaries are porous to poisonous air and water. Many of these people want to know whether the old surface patterns of Jewish life hint at deeper veins of precious metal, deeper truths from which we can learn new paths of life. In this book I explore these deeper possibilities.

For other Jews, Judaism has not been a joyful path, and the very effort to explore it may call up nightmares and demons from earlier generations of our families, nightmares from which we or our parents struggled to break free.

Nightmares perhaps of the limited roles assigned to Jewish women, or the distinctions concerning kosher food that to some of us seemed obsessive or hypocritical, or the whispered taboo on menstruation, or the conventional horror and contempt for homosexuals, or the habit that the little blue *pushke* for the Jewish National Fund was the *only* way of showing that we cared for others who were trying to make a better world.

And some Jews are gripped by the nightmare of Jewish claustrophobia—the fear that if we got "too Jewish" we might lock ourselves into our own grandparents' (or great-grandparents') ghetto.

Perhaps most basic of all, while some of us feel grateful for the sense of familiarity and community that may flow from Jewish law and custom, others of us fear being "commanded" by Jewish demands, constricted by these restrictions. For some of us may sense these commands as coming not from some ultimately benign and wise Reality, or from the necessities of communal life and the discoveries of countless generations, but instead from our immediate forebears—parents and grandparents from a narrow world who were unhelpful guides to the world we sought to live in. Unhelpful when they tried to guide us and infuriating when they tried to command us.

Indeed, for many of us the only "down-to-earth Judaism" we knew was restrictive, divisive, irrational, oppressive.

For those who bear the heavy burden of such nightmares and demons, these memories do have and should have real effects on what they make out of being Jewish in their own lives.

Yet perhaps some of us have let these nightmares weigh *too* heavily upon us—assuming that the rigid down-to-earth Judaism we inherited was the only form in which it could exist.

This book is *not* grounded in the notion that in order to be Jewish and draw on Jewish wisdom, we must cut ourselves off from modern society and culture.

It is grounded instead in the notion that all of us—those who grew up loving the tradition, those who grew up hating it, and those who grew up outside it or barely influenced by it—can now, as the heirs of Modernity, look again at the experience and the experiments of all the Jewish generations, to see what might be possible and usable.

We might do this for the sake of something that we more than half believe: that the personal is political, the personal is communal, the personal is cultural, the personal is spiritual—and that all of these are Jewish.

We may even find that some of that Jewish wisdom may be of use to other communities. Not because the Jews are a "chosen people," but because they have knocked about the planet for a long time, searched deeply into what the good life is, wrestled and danced in times of happiness and terror.

ॐ

Some guides to the use of this book:

First of all, *Down-to-Earth Judaism* will be easier to follow if readers clearly understand the historical periods through which I have shaped its pattern: I have treated Jewish history as if it could be divided into three eras: the Biblical, the Rabbinic, and the "whole-earth, whole-person, whole-people Judaism" that we are just entering.

Some people would add medieval and modern Judaism as separate periods. Why don't I do this?

Because I am defining the periods according to the patterns by which the Jewish people lived a "down-to-earth" everyday life, in each period, according to a different basic pattern. Between these historical periods have come times of profound crisis—a breakdown of the old pattern, and the renewal of Jewish life in a different basic pattern. During those crises the Jewish people has remade Judaism and Jewish culture:

- The first such crisis gave birth to what we call Biblical Israel, after the breakdown of a pre-Biblical Middle Eastern society that we can now only dimly imagine.
- In the Biblical period—the first era in which we discern what we now call the "Jewish people"—the Jews lived mostly in one land, and their culture and religion focused on the earth, the body, land. We might call this "body-Judaism."
- The philosophical and military triumph of Hellenism ended this period. After centuries of crisis, the Jewish people responded by creating a second great culture—Rabbinic Judaism. That culture lived in dispersed communities and focused on words and learning, both to hold together over great distances and to use honorably the newly learned powers that Hellenistic science, philosophy, and politics had taught the human race. The Rabbinic culture that was based on words and wide dispersion, and its new patterns of Jewish daily life, changed relatively little during the Middle Ages—certainly not as profoundly as it changed from the Biblical to the Rabbinic pattern. We might call this the era of "word-Judaism."
- Since then, the philosophical and military triumphs of Modernity, especially during the past two centuries, have dissolved much of the inner coherence of Rabbinic Judaism. Worse yet, the Holocaust destroyed its most intense, nu-

merous, and vital communities—just as Hellenism and the Roman conquest had done to the world of Biblical Judaism. From that perspective, "modern Judaism" is more a label for a time of crisis—breakdown and renewal—than a name for a new form of Jewish life and culture.

The turmoil of breakdown and the disappearance of a coherent pattern for Jewish daily life is reasonably clear. But what about renewal? If we are moving toward the creation of a third great Jewish culture, on what terms might it be built?

Today, Jews are *both* in touch with their bodies and adept with words. The whole people—women as well as men, those deeply learned in Jewish lore and those whose learning is in other arenas of life—are in a position to guide their collective future. Jews live *both* concentrated in the Land of Israel and scattered around the globe. And in *both* arenas, Jewish communities have much more power to shape human history than has been true for millennia.

Perhaps some focus will emerge in this new era of Jewish peoplehood that includes Biblical "body" and Rabbinic "words," synthesizes them, and goes beyond them. It is very likely that just as Rabbinic Judaism reinterpreted Biblical tradition rather than ignoring it, so the Jews of today will keep struggling to reinterpret both Biblical and Rabbinic tradition rather than ignoring them. Evidence is growing that this reinterpretation will be as profound as was the Rabbinic reinterpretation, that it will embody a transformation rather than a mere reform.

But that is just my own view. Others believe that the changes will ultimately turn out to be as important as those of the Middle Ages, but no more so, that we will see the recovery of a renewed Rabbinic culture. It will take centuries to understand fully and to name accurately what we are doing. In the meantime, this book is aimed not only at understanding the Jewish past better but also at making it possible for Jews to choose more creatively and consciously from the past to shape a down-to-earth Judaism that works today—some of it old, some of it new.

Down-to-Earth Judaism centers on questions about our own lives. Even the questions I found myself asking about food, money, sex, and rest in the Jewish past came very clearly from my own efforts to live in the Jewish present and future. So I could not fence off "that's the way it used to be" and "here are some ways it might become" from each other.

You will find that in most of these chapters, whether they are about a pattern of Biblical life or the Middle Ages, about an emerging practice of some communities in this very decade or even an imaginative picture of what might come to be, our explorations of today and yesterday and tomorrow will be intertwined. At many points I explicitly raise questions about what new approaches might arise from listening to this or that ancient practice. Sometimes, as in a chapter on our present generation, I suggest possible answers to these questions. Sometimes I leave the questions open, unanswered, soaking into our minds and hearts to affect how we think and feel as much perhaps as what we do.

Although the book is divided into four sections, the four arenas cannot be utterly separated from each other. Issues of food and money overlap, issues of food and sex intertwine, and issues of "rest" pervade the other areas.

Through most of Jewish history, food, money, and even most aspects of sex have been about work—production and reproduction. Today, the work of filling up the earth with human beings and the work of subduing the earth to human will and intelligence have been accomplished—and despite this are relentlessly continuing! So we need to think in new ways about "rest." We need to examine whether we should be bringing the category of rest *within* the categories of food, money, and sex. So, as you read, you can expect to find that some themes will reappear in the different arenas.

If you want to focus on just one area, you may find that it stands well by itself. If you want to explore what "the next Judaism" might look like in all four areas, you can read the last two chapters in each of the four sections. (In Part IV, Rest, that means both chapters in the section.)

The questions that moved and haunted other generations may not be the questions that arise for us. I have tried to be clear about what is theirs and what is ours, always with the sense that this book is not for antiquarians with an academic curiosity about the past, but for people wrestling to find a way in the forest of our lives.

Wrestling—and conversing. Throughout *Down-to-Earth Judaism*, I write as if I am speaking—with you. That is because I am. For me, the best Jewish learning has come through overhearing ancient conversations (like those of the ancient Rabbis, for example) and through taking part in the conversations of today. For me, that has become the most natural way to write as well as to speak.

My conversations have involved many people and many texts, ancient and contemporary. Close to the end of *Down-to-Earth Judaism* is a section titled "Go and Study, Go and Do." In it I name and cite the people and writings with whom and with which I have been conversing. And I invite you to join this conversation as well, not merely to sit silent, listening. At the very end of the book is a write-back page to make that easier to do. Please join with me, with us.

"*Chadesh yamenu k'kedem*," says a verse written in a moment of despair, after the destruction of the Temple and the death march of exiles to Babylonia.

"Make our days new, as they were in the beginning."

Not—"Give us back the good old days."

Rather—"Make our own days new and full of life, as they were long ago."

❧

There is an ancient blessing, traditionally said whenever Jews came together to learn Torah, that I would like to say now, in a renewed form:

Blessed are You, Breath of all life, Who each day breathes into us a new life-breath and teaches us to renew our lives by soaking ourselves in the living waters of the Torah.

—*ARTHUR WASKOW*
23 Nisan, Maimouna 5755
April 23, 1995

Part One

FOOD

I. IN THE BEGINNING, FOOD

What can Jewish culture teach us about how and what to eat?

Just to raise the question is to invite a din of jokes: What else do Jews do but eat? What we say is that

—we are obsessed by the trivia of *kashrut*, the code of kosher food; or

—we are consumed with passion for the unkosher delights of Chinese food; and

—in any case we think food the most important element in a party, a business meeting, a political rally, or a religious celebration.

I remember my conversation with a psychotherapist. Somehow the question of food had arisen in our session. I turned it aside, raised something else.

"Wait," he said, "food is an important issue for you."

"I can't swallow that!" said I.

He didn't answer. I glanced and saw his face: eyes grown big, a grin barely able to hold in a burst of laughter.

For a full minute we sat silent. I was faintly annoyed, mightily puzzled.

Finally I chewed my own words over again. I gasped. *Swallow?*

And so for the first time, I came to believe in the existence of the unconscious and the power of food.

Today, what are the questions that stir in my own *kishkes*, my own guts?

- Why am I eating what the doctors say is "too much"? How can I stop?
- Some of my friends eat only kosher food, and some do not. In both groups, and in my own heart, the questions arise: Is there any good reason to keep kosher? Is it enough that this is an ancient pattern of Jewish eating? Is there any pattern behind the pattern—any reasoning beneath the whole set of rules of kosher food?
- Many of my friends and a couple of my children have stopped eating meat. Should I become a vegetarian? Or eat less meat?
- Should I eat chickens that have been raised in factory farms, practically unable

to move, fed hormones to speed their growth? What about tomatoes grown with pesticides? What about vegetables that come in elaborate packages? When these questions arise, I often feel like saying, "This stuff may be kosher, but it sure ain't *eco*-kosher." Should I pay attention to this gut reaction—or just write it off as a Jewish wisecrack?

- Sometimes I treat a meal like a fast stop at the gas station; sometimes I remember to make it a time of celebration, friendship, enjoyment, delicious delight. I usually feel better the second way. Is there a way to do more of that?

- Come to think of it, the gas-station analogy works in the other direction, too. What about the way I "eat" gasoline, or newsprint, or electricity? Is there a "kosher" or an "unkosher" way to consume these products that come from the earth but are not literally food? And here comes this odd word "*eco*-kosher" back again. *Now* do I want to pay attention?

- Every once in a while, I look at the food I'm eating and my mouth drops open: how amazing—that sun, rain, soil, and many many different people have conspired to grow this food, bring it all this way, cook it, eat it! When I have this shiver of awe, I feel refreshed and joyful. How can I have it more often?

- And—in some ways the most puzzling question of all—why are these questions bothering me? In generations past, so I understand, the Jewish community had a fairly clear and simple path to walk when it came to food. If I had grown up then, eating would have been simple. What did we lose and what did we gain that made these questions so complex, or at least so ridden with anxiety for me?

I ask myself: In almost four thousand years of Jewish eating, has any wisdom emerged from our people that I can still draw on today to help me with these questions? Maybe not "answers" but hints, pointers, seeds of possibility that I can fruitfully grow?

Shall I look at the earliest records of our thinking? It actually comes from a culture of shepherds and farmers that lived close to the land, grew its own food. Perhaps there I can find some interesting ideas about food and eating.

I look back at the Bible, beginning with the Five Books of Moses, those books of myth, history, warning, law, architecture, poetry, even one novelette, and a number of short stories, all stewed together in a pot of many flavors. I look with "food" on my brain, I search with a hungry appetite.

I discover that for thousands of years the Jewish people has believed that eating matters. *Really* matters: to history, society, the earth, the Cosmos—even God.

This belief begins at the beginning. The first story about food I find early in the Book of Genesis, in a tale about the very beginning of human history. What I find is no mere pleasant tale, no casual fable, but instead a story that echoes all the crucial issues of my own life. For when the ancient People Israel gathered in its tents to tell the story of Creation, the storytellers chanted that human history itself began when human beings violated a special Divine command of what to eat.

God said there was one fruit in Eden that should not be eaten. Was not what later generations would call "kosher." Eve and Adam ate it anyway—and thereby shattered the primordial Garden of Delight.

What followed? Conflict and struggle in two crucial spheres of life. The two in which fruitfulness continues.

In one of these spheres, there will be a struggle between Adam and the earth, which in Hebrew is called *adamah*. Since the word *Adam* means "earthling," the being shaped from earth, this moment testified to the deep experience that somehow human beings who are earthy, part of the earth herself, also suffer alienation from her. Alienation between earthlings and the earth, human beings and the humus.

In pain and sweat the humans will toil to bring forth food, and in hostility the humus will bring forth thorns and thistles.

Even with the animals there will be tension. In the original Garden of Delight, the human beings had one animal as friend and teacher—the snake. But even this friend becomes an enemy in the aftermath of Eden. And by the end of the Flood, there is fear between all animals and humankind. Wound the earth, and she will war against you.

The fruitful earth has become a sphere of conflict, and so has the fruitfulness of human beings. The shattering of Eden shatters the flowing relationships of women and men into rigid gender roles, subjugates women, and tangles sexuality and childbirth into painful, not simply joyful, aspects of life.

As I read this story, I find myself wearing an ironic smile. Many cultures, I realize, have a tale of the first rebellion, the first painful crossover into making painful history. In some mythic tales it is an act of murder. Or sex. Or stealing fire. Or creating knowledge. Now, of all possibilities, what did Jewish culture choose as the symbol for beginning history, making trouble?

Eating.

Did the Eden myth focus our anxiety about the world on food? Or did the reality of our everyday lives give shape to the myth? In a land where rain came and went and sometimes did not come at all, where there was no great river to irrigate the soil, where drought and famine afflicted every generation, perhaps every generation had a "depression mentality": Eat your food! Next year the table may be bare!

What is more, as you eat, be fully conscious how precarious is your relationship with the God Who brings forth all food from the earth! How precarious is your relationship with the earth!

For in the story is encoded the warning that if we make trouble for God, we will soon have trouble with the earth.

At the heart of this story is the assertion that since eating actually is a crucial connection between human beings and the earth, a flaw in the eating process— consuming what comes from the earth in some crucially incorrect way—would indeed lead to trouble between earth and earthling.

What was crucially incorrect about eating from the Tree? Was it simply dis- obedience, as most of us have been taught? Or was the choice of the Tree of separation, of good versus evil, itself a separation from the flow of life, the weave of life—and therefore brought on a separation from the earth?

And not only from the earth. For as I read the story, searching for its teachings about food, I cannot help but notice that it tells us also that men and women now are separated from each other. Now they are ashamed to see each other, and must wear clothing. Now the man will rule over the woman. From this flaw in eating, says the story, will come a break in the flow of their relationships.

Why? I wonder. Is the Eden story hinting that women have a special rela- tionship to food? It is Eve, Chava, "mother of all life," who both prepares and eats the fruit of the forbidden Tree, and then hands it to her husband. Is this an echo of the primordial sense that women provide children with their first food, the milk from their breasts, and that whatever men do in order to feed people is secondary?

Or does this legend echo the daily habits of Israelite society? Was it women who prepared the food?

Intrigued by these questions, I look at other Bible stories about cooking and providing food. They do not seem to single out women as cooks. For example:

- After Eden, the Bible's first description of a meal is in the story in which Melchitzedek, priest of God Most High, himself brings out bread and wine to greet and bless Abraham (Gen. 14:18).
- Later, three travelers come to the tent of Abraham and Sarah (Gen. 18). Even before these messengers announce that a child will be born, Abraham asks Sarah to bake cakes, and has a servant boy prepare a calf. Then Abraham serves the meal.
- When the child Isaac grew to the age of weaning, Abraham "held a great feast" on the day he was weaned (Gen. 21:8). We might note that this feast is the second life-cycle celebration in the history of the Jewish people. First came circumcision, focused on sexuality and procreation; then, as the first

the Bible says that the very reason for letting the land rest is "so that the needy of your people may eat." The food would come both from what had been grown and stored before the seventh year, and from what the land grew freely in the seventh year of its own unforced accord. A kind of manna.

Thus both land and people could savor in the present just a taste of the paradise of past and future—Eden when earth and earthling were at peace, and the Messianic Age, when earth and earthling would no longer be at war.

As I read these passages on the seventh year, I realize that this rhythm of work and rest was a way for the ancient Israelites to describe the exchange between humans and the land as flowing in two directions. If one assumes that in Eden, a human mistake was made in taking from the earth and that this brought about a flaw in the pattern of the earth's giving, then human beings needed consciously to shape *how they took from the earth.* How we eat from the earth affects how the earth feeds us.

From our standpoint, what comes from earth to earthling is an "inflow." It is shaped by specific rules of how to treat food. The "outflow" from earthling to earth is shaped by specific rules of how to treat the land in which that food grows.

We may ask why the Israelites focused so intently upon food as central to all questions of creation and procreation. Perhaps one answer is that in the ancient Land of Israel, this "land of milk and honey," the food supply was precarious. There are tales of famines that drove even shepherds Abraham and Sarah, Isaac and Rebekah, Jacob's whole clan into exile; famines that drove farmers like Naomi and her family into exile; droughts so long that a whole section of the Talmud is devoted to ways of fasting and praying for rain. Perhaps this precarious food supply dependent on precarious rain—so different from the regular flow of the Nile, the regular irrigation of Babylonia—was what drove the Israelites to put food at the heart of their sense of the sacred, and to believe that the land would be fruitful only if they chose right ways of eating.

In several stories from the period of Israelite kingship (when most scholars think that the crucial elements of the culture were shaped), intense fear of famine or hunger was connected not only with the danger of a natural drought but also with warfare between the Israelites and their neighbors.

One peculiar and powerful story, for example, describes a successful battle led by King Saul against the Philistines (I Sam. 14). Saul, presumably to screw tight the courage of the Israelite army, ordered and vowed that no one would eat anything at all until nightfall and victory. The soldiers obeyed, though they were famished and exhausted. But as the tide of battle shifted, Saul's son Jonathan, who had not heard his father's vow, grew giddy from hunger. He dipped his staff into honey from wild bees, sucked on the honey, and "his eyes grew bright again."

Saul's officers explained the vow to Jonathan, who said his father was mistaken and advised the army to ignore the order. So they slaughtered the enemy's flocks and ate well—even, in their intense hunger, consuming the blood instead of pouring it out on the earth.

Meanwhile, Saul tried to consult a Divine oracle to see how next to fight the battle. But the oracle would not answer. Suspecting that someone had broken his vow, Saul lined up the entire army on one side and himself and Jonathan on the other, and asked the oracle to discern the sinner. It pointed to the royal family. Then Saul asked the oracle to discern whether he or Jonathan had sinned. When the oracle pointed out Jonathan, he ordered his son executed. But the people resisted and rescued Jonathan.

This story may seem a mere idiosyncrasy: one day, one battle, one king's command. But it is not so easily dismissed. The king is ready to execute his own son and heir in order to punish his people for eating. The image is something like national anorexia—followed by national bulimia. Control of the kingdom, victory in battle, the rivalry of father and son, a threat of death, a curse of defeat, God's Own will and pleasure, all knotted up in whether or not to eat. Fasting out of control, eating out of control.

Indeed, it strikes me that this very moment could have deeply influenced memories of the journey from Egypt into the Wilderness. It could have given bite and stomach to the story (Num. II) in which the famished people demand meat and God sends them meat on which they gorge themselves. This meat comes so entwined with a Divine curse that as the people stuff their mouths (so full that the meat comes out of their noses), a pestilence begins to fell them by the thousands.

Or take yet another story of the kingdom period (II Kings 6, 7). More than a century later, the army of Aram, north of Israel, is besieging the Israelites of Samaria. So stringent is the siege that the Israelites are reduced to cannibalism:

> The king was passing by when a woman cried out to him, "Help, my lord, O king! This woman said to me, 'Give your son, so that we eat him today, and we will eat my son tomorrow.' So we boiled my son, and ate him; and today she has hidden her son.' "

The king is struck with despair so deep that he threatens to kill the Prophet Elisha for failing to invoke God's help to break the siege. Elisha prophesies that in just twenty-four hours, food will be abundant and cheap throughout the city. The king's lieutenant commander thinks this is so ridiculous that he calls out, "Even if God made windows in Heaven, this could not happen!"

Yet it does happen. During the night a weird panic strikes the Aramean army. It flees in confusion, leaving behind all its gear and all its provisions. By the next noon, food was plentiful and cheap throughout Samaria.

Could this dreadful ancient experience of food deprivation still be affecting us— me—today? Could the knowledge that a year of drought or an invading army or a capricious king might cause starvation have bitten so deep into the Israelite mind that even today, my own mind cries out for my belly to be fed when I am not really hungry? Could this terror have made food a central element of legend, and made distinctions about food a central element of daily practice?

Something to note about these stories: In both of them, the family context in which the eating occurred was twisted profoundly out of shape. Parents who had fed their children when they were young were ready to kill them over a matter of food, or even to eat them. (The horrifying image of mothers eating their children in time of famine recurs in the Bible, in Deuteronomy 28: 53–57, and Lamentations 2:20.)

The fear of hunger so deep, the taste of food so delicious: One of the greatest of all prophetic visions puts this tension into one supernal moment. Ezekiel, in Babylonian exile after the first destruction of the Temple, has just been over- whelmed by an uncanny visitation, a whirling, wheeling, four-headed Being—lion, eagle, ox, and human—full of flashing fire, culminating in a Rainbow that seemed like the likeness of the brightness of the radiance of God.

And from this vision came a Voice and a Hand, with it a Scroll. Written on the Scroll were words of lamentation, moaning, and woe.

And the Voice said: "Eat what you find. Eat this Scroll. Then go, speak to the House of Israel."

So Ezekiel opened his mouth, and ate, and filled his belly and his guts with the Scroll—and "it was as sweet as honey in my mouth" (Ezek. 3).

To eat the very words of God! and find these words of woe as sweet as honey!

It was then that a great wind lifted Ezekiel, and in the rushing wind he heard the great rushing shout of the words that would later become the great counterpoint to Isaiah's vision of God's holiness within the Temple itself:

Baruch k'vod YHWH mimkomo.
Blessed be the radiance of YHWH [radiating] forth from Its place.

The words breathed forth from God's mouth enter not our ears but our mouths, not straight to our brains but down our gullets to our guts, our streams of blood.

In exile, far from the shattered Temple, God's words of warning reach out from the secret place of holiness into the moving, whirling public sphere. They must literally be eaten, must become part of the people's very bone and belly. Part of a place that to others is hidden, but to each person is intimate and known.

How sweet to learn that even far from home, God's words can fill our bellies, not our minds alone. How sweet even are words of woe and warning, where we feared there might be utter silence.

Behind the jokes we tell today there is a delicious reality of long ago: Food was both so important and so problematic to the ancient Israelites that they gave it a central place in their culture—gave it publicly, clearly, consciously rather than covered and uncovered by jokes. They created what might even be called a sacred history of food.

Perhaps this is itself a teaching—that we do not need to be embarrassed to say that food is central, sacred. We have covered and uncovered this feeling with jokes because modern Jews are embarrassed to feel and speak openly about it in the midst of another culture that treats food as less central, less sacred. A culture that constantly advertises that the faster we eat, in places least connected with our homes, the better.

We Jews might ask ourselves a more precise question: If it is indeed a teaching of our culture that food is sacred and central, how can we give some teeth to that idea?

- What mood, what emotional orientation, do I want to have while I eat?
- Do I want to eat alone, or as part of a lonely crowd? Or do I want to make sure that my family and my community are truly my "companions"—those who share my bread—and to shape the kind of eating that strengthens the loving bonds of intimate friendship?
- Do I want to be able to track how food comes from the earth to my mouth, and what my body is doing with the food after it leaves my mouth?
- Do I want to share my food with those who are hungrier than I am? Do I want to ask those whose kitchens are fuller than mine to share their food with me?

How did the ancient Israelites go beyond their sacred history of food to decide how to govern eating in the everyday world?

—One major approach they took to hallowing food was to set aside some as sacred, others as forbidden.

—Another process for hallowing food was to take the products of the land to a single place, the Temple in Jerusalem, there to bring God near to them by consecrating grain and meat and bread and wine and olive oil and water.

Let us look more deeply into these approaches and explore how and why the Israelites might have made these decisions, in the hope that we can learn how better to shape our own eating.

When I ask myself what the actual content of my diet should be, I realize that all the foods of the earth stretch out before me. Summer fruits in the dead of winter; ocean fish a thousand miles from salt water; grains once isolated in the Andes; spices that could only grace an emperor's banquet table because they had to be carried by camel, horse, and runner ten thousand miles from India—all these I can pick up on a casual visit to the supermarket.

Not so for the ancient Israelites. Their technology and economics restricted their diet to the range of foods indigenous to the Land of Israel, the eastern Mediterranean, and the Near and Middle East. And then Israelite tradition chose to narrow the diet even further.

This self-restriction is an ongoing part of my life today. All around me, people are restricting their diets within a spectrum far smaller than what the supermarket carries. Some are following their doctors' advice to avoid foods high in fat or cholesterol. Some are choosing to eat only what is labeled "kosher" by some parts of the Jewish community. Some have decided to be vegetarians, or to eat nothing at all that comes from animals—not even eggs or milk. Some will not eat beef, or veal, but will eat fish. Some make choices on the basis of what foods are grown "organically"—that is, without the use of manufactured pesticides or fertilizers. Some refuse to eat foods that have been grown under conditions where the workers were ill treated or ill paid, or oppressed by reason of gender, race, or native tongue. Some avoid foods that have been packaged in such a way as to leave indigestible wastes to be poured back upon the earth after the food itself is eaten.

Such a myriad of values by which to judge! And so I ask myself, What wisdom may I learn from Jewish practice?

I search for the value choices involved in what the Israelites thought was proper to eat. What specific values these were are not always clear to modern eyes—at least to mine—and I find myself mulling over the list of their permitted foods, in order to infer what was in their minds from what was in their mouths. But the clearest fact is that they made decisions. Not every available food was to be eaten. In that sense, the myriad different choices we make all have some relationship—

perhaps even some ultimate origin?—in the assertion of the Israelites that choosing our food matters.

What were their choices? First of all, there is some relationship between the food that the Israelites are growing, and the foods they urge themselves to eat. Their tradition remembered that they began as seminomadic herders of sheep and goats (and, less often, of cattle). They never describe themselves as pig farmers. Later they became growers of barley, wheat, beans and lentils, olives, grapes, dates, and other fruits and nuts. According to the tradition, it was rare for Israelites to be hunters or fishers.

Indeed, the tradition went out of its way to describe hunting as "Other." Hunting was the primary path taken by two figures who had a close mythic connection to the Israelite community. Each had been a member of the primal Israelite family, but left and became the progenitor of a nearby hostile people. These individuals were Ishmael and Esau, described by the Biblical texts as archers and hunters.

They were members of the Abrahamic clan, but members on their way out of the family. Ishmael was brother to Isaac, Esau to Jacob—brothers in conflict and partial reconciliation. Isaac and Jacob were seen as bearing the origins and continuity of the Israelite community. The Biblical literature and, later, the Rabbis saw Ishmael and Esau not only as figures of the dim past, but as archetypes of tensions between the Jewish people and its neighbors.

For the Jewish self-image, it was important that the Israelite path dealt with domesticated animals, not wild ones. Mutton, milk, and cheese came from these animals. The other staples of the Israelite diet were bread (made from barley and wheat), beans and lentils, and wine. Fish and poultry were rarely mentioned. Green and orange vegetables were rarely used.

The pastoral tradition was so strong that sheep and goats became almost a totem for the Israelites, and certainly a metaphor for Israelite society, as in "The Lord is my shepherd." Not only foods but sacred objects came from sheep and goats—the parchment used for the scrolls of sacred literature; the ram's horn, or *shofar*, used to blow the alarm and to mark sacred time; the leather of the sacred boxes (*t'fillin*) worn on head and hand; the wool of four-cornered garments and their fringes (*tzitzit*).

Metaphors from growing grapes were also frequently used to describe Israelite society. One might say that the people saw themselves as God's ruminating flock, God's well-pruned vineyard.

These choices were not left merely to individual decisions within cultural probabilities. There were rules of what was permissible to eat:

- Among mammals, only those that both chewed the cud and had split hooves were permitted; among fish and other water creatures, only those with fins and scales; among birds, only those specifically enumerated (which included no birds of prey); among insects, only several species of locusts or grasshoppers. No reptiles or amphibians were permitted.

• With regard to the permitted mammals, no blood could be eaten, and no limb cut from a living animal. No animal could be eaten that died from its own sickness, from old age, or from being attacked by another animal. A kid was not to be boiled in the milk of its mother. Although the written Torah and later Biblical books do not specify means of slaughtering, such rules of slaughter had arisen, at the latest, by late in the Second Temple period.

• All species of plants and all their parts and products—fruits, grains, roots, stalks, leaves, beans, seeds, flour, juice, wine, oil, bread—were permitted. For one week each year—the week of Pesach—only unleavened bread was permissible to eat.

What are the origins and meaning of these rules?

Which of these rules were the most distinctive, and, to my eyes, most odd? The ones about which animals could be eaten, and under what conditions. And odd not to my eyes alone. These rules have provoked the longest and most involved discussions.

Four main hypotheses have been put forward to explain the Biblical rules:

that their sharp distinctions between permitted and prohibited foods expresses and strengthens the Israelite conviction that God's creativity is expressed through distinction-making: distinctions among different orders of life, and distinctions between the Israelites and other peoples;

that their goal is to express and address a deep ambivalence about eating any meat at all;

that their goal is to discipline and hallow the Jewish people by requiring everyone to apply Torah to even the most physical and animal of needs; and

that their goal is to encourage the eating of relatively healthy meats and discourage the eating of meats that might be likeliest to communicate disease.

The fourth, "medical," hypothesis may be the most comfortable for a person with a modern sensibility, living in a society where the "Pure Food and Drug Act" is intended to prevent disease. But I can find little to support it in the Biblical texts. The medical hypothesis emerges among some Jewish interpreters and commentators in the Middle Ages, as they learn more about human physiology and seek to apply the rationalist methods of Hellenistic science. It was put forward again in the modern period, when once again knowledge grew of human physiology and the origins of disease.

The Biblical text gives more support to the "distinction-making" and the "anti-meat" hypotheses.

The more I realize that these two approaches are not at all mutually exclusive and may even strengthen each other, the more they make sense to me. If the Biblical Israelites were ambivalent about eating meat, they might have seen precisely that attitude as one of the most important differences between themselves and other peoples. They might accordingly have shaped the rules of proper meats so as to separate themselves from other peoples. This outlook might have especially resonated with the Israelites' sharp distinction between their image of themselves as herders of domesticated animals, and their image of their near rivals-and-relatives as hunters. So let us look more carefully at these two notions.

IS MEAT THE PROBLEM?

One view is that much of the Torah's code of proper foods is an answer to one underlying question: What shall we do about killing animals for food?

The argument for this view begins not with the code itself but with several stories in Genesis and Exodus that express real ambivalence about eating meat.

In the first version of the story of Creation, God offers as food to the primordial Human "all plants that seed forth seeds that are upon the face of all the earth, and all trees in which there is tree-fruit that seeds forth seeds." There is no hint that any meat may be eaten (Gen. 1:29).

It is not until after the wanton violence of human beings has corrupted the earth and brought the Flood upon it that God offers as food for humans every living, moving thing—all wildlife, all birds, all fish, all crawling life. "As with the green plants, I now give you all." Even then, God sets one condition: "Flesh with its life, its blood, you are not to eat!" (Gen. 9:3-4).

But the tension and ambivalence do not end there. One of the other strands of Torah (Num. 11) tells a tale of the troubles in the Wilderness. One year's journey out of Egypt, the Israelites are swept by a craving for meat. Manna is not good enough.

God answers first by warning them that their mouths will soon be so full of meat that it will come out of their noses and they will come to loathe it. And then God sends what seems like a miracle of meat; a gigantic flock of quails that settle just where the Israelites can eat them. This works all too well. As the people begin to stuff themselves, a disastrous plague strikes many of them down. Those who had craved meat to eat ended as "dead meat" themselves. The place was named "the grave of the craving."

Both Leviticus (17:8–16) and Deuteronomy (12:20–28) deal with the desire to eat meat outside the sacrificial system. But both insist with great intensity that the blood must not be consumed.

Leviticus demands that either the animal be brought as an offering to the central Shrine (where the blood can be sprinkled on the Altar) or else if an animal was killed elsewhere, that the blood be poured on the ground and covered with dust.

Deuteronomy notes—the tone is rueful—that some who live far from the central Shrine say, "I *will* eat meat, because [their] soul craves meat." So, says the passage, "You may eat meat, in accordance with all the craving of your soul." But then: "Pour out [the blood] upon the earth like water."

All this ambivalence over eating meat suggests that the prohibition of eating certain animals may have been a way of resolving the dilemma.

- On one level, the partial and specific prohibition could have functioned as a compromise. "All right," it said; "eating animals is a problem. So is not eating them. So we will eat some and not eat others."
- On another level, the prohibition forced people to make a more conscious judgment at the moment of killing an animal or eating meat: "Is this an animal I am allowed to kill? How come I am allowed to kill at all?"

If the idea was simply to create this kind of compromise or consciousness-raising, *which* animals were prohibited might not have mattered very much. So long as some meats were permitted and others prohibited, that might have been enough.

In actual fact, by limiting the consumption of meat to animals that chew the cud and have split hooves, the Bible ruled out all meat-eating animals. Even domesticated animals that ate meat, like the dog and cat, or sometimes ate meat, like the pig, were ruled out. Yet some domesticated animals that did not eat meat, like the camel and horse, were also prohibited. So while all carnivores were prohibited, not all herbivores were permitted. The "fit" was not perfect.

All right, I say to myself. Just suppose the idea was to require that Israelites eat only meat from animals that did not eat meat themselves. What was the point? Would this have had any effect on the people?

By eating only from the flock of ruminants, might we be more likely to see ourselves not as wild wolves and lions, not as scavenging pigs, but as God's ruminating flock? With God as our shepherd? If the Israelites could not eat animals that hunted prey for their food, and could not eat even permitted animals if they had been killed by predators or hunters, would this not separate the Israelites more fully and more deeply from their hunter neighbors? Might the separation be not only sociological—"We cannot eat what you eat, so we cannot eat with you"— but also psychological—"We are what we eat, so we are not like you. We are not predatory." (It goes better in German: "*Man ist was Man isst.*")

If that is indeed the point, then I begin to see the purpose of sacred slaughter at the Holy Temple. Since we humans *are* animals, not plants—and omnivorous animals at that, capable of being predatory—then we must consciously and constantly choose whether to be tame or wild, ruminants or predators. By giving the domesticated herbivores as sacred offerings, perhaps we can focus on what it is to be like them. Perhaps we can train ourselves to be more like them.

And if we bring the offering ourselves and are present when its blood is poured out on the earth or on God's earthy Altar, the slaughter is given an ultimate solemnity. Then the killing becomes not casual, not simply a sating of our own bellies' needs, but a sacred recognition that the earth has a stake in every killing.

So now the questions I ask myself become more subtle. For me, in my own generation, what kind of eating would teach me to shepherd the earth instead of tearing it limb from limb? What foods would remind me that all of earth is my community, that I want to distinguish myself from those who would treat other humans and the earth as prey? I also find myself asking more about the way I eat than what I eat. More about what the form and process of the sacred slaughter teaches me than what specific foods are good for offering.

I know that I will need to look much more closely at how the system of Temple offerings actually worked, both for the Israelite community as a whole and for individuals within it. But before I do, I am still interested in the whole idea that distinctions in what may and may not be eaten refer to the making of distinctions in the universe.

IS SEPARATION THE GOAL?

In making strong distinctions about food, were the Israelites affirming that distinction-making is the essence of life?

The main evidence that they were comes from a close examination of the specific lists of prohibited and permitted foods in the Books of Leviticus (Chapter 11) and Deuteronomy (Chapter 14).

The two books come from different strands of Israelite culture, bespeak different concerns about life, and address what to eat in somewhat different forms.

Leviticus is the priestly code of holy behavior. It was probably codified around the beginning of the seventh century B.C.E., about one hundred years before the Babylonians destroyed the First Temple.

What did it mean to be a *kohen*, a priest? The entire existence and function of the priesthood was focused on the physical body, not on the intellect or the emotions. Priesthood was hereditary, based on biology rather than intellectual or ethical attainments. Members of a priestly family who had bodily blemishes could not serve as priests. The priesthood dealt with animals, grain, wine, blood, the cycle of sun, moon, and earth—all aspects of the body of the universe.

In later generations certain people—Jews and others—have denigrated this physicality as a path of God. "How primitive, how pagan!" some have said. "How unspiritual!"

But as for me, I am more and more conscious of living in a generation when the body of the earth is wounded and may be in mortal danger. And I am myself also growing older, feeling more sharply the creaks and cracks of my own body. So I find myself thinking, It may be important to focus once again on the sacredness of the body. Not to treat all blemishes on great round earth or tiny earthling as disabling or disgusting, but to seek to strengthen and to heal.

If I had my way, I would start searching for means to shape a "priesthood" where the mind and heart, knowledge and wisdom, could be joined with bone and muscle. But—steady—first I should find out what the priests of Leviticus are saying.

Although Leviticus centers on the rituals of body and purification of the body, some parts seem also to address the healing of the body politic. Most of the book seeks to define what events or objects convey ritual taboo that alienates the community as a whole from God's natural order or that alienates individual people or objects from God's communal order. It specifies how to nullify these taboos so as to restore communal connection and wholeness, both by enforcing social justice and by doing "ritual" acts, such as offerings, that restore the balance of nature and community.

The priests evidently saw an ordered relationship with the earth and just relationships within society as part of a continuum of orderliness in God's universe. So they did not make as deep a distinction as does modern society between "ritual" and "social justice."

The Book of Deuteronomy is written from a prophetic, not a priestly viewpoint. It presents itself as being Moses' final speeches as he prepares to die and the people prepare to enter the Land of Promise—speeches full of warnings that once the people enter the land, they may break their covenant with God, and suffer terribly as a result. Most modern scholars believe that Deuteronomy was written in Moses' name by some prophetic writer(s) who lived around the end of the seventh or the beginning of the sixth century B.C.E., shortly before the Babylonian Conquest.

At this point in Israelite history, internal social conflict between rich and poor was intense. The memory of Assyrian conquests and the fear of Babylonian Conquest were overwhelming. Prophets who foresaw great danger may have tried to command the people's ear by writing in Moses' name what they thought Moses himself would be saying if he were alive. Or they may have embroidered their own midrash into ancient tales about Moses and ancient versions of his teaching.

So Deuteronomy was far more concerned that social injustice and idolatry were polluting the land, weakening social unity, and bringing on exile and destruction than about performing rituals incorrectly.

We might expect the two texts—Leviticus and Deuteronomy—to be very different in the way in which they dealt with permitted and prohibited foods. There are indeed differences between them, subtle ones that have led to some interesting thoughts about the meaning of the code of proper food. It is also true that both Leviticus and Deuteronomy are clearly drawing on very similar understandings of what is proper to eat.

Some of the Biblical passages themselves give reasons for the prohibitions. In regard to not eating meat from animals that "died of themselves" or were attacked by other animals, and to not eating "swarming things that move upon the earth," the Torah asserts that as God is holy, so the Israelite people must be holy.

- Since the word for "holy," *kadosh*, also means "separate," there may be a link between the sense that just as God is separate from the world, the Israelites are to be separate from other peoples. Perhaps they are especially separate in that they define God not as part of nature, not as the world itself, but as separate from the world—much more separate than did most other peoples of that time.

According to this approach, Israelite food must be different enough to be an emblem of separateness from other peoples. But—more important still—the Israelites' emotional and spiritual investment in the difference must be so intense that people from the two communities cannot sit calmly together to eat their different foods. The Torah ascribes just such feelings to the Egyptians, who will not eat lamb and abhor the Israelites because they do. Separating one food from another separates one people from another.

Aside from the *kadosh* passage, some scholars point to the prohibition on boiling a kid in its mother's milk that appears three times in Torah (Ex. 23:19; Ex. 34: 26; Deut. 14:21). In two of these passages, it is connected with the teachings of how Israelites are to celebrate the festivals. Some scholars believe that the taboo appeared there in order to prohibit a specific practice being performed by other Middle Eastern cultures to celebrate their festivals. This view strengthens the notion that the regulation of food was intended to distinguish the Israelites from other peoples.

For me, this raises a whole set of quandaries. I take joy in the special celebrations of the Jewish people—for example, the Shabbat and the festivals that are not like the holy days of other peoples. But I am not altogether happy about using food to separate communities. I would like to be able to eat with members of other communities and cultures. If the whole point of having special foods is to make this difficult, then I am in a quandary.

So I press on, looking deeper into this matter of distinctions. In our own day, the importance of "distinction-making" in the regulation of food has been given some new direction by scholars who draw on anthropology to explain the specifics of the prohibitions. Mary Douglas and Howard Eilberg-Schwartz point out the analogy between the three world arenas of the Creation story in Genesis I—water, sky, and earth—and the way that animals that can be used for food are divided into three categories: fish, birds, and mammals, according to the elements of water, air, and earth that they inhabit.

The Creation of the world proceeded by making separations between those three arenas. In each arena, there is a "proper" way of getting around—swimming, flying, or walking—and even an especially "proper" way of doing it. Animals that do not behave properly for their particular arena obscure the distinctions and are not to be eaten. Thus amphibians (like crabs) that live in the sea but also walk on land; land animals (like snakes and ants) that crawl instead of walk; fish (like sharks and whales) that are not "properly" equipped with fins and gills for swimming; flying things with four legs instead of two—all are forbidden.

To this extent, both the Deuteronomy and Leviticus passages track the three-story universe of water, land, and sky that is laid out in Genesis. But there are differences in the wording of the two lists of prohibitions. Eilberg-Schwartz points out that the priestly authors of Leviticus not only drew on the land-water-air distinction, but also used words similar to those in Genesis that distinguished between three different kinds of land animals—domesticated, wild, and swarming.

He suggests this was no accident. He thinks that Leviticus consciously reworked the language of the prohibitions in order to echo much more closely the language of the Creation story in Genesis.

Eilberg-Schwartz suggests that these priests had two traditions—the Creation story, and what was actually eaten and prohibited. They understood the food regulations in terms of Creation because they understood Creation as a process of classifying and distinguishing. That was the way they, in their priestly function of overseeing proper eating, went about making the people holy; and that was how they saw God making the universe holy.

So they wanted the language of the rules about food to echo the story of Creation. Just as God made the universe by dividing it into thirds and then dividing the third part into thirds again, so they would "make" the Israelite people, or at least make it holy, by distinguishing its food in patterns of threes.

The priests would become, as it were, imitators of God, creators themselves on the microcosmic level. And the people of Israel would become a microcosm of the universe.

As I absorbed the whole story up to this point, I felt excited by the whole notion of eating in such a way as to replicate the story of Creation. My dinner table becomes a miniature universe, a Model Earth. If I know how to eat, then I am not just completing but repeating the work of God.

But the Bible's particular code of proper food works for me only if I—today— believe in the three-story model of the universe that Genesis lays out. What if I have a different view? How can my dinner table recapitulate the universe if I am awed by the spirals of the galaxies and DNA? by the intricately interwoven web of life on earth? by the knowledge that somewhere in my body is a proton that burst into being a billion light-years from my planet? by the knowledge that my inquiries themselves may change the shape of matter in its fuzzier margins? that indeed I am, through all my thoughts and gazings, the co-creator of the universe?

If *that* is what I think, what shall I eat?

I let these questions settle in my soul, for now without an answer. Sometimes there is a benefit in asking a question without leaping to an answer. Now I turn back to a different aspect of the story. For the story is also about the nature of the telling, also about the interaction between what we believe and what we do.

For after all, the foods we eat and the earth we live on do not fit perfectly together. Some of the specific animals that are permitted and prohibited do not fit perfectly into the categories of Genesis. Why not?

If the Creation story had led in a straight historical and logical line to the list of prohibitions, then the fit between the story and the prohibitions would presumably have been perfect.

Or if the list of permitted and taboo foods had been well known and fully accepted before the Creation story was written down, then also the fit between the story and the prohibitions would presumably have been perfect.

But what if the story and the practice had evolved simultaneously? If the prohibitions developed in actual practice alongside the development of the Creation story, then it is not surprising that there is some fit but not a perfect one.

If all this is true, then maybe there was a certain pattern of eating among the Israelites. It was loosely connected to the idea that the universe, or at least this planet, had three basic habitats: water, air, and earth. Some great priest-poet gave a clearer shape to the Creation by writing the first chapter of Genesis, and then the great poetic story gave still clearer impetus and direction to the prohibitions.

The priests took this process an extra step by going even farther toward using the language of Genesis when they wrote the code as it appeared in Leviticus. As for the nonpriestly authors of Deuteronomy, they had much less investment in trying to make the rules of practice match up with the Creation story. So they were content to use the earlier, fuzzier version of the rules when they made the list in Deuteronomy.

If Eilberg-Schwartz is right, the priestly authors of Leviticus were already, some 2,600 years ago, asking why certain foods were permitted and others prohibited. Their puzzlement was not unlike our own. And they answered their own question, not quite explicitly, by using words that echoed the Genesis story of Creation and underlined the importance of distinction-making in the process of hallowing the world and the people of Israel.

For me, this twirl in the story gives a new twist to how our eating mirrors God's creative act.

How we eat changes the story, and our storytelling changes the eating. *Both acts of creativity mirror God.* Not because the universe is made up of air and earth and water, but because we are always pushing act and idea into a kind of leapfrog with each other.

We can ask ourselves a riddle: Which came first, the rules or their reasons? action or theory? poetry or practice?

At once we realize that the only answer to that riddle is to remember the other riddle "Which came first, the chicken or the egg?" The answer is: *Both.* The relationship between chicken and egg, egg and chicken, chicken and egg, is a spiral. Changes and recombinations in the egg lead to a different chicken; events in the life of the chicken lead to selection of the egg. And so forth.

This riddle, of course, is about food. And about the universe.

TIME OUT FOR A WORD ON TIME

The spiral of moving from action to thought to more defined action to more poetic thought—appeals to me immensely, as a model through which to understand the world. So I want to pause for a moment from looking at the specifics of food to say that often in the rest of this book I will draw on this pattern of thinking about down-to-earth Judaism. For it seems to me one of the most important aspects of Judaism is that it has operated in this way.

This is the way the spiral works:

1. A story or practice that the Jewish people has received from the **past**
2. influences what it sees as most salient and most important in its **present** life.
3. Out of its **present** situation, the people then
4. chooses what to emphasize for the **next** generation. Not only what to emphasize in what it will do next, but also
5. what to enrich and embroider in what it **used to be**—that is, in the stories and life-paths it has inherited.

So the past shapes the present, and then the present not only shapes the future but also reshapes the past.

By assigning a reason for what has already been done, the people gives a special twist and direction, a new curve on the spiral, to what is to be done. As a result practice changes, and gives rise to still newer theory—often phrased as if it were old theory now newly discovered or better understood.

Sometimes historians, anthropologists, and sociologists have said that if this is the way religious practice evolved, out of the changing life of the people, then it means there is no religious significance, no whiff of the Eternal, no holiness, no God, in the process. It is mere anthropology, mere sociology, mere history.

But we can choose to understand this dance of past, future, and present as itself a holy process, as itself God's spiraling dance into the world, a dance that becomes visible because a living human community—in this case, the Jewish community—is, generation after generation, endowing it with a visible form.

We can, in fact, give a name and a visual image to that particular Jewish form, that Jewish dance. I have already referred to it as a "spiral dance" because the way in which the Jews go back into the past in order to make a new future is a spiral process.

This time-set is unlike the time-set either of Modernity or of some traditional peoples. The time-set of Modernity sees change as a straight-ahead, straight-line progress, always moving forward. Some traditional peoples see time as circular, always repeating itself, always coming back to restore the time of beginning. The Jewish time-set is a spiral that curves backward in order to curve forward. For Jews, progress happens only when one draws on the past, deeply digesting it, in order to reinterpret it and shape a new future. We do not simply repeat the past, we do not simply invent the future.

It is not just new Jewish ideas and practices, like how and what to eat, that emerge this way. The very fabric of Jewish time, the Jewish sacred calendar, also does this, as we will see when we look in more detail in the section titled "Rest." The pattern of the week, the month, the year, the seven-year cycle, even the cycle of seven times seven years make spirals within spirals the shape of Jewish time.

When we go back into the past in order to make a new future, that is a spiral. But when we add to this that the future is always remaking a new past, that we are constantly remaking our memories to fit our new reality, then we see the spiral curving back upon itself. Then the spiral become a Möbius strip, which curves in space in order to reshape its single surface.

As the Prophet Ezekiel in one great vision saw the curving Rainbow, that strikingly beautiful synthesis of an infinity of colors into one shape, as "the appearance of the likeness of the radiance of God," so perhaps in our generation we can see the Möbius strip, that Spiral of a Spiral, as "the appearance of the likeness of the dance of God."

❀

If we keep this Jewish way of thinking in mind we will find more than two ways of understanding the Biblical outlook on food. Long after the Torah text was "closed" and transmitted to the future, efforts have continued to reexamine and reinterpret the rules of proper food. At least two other hypotheses have been put forward.

One is the suggestion that the prohibitions themselves, not the specifics of what was prohibited, were intended to educate and uplift the people. The people would learn humility, self-restraint, and obedience to Torah by applying Torah to even the most physical and animal of needs.

The other suggestion is that the permitted foods were healthier to eat than those prohibited. We will return to these reinterpretations when we examine how the Jewish people in the era of the Rabbis, during the Modern Age, and in our own generation have been looking at food issues. In the meantime, the Biblical rules of what to eat and what not to eat have raised several important questions for us to consider as we choose what to eat:

- In both approaches that we have examined in detail, the "meat-ambivalent" and "Creation/distinction-making" models, the fit between the theory and the facts of the prohibited animals is not perfect. One of the main reasons is that outward physical characteristics like hooves and cuds, not biosocial categories like "herbivorous" or "walkers," are used to define which animals can be eaten. As Howard Eilberg-Schwartz points out, this type of categorizing is characteristic of the Israelite priesthood with its focus on bodily characteristics. If this is so, it seems to have affected not only the language of the priestly code in Leviticus but the prophetic code in Deuteronomy as well. In other words, it pervades Israelite thought. Much of the effort post-Biblical Jews have put into figuring out some "deeper" ethical or ontological categories beneath the hoof and cud can be laid to a sense of discomfort about the focus on the physical body. How do we ourselves feel about this focus?
- How do we see the process of Creation, and the role in it of distinctions and separations? Do we see the differences between earth, air, and water as the crucial dividing-markers of the universe? Do we see the different forms of locomotion in each of these domains as the crucial distinctions between different kinds of animals? Do we want to tie our decisions of what to eat to our sense of these demarcations?
- How do we see the boundaries and connections between the Jewish people

and other peoples? Do we want to choose the foods we eat in order to affirm and demark those boundaries and connections? If so, how much do we want to rely on the traditional distinctions and how much on new ones to make those markers?

• How do we feel about the assignment of some foods to a special time in the yearly cycle, as in the special limitations of Pesach?

III. SACRED FLOW AND SACRED CELEBRATION

More and more in my own life, I try to infuse the everyday with a sense of sacredness. Whenever I think consciously about it, my intellect believes that when I am eating, breathing, writing, making love, that "ordinary" moment shares in fact in the Wholeness of the universe. But in the constant doing, that fact is easy to forget. How can I help myself experience the deepest spiritual pleasure that I know, the one that comes when I can feel in my bones and *kishkes* that what I am doing *right now* embodies God? How can I infuse the unconscious sacred flow with conscious sacred celebration?

If this exploration into food and Judaism is to have the strongest meaning for me, I must find answers to this question. Or—not necessarily answers. Hints, pointers from which I can shape my own answers.

And the hints are there, in the Biblical tradition. For the Israelites, there was a general rule that all food in some sense belonged to God. One way of affirming this was that on special occasions (national or familial or individual), food must be brought to the Temple as an offering to God. For the people as a whole, these special occasions came when the natural cycles of sun and moon and earth spiraled round to the times of harvest, sowing, rain, and heat, the times of chill and dark. For families or individuals, these special occasions came with an experience of prosperity or despair, a death or a healing, guilt or joy.

HALLOWING ALL FOOD

But if the goal was to remind people that on *all* occasions God is present, then food offerings on special occasions were not enough to set that truth deep into their consciousness. So the Biblical outlook required that some of every crop and flock must be consciously set apart to recognize God's Ownership (Num. 18).

There were several mechanisms by which God's Ownership was made clear: "first fruits," or *bikkurim*; the formal designations and rituals of *terumah* and *tenufah*;

and tithing. In most of these ceremonies, the priests and the poor were God's representatives.

To begin with, the firstborn of cattle, sheep, and goats; early fruit from a young fruit tree; the early part of each year's barley harvest; and the first processed foods of each season (wine, olive oil, dough, leavened bread, and date jam) were set apart for God. Only when that was done—as if to pay "rent" to the Owner—could the rest of the offspring, crop, or processed food be eaten.

Fruit trees went through a special procedure. For the first three years, none of their yield could be eaten. Then the fruit were dedicated as holy to God, and eaten only in Jerusalem. Only from the fifth year on could the fruit be eaten in the ordinary way. In the literal language of the Torah (Lev. 19:23–25), this process was called *orlah* (foreskin). The "foreskins" of the trees were being "circumcised." Perhaps this image was a visual echo of male circumcision: As the foreskin was trimmed to symbolize the covenant with God for future fruitfulness, so the fruit were trimmed as a sign of that covenant. Or perhaps the image was more metaphoric: The double pause before the fruit could be eaten, like the pause of eight days before circumcision and then the pause from infancy till adolescence for the male to become "fruitful," bespoke the covenant with God for future fruitfulness. Only self-restraint, pausing, could bring bounty. Or perhaps in both cases, the covenant required both a human pause to let God act, and a human action to affirm God's pause.

In regard to all the plant offerings, these set-asides were announced through *terumah* (uplifting dedication), and then for some of them, a ceremony of physical elevation (*tenufah*) at the Temple. The firstborn animals were offered on the Altar. All this food then went to the priestly families to be eaten.

All grain, new oil, new wine, cattle, sheep, and goats were subject to a tithe—the giving of one tenth to the tribe of Levi, who had no land of their own but dedicated their lives to sacred service, either at the Temple or around the country. The tithe was also subject to the ceremonial dedication of *terumah*.

In most years, the tithe went directly to the central Temple. But every third year, according to Deuteronomy (14:28–29), the tithe stayed in the local district and went not only to the landless Levites, but also to the landless poor: the orphan, the widow, the sojourning foreigner. This innovation may represent Deuteronomy's stronger concern for social justice in Israelite society—perhaps because the book was written at a time of social crisis, by one or more prophetic figures much like Jeremiah. We shall notice this concern again in the way that Deuteronomy understands Shabbat.

After the Babylonian Exile, there was some doubt whether farmers in general were fully complying with the tithe; and as a result those who were most concerned with careful observance of Torah began to set the tithe apart and do *terumah* themselves on what they ate.

From year to year and generation to generation, these practices affirmed that fertility and fruitfulness were a matter not only of biology but also of society and spirit. For one generation of barley and grapes and olives and sheep to follow another, the whole society had to affirm some Wholeness, some Unity, beyond biology.

Indeed, this process defined what actually was "society"—what was the in-group of people who had to feed each other and not feed *on* each other, who together had to make sure that the human generations followed one after another.

There are echoes in the Torah of an earlier pattern in which the oldest son of every family was its priest. But the tribe of Levi became the substitutes for these firstborns. For good social-spiritual reasons, the Torah describes in precise numerical detail how the substitution was made. For it to "work," it was crucial that there be almost exactly the same number of adult male Levites as there were firstborn sons. Otherwise, the new arrangement would have supplied too little sacred energy for the people's needs—or perhaps too much.

By substituting one tribe for the firstborns of each family, Israelite society made each clan, each tribe, interdependent with the others. No longer could one clan or tribe separate and expect to find prosperity on its own. For the ability to "prime the pump" of God's blessing—to offer barley so that barley would grow and pour water so that rain would fall—had been handed over to the Levites. Now every family, every tribe, had to connect with Levi. Just as no family could live well on the food it grew alone, just as the whole Land of Israel made up one economy, so its people had to be organically intertwined in one spiritual network.

The Levites were in a sense the bloodstream of Israelite society. They made up the distinctive organ system that ran throughout the body. Only if food is infused *into* the bloodstream can nourishment come forth *from* the bloodstream. One reason to share each harvest with the Levites was that they themselves needed to eat. Another reason was to put food itself into the social circulatory system.

Shortly after the Temple offerings ended, the great Rabbi Akiba recalled that it took an offering of barley to make the barley grow, an offering of water to bring rainfall. So the tithes had to be in oil and grain and fruit if olives, barley, and trees were to flourish. It would not have worked for the Levites to be given gold and silver alone (though there were some provisions for commuting part of the tithe into money). The overarching Unity needed to be nurtured by receiving what It also was to give. What from the human standpoint was an inflow needed to be fed and balanced by an outflow.

In the entire spectrum of actual eating, the Biblical pattern integrated the physical act with spiritual concerns. Whether through sacred offerings, prayer, or self-control, each Israelite learned that food was an integral element of the Unity of body, emotion, intellect, and spirit—within each person and within the world as a whole.

At first glance, I feel a little baffled by this approach to endowing food with spirituality. These folk were farmers and shepherds; I am not. They could bring the food they themselves grew as tithes and offerings; I cannot.

But—is this really true? Why can I not *become* a farmer, albeit on a tiny scale? In my backyard, or in a vegetable garden at my synagogue, or in a neighborhood garden that I share with Jews and members of other cultures and communities, or even in a flower box on a windowsill in my apartment, I could grow tomatoes, squash, onions, blueberries, mint, corn, beans.

I could eat some, give some to the poor, bring some to a neighborhood block party. I could share these fruits of our sun, our rain, our seed, our labor with a group of my friends that prays or studies or reads books together. I could bring them to a Kiddush or oneg shabbat on Friday evening or Saturday afternoon, to a brunch on Sunday morning.

Most important, I could tell the others and myself what I am doing. Tell them these are tithes of my small farming. Describe what it was like to raise the plants, how if felt to bless their growing.

THE TEMPLE OFFERINGS

So now I want to know more. I want to know about those "special occasions" when food was brought with an intensely sacred focus as a special offering to God—originally at various places around the country, and later at the Temple in Jerusalem.

I am intrigued, to begin with, by the Hebrew word that the Bible most often uses for these food offerings: *korbanot* (singular, *korban*), which means "that which is brought near." A closely related Hebrew word means "innards," as in "guts" or "intestines." *Korbanot* bring the inwardness of God near to the innards of humans.

Today in English, the word most often used to translate *korbanot* is "sacrifices." Literally, that word means "making sacred"; in practice, it has taken on the some-what ascetic flavor of "giving away." "Offering" or "gift" expresses more of the taste of intimacy that the Hebrew implies; but even these words sound more like "sending away" than like "bringing near." To get really close to the Hebrew meaning, we would have to use as nouns such English words as "nearing" or "innering" or perhaps "endearing": Israelites brought "innerings" to the Temple.

With the word *korbanot*, the Bible puts every human speaker, every human reader, in the position of receiving food, not giving it away. But at the Temple, who is receiving food? God. So every human who brings food to the Temple thereby stands in the place of God—receiving food. The face of everyone who brings the food is a face of the God Who savors the food.

God is not left to hunger in loneliness, not left to weep unfed. And therefore—neither are the people.

The sacred offerings of food were "brought near" in two patterns. One was a national public rhythm that involved and represented every member of the People Israel. The other had no public rhythm, but grew out of the unique and individual life events of a family's or a person's path.

What kinds of food made up the offerings? First of all, the Torah forbade some foods that may have made up special festival offerings of the nearby Canaanite peoples: "You shall not offer the blood of My sacrifice with anything leavened; and the fat of My festival offering you shall not leave till morning. . . . You shall not boil a kid in the milk of its mother."

Almost all the offerings required the killing of an unblemished animal (at least eight days old) and its presentation to God. The animal might be a sheep or goat, a bull, or a turtledove or pigeon, depending partly on the intention of the specific offering and partly on the wealth of the household. In any case it had to be the property of whoever brought it, and an animal raised for food, not one from the wild or one intended to do work.

After the animal was ritually slaughtered, its blood was sprinkled on the sides of the Altar. Depending on the kind of offering, part or all of it was burned on the Altar. The parts of the animal that were not burned were waved by a priest in the six directions of the universe. Some of the meat was eaten by the priests, the rest by the household that had brought the animal to the Temple.

The animal offering was accompanied by loaves or wafers of unleavened bread or griddle cakes of wheat flour, oil, and the savory frankincense, seasoned with salt. Parts of these were burned upon the Altar.

Some of the offerings also included a pouring of wine and, once a year, of water.

THE PUBLIC RHYTHMS

As I turn my attention to how the Biblical Israelites brought offerings of food to celebrate the great national festivals, I take stock of how I do this today, in America.

At once there leap to mind just two occasions, one "Jewish" and one "American," when the main event of a festival is a special meal: a great dinner in the spring, for Pesach, and one in autumn for the American Thanksgiving.

For many of the other Jewish festivals there are special foods that float across my tongue: apples and honey for Rosh Hashanah, fasting for Yom Kippur, potato latkes for Hanukkah, fruits and nuts for Tu B'Shvat, hamantaschen for Purim, blintzes with sour cream for Shavuot.

But for other American festivals, no taste arises: not for the Fourth of July or Labor Day, not for Memorial Day or Presidents' Day, not for the days that honor veterans or Martin Luther King. Only for the harvest itself, only for Thanksgiving, do turkeys and cranberries and pumpkin pies come dancing on my palate.

How sad! I think, quite startled by the discovery, and at the same time grateful that even with the Temple gone the Jews have preserved some special tastes for times of celebration. Or rather, perhaps the tastes have preserved the festivals, kept them alive when otherwise they would have withered away, in exile from the place where goats and griddle cakes were brought to mark them.

How did it work in the days when there was a single central place to hold these festive meals?

Most basic of all, every national offering of food from the earth celebrated the rhythms of the earth that nourished the food. The offerings were keyed to the daily spinnings of the earth in order to face and shun the sun, to the cycles of the moon as it shadowed or brightened the night, to the broader yearly ovals of the earth—and to the unique ability of humans to count the seventh of each of these different cycles.

- Each day, one lamb was offered soon after dawn and another one in the afternoon.
- On Shabbat there were two extra lambs (called the *musaf,* or "additional" offering), and twelve new-baked loaves of *lekhem panim* (literally, "bread of faces"—often translated as "bread of the presence" or "shewbread") were placed on a golden table before the Altar.
- On the New Moon, two bulls, one ram, seven lambs, and a goat were added to the regular offerings.

In the round of the year, each of the festivals included a goat as a collective sin-offering, and each had its own special pattern of other offerings as well.

Originally, the year was understood to begin in the spring, when the winter rains came to an end and—if the rain had been plentiful—lambs were born and barley sprouted. Indeed, the spring festivals were keyed to the arrivals of these foods.

- The offerings of Pesach celebrated the experience of both shepherds and farmers, and the unification of both kinds of food growers into a single peoplehood.

On the first evening of Pesach, each family throughout the Land of Israel brought a lamb to the Temple (or if the family was too small to afford a lamb, then a group of families together). In some years more than three million people participated.

Each of these groups of people offered the lamb on its own behalf rather than leaving this for the priests to do, echoing at this one time each year the ancient sense that each extended family held its own priesthood. The priests stood close by to catch the blood in gold or silver basins and passed the full basins from priest to priest until they could be tossed against the Altar.

Then the lamb was roasted by each group that had brought it, and members of that group ate it together around a campfire that night.

On the next day, and every day of the festival week, the priests offered up two bulls, one ram, seven lambs, and a goat as a sin-offering, in addition to the regular daily offering.

On the second night of Pesach, an *omer* (approximately a bushel) of the first barley of the new season was brought to the Temple. During the following day it was ground into fine flour, and on the day after that it was mixed with oil and frankincense and made into griddle cakes. Some of the cakes were burned on the Altar while the rest was eaten by the priests.

Seven weeks after Pesach, when the barley crop was complete and spring wheat and other grains had just begun to be harvested, came the festival of Shavuot. The special offering that had been made for Pesach was offered again: two bulls, one ram, seven lambs, and a goat. In addition, on this occasion only two loaves of *leavened* bread, the bread of civilization rather than the primitive unleavened *matzah*, were waved before the Altar. First fruits—that is, the first part of the spring wheat harvest, other grains, and possibly the fruit of trees that had just become three years old and therefore available for food—were also brought to the Temple. The procession of these first fruits was led by an ox, which was then sacrificed.

Counting from the month of Pesach, lambs, and barley as the beginning of the year, the seventh month came in the fall, when the fall crops were harvested and normally the rains began again.

In the Biblical era, this seventh month was treated as the Shabbat of the months. It was unique in that four different festivals were celebrated—one at each phase of the moon.

- On the New Moon of that month (which over the centuries became known as Rosh Hashanah) a special offering was added to the regular New Moon *korban*. This Rosh Hashanah offering provided a leitmotif for the seventh month, in that it was repeated on two of the other festivals. It was as if the New Moon came again, and the people could again experience their own rebirth, on the tenth and twenty-third of the sabbatical month.
- On Rosh Hashanah this special offering was one bull, one ram, seven lambs, and one goat as a sin-offering.
- On Yom Kippur, in addition to the Rosh Hashanah offering, the sacrifice was one ram for atonement by the high priest, and another for the people. One goat was killed at the Temple, and another (the "escape-goat" or "scape-goat") was driven into the Wilderness.
- During Sukkot, the seven-day fall harvest festival, water as well as wine was poured each morning before the Altar. The Sukkot offerings were especially expansive—seventy bulls during the festival week in addition to goats and many sheep each day. Haunches of meat were waved as offerings in the six directions of the earth, and there was a special Sukkot waving of the branches of three trees (palm, myrtle, and willow) with the *etrog* (citron).
- On the day after the seven days of Sukkot, as the moon of the seventh month began to wane, the winter-greeting, inward-looking festival of Sh'mini Atzeret (Boundary-Making Eighth Day) was marked by a return to the relatively spare and inward offering of Rosh Hashanah.

Besides the permanent rhythmic celebration of the festivals, there were also special national celebrations during which offerings were made to mark victories in battle, the end of droughts or plagues, the dedication of the Temple, and the acclamation of a new king.

As I absorb the rhythms through which the specific foods and numbers of each offering changed through the years, I taste again with sadness the nontastes of my American festivals. Perhaps there is something deeper missing, a deeper reason for the absence of symbolic foods. These festive days are not keyed to the rhythms of the earth, but only to the anniversaries of political events or the birthdays of political heroes. Thanksgiving for the harvest is the one exception, and that is the one time when foods become the medium of our celebration.

The deeper teaching of the Israelite festival offerings is that we need to reconnect our public celebrations with the rhythms of our wounded earth. Perhaps the misuse and wounding of our earth are intimately intertwined with the abandonment of the festivals of earth? Now that we know how crucial to our existence are the rhythmic shrinking and swelling of the ozone layer in the global atmosphere, do we not need festivals to mark that rhythm? Do we not need festivals for the tides, the rain, the rivers, the reappearance of the bears from hibernation in the Yellowstone, the year's first sighting of a fledgling eagle, the rising of the syrup in the maples of Vermont? And if we created such festivals, would their foods of celebration come naturally, organically, to us?

INDIVIDUAL OFFERINGS

For ancient Israel, national celebrations, each with its characteristic food offering, were not enough to heal and renew the ecosystem-cum-community in which sun, rain, soil, grapevines, goats, and the Israelites each formed a part. For households and individuals, too, experienced special occasions in the weather of their local lives. From deadening guilt and transports of joy, from walking the threshold of life and death, there needed to be a moment of release.

And as for the nation, so the household: Food must be part of these observances if the experience is to be fully digested. That is why people brought offerings of food to mark the annual reunions of their clans and families, to give thanks for successful livelihoods, to acknowledge sin or seek recovery from illness or rebalance the psyche after a menstrual or seminal flow or fulfillment of a special vow. When someone had cheated someone else of property or service due, the guilty party was not only required to make restitution of the amount owed plus some extra, but also to offer a ram in expiation.

From our perspective, these moments would seem to be times to consult a psychotherapist, a rabbi, a physician, a lawyer, or perhaps a women's or men's group or a recovery support group. In almost all these cases, the actual practice of this consultation would be talking—unlike the Temple offerings, which were wordless acts of the body. Today, only the physician is likely to treat us as bodies with mouths and veins and tubes and muscles. As for food, it is possible that the physician might recommend a change in diet or give us medicine. The support group might encourage us to stop drinking or smoking or eating some problematic substance. Rarely would food be prescribed or expected to be a primary element in restoring balance.

There is perhaps one exception. If the tone of my special moment were celebration, then indeed I might expect cake and ice cream for a birthday party, dinner out for an anniversary or a graduation, champagne for a promotion. But the more these occasions are celebrated with food, the less likely they would include introspection, reflection, spiritual search, and growth.

Not so the special individual offerings at the Temple. They all seem to have required both deep personal engagement in thought and emotion—and engagement of the body, through food.

There were four different basic offerings brought by individuals to the Temple, and they were related to four different spiritual states of being. One type of offering was brought to repair a breach in relationship with God, resulting from a taboo body event or a mistake in ritual. The second was to expiate deliberate acts of injuring or defrauding another person or the community. The third was to seek a spiritual ascent, a deeper contact with God. The fourth was to celebrate a joyful event and express thanks to God.

Let us look first at the offering brought to repair a broken relationship with God. Most English translations and discussions have called it a "sin-offering," but this does not accurately catch the original meaning. In Hebrew this offering was called a *chattat*, from the root word *chet*, a term from archery that meant "missing the mark." The overtones of abysmal moral and ethical failure that pervade the word "sin" in English were absent from *chet* and *chattat*.

The *chattat* might be brought by someone who had experienced an uncanny contact with the frontiers where life and death meet, such as a seminal emission or a menstrual period; by someone who had made a mistake in ritual; or by someone who through withdrawal from the community, even in a sacred role like that of Nazirite,* had become separated from normal human responsibilities.

The kind and cost of the *chattat* offering were attuned to the wealth of the person who had sinned. The high priest brought a bull—the most expensive possible offering. (Male animals were especially costly because they could sire many offspring.) High officials brought a male goat; ordinary folk, a female goat or a lamb; the poor brought pigeons or turtledoves or even merely flour.

As with all animal offerings, those who brought the *chattat* laid their hands on their animals' heads before the act of slaughtering. Thus they identified their own lives with those of the animals, and symbolically offered their own lives.

Each animal was then slaughtered, and its blood sprinkled on the horns, or sides, of the Altar. For the *chattat* offering, part of the animal's body was burned on the Altar, and the remaining meat was eaten by the priests.

The second sort of offering was the *asham* or guilt offering, for cases where some person or the community had been hurt or defrauded. Here the sliding scale

---

*Nazirites were those (men or women) who took a special vow of spiritual dedication, the outward signs of which were letting the hair grow with no cutting, and refraining from eating grapes or any grape product. An untrimmed grapevine was called a *nazir*; the Nazirites became, in a sense, human grapevines who could not, of course, consume themselves. This was the only spiritual role open to individual choice, with no root in an inherited body role (not even gender) or in a special gift of prophecy from God.

of cost did not apply. Usually the guilty party had to bring a ram, an expensive penance. Its meat was given to the priests. Beyond that, it was necessary to repay the damaged person or the community the full amount for which it had suffered damage, plus 10 percent as punitive damages. For swearing falsely, the punitive fine went up to 20 percent.

After either a *chattat* or an *asham*, the Israelite was obligated to bring a special offering in token of spiritual ascent and surrender. This third type was called an *olah*, which literally means "what rises," though it is usually translated as "burnt offering."

The *olah* had three parts: an animal (bull, goat, sheep, or bird); a loaf of bread or a griddle cake made of flour, oil, and frankincense; and a pouring of wine. Since the point of this *olah* was spiritual surrender, an ascent to God, all of the meat was burned on the Altar so that it would "ascend," and all of the wine was poured out in the Temple. From the "meal offering" of bread or pancake the priest took a handful to be burned, and he could eat the rest.

The fourth sort of offering was called the *shlamim*, a "peace offering" or, better, "wholeness offering." This was brought not as an obligation but by free will to celebrate some joyful event such as the completion of a vow, a family reunion, or a successful harvest. Any domesticated animal might be brought, together with unleavened griddle cakes. Part of the animal was burned on the Altar, part given to the priests to eat, and the rest given back to the household that brought the offering. They would eat it as part of a festive meal held at the Temple for the family and its guests, including the Levite who served in their own community. The tone was one of praise and thanks to God.

Thus on a wide variety of occasions when an individual, a household, or the people as a whole were facing emotional and spiritual upheaval—grief or guilt, hope or joy—Israelite culture required the people to connect with God by offering food. Was this inevitable? No. There could have been other ways of dealing with moments of crisis: prayerful words, sexual celebrations, song and dance, competitive games, therapeutic conversations have all been used by other cultures (and some, like song and dance, were used on some occasions by the ancient Israelites). Biblical culture made a real choice when it decided that food was crucial in such moments.

By choosing food as the medium of sacred connection, Biblical culture was also saying something about its primal importance. This was, in a sense, a specialized version of an "economic" interpretation of history, in which one of the main tasks and functions of God, the great harmonizer, was seen to be the provision of food.

Long after these patterns were established, Rabbi Akiba (who himself grew up as a shepherd and probably had a stronger sense of the Biblical mind-set than most of the Rabbis) said that the Torah required that barley be brought as an offering at Pesach time to call down God's blessings on the barley crop just then ripening;

first fruits of wheat and the leavened loaves of wheat bread at Shavuot in order to invoke God's blessings as the spring wheat ripened; and water at Sukkot to bring down blessings on the rain that should begin then. In other words, if humans are generous in their offerings of food and drink, then God will be generous in blessing food and fertility.

For us today, what questions arise from this Biblical pattern, what possible choices can we make in how we eat?

- Do we want to mark the great seasons of the earth—harvests, rain, sun, shifts in the air or sea currents—by celebrations focused on foods that come from the sea, the air, the earth?
- Do we want to gather in some analogous way to mark disasters in our relation with the earth—oil spills, nuclear meltdowns, ozone depletions—and then also offer foods in a more penitential way?
- Since there is now once again a self-governing Jewish community in the Land of Israel, do we wish to create communal or national forms by which its national economy—especially the foods that grow and are eaten there—are offered to God or in some other way explicitly imbued with holiness?
- As individuals and households, do we wish to treat foods that come from the Land of Israel differently from those that grow in other countries?
- Do we want to mark the Jewish festivals, the cycles of the months and years, with special foods or special ways of offering food? If so, do we want to reinstitute the offerings that were made at the ancient Temple or to shape others?
- Do we want to mark the turns of each of our life cycles with foods, or to set aside some way of using food to mark other important changes in our emotional and spiritual lives?
- Do we want to shape a version of "psychotherapy" in which food and earth and body would play an important role?

Let us once more place these questions where they will stir our best thoughts toward the Jewish future, and turn now to learning from another era of the Jewish past.

One of the questions that came to me as I first explored the issues of food and Judaism was a question about the questions:

Only a couple of generations ago, most Jews seemed satisfied that they knew what and how to eat. What happened? Why are we so uncertain now?

What happened was the breakdown of a long-standing Jewish civilization. Out of the breakdown has come a puzzling set of experiments in what the future of the Jewish people should be. And of course it is not just the Jewish world that is experimenting. The old Judaism broke down because the old certainties in the rest of the world also broke down. It is an earthquake, a world quake, that we are living through.

The new uncertainty gives me enormous freedom, enormous excitement—and also the heebie-jeebies. I don't want to go back to the old, closed world—but I do want to dance with the earthquake instead of being buried by it.

I would be utterly astonished if the Judaism that existed before the earthquake came out of it unchanged. One thing is almost certain: The world around us is so different from the world that surrounded the Jews of the last two thousand years, that the next era of successful living Judaism will be deeply different from the preceding one.

Two thousand years or so ago, we went through an upheaval that was quite similar, so we already know that we can come out fully alive, quite different, and yet quite clear that we are the same community we were before. The last time we danced our way through a world quake, we emerged with a new geography, new languages, new symbols, new daily practices—indeed, new foods and new ways of eating!—still knowing that we were "the Jews." And feeling good about our new life-paths.

Twenty centuries ago, food was at the center of the earthquake—precisely because it had been so central to the spiritual life and religious practice of the Biblical Israelites. Once the new shape of Judaism crystallized, it became clear that one of the deepest differences from the old pattern was the way in which the people as a whole dealt with food.

In the first two centuries of the Common Era, the crucial Biblical connection among the people, food, the land, the Temple, and God—the very connection we have been examining so far—was shattered by the destruction of the Temple and the dispersion of the Jewish community outside the Land of Israel.

Severed from the single land that they had seen as specially given them by God, the Jewish people no longer considered food to be the single most important medium through which they could make connection with God.

Even so, food was not ignored or excluded from sacred celebration. It could have been. In many versions of the Christian spiritual path, for example, the ritual meal of the mass is important, but everyday meals are not. But for Jews, food continued to be important. The Rabbis who shaped a new Jewish culture described each family's dinner table as a holy Altar, and developed a code of "kosher" (proper) food that was elaborated far beyond Biblical simplicity.

This new way of treating food as sacred depended a great deal on a new way of connecting with God. We need to understand this approach before we can look in detail at the role of food in post–Biblical Judaism.

So I invite you to come along with me, on another brief "time out" from food. In this time out, I want to sketch my own summary of what we went through as a people two thousand years ago. I want to make clearer how I see *that* period of upheaval as a helpful model for us in our own time of upheaval. Food for thought, so that when we return to the topic of food again, our ideas will reflect more thought.

THE RABBINIC TRANSFORMATION

The people we call "the Rabbis" emerged roughly two thousand years ago as the shapers and managers of Jewish culture. They achieved this leadership position after two centuries of struggle within the Jewish people over how to respond to Hellenism, the triumphant imperial civilization rooted in Greco-Roman culture and power.

The Rabbis were not the only contestants in this internal struggle. There were:

—Priests, who sought to continue the Temple sacrificial system through accommodation with Rome;

—Zealots, who sought God's military help to expel the Roman legions from the Land of Israel;

—Christians, who thought that in the midst of such profound upheaval surely the Messiah must have come already and would complete the transformation;

—Hellenizers, who were as thoroughly convinced by the power of Greek philosophy as the land was conquered by the power of the Roman army.

—"Children of Light," purists who isolated themselves near the Dead Sea in monastic communities of ritual perfection to struggle against the "Children of Darkness."

All of them struggled with and against one another, each hoping to shape the Jewish future.

All were responding to the Hellenism that swept across the Mediterranean basin and deep into the Middle East. Hellenism embodied a complex of ideas and practices that had enormous power—military, economic, and intellectual:

The far-flung Roman empire created an economy based not on the flocks and crops of one small piece of land, but on massive granary-provinces, great cities, commercial entrepôts.

Its politics was based not on a citizen army from the countryside, but on the imperial legions.

Its intellectual and spiritual life was focused on philosophical dialogue for the elite and for the masses, obeisance to the emperors.

Its philosophers and bureaucrats were male, and much of their thought and practice was misogynist.

The Biblical culture that had been shaped around physicality was physically defeated by Hellenism. Israelite culture had been focused on a geographic land centered on a single physical Shrine that was itself centered on a single physical cube-shaped room, the Holy of Holies, and on an earthen Altar; a hereditary caste of priests with unblemished bodies; offerings of food; the physical politics of kings and armies. This Israelite body-culture was physically defeated by the Roman legions, its Shrine burned, its people physically dispersed and sold into slavery, its land sown with salt to make it sterile.

The next culture of the Jewish people responded to this physical defeat by playing a different game. It was a game the Hellenists also played; but whereas the people concluded after the Bar Kokhba revolt was smashed (135 c.e.) that there was no way to win the game of physicality against Rome, they felt that a workable way to preserve their own identity was to play—and at least among themselves to win—the game of words.

The Rabbis who won the people's support as new shapers of Jewish culture were an elite of mind and study, not of heredity and body (as were the priests). They built a bridge of words from the old Biblical model of Temple sacrifice to the new model of prayer by communities dispersed in many lands.

In place of food, they brought words as offerings to God.

Words of prayer and words of Torah, the study and reinterpretation and elaboration of the sacred text.

Words chanted aloud, not silently perused—chanted aloud even when study was carried on by an individual alone.

So the medium of sacred celebration shifted from what went into the mouth, to what came forth from the mouth, in what seems almost a simultaneous displacement and unconscious reinstatement of the organ.

How did the Rabbis make words into a bridge away from sacrifice? First they elevated into sacredness a new text, the Mishnah (completed ca. 200 C.E.).

On the surface, the Mishnah was a description of the actual life practice of the Jewish people in the Land of Israel before the destruction of the Temple. So on the surface, it accepted the centrality of priestly sacrifice.

But the Mishnah was the Rabbis' version of that culture. So it bespoke the deep differences in worldview that came from a group whose existence was built around intellect and study, compared with one rooted in heredity and body.

In the priestly understanding of the world, key distinctions in the universe came directly from God's distinction-making at Creation. In the Rabbis' understanding, human views and uses had much more power to define all boundaries. In the Rabbis' version of Judaism, there was far more room for human judgment and decision-making than there had been in the priests' outlook.

Then, in responding to the Mishnah, explaining it, enlarging on it, reinterpreting it, the Rabbis proclaimed that it was not just the record of a life practice. The Mishnah was also Torah—revealed on Sinai, even though its words had not been written down at the time of Sinai. This aspect of Torah survived as oral tradition from Moses on, and constantly reemerged through the midrashic reinterpretation of the original Torah text.

Thus the Rabbis called it the "oral Torah," as distinct from the written Torah. And around this oral "document" clustered thousands of oral commentaries, spoken in countless chanted conversations over hundreds of years, conversations not only among people in the same room but among people separated by centuries and deserts.

By the fifth century C.E., the Rabbis had woven thousands of words of commentary into thousands of pages of Talmud, reconnecting the newly emerged text of the Mishnah with the older texts of the written Torah and reshaping all of it to address the new situation of a people dispersed in many lands. Thus they made the bridge of words to connect a lived reality with the sacred text.

An oral Torah for an oral people—a people for whom both talking and eating were sacred.

The bridge of words was a spiral bridge. What the Rabbis did was to go forward by going backward. They drew on the ancient texts by reinterpreting them. They did not throw them out, but they did not stay stuck in them. Over and over, they found new meaning between the words and letters.

They explained what they were doing with a poetic lilt: The Torah, they said, was not written in black ink on white parchment. It was written with black fire on white fire. The black fire was the words and letters everyone could see, but in the white fire also—the whiteness of "empty" spaces—there was living Torah. It was simply necessary for every generation to read the deeper meaning in the white fire.

That is how the Rabbis were able to assert that the new life they were living was still a Jewish life.

In order for us to shape our eating, we want to examine in more detail how the Rabbis made the spirituality of words both reaffirm and transform the spirituality of food. But first let us pause a moment to note that this whole process—quite aside from the details of the result—may speak to our own lives.

For we, too, live in an era when the whole pattern of Jewish life as we have known it has been shattered by a powerful set of ideas and practices. For us, Modernity has played the role that Hellenism played for the Jews of two thousand years ago. It has brandished its philosophical and military power and turned us into an "endangered community."

Among us, too, as among our forebears, there has been intense debate about what path to take in response to this crisis:

—Secular Zionism?
—Yiddish socialism?
—Melting into the modern melting pot?
—Restoration of religious life as it was before Modernity?
—The creation of new religious forms that digest Modernity, neither spitting it out nor being swallowed up by it?
—Or . . . what?

More and more of us see Modernity as having come to a dead end in the Holocaust, the shattering of local, face-to-face communities, neighborhoods, families, the danger of a nuclear holocaust, global warming, ozone depletion—but we also see Judaism as we have known it, with its sharp separation from other peoples and its isolation of women, as not yet fully a sacred path of life for our generation.

Can we succeed as did our forebears in shaping a Judaism that is deeply rooted in the Biblical and Rabbinic pasts while it draws on the best truths of Modernity?

Can we learn to read the white fire of the Torah?

HOLY FOOD, HOLY FAST

Keeping these questions in mind, let us turn back to the specific question of what we might learn from how the Rabbis dealt with food.

In one major sphere of life, the Rabbis substituted words for food. That sphere was the everyday gathering of the people to connect with God. The Temple offerings of food had been timed for dawn and dusk. The Rabbis directed that with the Temple gone, the central form of connection between God and the community would be words of murmured prayer, said at the same times of day and night as the offerings had been made.

Indeed, the very first question addressed by the Mishnah, which therefore became the very first words of Rabbinic discussion in the Talmud, was this: "From what time may one recite the Sh'ma in the evening? From the time that the priests enter to eat their Terumah until the end of the first watch." Thus, just as Biblical Israel saw all history beginning with an act of eating in Eden, so the first Rabbinic words connected the central assertion of God's Unity with an act of eating.

Furthermore, some of the Rabbis asserted that the timing of prayer was to be based directly on the pattern of the Temple offerings. They explained the anomaly of the added nighttime prayer by connecting it to the nighttime burning of the animals offered up on the Altar. Other Rabbis disagreed. They claimed that the pattern of prayer three times a day went back long before the Temple was built, long before the Exodus, all the way back to the Patriarchs.

At first glance, this debate may seem so esoteric as to be meaningless to us. But it addresses an important question: Is prayer down-to-earth, or up-to-Heaven? Are the times of prayer defined purely by the Temple offerings of food, or by the Patriarchs' primordial responses to the cosmic movements of the sun?

The debate itself carries a message to us. Dancing in the earthquake of their time, the Rabbis often danced in different rhythms with and against each other. If we find that today, in our own earthquake, we hear different melodies as the ground shifts and shakes beneath our feet, if we become uncertain what to do, we can still enjoy wrestling with each other. We can still feel it as a holy process, even before deciding what practices will most enrich our lives.

As the Rabbis debated, even those who thought the Patriarchs originated daily prayer agreed that whatever Temple food offerings came outside the regular daily pattern must now be replaced by prayer. So the Rabbis provided for an extra prayer service in the synagogue on Shabbat, on festival days, and on the New Moon, because on those occasions an extra food offering had been brought to the Temple.

The Rabbis did not simply replace food with prayerful words as the grounding of a sacred life-path. In most circumstances they sought to fuse words with food. Let us begin with how the Rabbis transformed two powerful moments of the Jewish year, how they turned the two most powerful moments of Temple sacrifice into the two most powerful moments of fusing food and words. One of these moments was Pesach, or Passover; the other, Yom Kippur, the Day of Atonement.

While the Temple stood, Pesach was the time when every family not only brought its lamb for an offering, but actually performed the slaughter itself. Millions of people gathered in Jerusalem at the spring Full Moon, to celebrate the birth of lambs and the sprouting of the barley as well as the birth of the Jewish people and the birth of freedom. But for those Jews who lived beyond reach of Jerusalem—and after the Temple was destroyed, for all Jews—there emerged a *haggadah*, or a telling, words that shaped the first night of Pesach.

The Rabbis who shaped this telling drew on one of the most triumphant Hellenistic uses of words—the Greek philosophic dinner, as in Plato's Symposium—to proclaim the inner freedom of the Jewish people from Hellenistic power. In such a symposium (literally, the Greek means "drinking together"), the guests drank four cups of wine and the wisest of them questioned the others as a way of teaching them how to think correctly.

How did the Rabbis transform this symposium? They made the four cups of wine into symbols of four actions God took to liberate the Israelites. They turned the questioning inside out, so that children, the least learned, could freely challenge their elders and initiate the story. Every morsel of food—the flat, unleavened bread; a bitter herb, and two other kinds of vegetables; the meat or the blood-red beets that substituted for the now impossible lamb offering; salt water; an egg; the wine— became a symbol, intertwined with words to tell the story.

Where the Greeks held a philosophical debate in their symposium, you might say that the Rabbis *ate* their words. Each idea went not just from mouth to ear, but from the dinner table to the belly.

And the Rabbis wove into the fabric of the Telling the spiral process of going back to ancient words to find new meaning. Not only did they make a playful, midrashic reinterpretation of the Torah's story the heart of the Haggadah, they asserted that this process of reinterpretation was not for the past or present alone. They explicitly challenged every generation to retell and reinterpret the story in the light of its own slavery and its own liberation.

The Passover Seder thus became a masterpiece of irony. The Rabbis rejected the Hellenistic worldview in the very process of drawing on Hellenistic practice. They showed that Jewish freedom could be lived even in the nooks and crannies of triumphant Hellenism, by weaving the celebration of freedom into the very nooks and crannies of a Hellenistic ceremony. They fused the Israelites' ancient sacred medium of food and the newer one of words into one of the most powerful rituals in any human culture.

The power of Pesach in focusing holy consciousness on food does not end with the Seder. The requirement that all leavening, or *chametz*, be removed from every Jewish household was read by the Rabbis with such strictness that for one week each year, an additional dimension of *kashrut*—what was kosher to eat—was laid upon all other requirements. In a traditional Jewish household, separate dishes, cooking utensils, foods, and recipes replace all normal kitchen practices.

For centuries, in most Jewish households this meant a radical simplification of what foods were to be eaten during the week of Pesach—because those that were certifiably free of leavening were hard to find. The effect was to set aside one week a year in which people ate very much as the earliest human beings ate: with the simplest possible bread, roasted meat, and fruits and vegetables. Through its special food, Pesach acted as a reminder and renewal of how close we are to the earth. (Similarly, at the other end of the calendar, living for the week of Sukkot in the *sukkah*, a leafy, leaky hut, meant living close to the earth in the simplest shelter human beings could make.)

In recent decades, this function of Pesach as a time of "earthy eating" has been undermined by an enormous proliferation of certifications of food as being *kosher l'Pesach*, kosher for Passover. As a result, traditional homes go through a major upheaval as Pesach approaches, in order to transform all food-related arrangements—but on the other side of the transformation, food is almost as plentiful, varied, and "modern" as before. Even so, the Pesach transformation makes unmistakable that food is a major element in holiness, and holiness a major element in food.

For a very large proportion of Jews today, the Seder continues to work well as a way of fusing foods and words, the past with the future and present, friends and family with the broader community, particular histories and universal hopes. Even so, as I absorb how deeply the Rabbis changed the celebration of Pesach because their world had changed, I find myself wondering:

Has our world changed so much that for us, too, Pesach would be more powerful if we transformed its framework?

For us, half the Jewish people—women—have come more fully into freedom. In our lives, Jews are not slaves or outsiders. In our day, it would be possible again for us to gather in public to celebrate Pesach, as our forebears did when the Temple stood. In our generation, the aspect of Pesach that is about rebirth in springtime has new meaning: For us, spring itself, the cycles of the living earth now stand in danger.

So we may ask whether some new ways of experiencing the connection of Pesach with land and birth and spring and food would be important to us.

Pesach began as a time to address food in a mode of simplicity, so as to express holiness. Yom Kippur drew on total abstention from food for the same purpose. Yom Kippur had begun as a day of "negating the ego" (*la 'anot nafshateychem*). That was understood to mean fasting from nightfall to nightfall, abstaining from all food, water, sex, and other bodily pleasures, and of gathering at the Temple to witness special sacrifices and the High Priest's public chanting of the holiest Name of God as a token of reconciliation between God and the people.

After the destruction of the Temple, what Yom Kippur became under the guidance of the Rabbis was a day of intense and practically continuous prayer. In every Jewish community, everyone gathered to confess collective and individual sins, and to beg God and each other for forgiveness. The Rabbis went out of their way to connect Yom Kippur's abstention from food with speech and action. They drew special attention to a powerful speech about the meaning of food and fasting that comes down to us as Chapter 58 of the Book of Isaiah, and preserved this challenge for future generations by prescribing that passage as the prophetic reading for the morning of Yom Kippur.

The passage was probably actually spoken by a prophetic figure (most scholars would say "Deutero-Isaiah," or Second Isaiah) as a challenge and rebuke on Yom Kippur at the Second Temple, after the Exile in Babylon. "Lift up your voice like a *shofar!*" says God to the Prophet. And the Prophet then challenges the people to rethink what it means to fast on Yom Kippur. He insists that the real "fast" that God demands, the real shattering of ego, is that food be shared with the hungry, clothes with the naked, freedom with those in prison.

Much later, during the time when the Romans destroyed the Second Temple, in the large and sophisticated Diaspora Jewish community of Egypt, Philo of Alexandria suggested another way of viewing the Yom Kippur connection between emptying the mouth of food and filling it with prayerful words. Yom Kippur, he said, comes just before the harvest, the "meal" that feeds the people for an entire year. Before every meal, he pointed out, the people pause for a moment to praise God for the gift of food. So the great long "meal" of the yearly harvest requires a much longer pause from eating, a whole day, to chant long prayers of thanks. That, he said, is *why* Yom Kippur comes just before the harvest.

A WORD OF BLESSING

Pesach and Yom Kippur were probably the most powerful moments in the year for fusing food (or fasting) with words of holiness. But these moments were exceptional only in degree; they were emblematic of everyday practice. The connection between food and words was indeed one of the first concerns of the Talmud, that sea of words the Rabbis poured together so that in it they could swim toward their own vision of the Infinite Horizon.

Imagine an "on-line" computer Internet in which all those who felt sufficiently attracted by Judaism (as their past or as their future) could join to talk it over. Could explore what a renewed Judaism needed to be, ought to be. Could chew a piece of matzah as they sent their thoughts by modem across the miles and years, across the generations and the continents. And then could have their words distilled by a generation of editors who had themselves been profoundly shaped by these discussions—distilled so that what remained might speak to another thousand years of Jews.

That, in the technology of its day, was what the Talmud was.

The Talmud begins with a section called *Zera'im* (literally, "Seeds," and more generally, "Agriculture"). It includes subsections on how to share food with the poor, how to tithe from fig trees and grainfields and vineyards, what gifts to bring the priests, and how to offer up the first fruits in the spring. All food. But the very *first* subsection, the very beginning of the Talmud, is entitled *B'rakhot*—"Blessings." Just as we must bless the God Who gives food before we eat of the food, so we must talk about those blessings before we talk of the food.

For the Rabbis, the very notion of blessing is shaped by the assumption that what most deserves and needs blessings is the God Who feeds us. These blessings at the dinner table become another way of replacing the Temple offerings, in that they explicitly focus on food and hallow it. They give specific weight to a saying of the Rabbis: After the destruction of the Temple, the dinner table in every Jewish home is what replaces the Altar.

> For ourselves in our own generation, the memory that the Rabbis created
> these blessings over food can spur us to imagine a daily practice of our own
> that would affirm the Unity of human, food, and earth.

The starting point is that there must be words of thanks at the end of every meal. (What makes a "meal"? The eating of bread.) The Rabbis read the Biblical passage "And you shall eat and be satisfied and bless..." (Deut. 8:10) to mean that after eating, after feeling satisfied, we should bless the God from Whose bounty the food came.

But for them, this was not enough. They went on: "Granted that a blessing is to be said after eating, how do we know it is to be said before? If we say a blessing when we are full, how much more so when we are hungry!" And the Rabbis continued: "If anyone enjoys anything of this world without a blessing, he commits sacrilege." No, says Rabbi Hanina bar Pappa, "it is like robbery from God and the community of Israel." (B'rakhot 35a, 35b)

The Rabbis also felt it was necessary to begin even before the beginning. Even before words are spoken, the body must be prepared. A regular meal should be approached only with hands that had themselves been made sacredly clean. So any meal that includes bread must begin with a ceremonial handwashing. (The actual cleaning of the hands should be done first.)

Since the ritual washing requires focused attention, it is done not from a running faucet but from a pitcher or glass—often one set aside for that specific purpose—that sometimes has two handles so that it can be picked up one-handedly from either side to wash first one hand and then the other.

After the washing and before the hands are dried, the blessing is said: "Blessed are You, YHWH our God, ruler of the universe, Who has made us holy through commandments and commanded us about raising the hands—*Baruch attah YHWH eloheynu melekh ha'olam asher kidshanu b'mitzvotav vitzivanu al netilat yadai'im.*" (After drying the hands, some people lift them up in a gesture of thanks to Heaven.) Then, keeping silent or humming a wordless tune so as not to break the connection between this blessing and the meal, those who are participating in the meal come back to the table to say the appropriate blessing over food and to eat.

What is the appropriate blessing? Here the Rabbis think it is important to note what specific food we are about to eat.

For what grows on trees, the Rabbis of the Mishnah said, "Blessed is the One Who creates the fruit of the tree," except for wine, for which the blessing was "Who creates the fruit of the vine."

For what they called "fruit from the earth," they prescribed "Who creates the fruit of the earth," except for bread, for which the words are "Who brings forth bread from the earth."

These categories are obviously rooted partly in the origins of food. To the Rabbis whatever came from bushes, roots, stalks, seeds, seemed crucially different from what grew on trees. But what was the other factor, the one that distinguished bread and wine from other foods?

The next generations of Rabbis, in the commentary that became the Gemara, wondered whether the second factor was the degree of human intervention in preparing food. They conclude, however, that the crucial distinction was not the effect human beings had on the food, but rather the effects that bread and wine have on the human beings, in cheering and sustaining them in a way that apples, grapes, rice, and even other prepared foods like olive oil do not.

For anything that does not grow directly from the earth—meat, fish, eggs, cheese, for example—and for everything drinkable except wine, the Rabbis specified the blessing "By Whose word the All comes to be."

The Mishnah explains that there is a hierarchy in these blessings:

> If one says over fruit of the tree the blessing "Who creates the fruit of the
> ground," the obligation is fulfilled; but if one says over fruit of the ground
> the blessing "Who creates the fruit of the tree," the obligation is not fulfilled.
> If one says, "By Whose word" over any of them, the obligation is fulfilled.
> (Mishnah B'rakhot 6:I)

This seems strictly logical: The All is the root of earth, which is at the root of trees.

If this logic and the basic obligation were all we needed to know, it would be simplest to use "By Whose word" on all occasions. But the Rabbis preferred that those who eat give their attention to where in the earth's economy the food is coming from, not just depend on the sense that it all comes ultimately from God. So they said that one should focus consciously in advance on what foods are to be eaten, where they come from, and therefore which blessing to use.

Over the centuries since the Talmud, the Rabbis codified how to make these choices. Above all, if wine is to be drunk during the meal, the blessings begin there, recognizing how special wine is. If bread is to be used at the meal, it is assumed that it is to be the main food; therefore the blessing for bread is what should be said. But if one goes for a glass of water or a piece of fruit between meals, or eats other foods without bread, or at the meal eats something that is not usually served and therefore not "covered" by the bread blessing—then the specific blessing for that food would be made.

Traditionally, all these blessings begin "Blessed are You, YHWH our God, ruler of the universe . . . —*Baruch attah YHWH eloheynu melekh ha'olam* . . ." and continue as follows:

- For fruit from a tree (defined as having permanent branches, with the leaves appearing on the branches and the trunk but not from the roots): "Who creates the fruit of the tree—*borey pri ha'eytz.*"
- For produce from the soil (vegetables, potatoes, bananas, beans): "Who creates the fruit of the earth—*borey pri ha'adamah.*"
- For pastry made from any of the five grains widely grown in the ancient Land of Israel (several varieties of wheat, barley, and spelt), distinct from ordinary bread in that it is made with honey, fat, oil, juice, or eggs, or with fillings of fruit, cheese, and so forth: "Who creates different kinds of grain foods—*borey meeney m'zonot.*"

- For bread: "Who brings forth bread from the earth—*ha-motzi lekhem min ha-'aretz.*"
- For wine: "Who creates the fruit of the vine—*borey pri ha'gefen.*"

The blessings at the beginning of a meal are raised to a still higher level on Shabbat and festivals. The Kiddush, a special blessing that celebrates the unusual holiness of the day itself, is intertwined with the beginnings of the meal. On Friday evening or the eve of a festival, after lighting candles in honor of the day, the household turns to the dinner table. The Rabbis observed that Kiddush could be made over either wine or bread, but that wine was preferable. So the Shabbat Kiddush begins with a recitation of the Biblical passage about the creation of the seventh day, continues with the blessing over wine, and concludes with a blessing focused on Shabbat.

Then comes the blessing over bread. On Shabbat and many festivals, the bread is a special one that has been braided or shaped into a symbolic form. This bread is called *challah*, an echo of the name for a special gift of dough to the priests or to God. There are two loaves of *challah* on Shabbat, in memory of the double portion of manna that came to the Israelites in the Wilderness on the day before Shabbat, so that they would not have to gather manna on Shabbat itself.

The *challah* is covered by a cloth, out of respect to its own honor, so that it should not feel ashamed that the Kiddush is being said over wine instead of bread. This cloth is ceremoniously removed, the blessing over bread is said, and salt is lightly strewn on the *challah* in memory of the spices at the Temple.

The *challah* is either divided by human fingers or is cut with a knife that has been kept hidden during the reciting of the Kiddush so that a swordlike weapon does not defile the coming of Shabbat. For Shabbat is the foretaste of that day when swords shall be beaten into plowshares and bread shall come from joyful plowing, not from conquest.

In many households, the *challah* plate is handed around the table so that each person can take from it, and all can understand that bread comes from God, not from human hands.

At midday on Shabbat or a festival, an abbreviated form of the Kiddush echoes this process of hallowing the food. Just as there were extra Temple offerings of food on Shabbat and festivals, so through extra blessings the Shabbat or festival meals become a strengthened form of greeting God's gifts of the food.

"AND YOU ARE SATISFIED"

As we have seen, the Rabbis taught that after eating the meal and feeling satisfied, it was again necessary to bless the Source of nourishment. They drew this teaching from the logic of a verse of Torah, but no doubt it probably also felt important because of their own experience. From their own lives they knew to pause and bless the Source both when they might be driven by hunger into gulping the food without a higher consciousness, and when they might be fooled by comfort into relaxing without a higher consciousness.

The Rabbis taught that if a full meal had been eaten, symbolized by eating bread and beginning with "ha-motzi lekhem min ha'aretz," then the Birkat haMazon, the full Grace after Meals, should be said at the same table where one has eaten, with some food (at least some bread) allowed to remain on the table till the Grace has been completed.

If a quorum of at least three adult males (more recently, in most communities, three adults) was present, Grace would begin with an invitation (zimun) to join in blessing the One Who has given what we have eaten. There would follow a brief rhythmic exchange between the leader and the others, accepting the invitation and initiating the praise.

This assertion that three people can make up a special quorum for communal prayer is unusual. The ordinary arrangement is that from one person to nine, nothing changes; each person is a lonely individual, and it takes ten persons to make up a prayer community.

With food the assumption changes. Yes, the Rabbis said, there is a difference between individuality and community. But when there is food before us, this change happens in a different way. Food plus three people make up a community.

It is as if the presence of food could make up for the absence of seven people— as if food represented the entire Seven Days of Creation, the whole web of water, wind, sun, seed, soil, animal, and human that culminated in the fruit of the sacred Tree.

In this way, the Rabbis affirmed the power of eating as a way to create community, and gave to those who were hungry a deeper hunger to eat together so that they could be fed spiritually as well as materially. (The Rabbis did not erase the boundary of ten entirely; they provided that if ten or more were present, the responsive zimun formula would be enriched by adding "Eloheynu, our God.")

What followed the rhythmic responses of zimun was determined partly by the placement of a meal in the cycle of Jewish time—weekday, Shabbat, or festival— and partly by circumstance—which foods have we eaten? Is there time to relax?

The usual traditional form on an ordinary weekday includes four blessings, three of which end with the formulaic *"Baruch attah YHWH..."* and then add a specific aspect of God's nourishing presence.

The first of these blessings focuses on praising God's ever-present loving gift of food for all creatures, ending, *"...hazan et-hakol*—Who feeds all."

The second thanks God for having shaped the Jewish people in the past through the specific gifts of the Land of Israel, liberation from slavery in Mitzrai'im (Egypt), the covenantal act of circumcision, the teachings of the Torah, and ever-renewed nourishment, and it ends with *"...al ha'aretz v'al haMazon*—for the land and for food."

The third looks toward the future, with hope and pleading that the Messianic days of peace and justice come to heal the wounds of Jerusalem, ending *"...boneh b'rachamav Yirushalay'im, ameyn!*—Who through compassion builds Jerusalem—amen!"

The fourth begins with an alphabetical ecstasy of praises for the God Who moment after moment, day after day, past, present, and future, showers abundance upon us. In this blessing appear a number of invocations of *"HaRachaman!*—Compassionate One!" that celebrate particular aspects of God's compassion, and are open to individual additions by those present. The fourth blessing includes the conventional *"Baruch"* formula for the One Who makes peace, but ends with a series of verses from the Prophets and Psalms that celebrate God's gifts of love, strength, and peace.

We might pause for a moment to explore the logic of this four-part blessing. The first part is an overall affirmation of the One Who feeds all—all human beings, all species, the earth itself. Then the blessing turns to specific experiences of the Jewish people.

The blessings fall into categories that partly reflect aspects of time, past, present, and future, and partly the thoughts and emotions that accompany each of these different time periods. In the second blessing, we recall a past when we drew our food from a single land, and there was a spiritual unity between cultural nurturance and physical nourishment. In the third blessing, we look forward to a future when this will again be so. In the fourth blessing, we recognize that in the present, not only in our memories and our hopes, there is a bounty that comes from the whole earth and makes us joyful and thankful.

Traditionally, on Shabbat and festivals the blessings after meals are enhanced just as the blessings before meals (and the offerings at the Temple) were. On these days the Grace after Meals is begun—even before the *zimun*—by chanting Psalm 126, which compares the joy of liberation after the pain of exile to the joy of the harvest after the painful toil of planting.

Thus the Rabbis, shaping a life-path for a time and place of exile, make every Shabbat or festival meal a material and spiritual harvest. Each fulfilling, restful meal becomes a memory of past peace and plenty in the land, an analog of it in the present, and a foretaste of it in the future.

In addition, specific references to Shabbat and festivals were inserted in the blessings for meals on those days. In some communities, a final blessing over wine is said on those days, after the regular Grace is completed. Phrases are added at weddings and circumcisions, and during *shiva*, the time of mourning.

On ordinary weekdays, in some communities the *zimun* is preceded by Psalm 137, "By the rivers of Babylon," mourning our separation from the land that was once the earthly source of our food and the Holy City where we brought food to celebrate its spiritual Source.

The Rabbis expected there to be situations when time was too short to say the whole Grace, and they provided for shortened versions, in which the blessings for the Food-giver and the blessings for the land and Jerusalem were required. In great urgency, one might simply say in Aramaic, *"Brikh rachmana, malka d'alma, marei d'hai pita,"* or in English, "Blessed be the Compassionate Ruler, Who governs this bread."

If the meal includes no bread, then the full *Birkat haMazon* is not said, and one or another simpler blessing replaces it. One of these alternate blessings is to be said on occasions when the meal contains wine, pastries made from the grains that were characteristic of the Land of Israel, or fruits also characteristic of the land— figs, dates, olives, and pomegranates. The other blessing follows a meal in which only ordinary fruits or vegetables have been eaten.

❧

What questions does this whole pattern of blessings raise for us?

- How do we focus our bodies, minds, and emotions on what it means to turn food into our muscles and our life energy? Are washing our hands and saying words the best ways to do this?
- Does the pattern of blessings help us make conscious choices of what, how much, and how quickly we eat? If not, what practices might do this? How can we best restrain our tendencies toward gluttony or self-starvation?
- What are the distinctions we would make between one kind of food and another? Is the distinction between what is tree-grown and what earth-grown important to us? Would we seek to distinguish foods that come from animals and from plants? Or to distinguish what comes from living animals (eggs, milk) and from dead ones (meat)? Do bread and wine feel different from grain and grape, as they did to the Rabbis?
- Are there other things we ingest that would feel important to recognize and hallow? Air, for instance? Could we imagine a system of blessings over different kinds of breath as elaborate as this one over different kinds of food?

Or perhaps blessings over different forms of light and different forms of warmth? Would we want to bless sunlight, fossil fuels, wind, tides, nuclear radiation as different sources of energy?

Perhaps most basic of all, we must ask ourselves: In our own time of earthquake both in the world and for the Jewish people, do we need to rethink how to make food sacred as deeply as our forebears did? For them, food was no longer what they grew in a small land by dint of their own labors, but what came to them by ship and camel train. For us, food has more and more become what is manufactured, not just grown: It comes from crossbred and genetically engineered plants and animals; it comes with inserted vitamins; it comes heavily packaged, precooked, frozen, irradiated, invented.

What is even more to the point, most Jews no longer find useful as a sacred path the Rabbinic system of blessings that we have just examined. Is that because words said in a formula no longer carry such a weight of holiness for us? Would we find it more authentic to say an impromptu word of thanks and blessing at the moment we face the food? Or do we live today in such a flood of words that just silence, breathing calmly, and holding the hands of our companions at the table would help us focus more deeply on the holiness of food? Or do we need to reconnect with the earth and our bodies in some new way to bring home to ourselves the meaning of food? Or . . . ?

What gives me most hope is the knowledge that we have danced with an earthquake before. (I keep coming back to this metaphor; perhaps I should experiment with letting my arms dance a thanksgiving at the dinner table?)

If we do not yet have the answers to these questions, still I know from my reading of the Rabbis' Talmud that the exploration itself can be a form of holiness.

V. THE KOSHER KITCHEN

As we explore our own situation, living in earthquakes of change and trying to prepare ourselves for entering a transformed planetary household, it may be useful to absorb what the Rabbis hoped to achieve as they reshaped Jewish life.

They had two problems to solve.

One we might call "vertical": how to offer up food to God in the absence of a physical Temple. They tried to address that question through the patterns of blessings over food that we have reviewed.

The second problem we might call "horizontal": how to distinguish the Jewish people from other peoples, since Jews were no longer living separately in their own homeland, but instead were scattered everywhere among those other peoples. And therefore, how to make the Diaspora dinner table so distinctive that at every meal a separate Jewish peoplehood was reaffirmed. The Rabbis addressed this by shaping a code of kosher food even more elaborate than that laid out by the written Torah.

How do the requirements of this code play out now, elaborated by centuries of practice and decision-making?

First, let us note that today a large part of the Jewish community around the world—explicit secularists like many Israelis and Jews from the former Soviet Union, and the Reform and part of the Reconstructionist religious communities in America—has dropped much of the traditional system of *kashrut* from its Jewish practice. Yet—a rich and almost funny paradox—at the same time there is in America a wider variety of foods that have been certified as "kosher" by traditional rabbis than ever before in Jewish history. Since those foods are broadly available to everyone, not just Jews, more non-Jews are actually eating kosher foods than ever before in history.

Although the code of kosher food was partly intended to separate Jews from other communities in the way they ate—and therefore in the way they lived— kosher food itself is probably playing less of that role now than it ever has. The rules that go beyond the food itself, however—especially the ones about cooking and eating utensils—continue to distinguish traditional Jews from other Jews and other communities.

What are we to make of this? How much separation, along what boundary markers, do we want? Is there a spiritual value to the kosher code as it has evolved? To begin to address these questions, we will look at the Rabbinic approach as it stands today in Conservative, Orthodox, and some Reconstructionist circles.

There are four main categories of requirements:

1. Which species of animals, fish, and birds are legitimate to eat?
2. Which specific animals and fowl have defects in their own bodies or in the slaughtering and preparation processes that would make them unfit to eat?
3. What needs to be done to separate products containing milk and those containing meat from being eaten together?
4. What special requirements are attached to foods that do not come from animals at all—wine, bread, fruit, and so forth?

SPECIES AND SPECIFICS

In the first category, the Biblical distinctions of what is permitted and prohibited were developed by the Rabbis with little change.

What mammals are permitted is clear enough: cattle, sheep, goats, oxen, buffalo, and deer. Pigs, horses, camels, whales, and rabbits are among those meats that are prohibited.

Chickens, turkeys, doves, pigeons, quail, partridges, peacocks, and domesticated geese and ducks are the main birds that it is permissible to eat. (Some authorities have permitted pheasants; others, not.)

Fish with fins and scales are in general permitted. There is a debate about whether sturgeon and swordfish have true scales; most Orthodox authorities say no and prohibit them, while most Conservative authorities say yes and permit them.

The Biblical tradition that permits some locusts and grasshoppers continues among Yemenite and other Oriental Jewish communities; Western authorities have prohibited all species of insects on the grounds that they no longer know which ones are permitted.

The only permissible milk and eggs are those of permitted species. The ancient Rabbis ruled that honey from bees was permitted on the grounds that it was not produced from their bodies but transferred from flowers to the comb. (They turned out to be physiologically incorrect, but the ruling stood.)

IN THE BLOOD IS THE LIFE

How must animals and fowl be prepared for eating? The Rabbinic tradition developed an elaborate set of practices based on three elements of the Biblical culture: the intense and oft-repeated prohibition against any consumption of blood; the prohibition against eating an animal that had died of disease or by being attacked by another animal; and the sacred process of offering animals at the Temple, including the ritual practices that accompanied the offering.

As ritual slaughter shifted from the Temple to the widely scattered Jewish community, the practices that had probably been passed on from priest to priest by word of mouth were made more publicly available and more elaborate by the Rabbis, in the code called *shechita*. Its central element is the slitting of the animal's throat in a single uninterrupted stroke with an extremely sharp knife, without any stabbing motion and without any pressure, and without causing pain as much as possible.

The *shochet* (ritual slaughterer) is a highly trained religious official, who must be spiritually focused, Jewishly knowledgeable, and as skilled in the theory and practice of slaughter as the rabbi is in requirements of prayer. The *shochet* examines the knife before and after each individual act of slaughter, to see whether there are any nicks or dents on the blade. If any are found beforehand, the knife must be resharpened to perfection; if any are found afterward, the animal's meat cannot be kosher and the knife must be resharpened before *shechita* can continue.

Since *shechita* cuts off the blood supply to the brain almost instantly, pain is minimized; since the heart pumps blood through the severed artery, a great deal of blood is emptied at once from the body (in line with the Biblical command that it be poured out, not eaten).

Some governments outside of the State of Israel and some non-Jewish organizations have on occasion questioned the humaneness of *shechita*. Sometimes they seem authentically concerned for the protection of animals, and sometimes their concern seems to have an anti-Semitic bias.

These criticisms have focused mainly on whether animals should be stunned before slaughter. Most authorities on *kashrut* have ruled that it is not permitted to stun animals with a blow to the head or an electric shock before slaughter. This ruling stems partly from fear that such stunning will in fact not be thorough, and that the animal will suffer much more pain than in *shechita*; and partly from concern that stunning the animal will diminish the flow of blood that occurs when *shechita* is performed, thus leaving much more blood in the body and the meat.

Hoisting and shackling animals have been used to hold them immobile and permit a more deft and painless slaughter, but in recent years objections that this process causes pain to the animals have led to pens that are designed to hold each animal quiet at the time of slaughter without the need to hoist it. Some but not yet all *shechita* uses these special pens.

Among the unresolved questions about *shechita* that contemporary Jews face are about making slaughter painless and humane. First of all, is there any way to do this so long as animals are killed? Secondly, should efforts in this direction be constrained by the basic outlines of *shechita*? What if it became clear that more nearly painless slaughter was possible by using means that might not fit inside the rules of *shechita*? To which set of values should the Jewish community give precedence?

The Rabbinic effort to avoid using the meat of an animal that might have been dying or sick or killed by other animals (or human hunters) leads to an elaborate examination (*bedikah*) of the body after the actual slaughter. The presence of any of a number of defects makes the animal unfit for Jewish use—that is, *treyf* or *terefah*.

(Originally, *treyf* meant "torn by a wild beast" and therefore unfit to eat. The word has come to mean broadly unkosher, and its use, like that of "kosher," has spread beyond food to what is generally fitting or unfitting.)

Certain adhesions, perforations, discolorations, and unusual textures of the lungs, and certain defects of the skeletal, digestive, or circulatory system, make the animal *treyf*. In this way, the animal is held to two overlapping standards: one that is medical, since disease disqualifies the animal; and one that is spiritual, since blemishes that would have disqualified an animal from being offered at the ancient Temple disqualify it from being kosher today.

The overall requirement for the animal's lungs is that they be smooth (*glatt* in Yiddish). If the lungs are not smooth, but stick to the chest wall (have "adhesions"), the animal may be *treyf*. But if there is only one adhesion, there are certain tests and judgments to ascertain how serious it is. The meat may still be kosher. Normally, if there are two adhesions the presumption of *treyf* is very strong. Even then, if Shabbat is so imminent that there is no time to buy more meat, or if the family is poor, the ordinary *shochet* might consult a sage to ascertain whether even these adhesions might be harmless so that the meat could be kosher.

Among some Hassidic and other Orthodox communities, however, the custom has arisen of rejecting animals in which the lungs are not absolutely smooth, in which any adhesions at all appear—even some that would be harmless if the *halakha* (law) were strictly applied. This standard has become known as "*glatt* kosher." Some Conservative and some Orthodox communities or individuals have felt resentment at the hint of a superior *kashrut*, especially one that renders meat *treyf* that by strict halakhic standards is not. So they have themselves avoided using *glatt* kosher meat in order to avoid giving legitimacy to such a notion.

This distinction is one of many carved out by subcommunities that set different standards of what is kosher enough to eat. From a sociological standpoint, these distinctions serve the function of differentiating groups of Jews from each other in a very dramatic and socially powerful way: *Can we eat together?*

In this way, the specific points of *kashrut* act in miniature, within the Jewish community, a good deal like the way in which *kashrut* as a whole distinguishes the Jewish people from other peoples. One of the major issues facing our own generation is how to deal with this whole distinction-making process. In our own time, do we want to emphasize differences between Jews and other peoples and differences within the Jewish community by defining sharply which people can eat together—or do we want to encourage different groups to eat together? If the latter, how should we deal with our different views of what is proper to eat?

From a religious standpoint, these differences betoken serious efforts to understand the will of God—efforts that result in disagreement over interpretation. At that point, a religious understanding can move in one of two directions: either that one side or the other has misunderstood God's will, or that the Infinity of God is being played out in the multiplicity of human understandings. Each of these outlooks appears within the Rabbinic tradition at different times, from different individuals, and on different issues.

Let us return, then, to the specifics of the code of kosher meat:

After slaughter, the animal goes through a series of procedures known together as "porging" (*nikkor* in Hebrew, *treibern* in Yiddish) to accomplish the removal of as much of the remaining blood as possible; certain fats that are traditionally prohibited; and (in mammals but not in fowl) the sciatic nerve, which is also traditionally prohibited.

The prohibition against eating the sciatic nerve is explained in the Torah as a mark of respect for that nerve, because during Jacob's wrestle with God, as a result of which he was renamed "Yisrael," "Israel," the "Godwrestler," his sciatic nerve was damaged, and he limped "sidewise" the rest of his life.

This story is perhaps the Jewish version of the legend of the wounded hero who is transformed by a profound spiritual struggle but continues to bear the marks of it. In characteristic Jewish fashion, the story—which obviously lies at the very root of the identity of the people of Israel, the Godwrestling people—thus becomes reenacted in the code of daily eating.

Since it is very hard to strip out the sciatic nerve from the hindquarters through which it runs, most Jewish communities in the West have simply not used the hindquarters of a slaughtered animal and have sold that meat to their non-Jewish neighbors. Eastern Jewish communities, however, probably because they were often poorer and needed the meat, trained porgers in how to remove the sciatic nerve. In the modern State of Israel, that practice has been followed.

One of the main aspects of porging concerns the removal of every possible drop of blood from the meat. Much of this has to be done by the *shochet* or by the kosher butcher, who must learn how from someone who already knows; some aspects may remain in the hands of the household itself.

In order to draw out the blood that remains after slaughter and initial porging, the butcher rinses the meat and soaks it for at least half an hour, but less than twenty-four hours, in a special pot or vat set aside for that purpose. This process must be completed within three days of the slaughtering.

The soaking must be followed by salting the meat with a medium-coarse salt that will draw out any remaining blood in such a way that it can drain off. The salt must be placed on all surface areas of the meat and must remain for an hour (or in emergencies, no less than eighteen minutes). Then all the salt is removed by rinsing the meat three times.

The coarse salt that is often sold for this purpose is frequently called "kosher salt." It is not especially kosher in itself—pure salt cannot be unkosher—but is called that because it is used for this part of the process of making food kosher— that is, "kashering" it. It would be more accurate to call the salt "kashering salt."

Since blood accumulates in the heart and the liver, these organs are dealt with in special ways. The heart must be sliced open before being salted, and the liver must be broiled on a grill that is set up in such a way that the blood can drain off.

Broiling meat to the point of edibility (after which it can be cooked in any desired fashion) can be substituted for soaking and salting as a way of eliminating the blood, but it should be done on a specific grill that is set aside for "unkashered" meats only. This approach can be used for people on low-salt diets.

Eggs with blood spots from an unschechted embryo chick cannot be eaten. Many kosher households will first break an egg into a separate cup, check it for blood, and only then pour the egg into a bigger pot with other eggs, to avoid mixing a *treyf* egg into a batch of kosher ones and making the whole batch *treyf*.

This whole set of efforts to remove as much blood as possible from kosher meat may raise questions in our own day. What can we make of the assertion that "the life is in the blood"? What effect does it have to try so hard to eliminate blood from our diets, even while we continue to eat meat? Does the effort move us in the direction of eating less meat, or none? Or does the whole process seem pointless, and do we find ourselves pulled toward either eating meat with all the blood still in it or giving up meat altogether?

FOOD OF LIFE, FOOD OF DEATH

The third major issue in *kashrut* is the separation of milk from meat. We have already met the textual origin of this practice: the Torah's thrice-repeated prohibition "You shall not boil a kid in the milk of its mother." By the time the Mishnah was edited (in the second century of the Common Era), the Rabbis already assumed that not only the milk and meat of one particular mother-kid relationship cannot be cooked together, but neither can the milk of any mammal be cooked with the meat of any mammal.

The Rabbis went still further in extending the range of the prohibition: Since the Torah does not waste words, they said, the triple repetition itself must be communicating that more than the surface meaning is intended. They derived from this the sense that Jews (1) may not cook any flesh in milk or with a dairy product, nor (2) eat them mixed together, nor (3) derive any benefit from them mixed together (for example, by selling the mixture).

There is, by the way, a modern Jewish joke that both draws on and lampoons this method of interpretation:

Said God to Moses, "Don't boil a kid in its mother's milk!" Moses replied, "You mean you don't want us to make cheeseburgers?"

Said God, mildly shocked and bewildered, "I just said—not a kid in the milk of its mother!"

Moses frowned, twirled his beard, and responded, "You mean, don't even use the same plates for cheese and meat?"

God's face reddened. "Just don't boil a kid in the milk of its mother!"

Said Moses, "My God! You mean we have to wait six whole hours after eating meat before we can have some milk?"

God threw the Divine Arms wide into the Cosmos: "Have it your own way, Moses!"

And so we do.

There was some debate in Mishnaic times over how far to carry the meaning of "flesh." Since the "mothers" of fish and birds do not have any milk in which their offspring could be boiled, the question was raised whether it was allowable to mix fish or birds with milk or dairy products. The Rabbis decided that although in the strictest sense it might be allowable, the flesh of poultry was so much like that of mammals that if people began to cook chickens in milk, cooking lamb in milk would soon follow. So they insisted that poultry (which also had to undergo *shechita* in order to become kosher for Jews to eat) should be treated like meat. Fish, on the other hand, was not brought under the same rules.

Out of all this emerged three categories of food: *basari, fleishig,* or meat; *chalavi, milchig,* or dairy; and *pareve,* or neutral. Fish, eggs, vegetables, fruit, wine, water, and all other foods that had no perceptible amount of either meat or dairy products in them were *pareve.* (Traditionally, though fish could be eaten at the same meal as meat, it would not be placed on the same plate.)

In order to avoid the prohibited mixtures, the Rabbis required that all cooking and eating utensils be assigned to one of the categories. Typically, a kosher household has a full set of *milchig* and *fleishig* utensils and dishes. For making *pareve* foods it has not a full set but several pots, bowls, and other cooking utensils. After the *pareve* foods are cooked, they are then transferred to either *milchig* or *fleishig* dishes, to be brought to the table. Then in these new dishes, they cease to be *pareve* and become either *fleishig* or *milchig.* Some of the *pareve* food might be kept in *pareve* bowls to be held for use at another meal, with either meat or milk.

The utensils of different categories are washed, dried, and stored separately, with different sponges, dishcloths, dish drainers, sink liners, and towels for each category. Some people run their dishwasher empty at its highest temperature between *fleishig* and *milchig* uses. Others use the machine for only one category of utensils, or have two machines, or two dish racks for alternate use in one machine.

Utensils made of wood, pottery, or plastic, since they are porous and absorb the juices of milk and its products or meat, are considered impossible to change from *fleishig* to *milchig* or vice versa, and they are impossible to kasher if they have been used for nonkosher foods.

Glass utensils, which do not absorb liquids, are considered permissible to use for either *milchig* or *fleishig* since they can simply be washed. On these grounds, in early times it might have been acceptable to buy one set of glass dishes, and use that set alone to move back and forth between *milchig* and *fleishig* meals. Many Rabbis opposed this, however, because glass dishes were more expensive than pottery ones, and this practice would have allowed the rich to keep kosher with much less trouble than the poor. So kashering glass utensils was reserved for cases when mistakes had been made.

One-piece metal utensils are hard, but not impossible, to kasher. This is done by letting them sit unused for twenty-four hours, cleaning them thoroughly, and then totally immersing them in boiling water or playing a blowtorch over them. (The water must not drop below boiling point and must totally cover the utensil. One traditional way of accomplishing this was to drop a red-hot brick into the vat of boiling water, forcing the water to slop over the top at a boiling temperature.) Alternatively, such utensils can be buried in the earth of a garden or flowerpot for one year.

Ovens can be kashered with a blowtorch or by being heated for half an hour, empty, to their hottest temperature.

Perhaps the sharpest debate over separation of meat and milk focuses on hard cheeses. Most of these require rennet to harden. But most rennet comes from the stomach lining of a mammal. There are three different views of this question. One is that the rennet is still meat, and that no cheese made with animal rennet is kosher. Another is that only rennet from kosher animals that have been correctly slaughtered can be used in making kosher cheese. A third—accepted by most Conservative authorities—is that the rennet has undergone a radical chemical change and can no longer be identified at all as a *fleishig* substance; so cheeses using rennet are kosher.

There may soon be some rennet available that is made by bacteria that have been genetically reengineered by introduction of a mammalian gene. Is this distant enough from the animal origin to make the rennet non-*fleishig* in all eyes? Perhaps. Or will some consider the genetic recombination itself a violation of Torah prohibitions of the mixing of species? Perhaps.

There is also a debate over whether to use only milk prepared by Jews (*chalav Yisrael*) and products made from it, on the grounds that non-Jews might mix the milk of nonkosher animals into kosher milk. In Conservative and most Orthodox communities, present public laws against such mixtures are accepted as sufficient safeguards.

The Rabbis decreed a separation in time as well as space between *fleishig* and *milchig* foods. They required a delay after eating meat products before eating dairy products, in order to cleanse the mouth from particles of meat. In some communities this delay is six hours; in some, three; and in some, one hour. No delay is necessary after eating most milk products, except for the blessing that recognizes that the *milchig* meal has been completed. (Hard cheeses require the same delay before eating meat as meat does before eating dairy products.)

The Rabbis ruled that in some cases an accidental mixture of meat and dairy foods need not make the food inedible. In general, for example, if by accident a volume of meat fell into a volume of dairy food that was more than sixty times as large, the meat could be removed and the dairy food would remain kosher. There were, however, exceptions and cautions to such rules.

What are we to make of this extraordinarily elaborate life pattern, all focused on keeping meat and milk separate? All this—one may well think—from the basic prohibition on boiling a kid in the milk of its mother! Surely there is more at stake here.

Perhaps there is. The Jewish philosopher Abraham Joshua Heschel, who in his own life drew his ideas from Hassidic mysticism, German philosophy, and American political freedom, suggested that embedded in the original warning against "boiling the kid" was a deep empathy for the giver, the giving, and the given of life. The ewe that suckled, the kid that sucked, and the milk that carried all the nourishment of life—together they were the weave of life. To boil the child of one in the milk of the other shattered this weave, made a mockery of mothering, and thus of life.

So far, so good. But then why extend the rule to all meat, all milk? Was it perhaps because that was a way of making even broader and deeper in everyday consciousness the necessity of distinguishing between life and death? Between the milk that among mammals is preeminently the food of life, and the meat that is obviously the food of death?

Do these separations have the effect of strengthening our respect for life and for the nurturance that humans and other mammals share? What would be the most effective ways in daily life of teaching us not only intellectually but at emotional and practical levels, the protection of life?

To look at another aspect of the milk-meat distinctions: Do we believe that the time delays between eating meat and dairy products are useful in reducing gluttony by encouraging us to make conscious choices of what, how much, and how quickly to eat? If not, what practices do we think would best do this?

Finally, some have argued that in our own day, this area is the one in which the distinction-making of *kashrut* becomes most detailed and most apparent—some would say, most obsessive and most intrusive—in daily Jewish life. Therefore, this is the area in which the consciousness of Jewish "difference" is most sharply experienced. How do we feel about these distinctions and differences? Would we want to abandon them, make other distinctions the badge of Jewish difference, or add them to the traditional ones?

FRUITS OF THE EARTH

Let us now examine those aspects of *kashrut* that apply to foods that come from plants.

For the ancient Rabbis, wine and bread carried special weight. So they laid down special requirements for the kosher preparation of wine and bread.

After some debate, the early Rabbis prohibited drinking wine made by non-Jews—originally because it was often used in offerings to their gods. This prohibition was then extended even to wine not used in such offerings and to wine made by monotheistic communities not suspected of idolatrous offerings. The Rabbis were concerned that sharing wine with other communities could encourage socializing, intermarriage, and departures from Judaism. "Kosher" wines, therefore, were restricted to those in which no non-Jews took part in any stage of manufacture, from pressing the grapes to sealing the bottle.

In 1964, Conservative authorities ruled that since most American wines are made by automated factories, the prohibition does not apply to them. They therefore suggested that these wines are acceptable for ordinary drinking, but that "kosher" (especially Israeli) wines should be used for explicit religious observances, such as making Kiddush for Shabbat and festivals. The sense of the world that underlay this ruling seems to have been that in American society, social connection with non-Jews is a desirable, not a disastrous, practice; and that the more open view adopted by some of the ancient Rabbis should now prevail.

Just as the Biblical tradition had viewed not only the growing of grain by farmers but also the baking of bread by households as an important moment to connect with the priesthood, so to the Rabbis the baking of bread, as an especially important aspect of cooking, seemed a sacred moment.

In the Biblical mode, the first loaf (*challah*), baked of dough made from new-grown grain, was given to the priest. The Rabbis noted that this requirement applied only to bread made from grain grown in the Land of Israel, and only when the majority of Jews lived there. But they decided that even in the Diaspora there should be a symbolic echo of the original gift so that this law would not be forgotten.

This tradition has required that whoever bakes bread made from one of the five grains indigenous to the Land of Israel (wheat, barley, spelt, oats, and rye) that is more than one *omer* in volume (about 1¾ kilograms) take part of the dough and throw it into the fire, reciting the blessing ". . . *asher kidshanu b'mitzvotav vitzivanu l'hafrish challah* . . . —Who had made us holy through commandments and has commanded us to separate *challah*." For commercial bakers who make large breads, the taken *challah* must be ¹⁄₄₈ of the dough; for a householder, it must be ¹⁄₂₄, in practice, an amount about the size of an olive.

The Rabbis expected that in the home a woman would usually be baking the bread, and they decided that this separation of *challah*, along with lighting the candles for Shabbat and observing the menstrual laws, were the only time-specific commandments that a woman was obligated to fulfill.

The effect of these decisions and practices was to make at least one aspect of cooking into a sacred act, analogous to the sacredness of eating the food.

In traditionally careful *kashrut* practice, breads baked by Jews are kosher only if *challah* has been taken. The special Jewish breads of Passover—matzah—come with notations on the box that "*Challah* has been taken."

Although this obligation applies to bread of the requisite size and grains no matter when or why Jews bake it, the name *challah* came to be attached to the special breads, usually braided or shaped into symbolic forms, that were baked for Shabbat and festivals.

Finally, there are special limitations on eating certain products of the Land of Israel.

The Torah provides that fruit cannot be eaten from a tree that is less than three years old, and that tithes must be taken from produce of the Land of Israel—grain, wine, and oil. The Rabbis ruled that this meant also all fruit and vegetables, everything that came from the earth as a result of cultivation. Produce that does not meet these restrictions is not kosher to eat. The original purpose of tithing—*terumot* (gifts) and *ma'aserot* (tenths)—was to provide a living to the Levites and priests, who owned no land of their own and who served the community as a whole through the sacred offerings. Even after the collapse of the priestly system, the Rabbis ruled that a proportion of each fruit should be set aside, returned to the earth, before it could be eaten.

One provision of Torah that we have already discussed—that in every seventh year, the land should lie fallow—had an impact on what is permissible to eat. Food harvested during the seventh year from fields owned by Jews in the Land of Israel and food grown from seeds sown that year were not kosher to eat.

So during the Biblical period, for two years running, most people ate only food that had been set aside and stored before this *shmitah*, or sabbatical year. The practice was economically hard but doable. Even after the destruction of the Second Temple, Jewish farmers living in the land tried to uphold the provisions of the sabbatical year. However, since Roman repression and draconian laws and taxes after the Bar Kokhba revolt (132–135 C.E.) and the collapse of the Jewish economy made observance of the sabbatical year increasingly hard, the Rabbis relaxed its restrictions.

The higher the proportion of Jews who were living abroad in the Diaspora, the less these restrictions meant. For they all applied only to food grown in the Land of Israel, and after the Roman repression, little produce was shipped overseas. Once the Jewish people had been all but extirpated from the Land of Israel and had been scattered across the world, the limitations on eating from the growth of the seventh year, or from untithed produce, or from young fruit trees became very unimportant.

But today, with the emergence of a large and self-governing Jewish community in Israel, these limitations have for some taken on added importance. They apply directly to traditional Jews in Israel. And since Israel exports some of its homegrown produce to many other countries, these rules also raise questions for traditional Jews in the rest of the world who sometimes eat food grown in Israel.

Various Israeli rabbinical authorities review the application of the rules to produce that is grown in Israel. They grant or refuse a *hekhsher* (certificate of proper kosher status) depending on whether they think the *shmitah* requirements have been met. The Chief Rabbinate of Israel does this certification. So do a number of other rabbinical groups that may not recognize the Chief Rabbinate's authority. Jews living in the Diaspora who wish to observe these rules can do so by checking for a *hekhsher* from an authority they trust; or they can avoid eating any produce grown in Israel or by-products such as fruit juices. Traditional Israeli Jews can if they choose apply the rules more directly by setting aside part of each fruit they eat as a tithe.

We should note that within the traditional community, there is some debate over how to deal with the laws of the sabbatical year. In early Zionist days when the settlements were poverty-stricken, some rabbis arranged for a legal fiction that the whole land be "sold" to non-Jews for the duration of the sabbatical year, thus nullifying the restrictions. Others opposed this practice. The debate continues. Certain Orthodox kibbutzim grow food hydroponically during the sabbatical year, thus avoiding the use of the "earth." Some Orthodox communities seek assurances that Israeli food products are not produce of the sabbatical year, nor of fruit trees less than three years old.

Given the many complex issues and disagreements over *kashrut*, how can contemporary consumers assess food products in the marketplace?

In regard to national or regional marketplaces of packaged foods, various agencies—most of them under the auspices of different groups of Orthodox rabbis, and a few under Conservative auspices—apply specific symbols to the product labels. A letter U with a circle around it, popularly called "the O-U," is used by the Union of Orthodox Jewish Congregations; a plain letter K is used by various individual rabbis who supervise the product's manufacture, and whose names and credentials are usually available from the manufacturer; still other symbols are used by specific local rabbinical committees on *kashrut*. One of these symbols of rabbinical supervision, followed by a P, indicates that the product is *pareve*. Inspection of contents named on a label can also indicate whether meat products like beef bouillon or milk products like lactose, caseinate, or whey have been used.

In regard to restaurants and butcher shops, local committees of Orthodox or Conservative rabbis inspect and certify whether a particular establishment is keeping kosher. Occasionally there are conflicts between such committees, applying different standards.

The structure, ethical commitments, affiliations, and independence of judgment of most or all of these authorities have been questioned. For example, since the producers of kosher foods pay fees to finance the process of certification—on the surface, a reasonable arrangement—the possibility arises that a large producer, paying large amounts of money, might be given less careful scrutiny. One issue facing

the next generation of Jews is whether the present arrangements for public certification of *kashrut* continues to be the most effective way of safeguarding traditional
practices.

As we think back over the issues involved in the code of kosher food, some
overall questions may remain:

- How do we feel about the bond between food, holiness, and the making of
  distinctions and separations that runs all through the system of *kashrut*?
- How do we feel about the idea that what is proper to eat changes according
  to the patterns and rhythms of time, that, for instance, during one week in
  the year, the special foods of Pesach take us on a weeklong adventure into a
  different dimension of *kashrut*?
- How do we feel about the communal effects of this process of distinction-
  making: both the distinctions it makes between Jews and non-Jews, and the
  ways in which it gives rise to different subcommunities of Jews, or reinforces
  the communal differences and separations that may have arisen over other
  issues?

The Rabbinic way of dealing with food accomplished some profound and long-
lasting changes in the ways Jews ate. Where the foods of the Jewish people were
gathered and where the people gathered to eat them became much less important,
while the words that came forth from Jewish mouths and the specific foods that
went into Jewish mouths became relatively more important. It became possible for
the Jewish people to eat anywhere in the world, eat food that came from anywhere
in the world, and still have a sense of its own distinctiveness in keeping in touch
with the God of all the world.

VI. GRINDING CORN, BAKING BREAD

When I was growing up in Baltimore, an Orthodox family lived up the street—by far the strictest on our block. Beginning when my father was in his teens, and still a whole generation later when my brother and I were in our teens, Mr. Shapiro policed our Jewish neighborhood. He was the one who yelled at us if we carried books to the public library on Saturday—Shabbat. And of course his household kept kosher.

But when she was in her nineties our grandmother told my brother a story. It seems that every year just before Passover, Mrs. Shapiro secretly brought her whole stock of regular dishes down the street to Grandmom, and carried Grandmom's regular dishes up the block to her house.

Why? To use them during Passover as if they were the special dishes she had set aside in a hidden place all year, the special dishes that had never touched a crumb of bread, reserved for the special *kashrut* of the festival that has no crumb of bread.

Yes! My grandmom's regular all-year dishes—those are what Mrs. Shapiro told her husband were the special *pesachdik* set. And after Pesach the two women changed the dishes back again.

And he never knew. For decades they did this, and her husband never knew.

Why did they do it? Mrs. Shapiro, because her husband never allotted her enough household money to buy a separate set of Pesach dishes—so she said. My grandmom? Because she had given up on Passover, *kashrut*, and God when her wonderful husband died young. She didn't stop believing in God; she just believed that she was punishing Him for being so criminally cruel to her.

Why does this story rise up for me when I have just finished reviewing the Rabbinic rules of *kashrut*? Not because I think the story betokens widespread sabotage of the rules, but because it says something about who was actually expected to carry out the rules.

The women. The men wrote the rules, the men who were Rabbis interpreted the rules whenever a question arose, the men studied the reasons and the quirks; but the women knew what the rules were, and they carried them out. Or—occasionally—didn't.

Because the kitchen was the domain of women.

Indeed, in most of Rabbinic life, the cooking of meals became so totally the domain of women that hardly any Jewish men would have known what women were doing in the kitchen.

Says the Mishnah (Ketubot 5:5):

These are the tasks that a woman does for her husband:
Grinding corn,
Baking bread,
Washing clothes,
Cooking,
Suckling her child,
Making ready his bed, and
Working in wool.
If she brought him one bondwoman,
she need not grind, bake, or wash.
If two bondwomen,
she need not cook or suckle her child;
if three, she need not prepare his bed or work in wool;
if four, she may lounge in an easy chair.

Says Rabbi Eliezer,

Even if she brings him a hundred bondwomen,
he can compel her to work in wool,
for idleness leads to lewdness.

Says Rabban Simon ben Gamaliel,

Even though he place his wife
under a vow to do no work,
he should divorce her
and give her her marriage settlement,
for idleness leads to stupidity.

There is much to note here. First and foremost, it assumed that women, not men, were responsible to prepare food for the household; if not the householder's wife, then her maidservants. Second, it was of course a discussion by men, and only men, about the roles and responsibilities of women and men. Third, although the Mishnah assigned men the ultimate power to make crucial decisions about the household, it saw women as intellectually and emotionally mature: On the one hand, they were able to oversee servants and manage a household; on the other hand, they would find enforced idleness psychologically debilitating. Finally, the Mishnah did not expect women who had free time to do what men with free time would: study Torah.

So by the time of the Mishnah, the roles of men and women had been defined in a way that was not customary for the Biblical Jewish community.

Over the centuries of the Rabbinic period, almost all Jewish women assumed and accepted the role of the household cook. This was not their only role. Often they brought in the family income and managed it as well. And they made the kitchen a place for spiritual yearning and affirmation. Out of the past three centuries of Jewish life in Eastern Europe, there are written records of *tekhinnes*—prayers in Yiddish for use by women, many of which focused on one special aspect of cooking—the separation of *challah*. This was one of the few positive time-bound *mitzvot* that were incumbent on women rather than men.

A contemporary folklorist, Chava Weissler, has explored these *tekhinnes*. One book of Jewish practice directed at women, *Shloyshe She'orim (Thirty Gates)*, not only gave texts of the *tekhinnes* to be said when offering to God a portion of dough from bread about to be baked, but explained the origin of the *challah* requirement and pointed out that it was, since the destruction of the Temple, the last surviving aspect of the laws of tithing food.

Shloyshe She'orim taught that in ancient days, and now as well, the separation of *challah* was connected with abundance from the earth and prosperity for the household and the Jewish people:

> May my *challah* be accepted as the sacrifice on the altar was accepted.... In ancient times, the High Priest came and caused sins to be forgiven; so also may my sins be forgiven with this.... Thus may my *mitzvah* of *challah* be accepted: that my children may be fed by the dear God, be blessed... as if I had given the tithe.

Here the *tekhinne* not only reminds us of the ancient priestly offerings but turns the woman who bakes bread into a contemporary High Priest!

Even when the women's prayers did not go this far, they affirmed the holiness of cooking:

> Lord of all the worlds... I pray you to give Your blessing on what I bake. Send an angel to guard the baking, so that everything will be well baked, will rise nicely, and will not burn. May this baking honor your holy Shabbos.

And for making a *kugel* (noodle pudding) for Shabbat, two *tekhinnes*:

Kugel, kugel, I make you truly;
Truly will I make you. . . .
Into the oven you will go,
Then into the mouth just so.
May you be as good as Jacob
and as red as Esau.

And, in a rhyming free translation from a weave of Hebrew and Yiddish:

May it meet with God's desire
That you, O kugel, come delicious from the fire.
Although we have no sacrificing place,
May you come sweetly to our taste.
May old and young, large and small,
Delight in what will fill us all.

Down to the twentieth century, the traditional Jewish kitchens in Eastern Europe were women's territory. The study of the theory behind *kashrut* was the province of men; but knowledge of what to do in the kitchen to protect *kashrut*, including when to consult the rabbi, was up to women. As cultural anthropologists who studied the *shtetl* reported, a man "learns what parts of the hind quarters of beef must not be eaten, and the reasoning behind the regulation, but he might not recognize a hind quarter if he saw it hanging in a shop."

Girls, on the other hand, learned a large part of Jewish culture in the kitchen. They learned the importance of cooking on two levels: First, that cooking itself was central to Jewish life; and second, that the rules of cooking and *kashrut* were crucial in defining both the internal vision of what it meant to be Jewish and the external vision of what it meant not to be Christian.

Girls learned to cook elaborate dishes. Hardly any item they put on the table was served raw. If the food was not baked, boiled, or roasted, almost all of it was at least warmed. It was strongly spiced, and its tastes were enhanced with fat. Although breakfast, lunch, and dinner were named and emphasized, food was available all day to ease the momentary hunger of any member of the family, and to greet a drop-in guest. Only on Shabbat were family meals formally and ceremonially gathered.

Women, though they ruled the kitchen, served at the table. They might rarely sit for meals except on Shabbat and holy days. Generally, they ate as they cooked.

Implicitly and explicitly, food was a conveyor of love, honor, and kindness.

Everyone in the family was likely to believe that compassion toward animals was the main reason for the rules of *kashrut*, and everyone understood that the way to greet honored guests and to protect the poor was to serve them food.

This attitude toward food began with birth. Almost all mothers breast-fed their children, or if necessary hired a wet nurse. Children were breast-fed on demand, not according to a schedule; and weaning often waited till a child was two or three, possibly to delay the next pregnancy.

Constant eating, constant feeding, went along with constant talking. All around the house were murmurs of prayer, Torah study, conversation, admonition. So finally, not only in the theory of the Rabbis but in the daily practice of the Jewish household, the orality of eating and the orality of speaking were fused into an oral Torah of ordinary life. Both food and conversation became holy—the one, a sacred offering into every mouth; the other, a sacred offering out from every mouth.

Many of us today might welcome this result. For many of us, it would give new life to learning, to food, and to the household—new life to an aspect of living that has increasingly been drained of life. But for most of us, this way of making the household holy poses a problem. In a world where most women work outside the home and carry on an intellectual life as vigorously as men, it makes little sense to isolate men as learners and women as cooks. And yet it is precisely because no one makes the food, the home, into life priorities that the home has become so lifeless. If this task is not assigned to women, who will do it?

There are several possible answers, the most obvious being, both men and women. For that to work, men must not only learn to cook, but also learn the arts and joys of cooking. For instance, they could work on creating a specific delicious dish to mark a specific time and meaning (like Shabbat, or Torah study, or political action to heal the world, or a successful completion of some piece of work). Women must not only learn Torah as a body of action-directives, but the arts and joys of reshaping Torah and talking Torah. And those habits must begin in childhood.

But there is something more. Men and women for whom the workplace has become all-consuming will not be able to make the time to restore the loving, murmuring, sacred kitchen. Only a reduction of the hours of frenzied work can bring these changes. No household, no family, can choose a holy path of life in utter isolation from society. So for food to become once more an element of everyday spiritual life, we may need to explore some wider social changes: shorter workdays, less commuter time, a four-day workweek (what a delight for making Shabbat holy!), less overtime—one or more of these life-style modifications, with little drop in salary, or a broad rescaling of how much money each household needs to make.

What other directions could we take? Some scattered practices hint toward other possibilities. For example, some Jewish households feel so burdened by the special food requirements of Pesach that they go away for the Seders, which are cooked by professionals for large gatherings. Some communities have held retreats for Rosh Hashanah and Shavuot, not only to pray together in new ways but also to share communal meals. For such special occasions, synagogues and *havurot* might find that preparing foods communally and delivering them to members' homes would meet their emerging needs. Or the potluck meal, where congregants prepare special dishes and bring them to synagogue to share among themselves, could become a much more important aspect of Jewish life. (Some synagogues and *havurot* might have to reexamine what code of kosher cooking they would urge upon their members.)

We might even imagine the transformation of take-out and home-delivery food from mere instruments of speed into a value-conscious, communal process. Perhaps sacred cooking could take place outside the home so that sacred eating can be renewed inside the home. Could neighborhood caterers prepare food that is nourishing, healthful, delicious, and follows not only traditional *kashrut* but also the "eco-kosher" practice that we will discuss in Chapter XI? Could families agree with each other that on some regular rotating schedule one household will take responsibility to cook dinners for ten?

All these suggestions imply there are some major changes in how we define a Jewish household, at least toward the goal of both cooking and eating together in a sacred way. To some extent, we may need to remake "extended families," "extended households," not by blood relationships but by shared values and friendships. And to some extent, we may need to urge certain public changes to restore households as places of sacred companionship.

One of my friends, a psychotherapist, says that some of the people who come to her are not really "grown-ups," they are "blown-ups." They have swollen and overblown egos, and often it is because they still feel themselves to be famished, underfed children. They are so hungry that they try to gobble up the world.

Usually, what they are hungry for is not food, but love. Or spiritual strength. In the absence of those deeper goods, they may try to gobble up approval, wealth, or power. Or they may literally overeat.

The Jewish spiritual path encourages a healthy, balanced self: an ego that is neither swollen nor eaten up with guilt, a body that is neither gross nor famished. In regard to food and other kinds of physical consumption, what process and practice does Judaism teach that embody this intention?

For me, as for many of my generation, this is not an academic question. There is a real danger in eating too much. More than a danger: I *do* eat too much. Did something so famish my childhood that I risk becoming a "blown-up"? Is this the doom of depression babies, or the doom of the grandchildren of Eastern European Jews who were always afraid of having too little to eat, and who taught their families never to pass up a morsel of food? As I explore food in Jewish culture, I find myself wondering: Can anything from the Biblical tradition teach me how not to eat too much?

It is not just food in the literal sense that stirs me to this question. One way of seeing the whole human race at this moment in history is that it is "gobbling up" the planet; not just its food, but its energy, its forests, its minerals, its air and water.

As we have seen, one of the major concerns of Israelite culture was making sure there was enough to eat. Were the Israelites ever concerned about having too much to eat, or about eating too much? Were they concerned with the danger that human beings might "gobble up" the earth?

We have already noted one Torah passage (Num. 11) that explicitly addresses gluttony, in the story about the blizzard of quail that strikes the people of Israel with a terrible plague as they begin to gorge themselves. So much for gluttony! But how is such a raging hunger to be controlled?

THE FASTS OF COMMUNAL SELF-RESTRAINT

One Biblical approach to limiting one's food intake was fasting. This was viewed not simply as a physical act of self-restraint but as part of a communal and spiritual process. Sometimes individuals entered on a fast of their own; sometimes the leaders of a locale or of the whole nation proclaimed a specific fast; and especially after the destruction of the First Temple by the Babylonians, several fast days were proclaimed as permanent ones for the people as a whole.

These fasts were seen mostly as a way of coming closer to God. (Notice that both feasting and fasting, offering up sacred food and offering to refrain from food, played this role.) Moses on Mount Sinai, in direct communication with God, is said to have fasted for forty days. The apocalyptic Prophet Daniel fasted in preparation to receive Divine visions.

More fasts were connected not with a direct unveiling of God, but with a desire to call forth God's compassion in time of calamity. In this mode, the fast was a way of either symbolizing or bringing about *tshuvah* (literally, "turning," or repentance) on the part of one person or the whole people. The fast could symbolize *tshuvah*, if the fast bespoke a spiritual transformation already undertaken; it could bring about *tshuvah*, if the fast caused the people to turn inward, to strengthen their own sense of self-control, perhaps for a moment to share the experience of the poor.

The one fast enjoined upon the whole people in the Five Books is the fast of Yom Kippur, *"la'anot nafshateychem"*—to "afflict your souls," or "let the air out of your blown-up egos." Pre-Exilic Prophets like Joel (1:14; 2:13–17) and First Isaiah (1:13) refer to fasts as a given of Temple practice. These are times of purification, repentance, and reconnection with God. It is Second Isaiah, after the return from exile, who connects the fast with feeding the hungry, as if one purpose of a fast were to experience the hunger of the poor and then act to assuage it.

In time of war, drought, or famine, fasting was undertaken by the community as a way of reexamining its own behavior—"What did we do to bring on this disaster?"—and of imploring God to restore natural and social harmony. Similarly, individuals might fast in a time of sickness or death (II Sam. 12:21).

After the destruction of the Temple, a series of fast days were observed that commemorated aspects of the calamity. The tenth of Tevet commemorated the beginning of the Babylonians' siege of Jerusalem; the seventeenth of Tammuz, their breaking through the walls of the city; the ninth of Av (Tisha B'Av), the destruction of the Temple; the third of Tishri, the assassination of Gedaliah, a public official appointed by the Babylonians to govern the Jewish community that remained in the Land of Israel.

Of these four fast days, only Tisha B'Av was a full twenty-four-hour fast from all forms of bodily pleasure (eating, drinking, sex, washing, anointing, wearing leather) on the model of Yom Kippur. The others were fasts from food, from dawn to sunset. After the return of the Israelites from the Babylonian Exile and the building of the Second Temple, the question was raised whether these fasts should be canceled, but they continued in force.

As a path of self-restraint, more subtle than fasting was the Bible's teaching of how to share food with the hungry. At the corners of the family field, said the Torah, property rights to the produce of the land began to fade away. Even though the land itself was in the leasehold possession of a household, what grew in the corners of the field did not belong to it. It belonged instead to the poor, the orphan, and the stranger—those who had no land, and therefore nothing to eat. Similarly, the food that the gleaners missed as they first undertook the harvest could not be gathered by the owner in a follow-up harvest. Instead, it must be left for the landless to glean by their own work.

These were provisions for dealing with immediate need and hunger. The Torah also had more long-range approaches to solving the underlying problems of the landless, but we will take these up in the chapters on money. The provisions for sharing food were noteworthy in several specific ways:

First, they restrained the owner's physical gluttony for actual food by restraining his spiritual gluttony for total power over what he owned. The owner had the physical and economic power to assert full control over *all* his land, to the very edge of his property, and over *everything* that grew on it. He was required however, to let his control fade away at the edges—not only through a mathematical formula like tithing, but in a way that responded flexibly to the needs and work energy of the poor. If (like Ruth in the Bible) the poor were prepared to work longer and harder at gleaning, they might gather more food.

Second, this very process meant that the poor also worked in order to eat. Their food did not come from a government storehouse, but from their own labor. The special aid they received was simply access to land, since they held none of their own.

In the entire food-eating spectrum—from fasting to eating one's fill to sharing the food—the Biblical pattern integrated the physical act with spiritual concerns. Whether through sacred offering, prayer, or self-control, each Israelite learned that food was an integral element of the Unity of body, emotion, intellect, and spirit—within each person and within the world as a whole.

❧

As Rabbinic Judaism began to emerge, self-restraint in eating was closely tied to concern that the land would not give forth food in abundance. Normally, in the Land of Israel no rain would fall for the six months from Pesach to Sukkot. If rains did not begin soon after Sukkot and continue till Pesach, there was serious danger of drought, famine, and disaster to the community.

Such a failure of rainfall is the focus of the section of the Mishnah called *Ta'anit* ("Fasts"). It taught that if there had been no rains by the middle of the month of Cheshvan—about three weeks after Sukkot—then a step-by-step regimen of fasting should begin.

Well-known communal leaders took the first step. They refrained from eating and drinking during the daylight hours of one Monday-Thursday-Monday sequence.

If rain still did not fall, then the whole community began to fast. For an additional Monday, Thursday, and Monday, adults (except for the sick, or pregnant women) would not eat or drink, and during this time would not wash, wear leather, have sex, or anoint themselves (the rules governing the major fast days of Yom Kippur and Tisha B'Av).

If there were still no rain, then a third level of fasting went into effect. Seven more fast days were proclaimed—also on Mondays and Thursdays. For these seven days, shops were closed and an alarm blast was blown on the *shofar*. Six special prayers were added to the regular eighteen of the basic part of the service. The Ark that contained the Torah Scroll was draped in sackcloth and brought into the town's public space. Ashes were strewn on the Ark and on the foreheads of the townsfolk, and they wore sackcloth; but the people were admonished that in the Book of Jonah, God saves Nineveh from disaster not in response to the wearing of sackcloth and ashes but in response to the community's transformation of its behavior, turning from wicked acts to good ones. Leaders examined the community's behavior and called for the specific changes that they thought necessary to evoke God's compassion and restore the balance of nature.

If the drought still continued, then business transactions, marriages, house building, planting—all were curtailed. Leaders of the community resumed individual fasts.

The basic symbolism behind these actions is that if the land is not ready to give food, the community must assert more self-control over the way it eats in particular, and must reexamine its life-path in general. Although this pattern was originally worked out for use during a drought in the Land of Israel, Monday-

and-Thursday rhythm of fasting and the related ceremonies of mourning were used in response to other communal calamities—plague, war, famine. They were followed by Jews in other countries in accord with the climatic rhythms of their own locales.

The rhythm of a Monday-Thursday-Monday daylight fast was also used by some Jewish communities just after Pesach and just after Sukkot, probably as a way of controlling or doing penance for gluttony that might have been expressed during those two festivals.

Fasts as an aid to inward meditation also became customary on several other days throughout the year.

Among these each month, was the day before Rosh Chodesh (New Moon), which became recognized as Yom Kippur Katan ("Little Yom Kippur"), a day for reflection and redirection of one's life.

Brides and grooms would similarly review and renew their lives by fasting on the day before their weddings. Their first food would be the cup of wine they drank together under the wedding canopy.

On the morning before Passover, firstborns would fast in recognition that Egyptian firstborns had died and Israelite firstborns had been spared in the Exodus from slavery. Thus firstborns would contemplate the way in which they owed their lives to a God Who opened up the possibility of freedom. Many firstborns would cut short this fast by studying a passage of Torah or Talmud, and then celebrating the completion of their study by eating.

In some Jewish communities, Mondays and Thursdays—the only days besides Shabbat and festivals when the Torah was publicly read—were devoted to daylight fasts.

In all these ways, fasting became an emergency "hot line" to God. Since performing good deeds in the world were also considered to be ways of approaching God, fasting in times of emergency or special focus was deemed to be closely intertwined with seeking to do good deeds.

When the community's consciousness of this close interconnection between fasting and correct outward action diminished, either of two quite different responses to fasting might emerge.

On the one hand, some Jewish leaders worried that fasting might replace good deeds or even undermine the community. So they tried to limit and ease public fasts; to discourage individuals from fasts that might make them burdens on the community or might decrease Torah study; and to emphasize instead the community's turning toward good deeds of loving-kindness as a way of winning God's compassion in times of emergency.

On the other hand, some mystics and kabbalists used individual fasts to encourage ecstatic states, a special pathway to becoming close to God. Fasts that involved long periods of weeping, special bodily postures, visualizations of colors, chanting hymns of Names of God, and other ways of altering body-mind relationships are reported over a very long period of time, as for example by such an early "apocalyptic" writer as the author of II Enoch, by Rabbi Ishmael in the Talmudic period, and by followers of Isaac Luria in the sixteenth century.

Such ecstatic fasting was ordinarily pursued by only a few adepts. Whole communities tried to use fasts this way only in such extraordinary moments as the wave of Messianic hope that arose around Shabbatai Tzvi in the 1660s.

For us today, this pattern might raise a series of questions:

- In times of famine or fear of famine, do voluntary fasts offer a way of stirring empathy among the fasters for others, or their own future selves, who might have no choice but to go hungry? If they do not, what would be the best ways of arousing such empathy?
- Are fasts effective in stirring people, as individuals or as communities, to reexamine their daily life-paths?
- Do fasts, with or without other physical exercises and practices, encourage worthwhile spiritual searching? Are the effects different for small numbers of adepts and for large communities?

THE TREES YOU SHALL NOT DESTROY

When we look at the tradition for guidance about not "gobbling" the earth by other means than literally eating, we find a whole set of teachings about protecting both God's Creation and the results of human creativity.

The Rabbis labeled these teachings *bal tashchit*, or "Don't destroy." The Talmud sketches out the boundaries of *bal tashchit*, and roots the whole notion in one verse of Torah (Deut. 20:19):

When you shall besiege a city a long time, making war against it to seize it, you shall not destroy its trees by wielding an ax against them; for you may eat of them, and you shall not cut them down; for is the tree of the field human, that you make it face you besieged?

The Rabbis decided that if trees must be protected even in time of war, then—all the more so!—all sorts of natural and human-made objects must be protected under ordinary circumstances. And yet, of course, human beings must have wood, and cloth, and water to meet their own needs. How to strike the balance?

The Rabbis (Pesachim 56a) criticized King Hezekiah for stopping up the waters of the Upper Gihon, a stream near Jerusalem, even though he did so to prevent an invading army from using it.

Perhaps this is a special case. Like the fruit trees in the Torah verse, the Gihon was part of the natural world that no human being owned. But what about objects that belonged to someone?

One who kills his own mules (T.B. Hullin 7b) or cuts down his own plants (Baba Kama 90b) violates *bal tashchit*, the Rabbis ruled. However, these are still special cases for they, like the trees of the Torah verse, are alive. Does *bal tashchit* apply to inanimate objects as well?

Yes. The Rabbis taught that even renewable sources of energy must not be wasted. R. Zutra said (Shabbat 67b), "Whoever covers an oil lamp or uncovers a naphtha lamp infringes the prohibition of *bal tashchit* [for in either case, the lamp burns faster]."

Even in a time of mourning, when clothing was supposed to be ripped as a sign of sorrow, the Rabbis said that too much tearing would violate *bal tashchit* (Baba Kama 91b). Tearing silken garments breaks *bal tashchit*, unless the tearing is in the seam so that the garment can be resewn. In what may have been the farthest fringe of this attitude, the Talmud reports:

> R. Hisda, whenever he had to walk between thorns and thistles, used to lift up his garments [so that his skin instead of the cloth would be ripped], saying that whereas for the body nature will produce a healing, for garments nature could bring up no cure.

So when, then, may human beings destroy what God and they have made, to meet their own needs?

> A teak chair was broken up for [fire to warm] Samuel; a juniper-wood table was broken up for [fire to warm] Rav Judah; a footstool was broken up for [fire to warm] Rabbah. Abaye said to Rabbah, But you are infringing *bal tashchit*. *Bal tashchit* in regard to my own body is more important to me, he retorted. (Shabbat 129a)

The Rabbis were unwilling simply to leave the rule of *bal tashchit* as a deduction from the Torah verse with no broader meaning or intention. Rabbi Simeon ben Eleazar, speaking in the name of a line of his teachers, said:

Whoever tears garments in anger, breaks tools in anger, or scatters money in anger regard as an idolater, for such are the wiles of the Tempter.... R. Abin, citing a verse [of Psalms] that says, "There shall be no strange god in you," adds: Who is the strange god *in* you?—the one who resides within the human being's own self?—The Tempter! (Shabbat. 105b)

In this last case, it is not need that is fueling the destruction but a kind of sullen anger. On the surface, the anger may be aimed at other people, but in a deeper sense, it bespeaks a rage at God. That we feel tempted to waste and destroy what is around us signals that we are distancing ourselves from God—for the world is not ours to destroy. If we bow to this temptation and actually destroy, it is God's Creation we are destroying—and therefore it is the Creator we are rejecting. We are making a god of our anger, worshiping that instead of the One Who shapes all being.

Indeed, perhaps it is no accident that the Torah's prohibition on destroying fruit trees and the Rabbis' disapproval of Hezekiah's damming of the Gihon River both focus on a time of war. For perhaps the Torah and the Rabbis saw that, in war itself, there was a kind of sullen anger—seemingly aimed at other people— that was already a rejection of God.

So here we find the Rabbis making a spiritual and psychological diagnosis of wasteful and angry destruction. Just as heedlessly gobbling up our food betokens a spiritual hunger, an emptiness, so does heedless destruction of the world around us.

Today, these rules and this spiritual analysis point us in the direction of an environmental ethic that is Jewishly and spiritually rooted. It is an ethic that takes seriously the limits on our ownership of any part of Creation, while it understands that only the fullness of spiritual life can nourish people well enough to respect these limits. If we *can* drink deep of the Spirit, then we do *not* need to gobble up the earth.

As I absorb the extraordinarily detailed code of what and how to eat in Rabbinic Judaism, I find myself asking over and over, *Why?* And yet part of me feels this question is disloyal, a betrayal of my forebears. So it is with great relief that I discover that century after century, as almost all Jews ate according to the rules of Rabbinic *kashrut,* some kept raising the question—*Why?* What was there about eating, they asked, that required this degree of discipline?

By discovering that others have raised the question, I feel myself freed not only to ask it myself, but also to search out how these forebears of mine answered it.

I discovered that two major answers emerged: one that was philosophical-rational, and one that was mystical. We will look at each of them, to see whether they might be of help to us as we address the same question—*Why?*—in our own lives.

The medieval Jewish philosophers explained that God intended all the commandments, including those concerning food, to improve the lot of human beings, as part of a universe ordered by a magnificent and ultimate sense of reason. They saw reason as the superlative advantage that human beings had over the rest of life, and they saw God as the Ultimate repository of reason. So the notion that Divine commandments could have no reason at all or run against rational understanding was repugnant to them.

And so the most influential of the philosophers, Maimonides, writes that "every one of the six hundred and thirteen precepts serves to inculcate some truth, to remove some erroneous opinion, to establish proper relations in society, to diminish evil, to train in good manners, or to warn against bad habits." (*Guide of the Perplexed,* III:31)

And what about food? Says Maimonides, "The food which is forbidden by the Law is unwholesome." (*Guide,* III:48) All pork, he asserts, is too moist and has too much extraneous matter to be healthy; but even worse, the food and habits of the pig are loathsome. As for the blood and fats that are prohibited even when they come from kosher animals, Maimonides asserts that they are bad for human digestion. He explains that the Biblical signs of acceptability—split hooves, cud-chewing, fins and scales— are outward signs of the healthy animals and fish, not meaningful in themselves.

Maimonides perceives some ethical aspects to *kashrut* as well. He asserts that the prohibition on mixing meat with milk is partly medical, and also connected with opposition to the festival practices of idolators—since it is twice mentioned just after the teachings about how Israelites should celebrate the festivals. Finally, Maimonides explains that ritual *shechita* is required to be as painless as possible, to express compassion for animals and to teach compassion to human beings.

Although Maimonides was an honored physician as well as theologian in his own day—serving as court physician to the vizier of Egypt—most modern medical opinion is skeptical about his medical justifications for *kashrut*. There have indeed been some in the Modern Age who have argued a somewhat different medical case—that pork and shellfish were in Biblical times especially susceptible to contamination and disease. But whereas Maimonides's medical argument in his day strengthened adherence to *kashrut*, this modern medical analysis worked in the opposite direction. For this line of argument typically concludes not that *kashrut* is immutable but now that refrigeration and inspection by microscope and other advanced hygienic measures have become possible, *kashrut* has lost its purpose.

This result was to some extent inherent in the philosophical-rational approach to Torah. Although the medical Jewish philosophers affirmed Rabbinic practice and gave it a new underpinning by arguing that it met the highest standards of philosophical rationality, their interpretation also bore the seeds of reexamining and dissolving Rabbinic practice. For what were Jews to do if unfolding reason were to run counter to the Rabbis' precepts? It was one thing to harmonize the Talmud with Aristotle, as did Maimonides. It was another to harmonize Talmud with Locke, Newton, Einstein, Freud, or Sartre—or with all of them at once.

The other major response to the question *Why?* about the Rabbinic code of *kashrut* came from a series of mystics, Kabbalists and Hassidim. They saw the Jewish way of eating as a way of replicating and influencing God's Own Path. How Jews took nourishment from the earth would affect God's Nurturance, might tip the balance from shattering to healing the universe.

For the Zohar, or Book of Splendor, which in the thirteenth century c.e. became and remained the greatest single text of the Jewish mystical tradition, nourishing one's self from kosher foods nourishes the Shekhinah Herself, God's Own Indwelling Presence within the world and human life, an Immanent Feminine full of compassion.

Eating forbidden foods, on the other hand, interacts with God's aspects of *Gevurah* (Boundary-making/Judgment/Rigor) that seeds and feeds the *Sitra Achra* (the Other Side), the negative, destructive, and dangerous aspect of God.

To begin with, *Gevurah* is an attribute of Divinity that is necessary if the universe is to have structure rather than ceaseless flow. Normally, it balances and is balanced by *Chesed* (Overflowing, Unboundaried Love) and by other aspects and emanations of God.

But if human beings themselves cross over and blur the Divine boundaries by eating what the Torah says is outside the Boundary, they force God's *Gevurah* into greater and greater prominence. The more the walls of Boundary are breached, the higher and stronger and more forbidding they must rise, and so the Other Side becomes more powerful in the world. More negativity emerges.

This whole approach puts enormous weight on the act of eating (as it does on other actions, including those connected with money, sex, and rest). Not only the future of a single person is at stake, not only is there a danger of individual sin, but the Godhead Itself is nourished or poisoned by each human mouthful. Enormous anxiety and intensity are loaded onto both correct action and correct intention, every moment at the dinner table. Taking pleasure in the food itself, its taste or its bodily nourishment, pales beside the intensity of the intention to heal God.

As the Kabbalah continued developing under social conditions of even greater strain, the importance of proper eating and other proper action was reinforced. After the Jewish community was expelled from Spain in 1492, some of its most creative members settled in the town of Safed, in the hills above Lake Galilee, in northern Israel. In Safed there emerged a new school of Kabbalah, defined by Isaac Luria. Luria and his followers felt that some Jewish misdeeds must have made possible the Spanish repression, just as the Prophets and Rabbis had said that Jewish misdeeds made possible the Babylonian and Roman destructions of the Temple. What is more, they traced these misdeeds to a fundamental crack in the universe itself—a crack that could only be repaired if human beings replaced misdeeds with correct action.

Thus they traced their own exile to an Exile within God, and they believed that only if human beings acted to redeem God's Exile could their own be healed.

In the beginning of time as we understand it, they said, the All-encompassing Infinite Unknowable God contracted inwardly in order to open space for a finite, knowable universe to emerge, and poured holy Divinity into this void as the fabric of the new world. But the Divine was so intense that no finite vessel could contain it.

As each stage of the Infinite became a finite vessel, the vessel itself broke and some diminished amount of the Infinite poured down another level to make another vessel, this one more finite and less Infinite. But it too broke and poured Divinity into another level. Thus the World of Spirit or Being shattered and poured its leftover, cast-off energy into shaping the World of Creative Idea or Knowing, which shattered and poured its leftovers into making the World of Formation or Relating, which shattered and poured its leftovers into shaping the physical universe we know, the World of Doing.

At each stage, as the vessel shattered, from it fell shards and sparks of holiness. The separation of each spark of holiness from all the others with which it had originally shared the Divine fire meant that each separate spark was dulled and shadowed, just as hot burning coals removed from a fire and separated from one another become much cooler, duller.

The Kabbalists described this cooling with the metaphor that the holy sparks had become covered with "husks," or shells of alienation. The cast-off energy of the World of Doing was most beset by these alien husks, for there was no lower plane where they could be transmuted into holy vessels.

To reverse the process and heal the shattered vessels, humans would have to act in the World of Doing in such a way as to remove the husks, gather the sparks, and reunite them into a holy vessel of Divine Unity. Human action could heal and repair the world and the Godhead Itself—and that healing was called *tikkun olam.*

For Luria and his followers, eating properly was not just one among many aspects of correct action, it was among the most important. Why was this?

For one thing, the physicality of food and its closeness to the husks of alienation made its use most dangerous. To redeem these sparks and lift them back toward the upper worlds would take great effort. So Luria taught that only if the blessings over food were said with great intensity and conscious focus on the desire for this mystical redemption of the sparks in the food could the pleasure and nourishment of the food be turned toward good instead of sin. The way to do this was to say aloud a formula that celebrated doing the intended act for the sake of unifying the Masculine and Feminine, transcendent and immanent, aspects of God. Once again, the Kabbalah turned the focus of eating away from sensual pleasure and toward the mental effort to redeem the sparks.

There may have been another element to the Lurianic concern with food. After all, the Kabbalists of Safed were back in the Land of Israel. Perhaps for them, the relationship with the earth and what grew from it became more vivid, in a way few Jews had experienced since Biblical days.

Living in the seasonal rhythms of the Land of Israel, Luria's followers gave great importance to what had before been a minor seasonal event: Tu B'Shvat (the Full Moon of the midwinter month of Shvat), which marked the midwinter reawakening of trees in the growth patterns and seasons of the Land of Israel. They chose to mark this a new year of the tree chiefly by eating special foods. They drew on the model of the most festive meal of the Jewish year—the Pesach Seder—to create a Seder focused on the conscious eating of fruits and nuts from the trees of the land. Thus they created the only Jewish sacred meal that is in principle based on the Edenic diet: not only vegetarian, but fruitarian. Its foods do not require the death of even a plant—unlike the eating of a carrot or a loaf of bread.

The Kabbalists of Safed raised their celebration of these earthly trees to a supernal level by portraying God as the mystical Tree of Life. Eating the fruit of the trees of Israel, they explained, fructifies the Supernal Tree. The flow of Divine abundance that makes the whole earth and the whole universe fruitful depends, they said, on human intentionality in blessing the fruits of the trees. In this way they, like the Zohar, put enormous energy and weight into the human act of eating.

Not merely eating, but eating with intention and with proper blessings. The followers of Luria ultimately published a guide to the Tu B'Shvat Seder they had created, entitled *Pri Eytz Hadar* (*Fruit of the Beautiful Tree*). They quoted a line from the Talmud—"Whoever enjoys produce in this world without pronouncing a blessing is called a robber"—and gave a new twist to its meaning:

> For by means of the blessing one draws down *shefa* [the flow of Divine abundance]. The angel who is assigned to that fruit [which is eaten] is filled by the *shefa* so that a second fruit can replace the first. One who enjoys the first without blessing it . . . eliminates the spiritual element it contained. . . . As a result, the angel's power is annulled, since it no longer possesses the *shefa* [that it needs in order to replace the fruit].

In other words, human blessings invite the flow of Divine abundance into the world, and the human misdeed of not blessing can block the flow. The future abundance and fertility of the earth depend on the present attitude of all those who eat from the earth now.

What is more, the very act of chewing stirs the potency of God. The thirty-two teeth of a human being echo the thirty-two times that God is mentioned in the story of the Seven Days of Creation. When the Torah says that a person "does not live by bread alone, but by all that comes forth from the mouth of YHWH" (Deut. 8:3), it means that people live by the whole Creation—for all of it came forth from the Mouth of God, speaking thirty-two times in order to create. The thirty-two teeth of a human being replicate these acts of Creation and fruitfulness whenever they are used to chew food after saying a blessing.

And, *Pri Eytz Hadar* continues, the food also contains holy sparks that have been forced into exile by the shattering of the supernal holy vessels. Some of these sparks are souls of the righteous of the past—even our own forebears—and the only way to free these souls is to say blessings over the food, then eat with spiritual attentiveness and fervor.

This should be done at every meal; but to do it on Tu B'Shvat, the New Year of Trees, was especially effective in stirring the Divine forces of fruitfulness, according to *Pri Eytz Hadar*. On that day many kinds of fruit should be especially bought and eaten. In *Pri Eytz Hadar*, it is explained that three different kinds of fruit represented the Worlds of Doing, Relating, and Knowing:

> The first sort have hard outside shells to protect them from the encroaching forces of the Other Side, but soft and delicious interiors: walnuts, almonds, pomegranates.
> The second have softer exteriors, since they are more distant from the Other Side and can let surrounding influences enter; but their centers are hard

and inedible, since there is still a point of danger: olives, dates, cherries.

The third need no protection and so are edible clear through: grapes, figs, pears, strawberries.

As for the fourth world, the World of Being, it is so ethereal, so close to the Infinite One, that it cannot be represented by fruits that exist in the physical world.

In the Tu B'Shvat Seder, the fruits of the Four Worlds were "eaten" in four courses, signaled by four cups of wine of different colors. In this way, by blessing the fruits of the trees of the earth below on the day of the New Year of the Trees, the Divine *shefa* flowing through these trees was drawn down and the Divine Tree above was fittingly, for its New Year, stimulated to send new *shefa* flowing into the world.

These teachings walked a knife-edge between ascetic rejection of the bodily pleasures of eating that was accompanied with blessings and meditations, and an affirmation of the joyful reunifications that could be brought about in Heaven as well as in the human belly if blessings and meditations were done well.

The Kabbalists who walked this knife-edge were a tiny elite, both learned and intense in their devotion. As their teachings soaked into the broader Jewish world, they moved most Jews in down-to-earth communities more toward joyful affirmation than toward ascetic self-denial. In Middle Eastern and Oriental Jewish communities, the Tu B'Shvat Seder became a time of celebration. The Hassidic upheaval in Eastern Europe in the eighteenth century also took the ideas of Kabbalah in a celebratory direction.

For the Hassidim as for the Kabbalists, what human beings did on earth had a powerful effect on God. The Hassidim, however, were more intent on strengthening God's love than on easing God's rigor. For them the imprisoned sparks of holiness were more likely to be rescued by people who fully engaged in the world, including experiencing its pleasures in a holy way, than by people who avoided the physical realities in which the sparks were embedded.

The Hassidim drew on the Torah story of the elders who, at Sinai, "saw God, and ate and drank" (Ex. 24:9–11).

Man's [sic] thoughts when he eats should be attached to God more than at any other time.... When a man [sic] needs to eat he should free his mind from other thoughts so that it can soar aloft to think of God while each mouthful is being swallowed ... the body being nourished by the physical act of eating while the soul is sated, fattened, and satisfied by means of this intention." (Quoted by Louis Jacobs from Elijah of Smyrna, citing Bahya Ibn Asher)

Some of the Hassidim went further. Not merely the idea of God but the very letters of the Holy Name should be kept in mind, through meditation at each meal. Indeed, the rebbe, on behalf of all his followers, was to contemplate the letters of the Hebrew *aleph-bet* that made up the name of every food he ate. For the letters themselves were, at the supernal level, the essence of the food. Eating the food fed the human body; contemplating the letters fed God.

Others suggested that in the great process of recycling souls from the bodies of one generation to the bodies of another (*gilgul*, Hebrew for "reincarnation," literally means "rotation" or "recycle"), the souls of some of our righteous forebears would reappear in the bodies of kosher animals. How could these sparks of holiness be freed from the husks of alienation so as to help reunify the holy vessels? By mindful eating of the special kosher food.

In either of these forms of contemplation and devotion, the goal of most Hassidim was not to rid the meal of sensual enjoyment, but to turn that enjoyment toward reunifying the universe and God. For the goal to be not ascetic self-denial but pleasure, there would have to be some pleasurable physical manifestation of the spiritual transformation, some way in which the spiritual richness of food entered the physical plane. Some of the Hassidim said that this bridge between the spiritual and sensual worlds was the *taste* of food. What we would call calories and vitamins served the body purely; but taste served only the higher function of delight—and thus led straight to Heaven. Sweetness, for example, they felt was a taste of *Chesed*; sourness, of *Gevurah*.

Where the Kabbalists had required gymnastic feats of knowledge, will, and devotion that only a few could achieve, the Hassidim offered every Jew an opportunity to make eating holy. They said that the easy path, the one widely applauded, was to know and affirm that every meal gave one the strength to serve God by prayer and Torah study. The harder path, one often condemned as selfish and hedonistic, was to eat each meal with the consciousness of redeeming the sparks within the food, do each ordinary act of work with the consciousness of redeeming the sparks within the work. In other words, it is easy to *use* what is ordinary to affirm what is holy; it is harder, and more important, to penetrate *within* the ordinary to affirm that it holds holiness. Harder, yes; but possible for much of the community, not only for a few spiritual athletes.

For us today, then, the question is what thoughts and actions could without asceticism move us to feel holiness within the very act of eating. For the Kabbalists and Hassidim, this could only be done by following Rabbinic laws of what and how to eat, to which were added their meditations on the tastes and the names of food and on the release of the souls within them. In our own generation, can we draw both on the rationalism of the philosophers who suggested the possibility of revising those rules in accordance with science, and on the mystical sense that the eating itself is a way of affecting God? How would such a synthesis look?

IX. THE END OF THE MATTER

Perhaps the most down-to-earth passage in all of Torah is simply this:

> There shall be an area for you outside the camp, where you may relieve
> yourself. With your gear you shall have a spade, and when you have squatted
> you shall dig a hole with it and cover up your excrement (Deut. 23:13–14).

How many religious texts concern themselves not only with eating but with the
other end of the digestive process? The Torah sees the whole cycle of moving food
from the earth into the human and from the human into the earth as a sacred
process to be addressed by the sacred text.

Although the cycle as a whole is holy, the Torah prescribes different ways of
dealing with its different aspects. As it addresses the issue of waste, it continues
not with a blessing as it does for eating, but

> Since YHWH your God moves about in your camp to guard you and deliver
> your enemies to you, let God not find anything unseemly among you and
> turn away from you (Deut. 23:15).

The Rabbis went much further in making explicit the holiness of the earth-
destined part of the cycle. They wrote a specific blessing to be recited upon completing a trip to the toilet. It is usually called the Asher Yatzar:

> *Baruch attah YHWH eloheynu melekh ha'olam asher yatzar et-ha'adam b'chochma, u'varah vo*
> *n'kavim n'kavim chalulim chalulim galui v'yadua lifnai kisei k'vodecha, she'im yisateym echad*
> *mayhem o im yipatay'ach echad mayhem, i efshar l'hitka'yeym afilu sha'ah achat. Baruch attah*
> *YHWH rofei kol basar u'mafli la'asot.*

Blessed are You, YHWH our God, Sovereign of the universe, Who has
shaped the human with wisdom, and created within us holes and holes,
hollows and hollows. Before Your radiant Throne it is lovingly known and

clearly revealed that if but one of these that are open were closed, or one of these that are closed were open, we could not continue for even one hour. Blessed are You, YHWH, Who heals all flesh and does wonders.

Surely it is no accident that the *"kisei"* of the blessing, God's "seat" or "throne," is also the Hebrew word for toilet—as if we honor the sacredness of every toilet by seeing in it a shadow of the Throne in Heaven.

Yet even while the Rabbis affirmed that elimination is a sacred process, they extended the Torah's warning that the Divine Presence within the Israelite camp would not want to be directly confronted with the body's by-products. The Talmud (T.B. B'rakhot 22b–25b) forbids the recitation of such crucial prayers as the Amidah and the Sh'ma within four cubits (two yards) of a privy or of the body's products.

Furthermore, the Rabbis said, anyone who in the midst of prayer feels the need to find a privy should do so quickly and then return to pray. (T.B. B'rakhot 23a) Perhaps this was for the sake of being able to focus the mind and heart on prayer. Or perhaps the Rabbis felt that regardless of mental concentration and focus, the physical body must physically be in a specific stance, a posture, an orientation, a space. Perhaps this feeling was a remnant of the priestly attitude that the body counted without regard to intellect or ethic, that a physical blemish disqualified both the animal offering and the priest.

This outlook—affirming that the whole cycle of eating and elimination is sacred, but the waste products themselves are not compatible with the sacred Presence— was given an additional meaning in Kabbalistic and Hassidic thought.

In the eighteenth century, the Hassidic rebbe Elimelekh of Lizensk picked up the imagery of the holy vessel shattered into scattered sparks that Lurianic Kabbalah had applied to food. If sparks of holiness were at the heart of all nourishment, including food, and if meditative and prayerful eating liberated the sparks to reunite and remake the sacred vessel of the universe, then what were the husks of alienation that encased the sparks?

Elimelekh answered that when the sparks had been freed by prayerful chewing and digesting, what the body could not use for nourishment must be the husks of alienation.

Whoever eats and drinks [with sacred intention to unify the sparks] . . . his soul will then benefit from the inward part of the food, the residue becoming waste matter to be expelled for the outside ones [demonic aspects of the Other Side]. He should also have in mind that, as soon as he will feel a need to evacuate his bowels he will not, God forbid, keep the waste inside his body to contaminate his mind and render his soul abominable by keeping the excrement and urine inside his body for a single moment.

In this way, Elimelekh broadened the Talmud's assertion that one should not continue to pray the Amidah or the Sh'ma while needing to eliminate waste. In effect, for this Hassidic master, all life became a time of intense prayer, and every human body became the "camp" within which God is always present, and from which all waste must be excluded.

For our generation, this attitude raises some important questions. From the Torah through the Talmud to Hassidism, the tradition reminds us that what flows out of our bodies is as much a matter of spiritual concern as is what goes into us. It reminds us not to be prudish, and so the form and style of discussions of these matters has much to say to us.

On the other hand, its content may be more problematic. In days gone by, the earth seemed so large and the human community so small that we could indeed "get rid" of our waste. We could find someplace outside the camp to bury it, and without much care on our part, the waste would return into the cycle of life.

Today the human race is much larger, and waste is not only what goes through a single human body but also what goes through the body politic. This waste is not always easy to recycle into the biostream, and the earth is much smaller and more vulnerable. For us, perhaps, not a single human body alone but the entire earth is the "camp" of the Divine Presence, and so there is no "outside the camp" where we can get rid of our waste.

For us, therefore, eliminating the husks of alienation as we free the sparks of holiness depends less on removing waste from our bodies and from society and more on getting the waste *into* the body of the earth—so that it can reenter the biological web and become food once again.

Getting our waste "out of sight" may still make sense, but "out of mind" is not a good idea. The Asher Yatzar blessing, with its reminder that we are an interwoven organism in which elimination is part of the sacred process, teaches us that we should keep our waste in prayerful mind.

Early in the 1970s, I went to visit an old college friend of mine in Baltimore. The conversation turned to food, and my friend's wife mentioned that she kept three sets of dishes: one *milchig,* one *fleishig*—and one *treyf.* That is, one for meat dishes and one for dairy, as in the strict tradition of Rabbinic *kashrut*—and one for foods that weren't kosher at all.

I blinked—what sense did that make?—and then said, "Oh! I guess you don't keep kosher but your parents do, so you have the two kosher sets for when they come to dinner."

My hostess smiled. "Good guess, but no. Actually my parents don't keep kosher either. But my grandparents used to—they're dead now—and my mother always kept the kosher sets for *her* mother's sake. That's the way I grew up, so that's what I do."

"Oh," I said, a little faintly. "I guess it's become a tradition."

The specifics of this story may be unique. At least I've never met anyone else who does it that way for that reason. But in a metaphoric sense, that's how many Jews live today: in/out of the kosher code, in/out of Rabbinic Judaism. Drawing on it or echoing it or keeping it well polished in the cupboard, even when they don't live by it.

When we look at the kitchens of "modern" Jews, we find that in most of them, the "rules" are much less complex and interesting than they were in the kitchens of Rabbinic or Biblical Jews. When it comes to food, modern Jewish culture has been a sort of thin cultural broth, rather than the thick stew of the past. The most interesting thing about food in modern Jewish life may be how much less interesting it is than food in Biblical or Rabbinic Judaism.

At the same time, the Jewish people as a cluster of groups and institutions has become much more complex, much "stewier," than in past Jewish life. As Rabbinic Judaism broke down under modern pressure, Jews went in many different directions. Each new experiment or version of daily Jewish life may have been thinner than Rabbinic culture, but the arguments and alternatives became much richer. That is what happens when a culture breaks down, before it reshapes itself.

As we have already seen, we may be able to draw on the teachings of Biblical

Judaism even though we no longer live in that world. For me, a similar equation applies to the teachings of Rabbinic Judaism: I can learn from some of them, even though I myself no longer live inside that world.

When I try to make sense of living in/out of Rabbinic Judaism as my friend did, it helps me when I reflect that Jews have dealt with this shattering before. What the Rabbis did in their day, we can do in ours.

The task may be harder. For Modernity has done even more to shatter the world of Rabbinic Judaism than Hellenism did to shatter the world of the Bible—and more quickly. It is true that enormous population growth, advanced industrial and information technology, worldwide changes in the environment, mass media, continental governments and global corporations, instant universal communication, mass lethal weapons, highly efficient medicine, and worldwide total war—all these have drastically weakened face-to-face communities of family, village, or neighborhood, in favor of numbers without names or faces, numbers of voters and purchasers. Most of our culture has shifted its attention from the spiritual and the Divine to material prosperity and scientific progress.

For Jews in particular, this has meant both sheer physical destruction (the Nazi Holocaust of the largest and most vibrant centers of Rabbinic Jews and of Yiddish-speaking Jewish Modernists) and a more subtle cultural, philosophical, economic, and political transformation. Most Jews have found many aspects of Modernity attractive and compelling. It has solved more of their immediate problems than did Rabbinic Judaism. Even Jews who have chosen to live by the Rabbinic code are really doing so in a profoundly new way: They get to choose their path. No one has erected a ghetto wall around Brooklyn's Borough Park or Me'ah She'arim in Jerusalem.

One of the results of this thorough shattering of the Rabbinic communities is that today the dinner table no longer represents a totally Jewish time and space, infused with explicit spiritual meaning. Most of us live far from our families, far from the neighborhoods where we grew up. More and more we eat alone—or if with others, not just with other Jews but with people who are the citizens of many lands and cultures.

The choice before us at the table is no longer between *kashrut* and the foods of the culture in which our own specific Jewish community lives. Instead, we find ourselves encountering foods of and eating with people of every culture on the planet. We meet people who eat according to other spiritually rooted patterns: vegetarianism, macrobioticism, boycotts based on how food producers treat workers or the land. Many of our meals are cooked and eaten not in our homes but in commercial centers, far from our friends and families. The distinctive roles of women and men in growing, preparing, and eating food are being dissolved or transformed.

The food itself comes not only from the farms and oceans of all the world, but now from its factories, too. The nature of the food is affected by mercury poured from industry into lakes and oceans; by pesticides sprayed onto huge areas of farmland; by urbanization of other huge areas of forest and farm; by the use of crossbreeding, selective breeding, and genetic recombination to change the plants and animal species that we use for food.

All this is true. So, what now?

Just as there were disagreements among and sometimes struggles among Jews of the Talmudic age about how best to respond to Hellenism, so in our own day there are disagreements about how best to respond to Modernity. For the last century or so, the arguments proposed by the adherents of these different responses have contributed to the richest aspects of Jewish culture, a legacy from the word-Judaism of the Rabbis to the post-Rabbinic world. As the cooking has gotten less Jewish, the words have had to carry more of the burden of "Jewishing."

These different responses include:

1. Wholeheartedly joining the "Modern" life-path and severing or minimizing ties to the life-path of Rabbinic Judaism. (This is analogous to the whole-hearted espousal of Hellenism, as some Jews did.) There are three categories of this path:

—becoming Western Modernists indistinguishable from all others;
—creating a Modernist Jewish culture based perhaps in the Yiddish language, but divorced from previous Jewish religious life;
—creating a Jewish homeland and state in the Land of Israel that would be secular and Modern but distinctive through its use of Hebrew and its interest in the Jewish past.

2. Using a modified or minimized Rabbinic Judaism to express many Modern values, meanwhile smoothing away the rawest, roughest edges where Rabbinic Judaism rubbed against Modernity. (This is the approach taken by some of Reform, Reconstructionist, and Conservative Judaism, analogous in method, though of course not in content, to what Philo and the other Jews of Al-exandria did to recast Judaism as a Hellenistic allegory.)

3. Restoring as much as possible of the world of Rabbinic Judaism as it was before Modernity. (This is the approach of Orthodox and Hassidic Judaism, and some aspects of Conservative Judaism, analogous to the Sadducee and Samaritan efforts to restore the Biblical sacrificial rhythm, or perhaps the efforts of the Dead Sea communities to isolate themselves in order to practice a ritually pure Judaism apart from the Temple.)

4. Creating a transformed post-Rabbinic Judaism—feminist, holistic, eco-centered, body-affirming, yet *deeply* rooted in the Jewish past, both affirming and affirmed by most of the Jewish people. (This is analogous to the Rabbis' creation of Judaism without the central Shrine or land, profoundly different from the Biblical world, yet deeply rooted in the Biblical tradition.) Many Reform, Reconstructionist, and Conservative Jews are moving in this direction.

5. Creating a new path altogether, perhaps an amalgam of Judaism, modernism, Christianity, feminism, Buddhism, which might, because of its "universalism," appeal to some Jews but perhaps even more so to other people (analogous to the emergence of Christianity during the Hellenistic period).

I myself am most attracted by the fourth option—renewing our Jewish roots in order to transform our Jewish future. In order to walk that path intelligently, I have found myself wanting to know and to draw from the spiritual efforts of all the previous centuries and millennia of Jewish life. Of course, the fourth path is not the only one of the five in which it is important to know and understand what the Rabbis, as well as the Bible, taught. In fact, Modernity is the only path that rejects Rabbinic Jewish wisdom altogether, calling it irredeemably unscientific, elitist, and ineffective.

You might think that if Modernity excludes ancient and Rabbinic Jewish wisdom, there is nothing that a spiritual Jewish path could learn from it. But from a spiritual perspective, since God's world is mostly good, Modernity is not likely to be wholly bad. There might be many elements of the modern world that bespeak God's truths. For example:

- Most Jews are now convinced that the equality of women and men is a God-given truth and goal, which was veiled by the way in which previous Jewish civilizations lived.
- The whole notion that people should rule themselves, not be subject to the commands of a king, a dictator, or an oligarchy, today seems a deep truth, glimpsed by Torah, that was obscured by the limited vision of the people and especially of their leaders.
- Some aspects of modern science—both content and method—seem to proclaim the depth and grandeur of Creation in a way that spiritually open Jews can celebrate, quite different from the "scientism" that sees the world as merely a dead object to study, exploit, and manipulate.

Of course, many Jews today who are wrestling with tradition—not turning away from it and not bowing down to it, but wrestling and dancing with it—seek to incorporate these truths into a deeper, renewed, reshaped version of Judaism.

In the most gloriously attractive and the most victoriously destructive days of the Modern Age, it was the first two options for how to respond—leaving or minimizing Rabbinic Judaism—that were tugging at most Jews.

But along the way—for some in the wreckage of World War I, for others in the wake of the Nazi Holocaust and the atomic bomb, for still others in the American cultural and political upheaval of the sixties—doubts about Modernity began to grow. Parts of it began to look more and more ugly and dangerous, not only to Jews but also to the whole human race and to many forms of life on the planet. Then the third and fourth options—the restoration of a pre-modern Rabbinic Judaism and the renewal/transformation of Jewish life to create a new form of Judaism—began to attract more interest and excitement.

ð

We need to take some time, therefore, to understand how these different responses to Modernity affected the food Jews ate and how they ate it.

Many who found that much of modern life and modern science was attractive came to disagree with one or both of the main arguments for the distinctive pattern of Jewish eating:

Was *kashrut* God's command? As modern scholarship and a scientific worldview spread, more and more Jews decided that the Torah's rules of what and how to eat, like analogous rules in other cultures, had little or nothing to do with God or a spiritual life.

Was *kashrut* a way to preserve the separation between Jews and others? To many modernized Jews, this seemed a detriment, not a benefit. The more attractive and open the modern world became, the fewer of them wanted to live in a ghetto—whether geographic or symbolic, compulsory or voluntary.

There was a more profound reason for the decline of *kashrut*. To the extent that *kashrut* was a way for human beings to limit their own power over the earth, the spirit of Modernity ran directly contrary to *kashrut*. For the success and the joy of Modernity lay precisely in that it increased humanity's power of subduing the earth, through science, technology, and more rational political and social controls.

In accord with these elements of the modern worldview, two approaches to food and the earth won wide currency:

- One was that the earth from which food comes is simply a tool, an instrument, a dead thing available for whatever human use and exploitation will bring about its most efficient production of food and of other consumable goods.
- Its twin idea was that food is simply an instrument of individual nutrition,

and perhaps flavor, that helps people most effectively to do their work (which is basically to produce more food).

How did the Jews of late-nineteenth-century Europe respond to this? Large traditional communities in Eastern Europe continued to observe *kashrut* as they always had. But to all three of the main new versions of Jewish community, modernist synagogues, secular Yiddish-focused socialism, and secular Zionism, *kashrut* made little or no sense.

The Reform synagogues (which emerged in Europe but became especially strong in the United States) viewed "ritual" as merely the transient clothing that past generations had used to protect deeper religious truths of reason and justice. At first, some Reform thinkers adhered to the Biblical prohibitions on such specific foods as pork and shellfish, while dropping the Rabbinic rules for separating milk and meat and the dishes for each. They made this distinction on the grounds that Torah might be Divinely inspired, but the Talmud was clearly the work of human minds.

When modern scholars argued that Torah was itself a weave of different historically conditioned documents, most Reform leaders dropped the distinction between the Biblical and the Rabbinic. It was swiftly overtaken by a broader rejection of dietary regulations altogether. By 1885, the crucial Pittsburgh Platform of the Reform movement in America asserted:

> We hold that all such Mosaic and Rabbinical laws as regulate diet, priestly
> purity, and dress, originated in ages and under the influence of ideas
> altogether foreign to our present mental and spiritual state. They fail to
> impress the modern Jew with a spirit of priestly holiness; their observance in
> our days is apt to obstruct rather than to further modern spiritual elevation.

God, the Reform movement concluded, had much to do with scientific reason and with social justice, but not with rules of *kashrut*, which were devoid of both. The rules that protected the poor and the stranger were sacred, but avoiding pork was not. The Reform movement raised one aspect of the ancient Prophets of Israel to greater religious importance. In Reform thinking, some of the Prophets had proclaimed it was sinful to pretend that Temple offerings of food could be made holy when the society as a whole was unjust. So the Reform movement attacked those who followed Rabbinic rules of *kashrut* while ignoring issues of justice and peace—and indeed often suggested that too much attention to ritual and practice might distract one from the pursuit of social justice.

As the Reform movement in the United States gathered institutional strength, it made clear its opposition to *kashrut* not only in the words that came forth from

Reform mouths but in the food that went into them. In 1883, a major foundational banquet for the Hebrew Union College in Cincinnati, the seminary created by and for the Reform movement, included shellfish on the menu in what became famous as "the Treyfa Banquet." Even though the organizers seem not to have deliberately decided ahead of time to reject *kashrut*, once the shellfish appeared they felt it unnecessary to apologize for or defend its inclusion. *Kashrut* was irrelevant.

During the mid-twentieth century, however, especially in the wake of the Nazi Holocaust, many Reform Jews found themselves more drawn to affirming a sense of connection with observant Conservative and Orthodox Jews. They began to feel that some limited observance of *kashrut*—especially by Jewish institutions, as distinguished from individual households—could contribute to that sense of connection.

The Reform community published a guide to life practice, *Gates of Mitzvah*, that asserted, "Judaism has always recognized a religious dimension to the consumption of food. The range of options available to the Reform Jew is from full acceptance of the Biblical and Rabbinic regulations to total non-observance." In 1979, a committee of Reform rabbis, chaired by Rabbi Walter Jacob, in answering a query, noted that the observance of *kashrut* might remind people of Jewish ideals and encourage ethical discipline, and might link all Jews with each other today and with their history.

The second major expression of Modernity to emerge in Europe and among Eastern European immigrants to America was Jewish socialism, in the revolutionary Yiddishe Arbeiters Bund (Jewish Workers Union) and such more moderate groupings as the Arbeiter Ring (Workmen's Circle). These groups believed that what was crucial about food was issues of social class: Who owned or controlled the means of producing food and therefore could set its prices, and who had no such control and so were at the mercy of the owners?

In the view of these Jewish socialists, when the rabbis insisted that observing *kashrut* would be rewarded in *ha'olam haba* (the world to come), they were distracting desperate and impoverished workers from seeking a good life in this world. Even worse, they argued, *kashrut* separated Jewish workers from other workers with whom they would have to work and eat if society were ever to be radically changed; and it misled Jewish workers into thinking that Jewish owners and workers had their peoplehood in common, thus taking attention away from the real class differences that were keeping workers powerless and poor.

On the other hand, when the Bund had a strong political base in the Jewish community of Poland between the world wars, it defended the right of Orthodox Jews to provide themselves with kosher meat, against attempts by some anti-Semitic Polish political parties to interfere.

For the third major expression of Jewish modernism, secular Zionism, the issues of food focused more on land than on social class. Secular Zionists who worked to create a free Jewish community in the Land of Israel did not see why liberated Jews should have a special diet any more than liberated Italians or Poles. But some of them hoped that this new community would be not only politically free but culturally and spiritually transformed, would create new spiritual values from growing its own food, working directly on the land, building the relationship with the earth of the Land of Israel that had been denied them by living in the Diaspora.

Many of these early Zionists were deeply affected by the ideas of Aaron David Gordon, a white-collar business functionary who at the age of forty-seven moved from Poland to Palestine and became a farm worker. From 1912 till he died in 1992, he published a number of articles and pamphlets that won wide influence, especially among kibbutz and socialist leaders, by setting forth a secular Jewish spirituality of work and nature:

> And when, O Man, you will return to Nature—on that day your eyes will open, you will gaze straight into the eyes of Nature, and in its mirror you will see your own image. You will know that you have returned to yourself, that when you hid from Nature, you hid from yourself. . . . On that day you will know that your former life did not befit you, that you must renew all things: your food and your drink, your dress and your home, your manner of work and your mode of study—everything! ("Logic for the Future")
>
> The Jewish people has been completely cut off from Nature and imprisoned within city walls these two thousand years. . . . We lack the habit of labor—not labor performed out of external compulsion, but labor to which one is attached in a natural and organic way. ("People and Labor")
>
> It is life we want . . . our own life feeding on our own vital sources, in the fields and under the skies of our Homeland. . . . We come . . . to be planted in our natural soil from which we have been uprooted, to strike our roots deep into its life-giving substances, and to stretch out our branches in the sustaining and creating air and sunlight of the Homeland. ("Our Tasks Ahead")

Some saw the kibbutz, a collective farm where every member of the community had an equal, earthy, and intimate work relationship to the specific piece of communally owned land, as the deepest expression of Zionism. In the spirit of A. D. Gordon, many kibbutzim that called themselves "secular" created new forms of celebration for such agricultural festivals as Shavuot and Sukkot.

In Israel, however, the hopes of these cultural Zionists have in the main not been fulfilled.

On the one hand, against all their expectations there has grown a sizable rabbinically defined community that, like the rabbinic communities of the Diaspora, lives in cities, adheres to *kashrut,* and has won enough political and social power to impose *kashrut* on some secular institutions.

On the other hand, though most Israeli Jews have taken great pride in "making the desert bloom," few outside the kibbutzim have sought to create a new Jewish culture of the earth.

So by the late twentieth century, modern approaches to food had generally won out over the Rabbinic approach in most Israeli and Diaspora communities. Especially after the Holocaust destroyed the largest communities committed to traditional *kashrut* (as well as many secular communities), the majority of Jews in almost every country in the world no longer observed the rules of Rabbinic *kashrut.* Some had made their own individual adjustments or compromises, keeping a few elements of *kashrut* while dropping others, so as to keep some sense of a distinctively Jewish diet. But for many, the requirements of *kashrut* became not a cause for celebration but an irrelevant curiosity from the past, or even a cause for shame and avoidance.

And yet the forces of the modern commercial marketplace were at the same time bringing about a perverse and ironic twist of history. In North America, at the very moment when a smaller proportion of Jews than in all previous history were eating according to the code of *kashrut,* there were probably more *non*-Jews eating certifiably kosher food than ever before in history.

How did this happen? In a mass consumer market, small fractions of the buying public who bring a single issue to their buying can have a disproportionate effect on the market as a whole, so long as nobody but them cares one way or the other about their issue.

That's what happened in the United States. By the 1950s, Orthodox Jews had set up mechanisms for certifying kosher food, for meat first, and then all sorts of nonmeat items. How could one be sure that a meat-based fat was not used in a cookie, or a breakfast cereal, or even in a cheesecake? How could one be sure that butter was not used to bake a bread that might be eaten at a chicken dinner?

At first, local rabbis went to inspect local bakeries and dairies and canneries, and put their *hekhsher*—a certification of how and whether the food met the requirements of *kashrut*—on the label. They might attach their names, or let customers check their bona fides with the store or the manufacturer. Then the Union of Orthodox Jewish Congregations set up a national inspectorate, charged the food industry fees to support the inspection service, and put the letter U on the labels of the approved foods. Jews who cared about *kashrut,* even if they weren't members of an Orthodox congregation, did not see much point in duplicating the UOJC mechanism.

When observant Jews could choose between one brand of cookies that had a *hekhsher* and another that did not, they usually chose the one that did. Even some casually observant Jews made this choice when it was easy to make. Such Christian denominations as the Seventh-Day Adventists and many Muslims also found the kosher certification useful. The bigger the market, the tinier became the per-item cost of the kosher certification. Nobody was interested in organizing a boycott of kosher foods; so there was no counterpressure on the food companies. So it became worthwhile for more and more food companies to invite inspectors to check their products and issue the *hekhsher*.

As a result, a wide variety of foods in North America came to be manufactured according to kosher standards, and non-Jews bought and ate them because they were easily available. In this ironic way, the same Modernity that had undermined *kashrut* as an all-encompassing life-path within the Jewish community made it more available as a casual possibility among Jews and non-Jews alike.

This irony actually points toward a deeper implication for the Jewish future. What Jews have accomplished is "exporting" particular pieces of *kashrut* to the non-Jewish world—not all of *kashrut* as a holistic life-path, but only particular foods that have been certified as kosher. In a traditional Rabbinic mind-set, one of the hardest things to imagine would have been that non-Jews would be attracted by even fragments of *kashrut*. Now that we have seen this happen, we can ask a new question: What other elements of Jewish life that we have previously assumed were for Jews alone, part of the special Jewish covenant with God, might be useful to the world as a whole?

By looking at Jewish approaches to food from the Biblical era to the Modern Age, we have come to the edges of the present. To get a glimpse of the possible future Jewish attitudes toward food, let us begin with four unconventional questions:

1. Are tomatoes grown by drenching the earth in pesticides 'kosher" to eat, at home or at a synagogue wedding reception?
2. Is newsprint made by chopping down an ancient and irreplaceable forest "kosher" to use to make a Jewish newspaper?
3. What about windows and doors so built that the warm air flows out through them and the furnace keeps burning all night? Are such doors and windows "kosher" for a home or for a Jewish Community Center building?
4. Is a bank that invests its depositors' money in an oil company that befouls the ocean a "kosher" place for me or for the UJA to deposit money?

If by "kosher" we mean what we have so far called by that name—the traditional law code of proper ritual slaughter, proper separation of meat and milk, proper tithing of fruit—then the correct answer to all these questions is that the category of "kosher" does not apply to them. (Not even to the first question, which is at least about food!)

But what if we both draw on the ancient meaning of "kosher" and go beyond it? What if we move the word and the idea to a new place in the spiral of Jewish thought, and test out a new word—"eco-kosher"? What if by eco-kosher we mean a broader sense of good everyday practice that draws on the wellsprings of Jewish wisdom and tradition about the relationships between human beings and the earth?

Then perhaps the answer is that these ways of behaving may not be **eco-kosher**. Where does this word, and the concept behind it, come from?

The word *eco-kosher* itself was coined in the late 1970s by Rabbi Zalman Schachter-Shalomi, founder of the P'nai Or Religious Fellowship. Schachter-Shalomi made not only his ideas but himself an extraordinary fusion of old and new approaches to Judaism. As a teenage boy in Vienna, he studied Orthodox Judaism by day and secular socialist Zionism at night. With his family, he fled Hitler, was interned in Vichy France, and escaped to America. He studied for the rabbinate in a traditional Lubavitcher Hassidic yeshiva, and was singled out as so unusually bright and creative by the Lubavitch leadership that he was sent out to be one of their earliest outreach workers.

But he learned to listen as well as to teach. To his astonishment and the consternation of Lubavitch organization men who were stuck in conventional Hassidic theory and practice, he discovered deep spiritual meaning in the lives and thoughts of Christian mystics like Thomas Merton and Howard Thurman (Martin Luther King's teacher), Eastern yogis, Muslim Sufis, transpersonal Jungian psychologists, Gandhian social activists, and women who were exploring and creating feminist spirituality and politics.

He left Lubavitch behind, and began to integrate all that he was learning into an expanded notion of Jewish mystical thought and practice. Instead of reading in books what the great Jewish mystics like the Baal Shem Tov had done, he began to do what they did: see new life in, give new life to dried-out Jewish practice. The traditional prayer book, he said, was like a cookbook: a guide to eating, but not the food itself. Some people thought that flavor and nourishment could come from eating the pages of the prayer book, but in fact that made no sense. The prayer book, like the cookbook, was useful only as a guide to cooking food with new heat, fresh water, and newly chosen spices.

And the same thing, said Schachter-Shalomi, applied to the code of kosher food. So he asked—is electric power generated by a nuclear plant eco-kosher?

Schachter-Shalomi was both unique in the way he brought traditional Judaism into contemporary life, and not at all unique in expressing the needs of a Jewish community that was moving beyond the Modern Age—reaching back to learn from premodern Judaism, and reaching forward to a Judaism that does not yet exist. For just as the Jewish people experienced a crisis in welcoming and celebrating the Modern Age, so it is now beginning to experience a crisis as it sees dangers and feels doubts about the Modern Age.

THE POSTMODERN CRISIS

The triumph of Modernity profoundly affected the eating habits of the Jewish people. While part of the community adhered to the tradition of kosher food, the majority of Jews in the world abandoned the rules in their flight from ghettoized Jewish communities, and in their identification with secularism and "universalism" and the potential of modern technology (in producing food as well as many other things).

In our own generation, however, this triumph of Modernity has become a trauma. In order to produce more food and other "consumables," the human race has subjected the earth to pollution and destruction. And the whole earth is striking back by threatening atmospheric decay, desertification, drought, flood, famine, the extinction of species. On the one hand, the whole notion that food must be treated as sacred has almost vanished. And on the other hand, the whole notion of treating the earth as sacred through rhythmic sabbatical rest for earth and earthlings has almost vanished.

The crisis of the Biblical Eden appears in our own day with more sharpness than ever before. For Eden is an archetype: Its crisis was, is, that we become fully knowledgeable humans only in the process of splitting ourselves off from the earth, eating from the earth in a split-off way. The tragedy is that we are in truth both split off from the earth and not split off from it. We are the one species that is able to rise "above" the earth, see it as a whole, and therefore choose to act as if we were not really embedded within it. Since as biological beings we are in fact still embedded in the earth's biology, when we act as if we are "beyond" earth, we ourselves are shattered.

Today the breadth and depth of our knowledge is so great that we have acted with even greater power to separate ourselves than in the agricultural or industrial revolutions. The result is that we and the earth stand in much greater danger than ever before—the danger that we may be forever exiled from the one great earthly garden.

During the last three hundred years we have learned how to consume some of the fruits of Planet Earth, fruits of the Tree of the Knowledge of Opposites and Distinctions, which were hidden away throughout our history: fossil fuels, and nuclear energy. The result of this consumption has been both enormous wealth and a new kind of war with the earth. We have eaten so carelessly that we have poisoned the earth, and she is responding by poisoning us.

It is not clear that the planetary biosphere can long survive the careless treatment we are giving it. So we have made the gift of food from the earth more problematic than ever.

Technology has also transformed the medium of the relationship between earth and human earthling. Originally, food was the great connection. There were others—clothing, housing, wood for energy—but food made up the largest and most potent aspect of what we received from the earth.

That is no longer so. Much of the human race has created an economy in which many other products of the earth that are consumed by humans may outweigh food—in market value, if not in survival importance. What implications does this pose for Jewish practice?

At the same time that Modernity has deeply affected the relationship between human beings and the earth, it has eaten away at the close-knit communities that had populated the earth. Breaking down the ghetto walls has given Jews new freedoms, new equalities; it has also left them bereft of dependable and loving relationships and a sense of meaning in life and death that stem from living in coherent communities.

Out of these discoveries have come new desires and new searches. In the arena of food and eating, some Jews have concluded that pure individualism leads to the death of ethics and community, and that accepting communal standards for what to eat might make sense. For many, the ethical issues stem from a belief that all peoples eat from all the earth, and that a specific Jewish peoplehood does not address such broad concerns.

They may welcome communal discussions and decisions about vegetarianism, macrobiotic diets, or boycotts of food grown by oppressed workers, but feel much less comfortable in choosing a distinctively Jewish diet.

Or they may feel unhappy with *kashrut*, not only because it divides Jews from others but because its own patterns are so much in the form of "This you *must* and this you must *not*." For Jews who resist the external imposition of black-and-white distinctions upon their lives, this may seem one of the most unpleasant characteristics of *kashrut*.

In the last several years, some have been trying to reshape Jewish values so that they might affirm and protect the wholeness of the earth precisely by affirming and strengthening Jewish life. They have been attempting to reconnect the idea of *kashrut* with some broader values and obligations toward the earth that stem from Jewish tradition. They have drawn upon those underlying ethical concerns for the earth and its creatures that some have said were encoded in traditional *kashrut*.

On the other hand some Jews who have been exploring new meaning in *kashrut* have started to look beyond the traditional definitions. From this deeper exploration, "eco-kosher" has become more than a word. It has begun to take on reality in the world.

NEW WORLD, NEW PATHS

How this happened is itself a teaching of a new mode of walking Jewishly in the world. In 1990, I sent out a memo to a number of rabbis and Jewish teachers, asking them whether the time had come to explore new ethical dimensions of *kashrut*. I was acting on behalf of a group that is now called ALEPH: Alliance for Jewish Renewal. ALEPH sees itself as a seed bank of new approaches to Jewish life—drawing on specific good ideas from the Jewish past that, like seeds from past generations of a species, could be newly planted for the sake of coping with a transformed future.

The memo intrigued Marshall Meyer (may his memory be for a blessing) and Rolando Matalon, rabbis of an innovative Conservative congregation in New York City called B'nai Jeshurun. Together with ALEPH, they gathered about a dozen leaders of all four religious streams of Jewish life, plus Jews who were active in organizations concerned with consumers and the environment.

Our talks were religious and secular, halakhic and nonhalakhic. Some of us were deeply steeped in Jewish law, others were committed to Jewish forms of social action but skeptical of *halakha*, still others had barely any Jewish connection but cared about healing the earth. From all these perspectives, we agreed to look at some of the traditional Jewish values and ethics that might be connected with what we eat.

As we did this, layer after layer of new possibilities emerged.

The first layer was about food itself: What kinds of food protected the earth instead of wounding it?

Then we began to examine whether other kinds of "eating"—consuming energy, using paper, buying machines, investing money—might be enough like eating food that in our generation the guidelines of what is kosher and *treyf* might be applied to them.

Then we looked more carefully at the whole notion of Yes or No, On or Off, Kosher or Treyf—absolute distinctions—that has been at the heart of traditional *kashrut*.

At the first level, the gathering looked at some traditional Jewish ethical categories about relationships between human beings and the rest of God's Creation. The main ones were:

Tza'ar ba'alei chai'im—literally, concern for the "distress of those who possess life," usually understood as respect for animals. Some members suggested this concept could be extended to prohibit the raising of animals under superproductive factory-farm conditions and then one step further, to prohibit eating meat from such animals. Still others suggested extending it to respect for the identity of plants; for example, by restricting the use of pesticides and genetic recombination, and then by prohibiting eating food grown by such products and technologies.

Bal tashchit—literally, "not ruining" the earth or protection of the environment. This norm began with the Biblical prohibition against cutting down the trees of an enemy—and then was extended to protect all trees and other aspects of nature, and even to prohibit the waste of furniture or other objects in which human labor was tied to the products of the earth. The members of the committee suggested that *bal tashchit* might be extended to prohibit poisoning the earth with chemical pesticides in order to grow food and to forbid eating foods grown that way, substituting "natural" or "organic" foods.

Sh'mirat haguf—the protection of one's own body. This principle could be applied to prohibit eating foods that contain carcinogens and/or hormones, and quasi-food items like tobacco and overdoses of alcohol. It would also mandate attention to anorexia or overeating, problems that can cause deep physical and psychological pain and turn food into a weapon.

Tzedakah—the sharing of food with the poor—could be extended to prohibit the eating of any meal, or any communal festive meal, unless a proportion of its cost went to buying food for the hungry. Some of the committee pushed this approach even further, suggesting that in a world where protein is already distributed inequitably, it is unjust to channel large amounts of cheap grain into feeding animals to grow expensive meat protein, and that it is therefore unjust to eat meat at all when the grain could directly feed larger numbers of human beings.

B'rakhah and *Kedushah*—the tradition that when we eat we must consciously affirm a sense of holiness and blessing. Traditionally, this meant that those who eat together literally pause at the table, before and after the meal, to praise God for the earth's bounty.

Even the secular participants thought it might be important to use old or new forms for heightening the attention we give to the Unity from which all food comes—whether we call it God or not. They pointed out that this would help us maintain an awareness of the sad fact that at the most obvious level we must kill plants and/or animals to live, and at a deeper level that whatever we now do to live poses some danger to the planet that gives us life. Keeping ourselves conscious of these truths, they said, would make it more likely that we could exercise some self-control.

At this point, the participants who were knowledgeable about Jewish tradition noted that they had done little more than list and barely sketch the relevant ethical principles that are embedded in Jewish tradition. To draw on them in any serious way would mean to look more deeply at how the tradition shapes their content— not only at the specific rulings but at how they are arrived at. Not necessarily to follow the same paths of thought or decision, but to wrestle with a Judaism that draws on the wisdom of all the Jewish generations, not our own alone. Once we have done this, then indeed our generation must decide for itself.

The very decision to apply these ethical principles to the choice of what to eat would represent consulting the tradition without being imprisoned by it.

For instance, they explained, it is clear that every one of these ethical principles stands as a norm in the legal code, the *halakha*, as well as in *aggadah*, or extralegal symbol, metaphor, philosophy. But it is more problematic whether one is obligated not only to avoid misdeeds, but also to avoid benefiting from them if done by others.

With care not to impose impossible burdens, they said, it would probably be legally possible to bring together these principles with the Jewish sense of the importance of food, by forbidding the eating of the fruits of these misdeeds.

The participants then asked, Does it make sense now to draw on these basic principles to set new standards for what we actually consume, standards for an "ethical *kashrut*"? If we did, would we run the danger of obsessiveness, or even the danger that applying strict standards might result in drastically reducing the kinds of foods and any other products we could use?

Perhaps we can learn a lesson from the way different types of Jews practice traditional *kashrut* today.

For different Jews do have different answers to the question "Is this food kosher?" For example, some will only accept certain types of rabbinical certification on packaged goods, while others are satisfied with reading labels to verify that the ingredients are kosher. Some people will drink only kosher wine, while others believe this category is no longer relevant. Some keep "Biblical *kashrut*," abstaining only from Biblically forbidden foods. Some are willing to eat nonkosher foods in restaurants and in other people's homes, others are willing to eat only intrinsically kosher foods such as fish and vegetables on nonkosher utensils when they are away from home, while still others do not eat any cooked foods away from home.

A new *kashrut* that drew on the ethical strands of Torah would also demand that people make choices about how to observe the rules. For example, some might treat the principle of *oshek* (not oppressing workers) as paramount, and use only products that are grown or made without oppressing food workers (products, for example, grown in one's own backyard or neighborhood garden, or that come from a kibbutz where all the workers are also co-owners and co-managers). Others might make the principle of *bal tashchit* (protection of the environment) paramount, and put *oshek* in a secondary place, perhaps applying it only when specifically asked to do so by workers who are protesting their plight.

In a multidimensional ethical *kashrut*, choices may work differently from the way they work in traditional *kashrut*. For there might be so many ethical values to weigh that it would be rare to face a black-and-white choice in a particular product: This one is grown by union workers, that one with special care for the earth and water, another...

Choices would depend more on balancing and synthesizing underlying values than on an absolute sense of Good and Bad, more on a sense of Both/And than of Either/Or.

BEYOND FOOD

Up to this point, the groups that had gathered to discuss the new *kashrut* had focused on food alone as the nexus between human beings and the earth. But it was soon apparent that it is not the only connection.

Indeed, in our own generation, although food remains for many the most urgent and perhaps the scarcest link to the earth, producing it takes up much smaller a proportion of our work and capital than it did before the Modern Age. Many other products of the earth that are consumed by humans may outweigh food. And where cropland or pastureland was originally the basis for producing food, in the modern economy, money in all its forms takes on much of the productive role that land once had.

Should we in our generation apply Jewish teachings about food to other "consumables" that come from the earth, and also to the money that connects us with them?

The committee members pointed out that from the Biblical era on, Jews paid some attention to links other than food between earth and human, even though none was addressed with as much care and regulation as was food.

Rain, for example, was a crucial connection with the earth. Without it, no food could grow; and in the Land of Israel, rainfall was sometimes problematic. One of the main concerns of Jewish liturgy is intense prayer for rain; and the Talmud specifies an elaborate pattern of fasts and prayers in time of drought. In our generation, the purity and health of rain has become not a given but a serious issue.

Clothing was another link with the earth, and the Torah notes a kind of *kashrut* of clothes—not mixing linen with wool. The Rabbinic tradition did not greatly elaborate this rule.

Energy was another interface in the Biblical era. Wood and olive oil were the main sources of light and heat. Olive oil took on a sacred aura, since in the earliest memories of the people it was used for anointing sacred pillars and, later, for offerings at the Temple, for lighting the Temple Menorah (thus taking a central place in the origins of Hanukkah), and for anointing kings (thus giving the name "the Anointed One, Mashiach, Messiah," to the human being who would someday redeem history). The Talmud examines carefully the rules of making oil for sacred use.

As for firewood, the Bible describes its gathering as the first occasion for a legal case to define the prohibitions on exploitation of the earth that apply on Shabbat.

Breathing was another link. God's most intimate Name may have been based on a breathing sound, and breath/wind became the metaphor for life, soul, and spirit (as in the Hebrew words *ruach, nefesh,* and *neshamah*). As early as the Talmud, air pollution was occasionally a problem—when living downwind of a tannery, for example—but this was rare, and few rules were developed for the correct use of air. On the opposite end of the continuum of sweet air and foul air, the Talmud explores in detail what spices make up the incense that was burned at the Temple to make a sweet savor for God and humankind; and Rabbinic prayer books have continued to include these passages, even though—or because—there is no longer an Altar at which to burn the spices. Except for the ceremony that ends Shabbat, few Jewish communities continue to use spices or incense to sweeten the in-breath. Nonetheless, even this can remind us to explore what could become a *"kashrut* of breathing."

Those who had gathered to discuss the role of ethics in *kashrut* felt that in our own world, where food is far from the only problematic link between human beings and their environment, it is certainly authentic for Jews to work out Jewish guidelines for these other linkages. Our water and air are often polluted, and our main sources of energy—fossils that can be replaced and renewed only over millions of years, and nuclear radiation—pose profound dangers to the web of life on earth.

The committee asked itself:

- How would we develop rules of *kashrut* to apply to nonfood products, and how would we enforce them?
- Does it make sense to draw on the basic principles—*bal tashchit,* and so forth— to set new standards for what we actually consume?

So they began to look at several different areas:

Work—How do we choose what companies to work for and what work to do? Should engineers, secretaries, scientists, public-relations experts, nurses ask whether their work contributes to or reduces the danger of oil spills, ozone depletion, global warming, nuclear holocaust? Do Jewish tradition and the Jewish community offer any help in making such judgments? What help is most needed?

How could the Jewish community, or parts of it, decide whether specific jobs were "kosher"? Suppose it decided that a specific job was not kosher? Should and could the community provide financial help—temporary grants, low-interest loans, etc.—to Jews who decide to leave such jobs in order to carry into the world their commitment to Torah? Should organizing toward such a fund be a goal of the Jewish community?

Investments—How do we judge where to invest money, in which money market funds, IRAs, and so forth? What about institutional funds in which we may already have a voice or could create one for ourselves—college endowments, pension funds, city bonds? Should these funds be invested in businesses that spill oil or deplete the ozone layer or burn rain forests?

In the Jewish community, investment funds that might become "socially responsible" include community-worker and rabbinical-association pension funds, synagogue endowments, building-campaign accounts, pulpit flower funds, seminary endowments, among others. How would the community decide which investments are "kosher"?

Purchases—In deciding which companies from which to buy consumer goods should we as individuals, use as one factor in that choice what else those specific companies are producing? Should we ask synagogues, pension funds, city and state governments, PTAs to choose vendors on the same basis?

THE ECO-KOSHER PROJECT

Responding to all these questions, the religious and secular Jews gathered by ALEPH decided to create an ongoing project to explore these issues and bring them to the broader Jewish community.

And suddenly, for the sake of an ongoing project, words became important. What to call this effort?

The word Zalman Schachter-Shalomi had coined fifteen years before, "eco-kosher," entered the discussion.

This word shouted out its meaning almost without need for definition. By joining a Greek prefix with a very new connotation to a Hebrew root with a very ancient one, it signaled precisely the fusion of the ancient with the postmodern. By joining the most expansive sense of healing the earth to the most precise code of daily conduct, it signaled the importance of broadening kashrut at the same time as it signaled the importance of turning ecological consciousness into everyday action.

For some, however, the power of the word was a problem.

On the one hand, those in the Orthodox community who had taken on the responsibility for regulating traditional kashrut expressed concern that the term "eco-kosher" might cause confusion. What if a committee for a new approach to Jewish eating and consuming were to decide that for environmental reasons, what the Rabbinic tradition viewed as kosher was now "eco-treyf," or what was treyf was now "eco-kosher"?

On the other hand, some Reform Jews were concerned that members of the movement who had put great psychic energy into deciding that most of the categories of kosher food no longer had religious significance in the Modern Age, might reject the whole notion because its name echoed the traditional kashrut.

After long discussion, we decided to use "eco-kosher" because no alternative expressed so well the commitment to Jewish roots and values and the sense of a continuous daily practice and discipline. At the same time, we decided to take two precautions:

- to say explicitly that eco-*kashrut* stood outside of and independent from traditional *kashrut*, in a different rather than a competing sphere; and
- to carry out this assertion by leaving on one side, at least for the present, the main categories of "kosher" and *"treyf"* products—meat and dairy foods—and focus instead on issues and products not addressed by traditional *kashrut*.

So we made ourselves into the Eco-Kosher Project. We decided to focus on four categories of *individual* and *institutional* purchase and investment:

1. Fresh and processed fruits and vegetables. In the ways in which they are grown, packaged, and marketed, which of these products are most sensitive to protection of the earth?
2. Household and congregational consumables other than food—in particular, paper products and cleaning products
3. Finances—in particular, choices of where to place checking and savings accounts, investments, and so forth
4. No-cost or low-cost conservation and recycling of materials and energy

The Eco-Kosher Project decided to begin by focusing on institutions that have buildings and sizable purchasing/investing patterns—for example, synagogues, schools, camps, Hillel houses, Jewish community centers, nursing homes, hospitals, day care and other social service centers, Jewish journals and publishing houses. As these institutions pursued the process, individual households would find their path made easier.

It was also decided to approach two major categories of Jewish leadership:

- "Cultural-educational" staff like rabbis, religious school principals and teachers, JCC and camp program directors, Hillel directors, chaplains, editors and reporters
- Administrators and purchasing agents usually responsible for making purchases, choosing banks, and other financial matters

In judging what is eco-kosher, the Project would develop standards derived from the ethical earth-preserving elements of Jewish tradition such as *bal tashchit* (not ruining the earth), *tza'ar ba'alei chai'im* (respect for animals), *sh'mirat haguf* (protection of one's own body), and *shmitah* and *yovel* (the rhythms of allowing the earth to rest), as well as from contemporary secular work on protection of the environment.

The Project intended to explore if the Jewish categories can be extended and intertwined to address a number of newer questions. For example, what about determining a new kind of sabbatical year, perhaps a rhythmic pause or moratorium in new technological development while we reexamine its effects? Or requiring an environmental-impact statement before undertaking large corporate investments in new products? How about asking everyone, not just Jews, to set aside a special time each year for living lightly on the earth—like Sukkot, with its simplest of shelters, or Pesach, with its simplest of breads?

Some members of the Eco-Kosher Project expressed concern over what impact this new approach might have upon adherence to the traditional code of kosher food. They concluded that there are a number of possible permutations:

- Some who find traditional *kashrut* an important link with Torah and Jewish peoplehood might continue to observe it while observing eco-*kashrut* as well.
- Some who do not resonate to the traditional code might continue to leave it to one side while following the new path with its new way of connecting with Torah and Jewish peoplehood.
- Some who are newly observant followers of eco-*kashrut* might discover that it leads them to an unexpected value in the traditional form.
- Others who have observed traditional *kashrut* might find that the new one fulfills their Jewish sense more richly, and give up the ancient form.

It was concluded that there is no way to tell in advance how many people would go in one direction or another, and that since the need is great, the risks should be taken with as much care as possible.

CONTINUING THE WORK

In the long run, the members of the Eco-Kosher Project realized, the Project itself would not be enough. If the analogy to *kashrut* makes any sense, then what is needed is a kind of "living Talmud," a group of people who are Jewishly knowledgeable, ethically sensitive, and willing to become reasonably expert on questions regarding food, other consumer products, and money, so that their advice would be taken seriously by large parts of the Jewish community.

Such an Eco-Kosher Commission might periodically issue reports and suggestions on specific matters, listing specific products and perhaps even brands that it regarded as "highly recommended," and others it viewed as "to be avoided if at all possible."

Stepping back for a moment to look at the deeper implications of the Eco-

Kosher Project, we may see that it hints at a new role for the Jewish people. Its implications are that the Jewish people as a whole, not just individual Jews, would be consciously involved in *tikkun olam*, the healing of the world. At least since the Roman empire shattered the Jewish community in the Land of Israel, the Jewish people has mainly felt that it was powerless to affect history. The most that the community as a whole could do was to walk a decent, holy life-path of its own—and in dire emergency to seek survival by creating a state of its own against all odds. But to change the lives of other people, of the planet? Impossible.

Yet we have lived through a century of earthquakes, with more upheavals yet to come. In just fifty years, the Jewish people has experienced both the cruelest devastation and the most extraordinary political and economic successes of its history. Yet even at our strongest, we remain vulnerable to planetary crisis. Indeed, the earthquakes of change that are affecting the whole world have affected us even more, and sooner.

What should we do? Always before, the choices seemed to be between preserving our own uniqueness, and abandoning our Jewishness to fight the universal struggles. What the Eco-Kosher Project implies is that we can strengthen our Jewish distinctiveness and serve the needs of the earth as well; that we can strive to heal ourselves by helping to heal the earth, and help to heal the earth by healing ourselves.

If keeping kosher is partly about making distinctions, then keeping eco-kosher deals with the issue of "distinctions" in a new way: not by separating only, but by consciously connecting. Connecting what is uniquely Jewish with what is shared and universal. Choosing not Either/Or but Both/And.

And by asserting that Jewish wisdom can be of use not only to all peoples but all species, by choosing life in such a time of crisis.

XII. SEE GOD, AND EAT

Moving toward an eco-kosher practice is something every Jew could choose to do, whatever his or her other commitments in prayer, communal life, Torah study, or kosher eating. From Orthodox to secular, anyone could walk the eco-kosher path—could add it to whatever else he or she is doing. So we can imagine Orthodox + eco-kosher, Freudian + eco-kosher, Zionist + eco-kosher, Reform + eco-kosher, and so on.

Now I ask myself: What about those Jews for whom well-worn Jewish paths—those trails most blazed by Rabbinic lore, those trails most committed to secular Modernity—no longer lead to a fully joyful place?

What about those Jews who are both post-Rabbinic and postmodern, who may indeed be exploring Zen, or Sufi, or Jungian, or Native American, or Goddess forms of spirituality?

What about those Jews who keep trying various versions of Rabbinic Judaism—Orthodox, Reform, and Conservative—but keep finding that none of them quite meets their needs? Who feel a nameless thirst for an unknown wine?

What about those Jews who immerse themselves in Jewish literature, or in Israeli politics, or in efforts to defeat anti-Semitism—but who find that a secular modern lifestyle, even with a Jewish communal flavor, is insufficient? Who feel a nameless hunger for an unknown bread?

What might it mean if these different sorts of uncomfortable Jews were to begin shaping a new Jewish spiritual life-path? To include what is eco-kosher, but create a richer ceremonial and spiritual and intellectual life as well?

What would it mean to make their own midrashic spiral on the past—going back to draw on all the older tales and texts that we have studied in order to shape something new?

I turn this question inward, not to "them" or even "you," but to myself. Having so far studied and written about what large numbers of Jews were doing at various moments of our history, I decide to ask one Jew—one only Jew, one only Jew—what he, what I, would like to do. Perhaps others will find my answers useful. Perhaps not. More likely, I hope, they, you, will find *some* of them are.

So: If I draw on everything I have learned, what would my eating look like, smell like, taste like, sound like, if I were able to make my highest desires fully real?

In asking that question, I remember the extraordinary Torah passage that was so important to the Hassidim: "They saw The God, and they ate and drank" (Ex. 24:9–11).

I imagine sitting down to eat, looking at the food that sits before me—and seeing God.

What is it that I actually see? Not only the food, but the great web of life that lies behind it: earth and rain and sun and wind; rows of corn and cabbages; apple trees and squawking hens; the bleeding purple grape and foaming wine; the tug of the moon on the salt sea and on the jumping fish; the steel pipes that span a continent to bring a flammable gas from the belly of the earth where it has been cooking for a million years, to fire an oven in my kitchen; farmers and fishers, truckers and pluckers, inspectors and sales clerks who got this food to my grocery store.

I see them, and I remember the words of a Hassidic rebbe from the doomed town of Chernobyl, who taught two hundred years ago:

What is the world?
The world is God,
Wrapped in robes of God,
So as to appear
To be material.
And who are we?
We too are God,
Wrapped in robes of God,
And our task is to
Unwrap the robes and
Dis-cover that we and all the world
Are God.

I look at all this web of earthiness that feeds me, and I see its strands as aspects of the God Who is both One and Infinite.

And I know that what I want is to be able to see this fully and to say it fully and to act it fully. To eat in such a way as to celebrate that I, who wear a face of God, am eating from these foods that wear the many faces of God.

And I know that in no one meal will I be able to do this as fully as I want to. No one will really replicate or fully celebrate this perfect web.

But I can imagine many moments that would bring me close. There is no one meal at which I can make all these moments happen; but at any given dinner I can create several of these moments.

And at every meal, I can move in the direction of this kind of celebrating. My model will be not "keeping kosher" but "moving kosher"—in the direction of more sacred food. No one meal has to be perfect to be kosher.

Knowing that the Ultimate Unity is beyond all planning, all specifics, can I nevertheless map out the path in that direction, map out specifics that might get me further on the way?

To do this, I might draw on the successive eras of the history of the Jewish people, and on the four worlds of Jewish mystical thought: the physical, the intellectual, the relational, and the spiritual. I might direct four elements of my self toward "blessing" the sacredness of food:

- the gestures of my body (as in the Biblical tradition)
- the words of my mouth (as in the Rabbinic tradition)
- my social, communal, and political action (as in the modern tradition)
- my silent stillness (as in the mystical tradition)

Now how could I encode these four aspects of Unity into an eating practice? I will begin with where my first contact with the food begins, and then move through the process to its ending.

First of all, some of the food I would grow myself, if only a few sprigs of mint or parsley or spring onion in a window pot. If I could, I would mulch and grow a larger garden—in my own backyard or in a community lot. In either case, I would take what grew in the corners and somehow get it to the poor. (One synagogue in New England created a *Pe'ah* Project, named after the Biblical "corners of the field" whose produce was given to the poor. They farmed a part of the synagogue grounds and gave the food to a local soup kitchen. A Washington, D.C., rabbi, Eugene Lipman, invited young men and women from the inner city to join with him in learning how to grow and harvest a vegetable garden, then sending the results of their labors home with them.)

What I could not grow myself, I would buy from a co-op in the neighborhood, where together with other households I would make decisions about how to hire staff, how to share some of the work, where to buy the produce, how to set prices. As much as possible, I would choose foods that had been grown with the least wounding of the earth and the least damage to the human beings who grew it, transported it, packaged it. And as much as possible, I would buy foods that had been grown nearby, in my own region of the earth—and in the Land of Israel, childhood home of the Jewish people, where certain fruits and grains became the sacred symbols of our seasons in that land.

As I turned my attention to cooking, I would think of my kitchen and my dining room as rooms within the Holy Shrine and Temple where foods were brought as offerings. I would remember how the Torah describes great artists bringing their designs to the portable Shrine in the Wilderness, and the people bringing rich colors of scarlet, blue, gold, purple; rich textures of linen, fur, and wood. I would make sure that the rooms where my food became an offering were festive and delightful. I would choose foods that were themselves red, gold, and purple, and design the servings and the meal to fill and please the eye, as well as our mouths.

I would share the cooking with other members of my household. In order to overcome millennia of habit, we would make sure that both men and women were cooking the meals.

This decision to leave behind the established roles of men and women in cooking and eating may be quite easy to accomplish in the world of "thinking," and even relatively easy in the world of "doing." It may be a lot harder in the world of "feeling," where deep assumptions about how it feels to be a man or a woman may be hard to soften and change. For me, the crucial moment came in an unexpected, inward way—not even in a kitchen.

It was a windy, chilly day in January 1973. The small Jewish community of which I was a part had decided after a long discussion of Torah's outlook on war that on the day of Richard Nixon's second presidential inauguration, we would take part in a "counterinaugural" rally protesting his administration's brutal bombing of Vietnam.

As we trudged across the muddy Mall near the Washington Monument, I started feeding people from a bowlful of raisins and almonds that I had brought along—"*rozhinkes und mandlen,*" as the Yiddish song goes. My friends warmed up, full of joy that they were being fed. And I warmed up, joyful to be feeding them.

And suddenly I realized: "*Ess, ess, mein kind;* eat, eat, my child!" This is what Jewish mothers did, had always done, had always said. There was nothing wrong with it, nothing demeaning—so long as it was possible to join the feeding with the study of Torah and the marching for change. I could enjoy being a "Jewish mother" in my feeding moment because I was also being a "Jewish father" in my Torah study, and a "Jewish son and daughter" in my rebellious march. The sacred task, I realized, was to make sure that women as well as men studied and marched, that men as well as women prepared and brought the bowls of needed food.

So together, men and women should not only cook but intertwine the cooking with the study of Torah and the mending of the world. When we began the cooking for each meal, we could pause for a minute to focus on what cooking actually means: the application of heat to raw foodstuffs. Both the heat and the food are gifts from the earth and the sun: the heat, a gift from wood, coal, oil, gas, wind, water, radioactive atoms; the food, a gift from soil and rain and sunlight; both, a gift from human society that is itself a gift from earth. So the pause before cooking should include praise and thanks to the sun, the earth, the people—to God—for these gifts.

We should also take a moment to think about the place the food was going, to think about the people who will join us in eating it. They are pilgrims, traveling to the Altar from far and wide to celebrate this replenishing of themselves and this reconnection with the earth. Who are they, where are they coming from, what will this food mean for them?

There is no traditional blessing for the cooking of a meal. If we were to create one, it should perhaps focus on God as Creator of the sun, the source of most of the heat energy with which we cook. Since the traditional blessings for the sun see it as the source of light, not heat, a new blessing might use the Hebrew word *chamah*, which means the sun as a source of warmth, from the root *cham*, or heat. Thus, in Hebrew or English: *"Baruch attah* [or in the feminine, *Brucha aht*] *YAHH eloheynu ruach ha'olam borey* [or *boreyt*] *hachamah*. Blessed are You, the Breath of Life, Who creates the warm sun."

While still in the kitchen, we would physically set some food aside to be taken to a soup kitchen or otherwise shared with the poor. And one tiny amount, perhaps a bite's worth of bread, we would ceremonially dedicate to the earth itself—burn it like the traditional *challah*, or bury it under a tree, or set it aside for mulching. Perhaps as we did this we would say aloud, in Hebrew or English, either the traditional prayer for separating (taking) *challah* (see page 79) or a new blessing: *"Baruch attah* [or in the feminine, *Brucha aht*] *YAHH eloheynu ruach ha'olam borey* [or *boreyt*] *pri ha'adamah v'ha'adam*. Blessed are You, the Breath of Life, Who creates the fruit of the earth and the earthling."

To preserve the sense of the kitchen as a room of beauty in the Holy Shrine, we would take a little time to set it back in order and clean away some of the debris of cooking before we moved to the table where the offering was to be savored.

When the moment came for the household to eat, we would pause again. Here we might begin with the verse of Torah:

> *Va-yekhezu et-ha'elohim va-yokhlu va-yishtu.*
> And they saw The God, and they ate and drank.

And wait for people to look, to *see*, the faces of The God in the food and in the people around the table.

Then we could draw on the traditional Rabbinic blessings that vary according to what food is being eaten. (See pages 62–64.) We might sometimes use versions in which the Hebrew pronouns and verbs about God were in the feminine form, or we might sometimes use the forms pioneered by the poet Marcia Falk in an effort to bypass both Masculine and Feminine images of God: *"Nivarekh et-ein-ha'chai'im....* We will bless the Source of Life...."

Or we might go around the table, saying in our own words what blessing we hope to bring to and receive from this food.

We might want to draw on the Rabbinic approach but create new blessings that categorize the sources of food according to the level of consciousness of the food-giver, as outlined on page 136.

In any case, we would use a few hand and arm gestures to "embody" these words and to affirm that we are part of a larger community of humans and earth as we eat—for example, holding hands as we say the words. Or we might all put out a hand to touch the bread we are blessing, or to touch someone who is touching it. Or before taking any food ourselves, we might reach out one piece of bread to give to someone else at the table—straight from our hand to another's mouth, in token that no one makes his or her own food but that all food is the result of sharing from One great table.

Perhaps at the beginning of the meal or even at each major course, one of the cooks might explicitly say that the food is intended to nourish the body, not to overfill it. That hungers of the mind, heart, and spirit must be met by the quality of conversation and of silence at the table, not by gobbling to fill this emptiness. That one way to achieve this balance of embodied spirit is to eat slowly so that the body has time to become aware and signal back to the brain that it is satisfied. (Modern physiologists explain that it takes about twenty minutes for the stomach to tell us that it has had enough. In that lag time it is easy to keep eating and become overfull. Perhaps early in human life, when food was scarce, gorging oneself on a fallen buffalo had value for survival, but rarely today is that a healthy pattern. Today our minds, hearts, and spirits must remind our bodies when to pause.)

Perhaps this reminder to guide our own eating by what fills us, no more and no less, might then lead to our pledging to give some money to the hungry of the earth. One way to affirm and strengthen this Jewish obligation would be to donate to organizations like Mazon or the Jewish Fund for Justice, which affirm that *as Jews* they are helping the poor of all the nations to help themselves.

Now we are ready for the eating itself. What should we be encouraging ourselves to eat?

Larger and larger numbers of contemporary Jews are choosing vegetarianism, or are leaning in that direction, as an eco-kosher diet. What is the spiritual logic of this trend? First, it draws on the Torah's repeated assertion (from Eden to the Wilderness) that it would be best if we ate no meat at all. It extends the Torah's concern about avoiding the meat of predators so that we not become predators ourselves. It simplifies and rationalizes the daily practice of *kashrut*. It responds to the emergence of "factory farming" that distorts and degrades the lives of cattle and poultry, by refusing to eat the fruits of this kind of slavery. It responds to the environmental damage caused by massive beef farming in particular, and to the economic injustice caused by withdrawing huge land areas from producing grain for human consumption—a cheap source of protein—in order to produce meat—an expensive source of protein.

For those who find total vegetarianism unworkable, there might still be eco-kosher choices to make. We begin by accepting the truth that since all food comes from living beings, every bite we eat limits the lives of other creatures. We cannot eliminate this damage; can we minimize it? Can we imagine a ladder of *kashrut*, in which some foods are more allowable than others?

Suppose we decided that those forms of life that are most like the Divine in level of consciousness and caring are the ones we wanted to eat least often, and so on through the scale of life-forms?

- We might avoid eating red meat, birds, and fish—in that order of intensity.
- Some people might choose to avoid all flesh.
- Others might avoid eating only beef, lamb, and other mammals, or eat them on very rare occasions and with special rituals of respect. Perhaps, after all, when the Torah singled out the special prohibition on the meat of a kid boiled in its mother's milk, it was underlining the way in which mammals nurture their young longer than all other animals, embodying the Aspect of God Who is *HaRachaman*, the Womblike, the Compassionate.
- Perhaps we could choose to eat chicken only on a special Shabbat, and even fish only at times of special focus.
- We might eat dairy products with special honor for the food that sustains new mammalian life through its earliest dependency.
- We could make grains and vegetables the staples of our diet, as they were long ago.
- We could honor fruits and nuts as the foods of Eden and the Song of Songs—the foods that destroy or enslave no life at all. There is indeed one Jewish sacred meal, the Seder of Tu B'Shvat, the midwinter New Year of trees and of the Tree of Life, in which the only foods we eat are fruits and nuts.

All these food categories bear a strong resemblance to those described in the Biblical Creation story: mammals (the creatures of the Sixth Day); birds and fish (the Fifth Day); the sun, source of energy and heat for cooking (the Fourth Day); plants (the Third Day). We might draw on the basic Rabbinic pattern of blessings over different types of food and revise the specifics to reflect newer ways of understanding and choosing what goes to make up our meals.

Overlapping this ladder-of-consciousness approach to our foods, we could show our concern for the health of human beings and of the earth when we choose foods. The evidence is accumulating that for reasons of health, human diets should probably be far less based on meat and more on grains and vegetables—especially those grown without pesticides—than many American diets of the last fifty years have been. Additionally, some analysts have suggested that the enormous social machinery necessary to produce beef cattle in huge numbers is destructive to the world environment and economy. The use of pesticides, as the damage done by DDT has demonstrated, can poison the earth and then the human population decades after the pesticides are themselves used.

What might we choose to eat when the rules of traditional Rabbinic *kashrut* collide with the eco-kosher approach? For example, "kosher" chickens have been slaughtered correctly, with minimal pain, but many have been raised under factory-farm conditions and fed growth hormones. Free-range organic chickens have probably not been killed by kosher means. So, under these circumstances what can we eat?

One answer is to approach free-range organic farmers to urge them to invite a trained *shochet* to slaughter their chickens. Already in the New York metropolitan area kosher–eco-kosher chickens can be found. (We might also note here that some slaughterhouses have begun inviting Muslims and Jews to co-officiate over the slaughter of food animals, so that the meat is both kosher by Jewish standards and *halal* by Muslim standards.)

Another approach is not to eat either kind of "partially kosher" chicken, whether on vegetarian grounds or as a boycott, and perhaps send letters to eco-kosher farmers and Rabbinic-kosher slaughterers urging them to begin cooperating.

I have already mentioned that I might wish to become conscious of buying foods grown both in the region where I live and in the Land of Israel. This would also mean that most of the time, I would be eating foods that ripen according to the seasons where I live.

The seasons—how can I best celebrate them in my eating? What can I do to echo the special offerings that once were brought at every festival to the Holy Temple in Jerusalem?

Pesach—yes, we have special foods for the festival: matzah, the bitter herbs, four cups of wine. . . . And there is even a new Pesach food that has emerged as a result of Jewish feminism. Susannah Heschel, speaking in Florida, encountered a traditional Jew who said, "A woman belongs in the pulpit, in the rabbinate, as much as an orange belongs on the Seder plate!"—that is, not at all. Since then, with both good humor and serious purpose, more and more Jewish households have added an orange to their Seder plates. This orange can also be understood with a deeper meaning: It becomes the only seed-bearing fruit on the Seder plate, symbolizing the ability of Jewish tradition to become reborn in every generation—to give birth indeed to a form of Judaism that women can join in shaping, in which the metaphor of birth becomes a central element in the story of Pesach.

Other festive occasions are celebrated with special foods: *challah* on Shabbat, potato latkes at Hanukkah, fruits and nuts for Tu B'Shvat, hamantaschen at Purim, apples dipped in honey for Rosh Hashanah. For Shavuot, perhaps the weakest of all the ancient festivals in our own lives, there is also a weakness in the connection with food. The Rabbis found that it worked well to focus on the words of Torah in celebrating the festival that they defined as the time of hearing Torah. But perhaps our generation finds it especially hard to celebrate with disembodied words, and for that very reason has found it hard to celebrate Shavuot.

It is true that there is a tradition of eating blintzes and cheesecake for Shavuot, perhaps in reflection of the milky foods that shepherds, goatherds, and cowherds eat in abundance as their mammals freshen in late spring. But these dairy foods seem a weak way to echo the transcendent moment of receiving Torah at Mount Sinai, and especially so compared with the experience of the Israelite elders who ate and drank in God's very Presence at the height of Sinai. And weak indeed, compared with Ezekiel's experience of God's feeding him the Torah Scroll itself, and seeing the whirling vision of the Divine Chariot. These tales are the closest Jewish tradition comes to describing a psychedelic meal; but Jewish communities have not tried to reexperience Ezekiel's vision in the way in which some Native Americans have used the sacred mushroom as a mystical food.

Today, how would we reconnect the words of Torah with our bodies, in order to celebrate Shavuot? Is there a lesson in the story of Ruth and the barley fields that we could include as part of the festival? Would a meal of barley soup and blintzes, particularly if these foods were reserved for eating only on Shavuot, become a signal of Shavuot-time?*

Why do I like the practice of connecting foods with holy days? Because then each mouthful attunes me, reminds me that food comes not abstractly from the earth but from some special patch of earth, some bioregion; that food comes not indistinctly, when I chance to buy it, but at some specific season, some specific time in the spinning of the winds and rains and tides and sunshine. Biblical Israelites accomplished this attunement through the process of Temple offerings; I need to learn it in a different way.

---

*Perhaps not food but "drushodrama" would best bring word and body together. That is, to use improvisational dance, mime, psychodrama, and gesture to act out new stories of the space between the words of Torah, as a way of renewing and reopening the midrashic process.

What about the words spoken among us at the table? The Talmud teaches that a meal without talk of Torah is like an offering to idols. For us, "Torah talk" could mean asking each other what part of that day's routine has brought a glimpse of wholeness, holiness. It might mean talking about the day's world news not as spectator gossip but as a problem in *tikkun olam,* the healing of the world. Or it could mean taking just a few verses from the Torah reading of the week, and exploring how that passage might relate to our own lives.

ॐ

Assuming that we have cooked and have eaten with concern for the earth and consciousness of the sacred meaning of food, how do we complete the meal? As Jewish tradition has long said, we could express our gratefulness and satisfaction in reciting a blessing at the end. The traditional Birkat haMazon (Grace After Meals) is found in many traditional books and booklets. For Jews who are prepared to use new forms as well as old ones, there are a number of other possible choices.

- Among them is a mostly English version of the traditional Birkat ha-Mazon, translated by Rabbi Burt Jacobson in such a way as to fit one of the most widespread traditional tunes. It contains images of God that, unlike the conventional Father/King images, encourage the sense that a great deal of Divine power rests in human hands.
- Two other mainly English versions (by Rabbis Shefa Gold and Hanna Tiferet Siegel) are keyed to totally new melodies and celebrate the basic themes of the traditional blessings without following the line-by-line meaning of the words.
- Another possibility is to chant the one-line blessing specified by the Mishnah for moments when time is short: "*Brikh rakhmana malka d'alma, marei d'hai pita.* Blessed is the Motherly Master of the world, Who brings forth this bread."
- Or simply to chant "From You I receive, to You I give; together we share, and from this we live"—perhaps repeated four times; once to honor those who physically provide and eat the food; once again to honor the feelings of community and sharing that make such work possible; once more to honor the store of knowledge and ideas about food, the earth, and farming; and finally to honor the Unity in which all these aspects of food find their place.
- Or finally, a time of collective quiet, consciously dedicated to meditation and thanks for that web of life that has brought us and our food together.

In any of these modes, we might remember that just as the process of eating did not begin in the kitchen, so it does not end at the table. We could visualize the pathways by which the food we have just eaten becomes fully part of us, how our bodies use chemicals from the food eaten earlier to break down the food just absorbed, to send potassium here, sugar there, water and the vitamins and fibers somewhere else. Even what we eliminate plays its role in cooling our inner heat, exercising our internal muscles. All this we need to see with our mind's eye, to remind us that the Unity lives within us as well as in the fields and clouds around the planet.

Perhaps we could say aloud, or simply and silently remember, or use our own words to recite these thoughts from Marge Piercy's prayer-poem "Nishmat":

We are given the body, that momentary kibbutz
of elements that have belonged to frog and polar
bear, corn and oak tree, volcano and glacier.
We are lent for a time these minerals in water
and a morning every day, a morning to wake up,
rejoice and praise life in our spines, our throats,
our knees, our genitals, our brains, our tongues.

And we could make a conscious connection between the moment when we finish eating and the moment when we go to eliminate the leftovers that our body does not need. We will celebrate this part of the process, too, not because we are eliminating husks of evil and of alienation, but because what we send forth fits in a different way into the great economy of earth. Just as we begin with an outward *challah*, setting aside a portion that we must return to the earth, so our innards make a *challah* of their own. The Asher Yatzar prayer (see page 104) seems a fitting way to bless the process by which the holes and hollows, the openings and tubes within us, the microchemical plants in every cell do their work to keep us healthy.

We have looked from start to finish at how we might eat a "model meal" to reflect an emerging "whole-earth Judaism": a meal we ourselves cook and serve; a meal when we have time for playful spiritual exploration; a meal in the midst of a small and intimate community of friends and family, who whether they are Jewish or not are comfortable with a Jewishly informed spiritual search. But what about some special variations on this scenario: what about constricted time, what about restaurants, what about guests, what about eating alone?

Perhaps we can explore and affirm all the many aspects of a "whole-earth" Jewish meal only when we are most at ease, perhaps on Friday evening for Shabbat dinner, or perhaps on the Jewish festivals. Yet at every meal, even those eaten alone or in a bustling restaurant, we can set aside a moment for reflection. We can celebrate the web of life that has brought us to *this* table, with *these* foods.

- We can choose just one moment of blessing to begin the meal, and one to end it.
- Even a moment of silence can be a centering.
- Even the question "What is the happiest meal that you remember?" could evoke the thanks and gratitude that gives spiritual depth to a meal.

What about refraining from food? How might whole-earth Judaism address the fasts that our forebears viewed as an indispensable aspect of eating?

The great Hassidic Rebbe of Apt, the first Abraham Joshua Heschel, said that if it were up to him, all the fast days of the Jewish calendar would be abolished, except two:

- the fast for Tisha B'Av, for who could bear to eat, remembering the destruction of the Holy Temple?
- and the fast for Yom Kippur, for on that day of universal reconciliation, who would need to eat?

This teaching has three levels of meaning.

One is embedded within the condition "if it were up to him." It takes a community, not a lone individual, to carry out a life-affirming renewal of the Jewish people. Indeed, very large parts of the Jewish people have already come to agree with the Apter Rebbe about which fasts to abolish.

Second is its explicit content. Is it, as the Apter Rebbe suggests, healthy and healing for the Jewish people as a whole to experience all the way to the *kishkes* the passionate sorrow and the passionate joy that Tisha B'Av and Yom Kippur express?

Finally, the Apter Rebbe is implicitly teaching that one should undertake a fast not because "the rules" say to fast but because it is a profound personal and emotional experience that nullifies the desire to eat.

For us, "the rules" mean not only formally encoded ones, but also the social norms about slimness that have pushed some people into anorexia and bulimia. In these disorders, the desire to eat does not vanish; it is, rather, forcibly suppressed or brutally distorted. One of the tasks of Jewish renewal is for communities and teachers to affirm that a wide variety of body types are what God had in mind as the human images of God—and to act on that assertion. Moreover, some counselors who have dealt with anorexics report that for some, not eating is an effort to become "more spiritual" by "freeing" themselves from earthiness and food. At several levels, then, anorexia is in fact a "Jewish issue," and should be addressed by rabbis and synagogues at personal, communal, and political levels.

Indeed, this whole line of thought should remind us that in Biblical society, offerings of food were intimately connected with healing the psyche. Today, most psychotherapists raise questions of food only if their clients present an "eating disorder" to be addressed. Drawing on the wisdom of Judaism, we might explore how to reintegrate food into all efforts at spiritual and psychological healing.

The reconnection of body and spirit, body and words, underlies much of what we have been exploring. It is one of the most important aspects of an emerging current in the last generation of American Jewish life, a movement for Jewish spiritual renewal. It is a path, or a network of pathways, that draws on Kabbalah and Hassidism, and on the social activism of Modernity and feminism, and on Rabbinic communal commitment, and on the Biblical intimacy with the earth. From dancers and rabbis, teachers and writers, singers and literary critics and anthropologists and grass-roots community organizers have come the beginnings of a new synthesis of Jewish thought and practice.

One element in this emerging synthesis is that many in our generation find it very hard to connect with a God Who is simply Up There, King and Lord, Above and Beyond, yet also very hard to accept the modern secularist position: There is no God. Instead, many have begun to connect with images of an intimate God: "Breath of Life," "Wellspring of Life."

Why is our generation at this place? Because we received a gift from Modernity. We discovered that powers we would once have defined as Divine (like creating new species, bringing a Flood of destruction upon all life on earth, overthrowing pharaohs, transforming psyches) had now "entered" the human race. We ourselves could do all these miraculous deeds.

So the God Who was entirely Up There might seem dead. But a God Who is In Here is very much alive. That God needs to be addressed with other language. Because our breath is both within us and beyond us, because we would die if there were no breath in our lungs and would also die if there were nothing to breathe in the world outside us, because all aspects of life breathe each other into living— for all these reasons, the Breath of Life can for many of us now be a more authentic, more sacred way to image God.

In addition, the increasing emergence of women as full and equal partners with men in Jewish life—another gift of the modern world—has made it harder to live with images of God as simply male. Certainly many Jews, women and men, have found it fulfilling to image God also as Mother and Sister; but even more, the life experience of many women (as well as men like the Rebbe of Chernobyl) has encouraged God-images that are more infused and embodied within the world.

Some who are seeking their path to Jewish renewal use blessings that pronounce YHWH as "Yahhh," with a breathing sound, and that use *Ruach ha'Olam* (Breath of the World), *Chai ha'Olamim* (Life of the Worlds), or *Eyn ha'Chai'im* (Wellspring of Life) to address God.

Other changes also relate to the "embodiment" of prayer and ethics in the body and in one's behavior. Using body movement, gesture, dance, and dialogue between partners as forms of prayer; using "drushodrama" and improvisational dance and operas like Steven Reich's *The Cave* and Elizabeth Swados's *Job* as forms of Torah study; integrating food and eating into psychotherapy, these may be for some of us what sacrificial offerings were in ancient Israel.

Still other changes have been wrought by

- experiencing the fragility of the web of life on earth, and searching for Jewish ways to eat that will help heal the earth;
- experiencing a change in the boundaries between religious communities, from barbed-wire barricades and fences to permeable fringes, and searching for ways to eat while welcoming other peoples to the table;
- experiencing the isolation of individuals bereft of community, drowning in the sea of mass Modernity, and searching for Jewish ways to eat so as to strengthen communities of Jewishness.

How to cook in the kitchen and eat at the table in such a way that women and men share the work and the pleasure in both places; how to eat with respect for the earth; how to eat so that we see both our food and ourselves as aspects of God; how to eat while welcoming other peoples to the table, yet strengthening communities of Jewishness—all these have become questions for a renewed Judaism.

For millennia Judaism has been characterized by On/Off; Either/Or; Kosher/ Treyf; Masculine/Feminine; Jew/Goy. More and more, our own generation is living with gradations, a spectrum, a rainbow of colors and possibilities. Would it be possible to create a "rainbow Judaism," or would that be internally contradictory?

Part Two

MONEY

Money.

Why does it provoke in us such anxiety and fear, such extremes of wishful fantasy and nightmares of disaster, such envy, shame, and secrecy?

How can we deal with money in a more balanced and life-giving way?

These questions—emotional and spiritual as they are—lie beneath the practical and intellectual questions we usually ask about money, especially in public.

Perhaps for the very reason that they are emotional and spiritual, they are questions we may especially want to keep in mind as we seek in the Jewish past some wisdom to draw on for our own lives.

During the Biblical era, money was an important element of life but not the dominant one it has become. When the Commandments at Sinai warned against envy, they specifically forbade coveting a neighbor's house, or wife, or slaves, or work animals—but did not mention money.

The reason is clear. When almost everyone is a farmer or a shepherd, food and land are the most important elements of life. The land brings forth food; the food makes it possible to work the land so that it will bring forth more food. For the male head of a household to be more wealthy than his neighbors meant not only having more land, but having more servants and more animals to work the land; having not only a bigger house, but perhaps a more capable wife, or more wives, to manage the household and its economy.

Money was not the largest element in the equation.

But today money is the great medium of our work and our food and our living. We work not for food but for the money to buy food and many other things. And we use money, much more than land, to produce what we need to live. For us, money in small amounts is, as it were, "food." We even call money "bread." In large amounts money is "land." In ancient days, the great landholder had great power. Today, whoever controls large amounts of money controls the lives of millions.

There is a still deeper connection between land and money that we also need to be aware of. Money is, *in fact*, land: That is, all our money comes from what we do with and to the earth. In modern society, money is so abstract, so interchangeable, that we easily forget that only sunshine, soil, water, wind, green grass, human effort, only these make money. How we deal with money, where we put it, affect the earth itself; and what we do with the earth defines our money. *Money is a fluid version of the earth.*

Where the ancient Israelite tradition taught how to think about the earth, how to live as part of it, we need to read that wisdom carefully. We need to see how much of it applies to us—not only our behavior toward the air and the ocean, but our behavior toward our bank deposits. We need to keep in mind the differences between Biblical society and ours, but also to remember that on the most basic level, there are "eco-connections" that were easier for that society to see than for us, but that remain facts today.

What might we want to learn from the Jews of long ago?

How could we make choices of how to make a living?

- How could we balance our desire for work that pays enough to live on with the desire for work that gives a sense of worth?
- How much is "enough" to live on? What is worth buying? How much should we spend?

What does it mean to save, to borrow, to lend, to invest?

- How much should we give away, to whom, and for what?
- Is there any way to dissolve or lessen our fear and envy of money?

As we have seen, the Biblical life-path embodied a strong back-and-forth flow between *adam* and *adamah*, humus and human, earth and earthling. In the flow from earth to earthling, food—how human beings ate—seemed the most important element. In the flow from earthling to earth, the complementary process was how human beings treated the "humus," the soil, the land. Just as the Israelites worked out detailed rules for making offerings of food and how to choose what to eat, so in the other direction there were detailed rules about how to treat the land.

To a large extent, for Israelite shepherds and farmers, land was capital. For most people, the "means of production" were the fields on which crops could grow and sheep could graze. Later in Jewish history, as the people became separated from the land, money became a more explicit and important part of their lives. We will see how the Judaism of the Rabbis and other later Jewish cultures dealt with money. But first let us look at the Biblical society that was still rooted in the land.

Even for the ancient Israelites, money mattered. There were ways in which land became converted into money, especially through leasing and lending. The rules of land ownership, rental, debt, and the payment of interest were intertwined with the rules of how to treat the earth.

There were also a few large pools of money, machines, or information. Certainly these pools were fewer, and each much smaller, than we have in the modern world. Yet we should note that the pharaohs of Egypt and the rulers of Babylon and the kings of Canaan, including some Israelite kings, amassed treasuries of gold and silver. And among the Israelites, the priests and sacred ministers of the tribe of Levi, who owned houses in special villages but no productive fields, did "own" and make their living from dispensing information about holiness, health, and justice.

THE RHYTHM OF RELEASE

The grand outline of how Israelites should treat the land was set forth in Leviticus 25 and 26. These chapters focus on the sabbatical/Jubilee cycle and what will happen if Israel ignores it. They are viewed by modern scholars as part of the Holiness Code, a set of rules directed at the everyday lives of Israelites that was incorporated in the larger priestly document of the rhythms of national life.

Since the Holiness Code is especially concerned with the danger that children may be sacrificed to Moloch and that wizards may consult the dead, it may come from the time of Kings Ahaz (743–727 B.C.E.) and Manasseh (698–643 B.C.E.), when these rituals are said to have spread. Chapters 25 and 26, however, seem to be a special subsection within the Holiness Code, and may have existed earlier and been attached to it later.

The sabbatical/Jubilee passage in these chapters seems unique not only in some specific language and themes, but in the way it treats as a unity issues that today we would probably categorize as "social justice," "the environment," and "rhythmic ceremonial." The passage asserts that no Israelite person, clan, or institution—not even the people as a whole—owns the land. "The land is Mine," says God, "and you but wayfarers on it, visitors with Me."

What is both symbol and practice of this Ownership? Once every seven years, for an entire year, the land must rest. It must make a Shabbat to YHWH, the Breath of Life. This "sabbatical" year was called a *shmitah,* a year of release. And in the year after the seventh seventh year, the fiftieth year, the land once again made Shabbat for an entire year. This year was called the *yovel,* or Jubilee year, a name that probably comes from a special blast of the *shofar* (ram's horn) that was blown on Yom Kippur of the fiftieth year to announce it.

For the land to rest, the people must also rest. For an entire year there was no organized cultivation or harvest. The people ate what had been stored before, or what came from the freely given, unorganized produce of the earth.

In each *shmitah* year, all debts were annulled. And in the fiftieth year, the year of Jubilee, each family got back the equal share of land that its forebears had been allotted when they first settled in the Land of Israel. Everyone who had become a slave or indentured servant, even those who were in the midst of their seven-year term of service and those who had decided they preferred to live as lifelong servants, were freed. (Now, indeed, they had somewhere to go.)

All this made a difference to land prices. No one could buy permanent ownership of land, since no one but God owned it in the first place. People could buy only the right to *use* land—only "the number of crops"—until the next Jubilee. If that year was coming up soon, the price must be kept low. And there were implications for other aspects of money. There was a whole different way of thinking about loans. The community was to act like a family. Of course, people in need got help, loans, when necessary. But members of the community did not charge each other interest. Giving help did not turn the giver into a permanent overlord, or the recipient into a permanent supplicant. For in seven years at the latest, the debt would dissolve.

If someone got into bad enough financial straits so that some of the ancestral family land had to be sold, then a family member could "redeem" the leasehold—buy it back at a price based on the number of years remaining till the Jubilee. Or at any time when his fortunes improved, he could redeem it himself. And if even that were impossible, then at the Jubilee the flow of time itself, or God, would redeem it. The land would come back to him anyway—unencumbered.

For the tribe of Levites, whose livelihood did not come from farms or flocks but from tithes given them by the community whom they served with sacred ceremonies and with crucial information, the levitical villages were like fields. If a Levite had to sell a house, it could be redeemed at any time, and in any case the original owner would receive it back when the Jubilee came.

Big-city properties were dealt with differently. For one year after selling a house in a walled city, the seller had the right to redeem it. After that, the house belonged to the buyer. In other words, urban houses were not recycled, perhaps because shepherds and farmers regarded them not as "means of production" but as mere gewgaws of pride.

These provisions of Torah dealt not only with landholding but also with personal economic status. Some people might become so poor that they had to sell not only land but also their own work lives—that is, commit their labor as indentured servants to someone who took on a role somewhere between employer and master. Such contracts were limited to seven years. Even in the midst of the seven-year term, however, servants could be redeemed if some family relative came to "buy out" their contract, with money according to the number of years of service they still owed.

In any case, in the seventh year of indenture the contract came to an end. At that point the employer was obligated not only to allow the servant to leave, but to pay a severance fee of sheep, grain, and oil (Deut. 15:12–15). Some servants preferred to stay, and were allowed to do so if they were prepared to stay for life.

Personal economic status, along with landholding, was transformed by the Jubilee. Even for one who had chosen a lifetime of servitude, or for someone who was in the middle of a regular seven-year indenture, the Jubilee year changed everything. The term of service came to an end. The Jubilee ended the contract and the servant went back to the family land for a fresh start.

When the Jubilee came around, no matter what had happened in the meantime, no one was exempted from equality. No one who was poor, no one who was rich. And in the very moment when everyone was restored to an equal footing, no one could work the land that was the family holding. If everyone celebrated sacred rest, then for a year even the lazy, so to speak, became equal.

How does this whole pattern match up with anything that "modern" economists and politicians might say? It is quite different from all of them in any flavor: conservative, liberal, or radical.

On the one hand, the Biblical pattern encourages getting ahead in the world through hard work, thrift, expansion, ownership, and putting lots of indentured employees on the payroll. Surely most modern capitalists would applaud this. Yet on the other hand, every seventh year this process pauses in midstride as people are forbidden to get ahead by working the land, and as those who have fallen into the pit of debt clamber out. Even more extraordinary, once a generation the Torah tries to dissolve "getting ahead" altogether, and affirms the social, economic, and political equality of all Israelites. Once a generation, it cancels out all success and all failure by sharing the most important element of the Israelite economy: land.

Most modern secular socialists might hail such a transformation as "the Revolution"—once and for all! The Torah does not. Instead, it expects and affirms that once equality is achieved, it will not and should not stay put. For then the process of "getting ahead" and "falling behind" will begin all over again. And it will keep on, with pauses every seventh year, for another forty-nine years.

The notion that ownership, working status, and money should all constantly change through a sacred cycle of time is a unique vision of Biblical economics, different from anything that the Modern Age has proposed or carried out.

And the vision is not only economic, not only ecological, not only political. It is all of these—and through them "spiritual" as well. As Rabbi Max Ticktin points out, the Jubilee challenges ancient and modern ideas of making oneself immortal by piling up material goods. The Jubilee brooks no pharaoh with jewels buried in a pyramid, no billionaire who believes that "whoever dies with the most toys wins."

The Jubilee replaces "having more" with "going deeper," deeper into one's own self as part of the One Self that unifies the world.

Was the vision carried out? Part of it was—especially the seventh-year Shabbat for the land and the annulment of debts. The fiftieth year's wholesale redistribution of land was rarely, if ever, actually done. Yet the vision survived.

Early in the sixth century B.C.E., for example, Jeremiah demanded (Chapter 34) that the people make a Jubilee by freeing all their slaves. When they failed, he prophesied disaster. If they would not free their slaves, they themselves would all become slaves. If they would not share their land, they would lose it.

Yet Jeremiah also invoked the Jubilee vision as a vision of hope (Chapter 32), even though the Babylonians were on the verge of conquering the land and he was prophesying their victory. At this dire moment Jeremiah, using precisely the legal form delineated in Leviticus 25, paid seventeen shekels to redeem a plot of land in his tribal village. He placed the deed of its redemption in a pottery jar, to remain buried until someday when the redemption could actually take place. And he proclaimed that someday the whole land would be redeemed as well, so that houses, fields, and vineyards could be bought and sold again.

Thus he affirmed that the great liberation of the Jubilee applies both to each individual and to the whole people.

Does this vision from another age have any implications for our time?

In this vision, there is a coherent model of a "sustainable economy" in which the people are fed for many generations and millennia, and the land is not tortured into desolation. Today, ecologists and economists focus on how to create just such a sustainable economy. This is no abstraction: It is as personal as Jeremiah's pottery jar. When people who are struggling over how to protect ancient forests and to use lumber resources properly define their battle in terms of "spotted owls" versus "logger jobs," that is what they are fighting over.

This vision contains a coherent model of how to encourage both entrepreneurship and equality. Political theorists and activists struggle over which of these values is more important, and how to balance them. When people battle over "safety nets" and "tax incentives," over "welfare" and "empowering the poor," those are the issues they are fighting over.

This vision is not only about the grand design of a society, it is also about the details of everyday life. It presents us a coherent model of how families and individuals should borrow from and lend to each other, how they should buy from each other, and contains many other teachings about interpersonal ethics over money, issues that we encounter in our lives every day.

XIV. "SILVER AND GOLD HE SHALL NOT MULTIPLY"

The basic rhythm of "leasing" land from God and then "releasing" it provided the overall framework for the Israelite economy. Since God was at the heart and in the limbs of economic life, there was hardly any separation between what we might call economic and spiritual domains.

The Israelite spiritual, economic, and political worldview saw God as the rightful Owner and Ruler of the world, and looked askance at any earthly or heavenly competitor who might claim the obedience of the Israelites. Therefore, even during a monarchy, the decentralization of wealth and power was encouraged. We have already seen how the rhythm of the sabbatical and Jubilee years aimed at decentralizing control of the economy to households, clans, and tribes.

Yet there were public needs, national needs, as well. How were they to be met, especially since the Torah did not want to establish a huge central treasury?

Taxes for support of the monarch, the poor, and the priesthood (a tribal bureaucracy that encompassed what today are separate cultural, medical, religious, legal, and economic tasks) were among the ways that ancient Israel met these public needs. Let us see whether eavesdropping on the Biblical teachings can help us address these issues in our own lives.

When the Torah talks about the king, it limits his power, both in money and troops: "Silver and gold he shall not multiply," it proclaims, in the same breath that it prohibits multiplying horses so as to prevent an overbearing royal cavalry (Deut. 17: 16–18).

Instead, the Israelites sought to meet the people's needs in decentralized ways. There were two basic sources of public income. One was an annual head tax of half a shekel on every Israelite male who was twenty years old or more. The other was tithing—that is, an income tax of one tenth of the produce of every landholder.

As we examine these two arrangements, what could we learn from this delicate balance: a tax of equal, absolute numbers alongside a tax of equal proportions? What do these two different forms of taxation say about the shape of society? What did they teach the Israelites about how to see and treat each other?

HEAD BY HEAD

The first report of the half-shekel tax is in Exodus 30:11–16, where it is closely connected with a census of all Israelite males over twenty. The census occurs in the Wilderness a year after Israel's liberation from slavery in Egypt. It comes in the midst of the building of the Mishkan, or Shrine of the Divine Presence, and the money is to be used for the building of the Shrine. The Torah goes out of its way to specify that the rich should pay no more than a half-shekel and the poor no less.

The text mentions that collecting the half-shekel will avert plague from the Israelites, and that money for the Shrine will act as atonement for the people. Paying the tax under these conditions is an act of great spiritual power. What is it about the half-shekel tax that gives it this power?

- Is it the ritual quality of a tax collected from each male, each paying the same without regard to economic standing, each stepping forward to be solemnly counted and perhaps to have his name solemnly recorded as a member of the community?
- Is it the specific dedication of the tax to the building of the Shrine that was to be the center of the people's spiritual life—indeed, the earthly dwelling place of God?
- Is it both—the simultaneous mirroring of the individual, unique, and equal Israelite male with the individual, unique, and mostly male God—those unique beings who met in the Shrine each to be counted as one, one, one, one, and One?

To modern ears, the very notion of a spiritually transformative tax may come as strange. It might be easier to think of the Shrine in the light of the Names Quilt of our own day. The Quilt was made by thousands of people, mostly members of a newly liberated gay community, who joined in sewing it, square by square, so as to place in collective memory—name by name—those who had died from the plague of AIDS. It was intended not only to serve as a memorial, but also to be carried from city to city, to call forth the spiritual, financial, and political power to bring that plague to an end.

The Mishkan, a Shrine intended to be carried from place to place during the Israelites' journey in the Wilderness, was built by a band of runaway slaves who for several hundred years had been forbidden to express their own identity in any public way. It was their first public and communal act of religious devotion, their first public and communal work of art. To build it, every member of the group—every man and woman—brought jewelry, cloth, wood, colorful dyes. And every adult male brought half a shekel. So when the men brought this money to build the Mishkan, they probably came both with deep sadness over memories of slavery and with an ecstasy of joy in liberation. Each knew that with this money they were inviting the presence of the God of Transformation, the God Who had made possible their freedom. And so the tax could bear the power of their own spiritual transformation.

The more deeply we see the half-shekel tax as profoundly transformative, a ticket to spiritual identity and citizenship, the more deeply we must ask ourselves: Why were only adult males required to pay the half-shekel? What were the implications of ignoring women in this practice, and ignoring people who were younger than twenty?

More clues to these questions may come from the Book of Numbers (1:1–4). It describes the same census as the one in Exodus 30. It does not mention the half-shekel tax, but it mentions something that Exodus does not: "All who are able to go into battle" shall be counted. So there seem to have been two overlapping assumptions about the census and the tax: that military capability and economic independence were what "counted," literally—and that only adult males fit both definitions. Only they could fight, only they could work to make money, and thus only they could be full spiritual citizens. Possibly it was also assumed that only men fit *either* definition.

Was this actually true at the time of the Exodus?

First of all, let us look at the issues of age. Children younger than thirteen (or perhaps twelve for girls) were almost certainly not thought to be capable of military, economic, or sexual (or, presumably, spiritual) adulthood.

As for teenagers, today we call them "adolescents," those who are in process of becoming, but not yet, adults. But in ancient days they were far more likely to be already economically and sexually adult. Why then wait till twenty to count them? Elsewhere the Torah (Deut. 20:5–9) expresses a desire not to send young adults to war who were just beginning to beget children or farm the land. Precisely *because* younger people were already in the first life-affirming flush of their adult lives, the Torah held back from sending them into the tasks of killing and dying—a prejudice exactly opposite to modern armies that depend on eighteen-year-olds. So it may actually be the choice of who is culturally and spiritually most appropriate for these death-oriented tasks—not a choice of sheer military efficiency—that made the dividing age twenty.

And what were the implications of leaving adult women out of the half-shekel tax? Had women been unimportant in the Exodus itself? Not according to the Torah's own history of those events! Certainly women like the midwives Shifra and Puah and the prophet Miriam had, according to the Torah, just recently been among the leaders of the people in their effort toward liberation. On the nomadic Wilderness trek itself, neither men nor women were landholders.

In the later history of the people, especially during the monarchy when the memories of Exodus may have been codified into sacred history, men did own almost all the land. In a few specific cases, women were economically self-sufficient; in very, very few, women are described as bearing arms in defense of Israel. Yet it is clear that these are exceptional cases. It is even clearer that the tasks women certainly undertook, such as bearing and raising children and nurturing family and household, were not regarded as part of the money-generating economy.

Still, in sacred history this moment of the building of the Shrine, the census of the people, and the payment of the half-shekel tax came precisely when the women who had been leaders in pre-Exodus times were disempowered. Since Exodus describes the half-shekel tax as itself a transformative spiritual act that redeems the whole people, we must take into account that women were kept at the margins of this transformation. They received its benefits but did not actively bring it about. How did this affect their attitudes toward the Mishkan, the rest of the Wilderness trek, the settlement of the land, and the future life of the people? Especially how did it affect their sense of money and its spiritual significance?

Since women rarely got to make their own voices heard in Biblical society—at least in the records and texts and stories that have come down to us—we cannot be sure. We can only try to sense what their views were. It seems likely that many women would have felt more peripheral to the central themes of economic, military, and spiritual life in the Israelite community.

How did the census affect men's attitudes toward women? For if, after the midwives and Miriam, women had been counted equally, a very different social history might have followed. Was the census simply following the existing social norms? Or was it actively seeking to channel the future social system in the direction of male dominance, perhaps in the teeth of opposition from women and men who had learned a different sense of holiness from the Exodus itself? (In many modern revolutions and liberations, like the Israeli War for Independence and the American war effort in World War II, a period of remarkable participation by women in social transformation is followed by an effort to put them back "in their place.")

Over the centuries, the function of taxation changed—even the role of women in it. After the people had settled in the Land of Israel, the half-shekel became a yearly obligation to pay for the repair of the Temple in Jerusalem.

The Book of Kings (II Kings 12:5–17) reports that during one king's reign, the priests who had received the public's money to repair the Temple were failing to make the repairs. So the king took both the money and the responsibility for the repairs out of their hands. Instead, a chest was placed beside the Altar, with a hole bored in its lid, where the people deposited their half-shekels as they came to worship. (The chest was shaped like a ram's horn, narrow at the top for coins to be inserted and broad at the bottom where coins could settle, so that theft became difficult. The chest was thus truly a horn of plenty—in Hebrew, a *keren shefa*; in Latin and English, "*cornus*," "horn," a cornucopia.) The king's scribe and the High Priest were responsible for collecting the money and paying the carpenters and masons who repaired the building.

After the destruction of the First Temple by the Babylonians and the return from captivity, Nehemiah (10:33–34) describes how the tax was reinstituted. According to the Mishnah (Shekalim I:I), during the Second Temple period, the ritual character of the half-shekel obligation was reinforced by issuing a formal public reminder on the New Moon of Adar, two weeks before Purim and six weeks before Passover. Many from the public brought the half-shekel when they made the Pesach pilgrimage, or at one of the other festival times.

By this time, one aspect of the Wilderness tax had been reshaped: Women and minors were now welcome to contribute the half-shekel if they wished, but were not obligated to do so.

Appropriations from the treasury to make necessary Temple repairs were made two weeks before the festivals of Pesach, Shavuot, and Sukkot (for the last of these, on the last day of the month of Elul, the day before Rosh Hashanah). The division of the money for Temple repairs was done as a ritual, with the appropriator removing and allocating the money only after asking public permission: "Shall I remove them?" and receiving the reply, "Remove, remove, remove."

Since the destruction of the Second Temple, the half-shekel tax has been in abeyance, but the Rabbis set aside the Shabbat two weeks before Purim to read the Torah passage that describes the first payment of the half-shekel in the Wilderness.

All of this shows how the payment of the half-shekel tax was given ritual and spiritual meaning. Since only the half-shekel was assessed without regard to economic standing, it seems to have represented the primal equality of those who paid it. For us, it may raise the question how we could create a kind of tax or contribution so full of ritual power that it symbolized the equal responsibility of all to honor and support the community as a whole—and yet not so high as to make the poor desperate, as have some modern poll taxes.

Perhaps a tax on time—a requirement for putting in a certain and equal amount of time in community service—would meet both criteria? Since all of us start with equally uncertain expectations of our life-"times," we could agree that everyone must set aside, say, two hours a week plus one day a month to work for a communal group or agency. This would truly be a tax that would have equal impact on the rich and the poor, and would signal to each that they were equal in God's sight.

HARVEST BY HARVEST

The other major tax that Israelites paid was explicitly tied to their income. It was the tithe, the obligation to pay one tenth of the produce of one's land and flocks.

Even more than the fixed half-shekel tax, tithing the income of individuals and households was a way of asserting that they do not carry on economic enterprise in a vacuum. To whatever degree people are successful, part of that success comes from the whole society and even beyond—from God. So they owe part of their income to the greater reality.

First of all, who owned tithes? Landholders and nomadic owners of sheep and goats. Their slaves, servants, and employees did not, just as their children and their wives did not. Indeed, the Bible did not directly address, did not say "You shall" or "You shall not," to those who were employees or servants, just as it rarely said "You" to women and children. Instead, Biblical commands about relationships between bosses and hired hands were directed at the bosses, as if they were the "normative" Israelites—just as commands about relationships between men and women were almost entirely directed at men. The employer was commanded not to oppress his hired hand; the hired hand was not specifically addressed.

The "norm" was being an independent entrepreneur—probably a farmer, who might hire workers—not being a hired worker oneself. Indeed, in a pastoral-agricultural society there may have been few landless people, and it may have seemed obvious that they could not function fully as citizens if they did not have a full economic competence.

Workers were, however, seen as part of the community. They were to be protected and every effort made to annul their debts and restore them to full citizenship. However, the form of these protections shows that in some ways workers were seen as a separate class within the community, temporary second-class citizens.

The givers of tithes, these individual landholders and flockholders, represented the strand of individuality within Israelite society. Who then, as recipients of tithes, were to represent the binding forces of God and the broader society?

As might be expected, this was a difficult religious and political question, and the answer changed during Israelite history—indeed, it seems to have changed twice. Both changes encoded what happened to the Israelites' religious and political values with regard to the control and use of money. The first change involved moving from a decentralized social entity toward a central power; the second, from top-down wealth and power toward social justice.

The earliest stratum of the Torah's provisions for tithing (Lev. 27) hints that the tithe may be voluntary, not a compulsory tax. It directed that the tithe be turned over to the priests and the local shrines or, slightly later, the central Shrine which had been placed at Shiloh. Tithes were used to pay for the upkeep of these shrines. The food was either given directly to the priests to eat, or was sold to buy supplies. Although the Torah declared a norm of sharing income with the priests, the impulse to carry out the norm seems to have come from the people's willingness to do so to feed a loose and decentralized network of priests.

Then, as David consolidated the monarchy, there seems to have been a shift (Num. 18). The tithes became compulsory. They went to the Levites, a "national tribe" that lived in cities scattered throughout the kingdom. These special cities seem to have emerged or been assigned to them during David's reign. From the tithes they received, the Levites gave one tenth to the priests, who were a subgroup within their tribe. Even though the priests still received the benefit of the tithes, they had evidently lost control over them. The Levites had won greater power. It seems possible that the Levites were connected with the growing power of the king, and that in these special cities they acted both as his functionaries and as religious bureaucrats.

Was there a struggle over this shift from local and loosely enforced taxation to central and compulsory taxes? There are certainly indications in the Bible that taxation by and for the king was controversial.

When the Prophet Samuel and the Israelite people debated whether they should crown a king or not (I Sam. 8), Samuel warned that a king would tax a tenth of their produce, and could conscript men to serve in the army and women to serve in the royal kitchens. Even if this is interpreted as an exaggerated warning, it makes clear that royal taxes in food, money, and personal service were to be expected— and that Samuel thought that reminding the people of such taxation might chill their ardor for a king. It did not.

Later, however, under Solomon and his son Rehoboam, taxes grew heavy enough to spark a rebellion, the assassination of the chief tax collector, and the division of the kingdom. Perhaps it was Rehoboam's heavy-handedness that got written retroactively into Samuel's warning by a writer who was editing an earlier story. Similarly, it may have been either prescient fears or the actual experience of Solomon's and Rehoboam's behavior that caused the passage to be written into the Torah (Deut. 17:16–18) that forbids a king to amass silver and gold, wives, or cavalry—three key symbols and tools of overweening power.

Samuel connects his warning about the politics and economics of a centralized monarchy with a spiritual proclamation: The people already have a king, he says. Their King is God, and crowning an earthly king may well trap them in idolatry.

Just as asserting that God alone is the great Landowner decentralizes landholding, so proclaiming that God alone is the great King legitimates grass-roots political power and the semivoluntary character of taxes.

But the Bible reports that in this decentralized society the people felt scattered and vulnerable to foreign powers. They did want a king, and the monarchy did become centralized, probably with the Levites as the tax-collecting and tax-spending bureaucracy.

That made possible the glories of the Solomonic kingdom, with its large territory, abundant economy, and resplendent Temple. With these outward glories came the spiritual satisfactions of a sense of security, a sense that the God of Israel was able to protect the people of Israel, a sense that the earlier struggle and pain had been justified.

The Bible also reports that the people began to suffer from the erection of overbearing wealth and power into idols. Ultimately this led even to the erection of a physical idol, a golden calf, in the central shrine of the Northern Kingdom. While some of the people felt the spiritual rewards of abundance, power, and comfort, others were feeling spiritually betrayed. Even the adherents of the God of Israel were acting like oppressive pharaohs. Some experienced a spiritual crisis. Was the God of Israel the Celebrator of comfort and abundance, or the Protector of the afflicted and the desperate?

And so there emerged a wave of social and spiritual protest, given words by those whom we know as "the Prophets"—Amos, Hosea, Jeremiah. From this ferment came the writing or the public disclosure of the Book of Deuteronomy, which called for a second great change in the structure and purpose of tithing.

Deuteronomy affirms and indeed intensifies the geographic centralization of Israelite political and religious life, wiping out the regional levitical shrines and the levitical bureaucracy in favor of the Temple in Jerusalem. From Deuteronomy's standpoint, the levitical cities had become not symbols of regional decentralization but exemplars of corruption, and the Levites, dependents on and supporters of overbearing wealth.

So Deuteronomy 14 shifts the uses of the tithe in two directions. On the one hand, it requires that the tithe be brought to the Temple directly and there be eaten by the celebrants themselves (rather than turned over to the Temple upkeep). Perhaps in this way the Deuteronomic reformers hoped to forestall bureaucratic corruption. To make this tithe easier to deliver, Deuteronomy provides that it can be converted into money, and then at the Temple this money could be used to buy "cattle, sheep, wine, strong drink, or anything else your soul desires," there to feast and rejoice.

On the other hand, Deuteronomy requires that in every third year, the tithe be kept in every local settlement and used to protect the poor, the foreigner, the widow, and the orphan. Struggling to affirm the old pro-Levite rules at the same time as they transformed these rules, the authors of Deuteronomy repeated that this third-year tithe was also for the Levites, but now the Levites were defined as landless and penniless, like the other poor.

In order to strengthen this new approach to the tithe, Deuteronomy (26:12–14) requires that in every third year, after completing the tithe, each landholder declare before God:

> I have cleared out what is holy from the house, and I have given it to the Levite, the foreigner, the fatherless, and the widow, in accord with all the commands with which You commanded me.
>
> I have neither transgressed nor forgotten any of Your commandments. I have not eaten of it while in mourning, I have not cleared out any of it while I was in a taboo state, and I have not left any of it for the dead. I have heard the voice of YHWH my God. I have done just as You commanded me.
>
> Look down from Your holy dwelling-place, from heaven, and bless Your People Israel and the earth You have given us, a land flowing with milk and honey, as You swore to our forebears.

The logic is clear:

> Since from my house I have taken what is holy because it is due to the poor and have given it to them, look down from Your holy house and give us what is due to us, who without it would be poor.

The great flow of prosperity between the land and the people must be primed with the small flow of prosperity between the landholder and the landless.

This approach to the tithe is unique to the land of Israel. In the Mesopotamian and Babylonian law codes, there are clear provisions for tithing to the king and to the royal temple. But there are no provisions for using the tithe to support the poor.

This Deuteronomic version attempts to resolve the spiritual collision between a sense of God as Giver of prosperity and a sense of God as Protector of the poor. The history of this collision of spiritual values within ancient Israel may be of use to us today. Jews who have often (and until very recently, accurately) seen themselves as the poor, the marginal, the oppressed, have in our generation become fairly prosperous. This is bound to affect our sense of the spiritual meaning of abundance.

If today we are struggling toward a new understanding of the Jewish ethic of the use of money, then we should notice that there are three alternative visions of

God that seem to have been put forward in this crisis of Israelite history: God as Guarantor of security and abundance, God as Defender of the poor, and God as the One who provides prosperity to the people as a whole if the people will protect the poor. This third image of God may offer us a spiritual outlook on money that takes into account both our past poverty and our recent prosperity, the experience of both others and ourselves.

We should also note that Deuteronomy connects what we might call "environmental" and what we would call "political" or "economic" matters. The rain, the sun, the soil cannot be divorced from issues of money and power. The spirituality of this book of Torah lies precisely in the assertion that these two spheres of life are intimately intertwined under God's governance.

And finally we should note something basic about the method the Deuteronomic reformers used in carrying out their reform. They did not throw out the previous tradition, the older version of the tithe, they gave it a new meaning and effect even while they went out of their way to reaffirm its connection with the Levites. As we have seen before and will again, this is a characteristically Israelite, and then Jewish, way of dealing with change, even great upheavals. The wisdom of the past is not abandoned but reinterpreted, and the identity and collective memory of the people are affirmed rather than violated.

As did those who came before us, we too may want to draw on the wisdom of the past without being trapped in it.

IF THE POOR ARE STILL WITH YOU

The same Israelite society that invented the use of the tithe to help the poor and the rhythmic release from debt to ease the burden on the poor also worked out other ways of limiting the distance between rich and poor.

First of all, there were commands not to oppress or exploit those who held no land and so had become day laborers (Deut. 24:10–19).

Whether [he is] a fellow countryman or a stranger . . . you must pay him his wages on the same day, for he is poor and urgently depends on it; else he will cry out to YHWH against you and you will incur guilt.

If you take someone's coat as a pledge for a loan, you must not walk into his house to seize the pledge but ask him to bring it out; and if he is poor, you must give the coat back to him at sundown. Otherwise, as the night turns chilly, how will he be able to sleep?

Above all, over and over the Torah repeats:

You were slaves and strangers in the land of Egypt; therefore you must treat the worker fairly, therefore you must not return a runaway slave to his master, therefore you must have one system of law for citizens and strangers, therefore you must love the stranger.

What if everything failed, what if the day laborer fell deeper into poverty?

In grainfields, vineyards, and orchards, whatever the harvester overlooked or had dropped to the ground was left for the poor to glean (Lev. 19:9–10; Deut. 24: 19–22; Ruth 2). In addition, produce that grew in the corners of the field, the vineyard, and the orchard was left for the poor to harvest.

From the standpoint of the poor, this practice, called *pe'ah* (corner), meant that there was always a right to eat, not from a handout but from doing work. There was a complementary absolute right to a job. No landholder could refuse to let the poor glean by claiming that they were less efficient, lazier, redundant. Capital, in the form of land, could not be fenced in against those who needed work and food.

From the standpoint of the landholder, *pe'ah* was a powerful physical assertion that no one's property stood apart, that no person stood alone, that "I" do not stop at a sharply defined fence or wall where "you" begin. Instead, my property and my identity fade away into that of the community, represented not by the king or priest, but by the poor. At its corners, the land I hold is not fully mine, because its produce does not belong to me. I secure my control over my whole allocation of land only if I agree that at the corners I do not fully control it.

At a more personal level, this assertion is physically represented in a rule of Israelite culture about clothing. My clothes become my second skin, the cultural edge of my identity as my skin is my biological edge. But I do not in truth live cut off cleanly, clearly from others. At the corners of my garments there must be a ritual fringe—an assertion that my clothing fades away into the world's air, that at the edges of my being I am both "me" and "us." Not good fences make good neighbors, but good fringes.

And what are "good" fringes? In a human community, it is always true that no person stands unconnected from the others. Fringes there are. But we can ignore them, pretend we stand alone; or we can with awareness celebrate our connections. We can affirm that what connects us with others is what makes us holy. So Torah teaches us to make *tzitzit*, fringes on the corners of our garments that are tied and knotted with the full awareness that they connect us to other people. When we look at these carefully planned and tied *tzitzit*, they remind us of all the many connections that bind us to each other and the earth, that make it possible for there to be *Echad*, the One.

In the case of *pe'ah* in the fields, this practice was not only a symbol, but a practical reality. Together with the right to glean food that had been overlooked, it protected the poor against emergencies of need. The provisions of the third year of tithing, the sabbatical year, and the Jubilee would over time help the poor in a more basic way, but in the meantime they could not be left to starve. What is more, they would be assisted not by some invisible, anonymous fund, but would become personally and emotionally present to the landholder, as visible as Ruth the gleaner became to Boaz the landowner. Visibly they would work, not eat from handouts. And the rich would visibly fulfill their obligation to provide a "job"— access to capital in the form of land.

Another form of aid to the poor was the rule that one Israelite could not charge another interest on a loan. Lest the wealthy conclude there was nothing for them to gain by lending money to the poor, since they would collect no interest and even repayment of the principal itself would be annulled in the seventh year, the Torah (Deut. 15:9) specifically warns that it would be sinful to refuse a loan, for your kinfolk will "cry out to YHWH against you."

The appeal to "kinfolk" is important here. This people saw itself as both a family and an intergenerational "social movement" seeking to transform the world of Canaan. Bonds of blood were intensified by shared vision and shared suffering. So within the broader family/movement, everyone must help anyone in trouble. Those who were outside the family, who did not share its social vision and practice, could be treated with more distance and more coolness. Could, for example, be charged interest on their loans.

What long-term vision did this "family" that also saw itself as a "social movement," hold about the poor and poverty? Some of them raged against those who hastened to end holy days so as to "buy the poor for silver and the needy for a pair of shoes" (Amos 8:4–6). They insisted to those who were well-off, "share your bread with the hungry, bring home the outcast poor, clothe the naked when you see them, do not hide yourself from your own flesh and blood" (Isa. 58:7). Some envisioned a society in which poverty had been abolished. "Each will sit under his own vine and fig-tree, and no one will make them afraid" (Mic. 4:4).

Deuteronomy has a more complex expectation. It asserts that if the people will heed God's teachings, then the land will be blessed with prosperity and "there will be no poor among you." Yet only a few lines later, it says, "The poor will never be absent from your land." How to resolve this seeming contradiction?

Perhaps the simplest answer is that the Torah is itself deeply skeptical that the people will ever fully heed its teachings, and therefore it expects the poor to remain.

Another answer is that the Torah is taking into account that some of its readers are optimists who expect the abolition of poverty; others are pessimists who believe it will last forever. The Torah fears that optimists will think nothing needs to be done about poverty because its final abolition is foreordained, and pessimists will think nothing can be done because it is all useless.

So the Torah says to both, "Do what I command you: open your hand to the poor!" (Deut. 15:7–11).

For us today, living in a world where extremes of wealth and poverty see each other not only on the television screen but in cities and neighborhoods where greed and degradation trade glances every day, these ancient teachings may point the way toward action. And for us today, the world has become so small and intertwined that there are no longer any walls between peoples. All the boundaries have become permeable. The fences have become fringes.

So for Jews, this raises a new question. Even if, like the Biblical Israelites, we became an intergenerational "movement" to heal the earth and empower the poor, once more a "family" with a purpose and a vision, we would still be in a place quite different from Biblical Israel. For we could no longer seal ourselves off from other peoples, as if there were walls and fences between us. We would need to take the symbols of fringes and corners, *pe'ah* and *tzitzit*, into the broader world.

What would be the *tzitzit* of the entire Jewish people? Among nation-states, would demilitarized zones be the equivalent of *tzitzit*? Among peoples and cultures, would *tzitzit* mean the common celebration of some sacred days in addition to the celebration by each community of separate festivals? (For example, could all peoples celebrate together the Rainbow Sign that symbolizes the multicolored faces of all life and the time when human beings acted to save all species from a Flood of death?) On issues of poverty and power, what sorts of actions would embody both the distinctions and the connections between different communities and cultures?

XV. THE TORAH OF WORK

Today, we are part of a world economy. When we look for some Jewish prec-
edents, some Jewish wisdom from the past to draw upon, for our economic situation we may find that the post-Biblical far-flung Jews of the Mediterranean basin
were more like us than the Israelites who grew sheep and barley and dates in a
single land. For the dispersed Jewish communities of the Mediterranean, like modern Jews, were part of a broad-based economy that they could not control.

Their anxieties over money were much like ours. They worried not only over
rain and drought, not only over kings who might raise taxes, not for relief of the
poor but to multiply their own gold and silver; they worried as well about great
waves of inflation and depression, prices and interest and wages, loans and savings,
the poor in faraway lands, and monopolies in vital commodities.

We can imagine that the Rabbis who guided the emerging Diaspora culture
might have decided to leave economics behind as a matter of Jewish concern. They
could simply have said, "Under these new conditions, Torah is about prayer and
festivals and *kashrut*. As for how to make a living, how to spend your money, do
as you like in your own country, your own situation. On these matters we can give
no guidance."

But that is not what the Rabbis said. They viewed the Jewish culture as a sacred
path of life in which the uses of money, like every other aspect of the path, must
be made holy. They recognized that the new situation in which the people found
themselves demanded that the path take on new forms; and they were ready to
draw on Torah in new ways to shape those forms.

For Jews in our own generation who live around the globe, what the Rabbis
did to shape a Jewish approach to money may be useful to understand.

HOW TO MAKE A LIVING

One of the first money issues that we face in our lives is what occupation, what
career, to choose. Indeed, for more and more of us this choice comes not once but
several times. The economy changes so rapidly that in a single lifetime we experience

both the opportunity of new vocational choices and the disappearance of old ones. At exactly the moment when the long-run payoff of prudent choices becomes much greater, the possibility of making prudent long-range choices drops.

There are two overlapping worlds that we must try to understand: our own predilections, and the economy around us. What are the questions we should ask ourselves? One is: What jobs are we likely to do well—by reason of our abilities, our experience, and our desires and values?

The other is: What jobs will win us respect because we ourselves and others around us believe that they embody worthwhile work that enhances rather than degrades the universe, and at the same time pays us enough to live in the ways we want to live—this coming year, seven years from now, fourteen and thirty-five and fifty years from now?

What help can the Jewish past give us in answering these questions?

What jobs can we do well? Many of our individual abilities are inborn, or shaped in ways we do not consciously control. We can, however, choose which abilities and values we will try to enhance. Those choices will make some futures easier to choose and others harder.

In regard to what jobs will pay enough money and respect, compared to that which we feel we want and need: Collectively, rather than individually, we (that is, our society) choose what industries to expand and what to contract, what education to provide and what to ignore, where to invest and where to divest—and therefore what jobs will exist and how much they will pay and how much they will be honored. Society—that is, ourselves as a collective body—also tries to teach us what level of income we "need" and "want." In this sphere, however, we are more able to make individual choices; if we like, we can draw on Jewish wisdom and experience from the past.

As the scene of that past shifted from the Land of Israel to the Mediterranean Diaspora, as fewer Jews derived their livelihood from the land, as economics became more impersonal and the other actors less likely to be Jews, how to make a living became a matter of conscious self-examination, rather than simple acceptance. The Rabbis who shaped Jewish thought viewed some occupations with suspicion; others, with pride and honor.

What the Rabbis thought about making a living still has an impact on Jewish life, in two ways. One of these is their preferences: What they deemed a desirable occupation still colors Jewish lives today. Secondly, the process by which they judged occupations offers us some guidelines for determining for ourselves what constitutes good and bad work for Jews to do.

THE WORK OF TORAH

The Rabbis' favorite occupation was their own. During the period in which they shaped the Talmud, to be "the Rabbis" meant to engage in the study and reinterpretation of Torah. It meant being intellectuals, but not in an ivory tower. It meant dancing and wrestling with ancient texts, with other interpreters—some long dead—and with one's own colleagues, so as to shape the ongoing life of the Jewish people. It meant tasting the joys of musing on God, making puns and wordplays, legislating economic justice, creating powerful liturgy, defining good medical and sexual practice, doing stand-up comedy. It meant being an intergenerational community of hundreds of writers and speakers (some as straightforward as Ernest Hemingway; some as complex and convoluted as James Joyce) who wrestled and danced with each other for hundreds of years into their own pasts and their own futures, whose speaking and writings made up the laws and economics of a far-flung people. Sometimes it meant experiencing torture and death at the hands of a foreign empire.

It is not surprising that intellectuals who held such public power and esteem saw the study of Torah itself—not farming, war, handicrafts, commerce, or statesmanship—as the occupation of highest honor. We should remember that the Rabbis were precisely the heirs of the earthquake in Jewish life that shattered the process of raising food in the Land of Israel as the link between God and the Jewish people. It was they who made the words that came forth from Jewish mouths the sacred equivalent of the food that had gone into Jewish mouths. It was they who turned the sacred cycle of food—shepherds' and farmers' handing the products of their labors (food) to priests, who offered it to God so that God would continue to shower food upon the farmers—into a sacred cycle of words. So they saw their vocation as the one that went farthest to repair the shattered universe.

The Rabbis identified this work with the sensual joy of making love. All of them were men (with but one or two possible exceptions over hundreds of years). They drew on frankly erotic images to express their love of Torah, envisioning the Torah as a delicious, ethereal, Divine "woman" with whom it was delightful to make love. If finding erotic joy in one's work itself defined a "good job," what did they experience as erotic joy? We know that they learned together in intense companionship. We know that what they said mattered—changed a culture, shaped history. We know that they were always conscious that the subject of their work was God, that is, the flow of Unity that gave themselves and all of life coherence. Their work made them feel intensely alive, deeply connected, well loved, courageous.

When the Rabbis read the sensual love poems of the Song of Songs, they experienced them as the lovemaking conversation between God and Israel. The connection between the two lovers was Torah. And every day of their lives, they were able to take part in that flow of intimate joy!

Perhaps, drawing on their wisdom today at the deepest levels, we could say that a good job was whatever brought a sense of joy to the worker, whether it was Torah study or something else.

The priests had eaten the food they were brought. But the Rabbis could not live by words alone. Could their sacred vocation bring them a livelihood?

The Rabbis were mostly opposed to making a living by teaching or learning Torah. "Do not use Torah as a cow," they warned. Instead, many of them had their own work, and some were independently wealthy. Some were supported by their wives while they studied. Most of them agreed that one should teach a son both Torah and an occupation. Yet others were supported by the community as a whole. Rabbi Nehorai even said that he taught his son only Torah, not a trade, because when a man grows old he will be unable to practice his trade and so will starve, but Torah study "guards him from evil in his youth and gives him a future and hope in his old age." (Mishnah, Kidushin 4: 14) Perhaps this thought was based on the assumption that the community would support an aged Torah scholar.

The Rabbis' more usual approach—carrying on a paying craft and studying Torah as well—suggests that not only is the paid work we do important to assess in the light of Torah, but also what we freely do as volunteers, unpaid and playful. Can we find the passion the Rabbis found in Torah study by laughing with our families, reading poetry, playing jazz, organizing a community garden? Can we make all of these activities a form of Torah by infusing them with the loving knowledge of Torah and community?

THE MORAL CALCULUS OF WORK

Study Torah—and learn an occupation. For the Rabbis were still heirs of the Biblical belief that human work to tend and heal the world was commanded by God. The question was: What occupation? On what basis should one choose a trade?

What had been a comparatively simple matter in the Land of Israel was no longer so simple in the more complex world economy. Yet the Rabbis clearly state that people should not choose a trade by calculating its likely income. For as Rabbi Meir says, "Always teach your son a clean craft, and then pray: for there is no craft that leads always to riches and none that leads always to poverty."

Rather, the Rabbis had in mind the ethical and moral implications of various livelihoods. One of them warned that no one should teach his son to be a donkey driver, a camel driver, a barber, a sailor, a shepherd (!), or a shopkeeper, for these crafts are the crafts of robbers. But another argues: Most donkey drivers are honest, most camel drivers straightforward, most sailors pious; but even the best among doctors is destined for Hell!

The Rabbis taught that certain occupations that disturbed the moral balance of the world would not bring prosperity. To modern ears it is not clear if they expected such occupations to bring down specific Divine or demonic interventions, or were warning of the intrinsic, systemic consequences of bad action. Perhaps to their own ears such a distinction was meaningless; perhaps to them "Divine intervention" and "systemic consequences" were the same.

One way in which prosperity could vanish was that public disapproval of an occupation might bring down the "evil eye," and so bring on financial losses. Those, for example, who bred goats and sheep that ate up grass and trees, and those who cut down beautiful trees for timber, were courting disaster. Did the evil eye here specifically refer to the disapproving eyes of customers who would not patronize the offensive business, or did such disapproval generate other levels of bad luck? Or was the evil eye the eye of God, Who did not look favorably on destruction of the earth?

Importing goods from overseas would not prove profitable, the Rabbis said, because importers depended on miracles to keep their ships afloat. (Is it possible that the Rabbis were warning that such high-risk ventures were bound to fail in the long run, or did they expect the universe to single out for rebuke anyone who depended on miracles?)

More subtly, the Rabbis named occupations that as sheer action in the world were praiseworthy, but if done for profit were unlikely to flourish:

- Explaining Rabbinic sermons to the public, because accepting payment verged upon working on Shabbat.
- Managing the money of orphans. Because the children were not competent to assess reasonable fees for the service, taking some of their money as a professional fee might verge on embezzlement.
- Writing sacred scrolls and documents, because scribes who viewed this as a profession might restrict their output in order to make more money.

WORK AND WOMEN

The Rabbis were especially concerned about the moral implications of livelihoods that brought men in constant contact with women. Perhaps this concern stemmed from the intensity of their own erotic fantasies, which began with women, then were translated into passion for the Torah, and often saw the Torah and women as competitors for their erotic energy. They themselves kept a great occupational distance from women, and they turned this into a general rule: "One whose occupation concerns women must not be alone with women, and one should not teach his son a trade carried on among women."

The first and most basic thing to notice about this dictum is that it addresses only men, as if only they existed in the ethical-social world of the Talmud. It expresses a simultaneous, and compulsive, attraction, fear, and revulsion toward women. It assumes that there are trades carried on among women—and evidently leaves them to women to carry on. Other remarks suggest that the Rabbis recognized two separate economic spheres, one of women's work and one of men's. (T.B. Pesachim 50b)

For example, under some circumstances women's work might benefit the family, under other circumstances it would not. For a woman to go from door-to-door selling wool, the Rabbis say, will bring no blessing. But for her to make cloth into clothing and then sell it, will, noting that Proverbs celebrates such a wife as a "woman of valor."

Evidently, selling either wool or clothing is restricted to women selling to women. Men should stay out of it. Why is it better to sell finished clothes than raw wool? Perhaps this is economic prudence: Handmade goods would bring greater profit than raw materials. Or maybe it is a way of affirming the industrious woman who puts work into improving the product.

On the other hand, perhaps the point is about selling door-to-door. Wool would more likely be sold this way than finished clothing, which would probably be sold at a shop. The Rabbis wanted women to be present in public as little as possible. They seem to have found the presence of women both an erotic temptation and a ritual danger to themselves.

But the Rabbis, and the millennia of Jewish civilization that they shaped, saw women as important economic actors. Inside the family, they had both economic rights and responsibilities. Indeed, we have already seen that certain tasks—grinding corn, baking bread, washing clothes, cooking, suckling children, making ready the bed, and working in wool—were defined as the woman's domain, either for the wife or, if she was rich, for hired servantwomen to carry out.

This was not slave labor. In exchange, women were entitled to be supported by their husbands. The Talmud defined the standards for reasonable support (Mishnah Ketubot 5:8–9), and the Rabbinical courts enforced these standards:

—not less than two *qabs* of wheat or four *qabs* of barley [a week];
—half a *qab* of legumes, half a *log* of oil, and a *qab* of dried figs . . . or fruit from somewhere else;

—a bed, a reed mattress, and a rush mat;

—a cap for her head, a girdle for her loins, and sandals at each festival;

—fifty *zuz* worth of clothes in the rainy season;

—a silver *ma'ah* for her [weekly pocket money]... and if he does not give her this [the income from] her own work belongs to her.

Normally, in other words, the income from wool she has spun or from similar work would be part of the household fund, for the husband to disburse; but she has a claim on it if he denies her her due.

Aside from their rights and obligations inside the home, women were economically active. If a woman was married, most of what she did in her economic role had to be approved by her husband, and most property she acquired during the marriage belonged to him. (But any payment from a third party for damages to her person belonged to her.) Any property that she had acquired before the marriage remained her own, though the income from its use (for example, rent from land she had inherited) was controlled by her husband as long as the marriage continued.

To a lesser extent, and for some sorts of transactions, husbands also needed the approval of their wives. Most basically, husbands could not invade the "marriage price" that had been set aside in the *ketubah* (marriage contract) to be paid to the wife in case of divorce.

Unmarried women—those who had come of age (at twelve and a half) without being espoused or married, widows, and divorcees—could act on their own and use their money as they saw fit.

The Rabbis expected women to choose their own work and to buy and sell their own property with an eye to economic prudence and effectiveness.

As Rabbinic Judaism evolved, these rules allowed and perhaps encouraged women to take an active role in the economic life of the Jewish community. Indeed, at least in Eastern Europe, the ideal pattern of many Jewish communities—achieved for only a relatively few families—came to be that the adult men would occupy themselves with Torah study, while the women carried on or oversaw all the tasks of *parnosseh*, bringing in the family livelihood.

ə

What out of all this might Jews facing issues of work today find instructive?

First, most Jews have clearly rejected the notion that the most important intellectual, spiritual, and political-legal work is reserved for men. Yet there is much we could learn from the impassioned, erotically charged stance that the Rabbis took toward their work. We could inquire into what might be called the "passional" as well as the moral, environmental, communal, and ethical implications of a job or a business. Does the job engage the passions of the worker?

As for the division of labor inside the family, today few of us would say that all of one sort of work devolves on men and another sort on women. Again there is much we could learn from the care and precision with which the Rabbis examined how to divide the household tasks and spend the household income. Today, we might say that within each household, the participants will as a family, not as individuals, work out these issues, talk together about what kind of work each feels drawn to, what level of income they feel is worthwhile, how to spend the money they have, how much to set aside for each member to protect his or her independence.

The notion that a household is a unit not only for purposes of companionship, love, sex, but also for economic sharing and decisions, could be the beginning and root of a "loving economics" in the broader society.

In such an atmosphere, we could learn once more from the Rabbis' outlook on work, jobs, and careers. We could ask ourselves, would a given task be more wisely done by volunteers than by paid jobholders, even if done with less skill? Would choosing to do specific work be greeted with communal support or met with intense communal distaste? If the latter, is the distaste purely cultural, or does it betoken a deeper disruption of good order in the universe? Are some business risks so extreme that to take them one must trust that miracles will happen—and then fall into deep and destructive despair if the venture fails?

ə

A business or a job: How did Rabbinic Judaism view the distinction?

As we have seen, in the Biblical mind-set the "norm" was an independent entrepreneur, probably a farmer, who might hire workers. Being a hired worker was the exception, not the norm. In the Rabbinic period, as might be expected in a much more complex commercial economy not rooted in the land, many more Jews were hired workers. To the Rabbis, the distinction between a commercial employer and a commercial employee did not seem nearly as great as the gulf between a landholder and a farm laborer had been in Biblical times.

The Rabbinic mind-set looked on employees not as a disadvantaged class needing special protection, but as independent contractors who were bargaining as equals, selling their labor as other business people might sell tools, grain, or clothing. Thus passages in the Talmud are couched in neutral language, as between employees and employers, not addressing one or the other as "you." (T.B. Baba Kamma 33a; Baba Metzia 76a, 110b) For the Rabbis, if any vocational group contained fuller citizens than others, it was neither landholders nor employees, but the Rabbis themselves.

In an economy where almost everyone was a bargainer and entrepreneur, was there still a need for safeguards as there had been in the Biblical pattern? Yes, but the pattern of the safeguards was quite different. There were three different kinds of safeguards that the Rabbinic model of society provided:

1. If the free play of competition was crucial, then blockages of that free play—monopolies or price-fixing agreements, scarcities of goods, scarcities of investment capital, the exploitation of workers so that they could not participate in the economy, and so on—were wounds that needed to be healed.
2. The community as a whole, through its public institutions, needed to provide certain economic goods like safe transportation and an effective city wall that no single household or entrepreneur could or would provide.
3. Some individual members of the community needed special help—money or *tzedakah*. This was not "charity," as it is usually translated, but not quite the same as *tzedek*, or justice, not as sharp-edged, not focused on the sense that the world is divided between some who deny justice and others who are denied it.

    Tzedakah might better be translated as the "social responsibility" that everyone owes and anyone might need. Everyone, even the poorest, was responsible for giving some *tzedakah*, even the tiniest amount; and circumstances might arise in which almost anyone might need to receive it.

EMPLOYERS AND EMPLOYEES

Today, some of the most important and most painful money issues arise between employers and employees, not only over money per se but over working conditions and the dignity and rights of workers. It is not surprising that this was true as well through the period of Rabbinic authority. From the Rabbis' standpoint, there were reciprocal rights and responsibilities that employers and their workers owed to each other.

In line with the general rule that the protection of life was the highest Jewish value, employees were supposed to take reasonable care of their bodies against expectable risks of their work, and employers owed their workers a safe and healthy workplace. Employers who failed in this duty through negligence were liable for damages five times the worker's losses, among which were the loss of income, damage to the body, medical expenses, pain, and shame arising from the injury.

In some circumstances, employers owed medical care to injured workers even when their injuries arose out of ordinary circumstances of the job. Thus Temple priests who became ill from eating the meat of the sacrifices or from working in chilly ceremonial dress had their medical costs paid by the Temple treasury. Where a Jewish community felt that the worker could not be left unprotected but that the employer could not bear the whole burden of medical costs, it would divide the costs between the employer and the community as a whole through a *tzedakah* fund.

Wages were set by bargaining. Either employer or employee could cancel the contract, but had to pay whatever additional expenses the cancellation imposed on the other party. If the worker had forgone available employment to accept a job, and then the job was canceled, the employer owed what the worker would have paid to receive a vacation.

A major concern of Rabbinic authorities, as well as of the written Torah, was that workers be paid fairly and fully. They must be paid on time—a day laborer, for example, before sunset. This was required not only for financial reasons in the narrow sense, but to keep workers from anguish and anxiety over when and whether they would be paid. Whether employers could after hiring workers decide to change their payment from kind to money or money to kind, was up to the workers; they could not be forced to agree to this change. If a worker claimed that the employer had not paid wages due and the employer said that the money had been paid, the Rabbis presumed that the worker was correct unless proved otherwise, even though in most other cases, Jewish law presumed that a debt had been paid if the creditor said so.

Workers were also entitled to form guilds or trade unions in order to help one another. Members of the guild or union could agree among themselves about wages and conditions of work, but the Rabbis limited the conditions under which they could press nonmembers to abide by their rules. They could do so to prevent the destruction of their jobs, but not to prevent pay reductions. The Rabbis also limited the degree to which strikes should be used to enforce the decisions of the guild: To enforce an existing contract or protect customary benefits, strikes were legitimate; to improve wages or conditions, workers were supposed to ask for arbitration by a Rabbinical court or by the local communal authorities.

Aging or disabled workers were entitled not only to pensions, but to keep their jobs if they could do part of the work while their employers hired assistants for them. This suggests that the Rabbis saw that part of the benefit of work lay in the honor and self-esteem involved in the work itself, not only in the payment of wages; and sought to preserve the workers' dignity as well as their income.

In this ultimate affirmation of work as a good in itself, the Rabbis were taking into an age of commerce the values the Bible had put forward for an age of agriculture. Just as working the land as farmers and shepherds was to join in God's process of Creation, so was working as a weaver, a sailor, a seamstress. To work was not a sad necessity but a joyful possibility, to be infused with spiritual energy rather than counterposed to it. For the Rabbis as for the Psalmist (90:17):

U'ma'aseh yadenu kon'nah aleynu;
U'ma'aseh yadenu kon'neyhu.
The work of our hands, establish it for us;
The work of our hands, establish it.

Both for our own sake and for the sake of all-that-is, may You, God, support and secure the work that we do.

What is our task today, if we wish to draw on this approach of Rabbinic Judaism to work? It may be that we must choose for the long haul an occupation in which that attitude is possible, as well as to renew such work each day in order that our hands do what the universe needs.

XVI. JUST WEIGHTS, WHOLE MEASURES

Rabbinic Judaism tried hard to turn work and the relationship between employees and employers—an arena which the Rabbis understood always involved some conflict—into an arena of community, loving-kindness, and holiness. They faced the same questions and worked toward the same goal when they addressed another aspect of economic life—the tension between sellers and buyers.

Perhaps the most basic issue we face in the marketplace is whether it is purely the domain of *Homo economicus*—ruled by the desire to maximize gain at minimum cost—or a place governed by ethical, moral, and communal standards. That basic question takes many forms:

- What standard of living can give me reasonable dignity and comfort without making me addicted to buying more and more unsatisfying material objects that soon lose their kick and stir me to still more buying?
- What "labor-saving" devices actually save me work, and which ones push me to work yet harder to pay for them, operate them, and repair them?
- How do I distinguish between advertising that informs me what is useful, and advertising that turns my pleasant fantasies into thirsty needs?
- How can I choose between products that wound the earth, and products that sustain and heal it?
- How can I choose between products that strengthen my own and my household's autonomy and integrity, and those products that make me subservient to the mass media and political or economic fashion?
- If I am myself a producer or seller, how do I balance my responsibilities—in setting prices, or in choosing materials for manufacturing and packaging—to the earth, to myself, and to those who buy from me?
- How much communal regulation do we want and how much should we leave to individual ethical and economic decisions? If individual workers band together to shape their working conditions and affirm their sense of their own worth, how much honor and support does the community owe them?

The Rabbis insisted that the marketplace as well as the workplace operate within a basic commitment to justice, loving-kindness, fairness, and community. Some communal interventions to preserve justice, protect the poor, and keep prices fair would be needed to make sure that bargaining in an open market would not damage those goals.

There were three major situations in which the community intervened:

- cases of inaccurate weights and measures;
- cases of ona'ah (overreaching, wronging, oppressing): damage to the customer or to the seller by selling a product at more than one sixth over or more than one sixth under the fair market price; and
- cases of hafka'at she'arim (profiteering): cornering the market and jacking up prices on vital commodities—those necessary to life or to carrying out religious obligations.

❧

To achieve elementary fairness in the marketplace, the Rabbis elaborated on the Biblical law (Deut. 25:13–15): "You shall not have in your knapsack different weights, one large and one small. You shall not have in your house different measures, one large and one small. You shall have a weight that is whole and just [shleyma and tzedek], you shall have a measure that is whole and just."

The Rabbis asked (T.B. Baba Batra 88a–90a), why does the Torah say both "whole" and "just" when one word might have been enough? They read it to mean that a weighed-out bushel of grain should be slightly more than a bushel, to make sure that it was not only shleyma, whole, but just to the purchaser, slightly more than the buyer was owed, lest it unintentionally be slightly less.

They added that the punishment for false weights and measures should be even more rigorous than the punishment for prohibited sexual unions, citing an esoteric difference in the Torah texts of the two prohibitions to prove their point. It was worse than ordinary robbery, too, for ordinary robbers could repay their victims, but who could ever track down all the victims of false measures?

For these reasons, the Rabbis of the Talmud, and those in almost all autonomous Jewish communities since then, have appointed inspectors of weights and measures to make sure that these laws were communally enforced, not left to individual ethical decision alone.

In regard to the second major area of communal intervention, the Rabbis derived ona'ah, the law against "oppressive" prices, from the Biblical command "If you sell anything to your neighbor, or buy from your neighbor's hand, you shall not wrong [oppress, overreach] each other" (Lev. 25:14).

The Rabbis drew on the Torah text to affirm that economics is a subset of a broader Jewish ethics, not an independent sphere that is amoral. For just after prohibiting "wronging" in the marketplace, the Torah adds (Lev. 25:17), "You shall not wrong each other, but you shall fear your God; I YHWH your God." In the Rabbinic views, this second command was both broader and more serious than the first, since it did not specify prices and since it invoked the name of God. And so they regarded the economic aspect of *ona'ah* as a special case of a larger truth.

They applied this law especially to cases of humiliating someone by speech or other action. For example, one ought not to shame someone else even by referring to the actual misdeeds of his or her family. The Rabbis quote with approval (T.B. Baba Metzia 59b) a popular saying: "If there is a case of hanging in someone's family record, do not say to him, 'Hang up the fish.'"

One of the most powerful stories of the Talmud focuses on the tragedy of *ona'ah* in the form of humiliation. The great wonder-working Rabbi Eliezer invokes God's Own will against the majority decision of the Rabbis. They excommunicate Eliezer for this *chutzpah*. Deeply humiliated, profoundly the victim of *ona'ah*, he falls prostrate to pray. Instantly his prayer breaks through to God, and instantly the Rabbi who had taken the lead in excommunicating him falls dead. For even when all the gates of prayer are closed, the gate of *ona'ah* is open. (Ibid. 59a–59b)

So we see how seriously the Rabbis took the danger of "wronging" someone by overcharging.

In the marketplace, *ona'ah* applied to overcharging or undercharging when the victim—seller or buyer—was not aware that the price was out of line with a fair market value. To be effective, the prohibition required communal oversight. But what about a situation when the purchaser might know very well that the price was exorbitant, and yet feel compelled to buy?

The Rabbis did not allow this, and they developed the law of *hafka'at she'arim* (profiteering; literally, "breaking open the market price") to prevent it. (T.B. Baba Batra 90b–91b) They forbade raising prices for a vital foodstuff by cornering the market. Farmers might legitimately even cut the flow of their produce to market so that they would not have to sell a huge surplus at minimal prices and then charge high prices for food when it was scarce. But middlemen could not speculate in vital supplies. They could not even export vital foodstuffs (at least not from the Land of Israel) if that would drive up their prices in the localities where they had been grown. One Rabbi, however, said that exporting wine was legitimate because if its price rose and people drank less, alcoholism might be reduced, an exception on ethical grounds to economic controls that had themselves been established for ethical reasons.

The Rabbis disapproved of selling necessities like wine, oil, and bread through a series of middlemen, through which the price would be increased without improving the product. Some of them even opposed price increases by distributors who transported the product.

Since many Jewish festivals and celebrations have traditionally required buying special foods or ritual objects for use at a specific time, there was an opportunity for abusive price-raising by merchants who controlled these commodities. Meat at the time of the great pilgrimage festivals, *etrogim* (citrons, lemonlike fruit) just before the harvest festival of Sukkot, fish in some communities for Shabbat, were examples of such time-sensitive commodities.

Long after the Talmudic period, when rabbis faced price-gouging at times of celebration, they took a wide range of steps that contravened ordinary religious law in order to make sure that even poor Jews would be able to join in the celebration. Thus on various occasions, rabbis

- have threatened to permit the use of ordinary lemons instead of *etrogim* unless the price of *etrogim* was lowered;
- have ordered *etrogim* sold in sealed boxes so that competition for more beautiful ones would not distort prices;
- have ruled just before Shabbat that all fish were *treyf*, in order to break a monopoly that had raised fish prices so high that only the rich could buy it for Shabbat, thus humiliating the poor.

These principles of a just marketplace were not only moral strictures with no mechanisms for legal enforcement. The early Rabbis debated whether their courts should appoint price inspectors, or let the market achieve fairness through competition and individual ethical choices. Even though they agreed that the literal words of Torah required that there be inspectors of weights and measures but not of prices, they—and Rabbinical courts throughout the centuries and in many countries—did set fair prices for specific commodities and appoint officers to enforce them.

Today, these actions of the Rabbis and of Jewish courts over many generations seem to point beyond the individual and the household. Is the Jewish community responsible to address issues of economic justice in the broader society? If so, how can that responsibility be played out? We can imagine several possibilities:

Should the organized Jewish community use Jewish wisdom, past and present, to shape its approaches to the cost of synagogue memberships, tuition in Jewish schools, the investment of organizational money, the treatment and pay of staff, the support of elders, and similar economic issues? What new institutions would have to be created in order to do this effectively, justly, and democratically?

Jewish courts today do not (except in Israel) have the kind of power that

Rabbinical courts had to enforce just economic standards. But the Jewish community does not honor some of its members, and could shame some as well. Should it speak out publicly, explicitly, and vigorously against Jews who violate standards of economic behavior that Rabbinical courts would have enforced?

Should the Jewish community explicitly draw on Jewish thought and practice in working out what economic policies to propose to the larger society? Would this mean legislative lobbying, electoral coalitions, action within businesses and corporations?

For any of these approaches—even the most limited and internal—to make a serious difference either to the Jewish people or to the world at large, Jewish communities throughout the world would need to decide to provide a conscious alternative to the society around them, one that was not isolated and limited within ghetto walls, but would explicitly challenge and try to change the larger world. Are Jews prepared to take on the risks as well as the benefits of such a role?

Money flows, even when there is no obvious or immediate exchange of goods or labor. From your hand to mine, from mine to yours, from me to the community as a whole, from the community to me or you, the money flows—or abundance stops.

How does this happen? We lend some money, or we borrow it. We give it to someone else, or to the government—perhaps out of a sense of obligation or of generosity.

But—when, how, and to whom should we lend our money? When, how, and from whom should we borrow it? To whom should we freely give? To what governments should we pay taxes, and what taxes should we not pay? How do we decide these questions?

The Rabbis understood that in order to encourage the flow of abundance, it was necessary to encourage the flow of money from hand to hand. They told the parable of the difference between Lake Kinneret (the Sea of Galilee), in which fish and vegetation flourish, and the Dead Sea, which is indeed dead. Kinneret, they explained, receives water from, and gives it forth into, the Jordan River. So it stays alive. The Dead Sea receives water from the Jordan but does not give it forth. Since the Dead Sea takes without sharing, it deadens itself. (This parable turns out to parallel a scientific understanding: Since water leaves the Dead Sea only by evaporation, extremely high levels of salt build up, killing most life-forms there.)

BORROWING IS BUSINESS

In the case of money, how do we encourage a flow of receiving and giving? The Rabbis knew that it was important to be able to borrow money, either in time of distress to get over the emergency, or in time of opportunity to create some new economic possibility. They addressed this need in a quite different way from that in the Bible.

In Biblical times, debt was what the poor might fall into in times of distress. The Torah (Lev. 25:35–38) directed that Israelites lend money to one another without interest, and it required (Deut. 15:1–3) that debts be annulled in the sabbatical year. The Torah realized that these provisions might make the rich unwilling to lend money, and therefore simply legislated that they must. The authority of Torah and probably of the priesthood was evidently great enough that this command was enforceable, since Jews lived in a single land, with a single economy, under a single legal system.

The Rabbis lived in a different world and had a different task. Under Roman rule and under conditions of wide dispersion of Jews in many lands under many legal systems, the Rabbis were not able to insist that those who had money lend to those who didn't. In times of rising economic opportunity, no one was willing to lend money to someone else and then lose the entire investment, even though it might benefit the economy as a whole. Why not get for oneself the advantages flowing from a successful investment? And why give up not only the year-by-year advantages but lose even the principal itself when the investment would dissolve in seven years? So the rich were simply not lending money to the poor.

What to do? Led by Hillel, the Rabbis arranged a way around the annulment of debt. They decided that the intention of Torah had been to protect the poor, and that under the conditions in which the community now lived, the periodic annulment of debt was working against the poor. For now no one would lend them money when they needed it.

How to change the situation while honoring the Torah? The Biblical provisions required the release of loans "that are with your brother" (Deut. 15:2–3). The Rabbis ruled that this meant loans from an individual to an individual—not loans held by a corporate body. So if an individual lent money before a sabbatical year and turned over the bonds of indebtedness to a Rabbinical court, then after the sabbatical year, the court could collect the loan and repay the original lender.

Through a procedure called the *prosbul,* which Hillel instituted (ca. 10 C.E.), the lender could declare to the court, with its approval, that he would be entitled to collect even after a sabbatical year had intervened.

Since the rich would be able to collect the money, they would be far more likely to lend it. This arrangement also gave the Rabbinical court some opportunity to oversee the loans and perhaps to protect the poor.

In doing this, the Rabbis gave a new and previously unexpected meaning to the explicit words of Torah in order to apply its deeper intent to a new situation. They struggled to honor the words of Torah rather than simply shrugging them off, by looking with great care at the precise meaning of those words and at the space they left for a new approach in a changed situation.

To people who in our own generation are struggling with enormous economic changes, both the Rabbis' decision to change and their attention to the tradition are suggestive. How do we ourselves want to shape the ongoing life of a culture and community that has many of its roots in an ancient text? Do we too want to go back to the old to shape the new? If so, would we do this more or less as Hillel did, or in some other ways?

The question of charging interest on loans is another aspect of the Rabbis' attempt to address new economic situations. Biblically, Jews were forbidden to pay or accept interest on loans to other Jews. The whole people was treated as one family who should not be charging interest to its members. We should note that in an economy of farmers and shepherds (unlike a commercial or industrial economy), investment capital was not likely to bring huge returns. So perhaps nobody lost out a great deal by lending someone else capital instead of investing it in his own venture. In a commercial economy, however, one major way of making money is to invest it. So a free loan may cost the lender a great deal.

How did the Rabbis deal with the question of interest in their increasingly commercial economy?

First of all, they adhered to the Biblical distinction between loans from one Jew to another and loans between a Jew and a non-Jew. On a loan from one Jew to another, paying or receiving interest was prohibited; on loans to or from a non-Jew, a Jew could lawfully pay or receive interest.

Why this distinction? Most Rabbinic tradition has asserted that interest is not intrinsically evil. If it were (like robbery, for example), a Jew could never be permitted by Torah to pay or receive interest, nor could anyone else. Taking or giving interest is not even intrinsically "un-Jewish" in the eyes of Torah, like working on Shabbat or eating pork, which are prohibited to Jews but not to other people.

Why then was the taking or giving of interest forbidden within the community? According to some Rabbinic commentators, the prohibition arose from the special obligations among members of a family, a guild, or other close community. Indeed, since many of the purely economic reasons for lending money did not apply when no interest could be paid, the prohibition forced Jews to think of themselves as more like a family if they were to lend money to each other at all. If anything, it made economic development within the Jewish community harder.

For that reason, Jews explored various ways of encouraging the flow of capital that would not fall under Rabbinic condemnation. For example, the arrangement called *heter iska* (permission for business) emerged, in which someone with capital became an inactive partner in the business in exchange for a share of the profits— a share that might be limited and specified as an absolute amount, not a proportion of profits. This approach made the investor a stakeholder with a more active concern about the firm than a lender might have, although the resulting payments verged on interest. In our hypercommercial modern world, some Jews felt the use of *heter iska* came sometimes to the edge of exploitation under the cloak of piety.

Alongside such arrangements, throughout the Jewish world there appeared "free-loan societies" that made limited amounts of money available without interest, usually for emergency personal or family needs and often for education with a long-term economic payoff, rather than for the direct support of a commercial enterprise.

In the broader ancient and medieval world, Jews and non-Jews often had an economic interest in working together. Yet they were very unlikely to look on themselves as a family or a close community across religious lines. So economic and political benefit, including payment of interest, was the main reason to arrange a loan. To have extended the prohibition of interest to that world would have made loans less likely, and so would have damaged the general economy.

In that broader world, some wealthy Jews (a small proportion of the Jewish community) took on a special role as moneylenders to governments and businesses. Several factors moved them in that direction. First, Christian authorities frowned upon Christians' taking or giving interest on loans to other Christians, so that the economic benefits of lending were easier to achieve through loans between Christians and others. Second, Jews in one town or country often had close family or friendly relationships with Jews somewhere else, and therefore had information on far-flung business and political conditions that enabled them to invest more prudently than people without such connections.

And as the Jewish people took part in a broader economy, they tried to balance the values of the "family," and its interest in economic sharing and mutual assistance, with the market values of economic risk-taking, investment, reward, and development. This was reasonably workable so long as the "family" boundaries were strong and only a few Jews were directly involved in the larger economy.

But in our own generation, most members of the Jewish community, not just a few, are involved in lending, borrowing, buying, selling with other religious and ethnic communities. Strong friendships and "family" connections, literally and figuratively, are likely to crisscross back and forth.

What does this mean?

- That none of the economic wisdom from the Jewish past can be applied in our present world?
- That the Jewish community should strive to re-create an internal Jewish economic network?
- That the teachings from the past about what members of the Jewish "family" owe each other should be transposed into what people owe those who are members of a neighborhood, or a profession, or a workplace, or a group that is politically or philosophically like-minded?
- Or, at still another level, do these teachings suggest that in our own generation the issue is not to whom we lend money but the use to which the money is

put? Should Jewish values and concerns govern our loans and investments, whether they go to Jews or to others?

SHARING MONEY

Issues of what we term "charity" in English confront us anywhere, from the city street where a homeless person asks for a quarter, to the family discussion at the end of the year about how large the tax-deductible contributions should be, to a corporate executive's decision about support for the arts, hospitals, and universities.

For the Rabbis, the ethics of sharing money were different from the overtones that echo from the word "charity." As we have seen, the Hebrew word *tzedakah* invokes social responsibility more than it does individual generosity.

In the Rabbinic view, not only the prosperous but also the poor were obligated to give *tzedakah*. And not only the poor but also on some occasions the prosperous might receive it.

Of course, among those who needed the help that flowed from *tzedakah* undertaken as "social responsibility" were some who had neither property nor jobs, such as orphaned children and people with physical or mental difficulties that prevented their working for pay.

But people who had jobs or property might also need *tzedakah*. Almost anyone at one point might become specially needy. A sudden storm or fire, or robbery, or oppressive arrest and imprisonment, or financial mistake might shatter even the rich. Some who made enough money, day by day, to support themselves, day by day, did not make enough to rest and celebrate on Shabbat. So these people needed enough *tzedakah* to buy food, candles, wine for Shabbat, to release them from the workday's toil.

Just as almost everyone, rich or poor, was seen on a continuum of bargainers in the workplace and at the marketplace, so did everyone live on a continuum of reasonable and necessary income, which it was "socially responsible" to safeguard.

The Rabbis began their understanding of *tzedakah* with a poignant reinterpretation of the command (Deut. 13:5) "You shall walk after YHWH your God." This meant that human beings should—like God—meet the special needs of people in trouble. For example, just as God prepared Eve for marriage when she had no family to do so, human beings should provide dowries to brides whose families could not afford it. (Pirkei de Rabbi Eliezer 12) As God clothed Adam and Eve when their own clothing was insufficient; as God came to Abraham when he was recovering from the pain of circumcision; as God comforted Isaac with a blessing after his father Abraham's death; as God buried Moses—so for human beings to "walk after" God meant to clothe the poor, visit the sick, comfort mourners, bury the dead. (T. B. Sotah 14a)

Some of these obligations require people to physically participate in acts of loving-kindness (*gemilut chassadim*) toward their neighbors; others require giving money, and it was these that were generally termed *tzedakah*.

Over the centuries, generations of Rabbis sought to codify the obligation of *tzedakah*. The most famous of these efforts was that of Maimonides (or Rambam) in the twelfth century; who proposed eight levels of worth in *tzedakah*:

- The highest level, providing someone with the wherewithal to make a living so as no longer to need *tzedakah* (that is, "a fishing rod instead of a fish");
- Next, giving in such a way that the giver did not know who received the gift and the receiver did not know who gave it. In this way, Maimonides thought, people would be doing *tzedakah* for its own sake as a religious act, not in exchange for honor or renown; and the dignity of the recipient would be protected against the tendency to kowtow to a donor;
- Sixth, the recipient is known but not the donor (especially useful if the donor is not behaving honorably—perhaps has made the money in a lawful but not honorable way?);
- Fifth, the donor is known but not the recipient (thus honoring the rich but preventing them from overawing the poor);
- Fourth, giving from hand to hand, without being asked;
- Third, giving from hand to hand, but only after the poor person has asked;
- Second, giving in a friendly way, but less money than is appropriate; and
- The lowest level, giving with a scowl.

What are the issues we might face today?

First: How much of our own income ought we to give in *tzedakah*?

To this the Rabbis replied that no one could avoid giving altogether. Even the desperately poor, who received all their own income from *tzedakah*, should give small amounts of *tzedakah*. At the highest level, one might give one fifth of one's income, but no more than that, probably for fear that a too generous giver would end up becoming a charge on the community or would receive too much honor and power for the community's good. Normal was giving one tenth of one's income.

Second: How shall we choose to whom among the wide range of the poor we shall give?

The Rabbis replied that anyone who asked for food should receive it at once. Even a stranger whom one suspected of fraud should be fed. Hunger is a powerful emergency.

Those who were strangers to the community and asked for less urgent help should be queried. The community was responsible to give what they needed—and therefore to make sure how much they needed. Yet no one who asked should be turned away utterly empty-handed.

Those who were known to the community, and whose needs were known, should not have their *tzedakah* delayed.

Giving should be extended in a series of concentric circles: first, to the poor of one's own near relatives, then of the extended family, then of the city, and then of other cities and countries.

"For the sake of the paths of peace," said the Rabbis, non-Jews as well as Jews should be given *tzedakah*. This phrase has two sides. It can be understood either as grudging or as transformative. It might mean that although non-Jews are not really entitled to be helped, keeping peace in the world requires that they be given help. Or it can be understood to mean that for the sake of *shalom*, the highest communal good and goal, it is not only an obligation but a joy to help all human beings.

It may be whichever aspect of this phrase spoke most deeply to people—the fearful and prudential one, or the one that was visionary and hopeful—depended on what the relationships between Jews and their neighbors were in any given time and place. In our own generation, when most Jews are not oppressed or outcasts, both the prudential and the hopeful may fuse into one.

Third: How much should different recipients be given?

The Rabbis asserted that the psychological dignity of the recipients should be affirmed as well as their biological needs. Those who had been accustomed to a prosperous life should not be doled out a bare handful of food. The community is not responsible to restore their former wealth, but should not make them objects of scorn.

The effort—and sometimes the result—of this weave of ethics and law was to strengthen the dignity of the poor in their own eyes as well as those of the prosperous. Tales are told of poor people who went on strike, refusing to accept *tzedakah* that they deemed too stingy until the amounts were raised, as if their willingness to accept *tzedakah* were like the willingness of carpenters to build houses. Why would a community respond to such a threat? Only because everyone so strongly felt the obligatory nature of *tzedakah* that no community could live with a breakdown in its ability to give.

The questions facing us today are not only whether we carry out these Rabbinic principles, but whether we agree with all of them.

- Do we affirm the concentric circles of recipients of *tzedakah* laid out by the Rabbis?
- Do we agree with Maimonides that preserving the donor's and the recipient's anonymity achieves the best results?

- Since buying a poor person "the fishing rod rather than the fish" costs more, how do we measure the immediate cost against the hope of future transformation?
- Are large-scale fund-raising appeals, direct mail, telephone calls, and professional experts the most effective means of raising funds? Are they the *only* effective means? Do they change the process so much that it is important to preserve or restore face-to-face, community-based ways of giving *tzedakah*?
- How do we balance the values of meeting the poor face-to-face with the values of far-reaching modern welfare systems?

THE CENTRAL TREASURY

In all societies people confront a number of ethical choices about paying taxes: Shall I pay in full or get away with paying as little as possible? What if I disagree with a particular tax or a particular use of tax money? Should I refuse to pay as a public act of civil disobedience, or quietly evade as much of the tax as I can? Or should I pay in full because I accept that the government has the last word? What gives any particular government legitimate authority to set my taxes?

In a democratic society, citizens face the same choices about paying taxes; they also face choices about setting them. How much money does the community as a whole need to raise from its members, even if as individuals they would hate to pay? And for what purposes? And which people should be required to pay how much?

The Rabbis made clear how important the basic obligation is to pay taxes:

As a punishment for the neglect of *terumot* and tithes the heavens are shut up from pouring down dew and rain, high prices are prevalent, wages are lost, and people pursue a livelihood but cannot attain it.... But if they render them, they are blessed. (T.B. Shabbat 32b)

The Rabbis also realized that in their world, the matter was not so simple. To what government were taxes owed? In their day, the Jewish community was autonomous but not totally independent. Over the centuries, there were outside governments in whose choice the Jews had little or no voice—the Roman empire, Christian kings, Muslim caliphs and sultans. In different countries, these rulers sometimes gave more, sometimes less, authority to the Jewish community to govern and tax itself. Often the rulers not only set taxes for all their subjects, but also imposed special taxes upon the Jewish community, usually as a sum total, leaving the distribution of the tax burden to the Jews themselves to decide.

There were also internal Jewish taxes to provide education, walls and guards to protect the community, and some aspects of *tzedakah*. So the Jews had to work out how to apportion both sorts of taxes.

In regard to internal taxes, the Rabbis discussed whether households should pay according to their numbers, income, and wealth, or according to the amount of benefit they received from the town (specifically, whether they lived close to the town wall and therefore had more protection from its guardians). They concluded that numbers should not be used as a basis for taxation; that the rich should pay more than the poor; and that those close to the wall should pay more than those far away.

In general, the Rabbis held that they themselves were exempt from the payment of most taxes. The study of Torah was itself a protection from marauders, they said; so scholars need not pay for police and walls. On the other hand, they used the streets like everyone else, and so were obligated to pay taxes for their usage and upkeep.

Orphans and the unemployed also received partial exemptions from internal taxes.

As for external authorities, the Rabbis distinguished between the Persian government in Babylonia and the Roman empire in the Land of Israel. Normally, Persian taxes were considered legitimate: *dina d'malkhuta dina*, the law of the government is law. But the Roman empire's occupation of Israel was illegitimate—and so were its taxes. In the early generations of the Roman conquest, the Rabbis encouraged tax evasion. Jews who collected Roman taxes were considered robbers, and were excluded from many communal functions. As time wore on and Rome's authority came to seem both more "normal" and more overwhelming, tax resistance diminished, and ultimately the Rabbis opposed the evasion of taxes if they were "limited." Limited taxes meant those that were specified by the central Roman government and were not just left to local bureaucratic discretion, with the likelihood of extortion and illegitimate impositions. Unlimited taxes were not really decided by the legitimate government, and thus the rule of *dina d'malkhuta dina* did not apply.

What began with judgments about only two external governments—the Roman and Babylonian—became far more complicated. In the long history of the Diaspora, Jewish communities faced a multiplicity of different external authorities. Which behaved lawfully and which not? Whose taxes should be paid and whose not? Moreover, the Jewish communities, as they responded to different local cultures and governments, found themselves both more different from each other, and more set off in cultural or physical ghettos from the Christians or Muslims around them. As they became more autonomous, they tried to determine what Jewish patterns to follow or create.

Facing outsiders, the Jewish authorities often tried to distinguish legitimate from illegitimate tax laws—especially "limited" from "unlimited" taxes—and to oppose or resist illegitimate forms. But then, if they were put under extreme pressure by local authorities, the Jewish communal leaders would give in when necessary for protection of the community. When the alternatives to compliance were exile of the community from a given country and the death or imprisonment of its leaders, the Rabbis complied. Sometimes they explicitly invoked the rule that *p'kuach nefesh* (saving a life) transcended almost all other commandments.

Since tax situations varied enormously from one country to another, and since each Jewish community had to respond to the edicts of its own locale, Jews found it harder to keep a seamless universal Jewish culture in this context than they did, for example, in regard to food, prayer, sexual ethics, and celebration. But they were not satisfied to let different approaches to taxation blossom without regard to Torah or to Jews in other countries. Local communal authorities consulted with the Rabbis to adhere to Torah law as much as possible on these matters. Even when the Rabbis felt they must permit deviations from Torah tax law, they framed the deviations in a context of broader Torah concerns. Rabbis in different countries consulted with and learned from each other.

For example, despite differences in the ways in which outside governments imposed an overall tax on the Jewish community, the Jews apportioned it according to Jewish principles. In the Rabbis' understanding of Torah, financial ability to pay was primary. If a government named an overall sum to be collected from the Jews, even if it was a head tax or a sales tax on food, the Jewish community would levy it more heavily on the rich than the poor.

Another example: From what sources could the Rabbis draw rules for the responsibility of Jewish taxpayers to each other? They applied the Jewish law of business partnerships. One business partner was entitled to make another attest to an accurate list of their common property. Taxpayers were viewed as property-holders-in-common of the public wealth, who could therefore be required to swear that their list of taxable property was accurate. On the ground that no business partner could win personal exemption from the firm's debts, the Rabbis forbade approaching the external government for an individual tax exemption. The costs of a school or a wedding hall were assessed to everyone, not only those who had children or planned to be married.

Drawing on these Rabbinic approaches, we might ask a series of questions:

- Today, how do we define tax laws as legitimate or illegitimate? If we conclude that a particular tax has been imposed illegitimately, what is our communal responsibility? At what point should we refuse to pay? If such principled resistance leads to the danger of death or imprisonment for the community or its leaders, should the community back down?

- What about a system of "taxes" for support not of the government but of the broader Jewish community? Could the community be set up so that practically all Jews would think such taxes were legitimate? Who should pay these taxes, how, and how much?
- Should modern Jewish communities enter into public debates on tax policy? Should they try to apply principles of Torah to issues of taxation?
- Should rabbis and educators be addressing individual members of the Jewish community about their ethical responsibilities in regard to taxes?
- Is any group of citizens so crucial to the public culture (as the Rabbis thought they themselves were) as to be exempt from taxes?
- Do the Rabbis' views of what tax money should be spent for and who should pay more and less have validity today?

In this arena, as in all the others involving money, there is much about the economic world of the dispersed Jewish community of the last two thousand years that may seem familiar to us. But there are also enormous differences. Perhaps the greatest are not so much in the narrow realm of economics but rather in the spiritual and ethical context that the Rabbis wove around and into issues of money.

Today, most Jews lives' are interwoven with those of the larger community much more than the Rabbis ever envisioned. Rarely do ethical issues involving money arise only among Jews with each other, and still less among Jews who respect and use Jewish tradition. Distinguishing between a "particularist" ethics among Jews and a "universalist" ethics between individuals of all communities is harder, for the communities are much more intertwined than before. So the influence of rabbis today as spiritual and ethical interpreters of Torah covers much smaller areas of life. For rabbis today to act as ethical guides, they would have to draw on the wisdoms of other cultures as well as the wisdom of Torah.

Still, there are ways for rabbis to play exactly this role. For example, nowadays many business disputes are settled by arbitration or mediation rather than by lawsuit. There have been occasions when disputants have named rabbis as arbitrators—one party to the dispute naming one rabbi, the other party another, and the two rabbis selecting a third. If the disputants agree to accept the rabbis' decision as binding, it can be enforced in court. In this way, the wisdom of Torah and of those trained in the approach of Torah can be brought to bear even though a secular court might not itself use religious teaching to arrive at its conclusions.

To note still another possibility: Increasingly, Jewish organizations—generally communal rather than "religious"—have been filing briefs as *amici curiae* (friends of the court) in regard to secular legal and policy issues. Synagogues, *havurot*, and religiously committed individuals could begin to do this as well, presenting the varied Torah-rooted outlooks on public issues. Without trying to make Torah the constitution of a secular society, Jews could bring it forth from the exile of irrelevance and invisibility.

XVIII. FROM RUNAWAY SLAVES
TO SOCIALISTS

"We are a band of runaway slaves." So the Pesach Seder holds up the mirror to the Jewish people. In all the long centuries of exile, Jews looked year after year into that mirror, and saw themselves always as the oppressed, the poor, the outsiders. Slaves who had been promised a land of freedom and prosperity—but who were still only strangers on a journey toward that land.

Not only in the distant mythic past, but in the painful present. "In every generation," the Haggadah says, "one rises up to destroy us." "In every generation, we must look upon ourselves as if we, not our forebears only, go forth from slavery to freedom."

A century ago, the modern world beckoned many Jews toward freedom. Freedom from their ghettoization, and freedom from poverty and economic exploitation. They looked toward the shattering of Pharaoh's power—and for many of them, that meant the shattering of the economic systems that had made them slaves.

In the lifetime of my own grandfather, Eastern European Jews moved away from using and thinking about money in the same way they had for the last thousand years, into the Modern Age. My grandfather, "Pop," grew up in a small town near Kiev, in the Ukraine. It was desperately poor until a Hassidic rebbe and a Russian doctor moved to town. Then Jews came to the town to be healed by the rebbe, and Russians to be healed by the doctor; both brought money, and the town rose from despair to simple poverty.

Pop's grandfather was a tailor; Pop's father was a tailor; Pop was taught to be a tailor, and started working at it when he was eleven. The family was an economic unit. Twice a year, during Pesach in the spring and Sukkot in the fall, debts between families or between bosses and workers were settled, and agreements were made for work and wages between, as Pop wrote, "the poor bosses and the poorer workers." When Pop's father left for America, he and his mother supported themselves with more tailoring, even after money began to arrive from Brooklyn.

According to Pop's own memory of his childhood, he had been fiercely committed to the traditional Jewish communal values: combining hard work and shrewd judgment in individual enterprise with a sense of fairness, communal responsibility, sharing, *tzedakah*, and limits on conspicuous consumption.

Fairness: that was crucial. Demanding fairness at cheder from the *melamed*, fairness from the Russian police chief, fairness from the goatherds who stole Pop's bread and buttons and taunted him for being a Jew. Above all, demanding economic fairness—the right to be paid fairly by his own mother for the work he was doing as a tailor to support the family. And his right to protest through a slowdown (not quite a strike), when she wouldn't pay him more.

Then in 1891, only fourteen years old, Pop himself set off for America. He settled first in Brooklyn and then in Washington, D.C. A tailor he remained— even, at one point, the ship's tailor for passengers on the *Leviathan*, a fancy trans- atlantic steamer.

Sometime between 1891 and 1920—no one is quite sure when—he became a shop steward for the Amalgamated Clothing Workers union, and an organizer for the Socialist party. In 1928, my father, still too young to vote, begged Pop to trade with him: If Pop would vote for Al Smith, the Democratic candidate for president, who had at least a chance of winning, my dad would in exchange vote Socialist in 1932. No deal, said Pop. Instead he kept on voting "Shoshalist."

"Fairness" had won. Being-a-rebel had won. Somewhere along that journey, Pop decided that fairness for himself alone was connected with fairness for all workers. His doubts about the ethical shape of that tiny village in the Ukraine, governed as it was by Rabbinic law and lore, had become an outlook that pervaded all of life— in the same breath, an affirmation and a rejection of the Rabbinic path to fairness.

In this Pop was by no means unusual. Many of the leading political theorists and activists of Eastern European Jewry, as well as many ordinary workers, went the same journey. Why this great change?

First of all, entering Modernity meant entering the broader, non-Jewish society.

Before the Modern Age, when Jews lived mostly in separate communities, what Jews thought about the uses of money affected only Jews. Jewish attitudes toward money had very little impact on the wider society beyond the physical or figurative walls of the ghetto.

Then as various communities entered the modern world, what Jews thought about money began to affect the larger society. Jews started businesses that sold goods in the wider world. Jews wrote political pamphlets that were read in the wider world. Jews joined labor unions. Jews voted. How did they translate and transform their earlier understanding of the uses of money to fit this new situation?

There were two main factors in this process: First, since Jews were used to a combination of competitive enterprise and social welfare inside the Jewish com- munity, they sought some version of this combination outside. The modern capitalism the Jews were entering had plenty of competitive enterprise, but there was little provision for communal social welfare. That was what many Jews missed—and sought.

Second, practically all Jews felt like outsiders entering the broader society. In almost all European countries, the legitimacy of the state itself was rooted in its Christian character. The entrenched holders of wealth and power were those most likely to try keeping Jews outside. So most Jews leaned toward a politics and an economics that would be more inclusive of outsiders: themselves and others. Depending on how top-down, rigid, and hostile was the particular version of modern society around them, the Jews felt more (or less) outside. The more "outside" they felt, the more likely they were to support reform, transformation, or revolution.

So most Jews looked for allies among other outsiders.

They did not always find support where they looked. In czarist Russia, Jews who sought allies among the peasants were sometimes rejected because the peasantry defined itself as much by its religious and national solidarity as by its economic situation. In some cases, the peasant farmers looked on Jews as their most immediate antagonists, hired by landowners to collect their rents—and extended their fear and anger to all Jews.

In most of Europe, people who were uprooted from the soil or from small shops to become the new industrial workers included Jews; and many of these Jews became highly literate, tireless, and politically well-informed activists in the myriad of labor unions and socialist parties.

FIVE VERSIONS OF SOCIALISM

In the large Jewish communities that lived in western Russia, Poland, Lithuania, and parts of the German and Austrian empires, from the 1890s through the 1930s there was an astounding burst of political and cultural energy. Five main currents of labor and socialist theory and practice emerged—each with many subflavors and factions:

- Bundism (from the name of the Yiddisher Arbeiter Bund, or Jewish Workers Union), which organized Jewish workers in Yiddish-speaking unions and political parties, separately from Russian or Polish workers; strengthened secularist Yiddish culture and opposed Rabbinic authorities and traditional religion; insisted Jews should remain in Eastern Europe and organize against its czarist or right-wing governments, through armed resistance and revolution if necessary (as in Russia in 1905 and 1917 and Poland after 1939) or elections if possible (as in Poland between the world wars); and they hoped to create democratic socialist societies in which freely elected governments led by unions and left-wing political parties would control the railroads, the steel industry, and banks.

- Labor Zionism, which believed that only in the Land of Israel could Jews create a socialist society where Jewish culture might flourish and become a beacon of justice to other societies. Most Labor Zionists were secularists, but a minority were religious and interpreted Judaism as supporting a welfare state, labor unions, and so forth. Some Labor Zionists focused on organizing large labor unions, producer and consumer cooperatives, and political parties that could shape the future of the *yishuv*, or Jewish settlement, in Palestine; others focused on creating small communities (ultimately called *kibbutzim* from the Hebrew word for "collect" or "assemble") that would own land collectively, make all decisions through town meetings, and share all income, work, and child-rearing.

- "Universalist socialism," which argued that a separate Jewish society and culture, religious or secular, in Eastern Europe or the Middle East, was an anachronism, and that all workers should struggle together for a society in which divisions between Russians, Poles, and Jews would disappear. Some of these "universalists" (a tag I am applying to them; they called themselves variously Socialists, Communists, Bolsheviks, Mensheviks, Marxists, Leninists, Trotskyists) hoped for a grass-roots revolution and a democratic socialism. Others believed that only a centralized elite political party could bring about the necessary changes.

   In Russia some Jews adhered to the Communist Party, and after the Bolshevik victory in 1917 ultimately took an active part in stamping out not only Bundists and Zionists but also practically all other independent grassroots groups in the Soviet Union.

- "Pragmatic emigrant socialism" (again, this is a tag I am applying to many different groups and families on the basis of their actions more than their theories), which encouraged Jews to leave Eastern Europe for any Western country—chiefly the United States, but also Canada, Australia, England, and Argentina—that offered industrial jobs, minimal anti-Semitism, and open space for organizing unions and political groups. This worldview became the basis for Jewish labor organizing in the United States, especially in the garment industry, where Jews often led unions made up of large numbers of Jewish, Italian, and other immigrant workers; for Jewish participation in the Socialist party and later in some factions of the Democratic party; and also for the rise of the Arbeiterring, or Workmen's Circle, and similar social-political organizations.

   The emigration of Eastern European Jews to America ended almost entirely with World War I. One generation later, the widespread suffering of the Great Depression of the 1930s convinced a number of young American Jews who came from working-class backgrounds, and had a first-in-the-family college education that capitalism could not meet human needs. Some of them joined the Communist Party USA and others became members of various Trotskyist and democratic socialist organizations.

• "Anarchism" or "communitarian/utopian socialism," which argued that huge institutions like the state and labor unions with professional staffs could never provide workers with control over their own lives and actual equality. Instead, workers should focus on radically reducing or getting rid of top-down governments as well as top-down businesses. Workers would create their own face-to-face communities to run farms and factories and set up ad hoc committees to deal with intercommunity problems like transportation. Some Jewish anarchists or communitarian socialists, like Emma Goldman in America and Gustav Landauer in Germany, did most of their work in the general society. Others, like Martin Buber, focused their teaching in the Jewish community and wove religious themes (especially the thought and the communal life of Hassidic groups) together with modern anarchist thought. Some Diaspora groups, like chicken-farmer communities in New Jersey and California and (more numerous and important) Israeli kibbutzim, owed much to this strand of Jewish thought. Anarchism was stronger among Jewish workers in England and America than it was in Eastern Europe, but nowhere was it as strong as more state-oriented socialism.

One important fact to note about these new energies is that almost all rejected the model of Rabbinic Judaism and indeed of religion altogether. For many Jewish socialists, Rabbinic law and the Rabbis' control of the Jewish community felt as rigid and narrow as the exclusion of Jews from the broader society and the oppression of workers by the economic system. As they sought to democratize their political and economic lives, they sought also to democratize their community and culture. By choosing secularism, however, many socialists cut themselves off from much of the rich Jewish language of spiritual search and celebration.

For the first time in thousands of years, women took an important role in shaping and leading Jewish life, through the new socialist movements. In theory, almost all these movements affirmed the full equality of women. Even though that theory was not usually carried fully into practice, the fact that the equality of women and men was held even as a vision and goal was a profound departure from Rabbinic Judaism.

In many aspects of the great socialist upheaval, women did in fact emerge as leaders and activists, women like Emma Goldman, Rosa Luxemburg, Clara Lemlich, and Golda Meir. Thousands of Jewish women whose names did not enter the history books took major roles in organizing garment workers' unions, setting up kibbutzim, fighting in Partisan bands against the Nazis, and in many other efforts to transform society.

The rapidly changing Eastern European communities that seeded most of these forms of Jewish labor and socialist practice were badly damaged by the cataclysm of World War I, and were later practically wiped out by the Nazi Holocaust. What remained?

- In many parts of the Jewish world, there were strong impulses toward democratization in general and toward the equality of women in particular. These impulses colored both what Jews did about the general society, and what they did about the internal structures of the Jewish community.
- In the Land of Israel, a Labor Zionist community developed that shaped the major pre-state Zionist institutions and ultimately the government, labor unions, and many labor-owned businesses of the State of Israel. The Israeli economy remained basically capitalist, but with strong direction from the state, a very strong welfare component, and a strong sense that the Labor-owned businesses owed more to Israeli society as a whole than to their own profits. By the late 1970s, however, Labor Zionism became much weaker, intellectually, economically, and politically.
- In the United States and other Western societies, there arose loose religious and cultural networks of Westernized but Jewishly conscious liberal and progressive Jews, which by the 1970s were very rarely socialist, but typically were more suspicious of big business and more supportive of social welfare programs than most other ethnic or religious groups with comparable economic status.
- Inside the Soviet Union before its collapse, there were extremely weak cultural links and connections among Jews, extremely weak and mostly state-corrupted unions, and hardly any independent socialist thought among Jews or anyone else.

Of course, not all Jews fit into these different socialist categories, as broad and porous as they are.

The several million Jews who lived in the Muslim countries of North Africa and the Middle East did not experience Modernity in any way similar to European Jews—until most of them emigrated to the new State of Israel in the 1950s and 1960s. Their experience of Islam, of nonindustrial societies, and then of Israel did not result in their becoming socialists in the European manner.

During the nineteenth and early twentieth centuries, especially in Western Europe and the United States, a relatively small number of Jews found business enterprise individually rewarding and enriching. Although these Jews were somewhat more likely to support public education, Social Security, and similar government programs than were Christians in analogous positions, few of them became socialists.

Despite these exceptions, I think it is fair to say that most Jewish thought about money in this period of our history was given its basic coloring by a vision of a democratic socialism where the people would use their government to support economic equality and prevent economic disasters. Even many Jews who did not espouse this vision were drawn in its direction and saw merit in many specific reforms that were originally proposed by socialists.

GRASS-ROOTS COMMUNITIES OF MONEY

Even though most of these socialist outlooks focused on what governments should do, nongovernmental groups were created to deal in Jewish ways with questions of money. We will look at two important forms of these grass-roots Jewish "communities of money": the immigrant *landsmannschaft* and similar groups, especially in North America, and the Israeli kibbutz.

When Eastern European Jews arrived in an American city, one of their first efforts was to re-create a community something like the village, town, or region they had left. People whom they knew or had heard about, a local version of Yiddish or Hungarian that did not sound strange, connections back home with people who might or might not soon be arriving in America—all these were reasons to stick together.

What did the immigrants need? Somewhere to sleep and money to tide them over when they first settled, until they could find a job and a room. Later on, a source of money to invest in buying a sewing machine or a stock of goods to resell. When somebody got sick, money for a doctor, and enough money to live on when no wages were coming in. A burial ground.

In short, money. Money for urgent welfare needs and money for long-term investment, for economic development.

The *landsmannschaften* and such groups provided a way to meet these needs. When I was growing up in Baltimore, for example, my mother, grandmother, and two aunts, as well as many women on our block and at least a hundred from our neighborhood, were members of the Ladies Cooperative Progressive Society. They met one evening a month for a pleasant get-together, and at the same time deposited at least a specified minimum amount of money as a loan to "the Co-op." Then members were able to apply to a loan committee to borrow money at no or very low interest for medical expenses, college tuition, or similar family costs. The Society was a social club as well as an economic support group. Once a year, the women celebrated, with their husbands, at a gala downtown banquet. At least once a summer, several rickety school buses roamed the Baltimore Jewish neighborhoods to pick up Co-op families so that they could travel together to a beach on Chesapeake Bay. There they bustled around with huge thermos bottles of lemonade and dozens of roast beef sandwiches and pickles, sang Yiddish and American songs, swam or dangled their feet in the water.

The group was not political in the explicit sense. When the word "progressive" fell out of favor in the general American media in the late 1940s, because Henry Wallace's Progressive party was considered "pinko," the women had a long debate over whether to change their name. They decided that they had called themselves "progressive" long before Henry Wallace came along, that they were clear about their own identity, and that they would keep on calling themselves what they pleased. Later, however, when federal regulations insisted that groups not call themselves "cooperatives" unless they adhered to certain rules of structure and procedure, the women threw up their hands and became the Women's Beneficial Society.

Although the Co-op had no explicit politics and did not address the public issues of the day, there was a very important implicit political effect of its work. It empowered women; it empowered immigrants and their daughters; it empowered Jews; and it did all this on a one-person—one-vote basis, rather than one-dollar—one-vote, and at little or no cost for interest, rather than market rates. What is more, it assumed in all this that money and friendship were intertwined, not opposed; that a real community shared access to money just as it shared lemonade, or swimming, or singing, or learning how to organize a formal banquet. No one called this "socialism," either to acclaim it or to denounce it. It just seemed normal, or at least normal for Jews.

Some of the *landsmannschaften* were much more consciously political than this. Some were affiliated with various national Jewish political or labor groupings. Many of them kept in touch with Jewish communities in Eastern Europe, helped them when they were in trouble, tried to keep open their paths of immigration to America, spoke out in their support when the Nazi noose tightened.

All of them, explicitly political or not, were important instruments in empowering the immigrant Jewish community to enter and succeed in the American economy. Ironically, even if their internal arrangements were quasi-socialist economic democracy, they were crucial in making possible the entry of Jews into the professions and businesses of capitalist America.

For the period from about 1880 to about 1960, the *landsmannschaften* were also crucial in reaffirming the shared concerns and the ethnic (not religious) Jewishness of the community; at the same time they enabled the community to learn American mores and exercise American power.

Meanwhile, Eastern European Jews who headed for Palestine instead of North America were creating a different sort of grass-roots "community of money." Of all the experiments that workers, Jewish or otherwise, have created for trying to live the socialist vision in the flesh-and-blood present, the one that has probably come the closest, and certainly has lasted the longest, is the Israeli kibbutz.

Kibbutz membership was wholly voluntary, unlike the collective farms of the Soviet Union. Internal debates were vigorous and almost endless, resolved only by decisions of the entire membership in town meetings. And these debates were about every aspect of life together—from education to music to food to money to family life, and even to rest.

The kibbutzim were certainly Jewish, but in a new way. Their daily tongue was Hebrew, but few of them prayed or studied Torah together. They drew on the Bible as a cultural resource for contemporary Hebrew writing—but put aside the Talmud and most Rabbinic writings. As the basis for making everyday ethical and communal decisions, they used modern philosophy, political theory, and psychology much more than religious Jewish thought (except that in the broadest sense, they echoed the calls of the Prophets for social justice). Some of them did draw on Hassidic thought and approaches, especially when it was intertwined with Western thought, as in the work of Martin Buber. They voted on what food to buy and how to run the kitchen and the dining room; but few of them kept kosher. Farmers themselves, they observed the agricultural Jewish festivals, but not such spiritual ones as Yom Kippur. They viewed themselves as the front line of physical defense for the Jewish people—in the Land of Israel and elsewhere.

On issues of work and money, the kibbutz made collective decisions. The ultimate authority was the weekly town meeting of all adults. They decided collectively what crops to plant, what prices to charge, what tools to buy, what industries to enter, how to assign jobs, and how to allocate money for internal needs like food, clothing, shelter, and education.

Everyone was economically and politically equal (until, in the late 1950s, some kibbutzim began to hire temporary workers for specific jobs). All who joined turned over their private property and money to the kibbutz, and became equal owners of its collective wealth. For decades, kibbutz members got only the smallest individual allowances to buy items for personal use. Their food and clothing were bought collectively. The members ate together in large dining halls. Their houses were built and maintained collectively. Books, films, concerts were provided by the community. Children were reared and educated and generally slept in separate children's houses, while spending time with their own families each day. Whether children went to college was decided by the kibbutz, according to its own needs and resources and those of Israel.

The kibbutzim elected all their officials for short terms, and insisted on rotating these jobs so that a local power elite would not emerge. (Sometimes it did anyway.) The elected work manager assigned jobs to the kibbutz members, partly according to ability and partly to encourage rotation and flexibility. No one went without a job; no one went without an "income" in the form of equal amounts of food, clothing, shelter.

In the process of decision-making, women were far more nearly equal to men in the kibbutzim than in any previous Jewish communities. But even there, work assignments came to have a strong gender bias: women in the kitchen and child care, men in high-prestige agricultural field work with tractors.

Warnings that equal sharing would eliminate the competitive urge toward greater efficiency were refuted by studies that showed that as economic units, the kibbutzim were about as efficient as Israeli businesses of the same size—perhaps slightly more so. Co-ownership in such an intense community, where everyone felt responsible for the prosperity of everyone else, seemed to take the place of individual competition. Even the dinner table became a place for members to share ideas about how to increase production. Such conversations did not require the cost of financial "incentive pay," and indeed they enhanced communal morale.

As the kibbutzim matured into second and third generations, economic changes in Israel and the world pushed many of them toward adding industrial or service enterprises (like tourism) to their agricultural origins. Desires for emotional privacy resulted in some internal privatization: family telephones, televisions, kitchenettes, children's rooms. Yet the economic equality of all members and the collective ownership of housing, farmland, factories, and all other basic facilities continued. Those members who left the kibbutz complained much more about the limits that the life put on emotional, spiritual, intellectual, and artistic exploration than about kibbutz economics.

Throughout Zionist and Israeli history, the kibbutzim have also acted in the public sphere. They deployed settlements in frontier areas that were not necessarily desirable from a purely economic standpoint, in order to assert Jewish control over those areas. They provided key members of the officer corps of the Israeli army. They supported the Labor and Socialist parties and the nationwide Histadrut federation of labor unions and its associated businesses, health insurance system, and educational centers. At the same time that the kibbutzim supported the government's and Histadrut's welfare programs, they took a competitive part in the country's basically capitalist economy as if they were conventional businesses. As a result, they contributed to the strong "welfare capitalist" tone of Israeli society.

These two kinds of grass-roots "communities of money"—*landsmannschaften* and kibbutzim—show how the Jews from Eastern Europe carried their own centuries-old experience of face-to-face community into new places and a new age. Responding to the challenge of modernity, both simultaneously reasserted Jewish solidarity and helped Jews affect the larger society. In both approaches, there was an attempt to preserve a Jewish culture without the Jewish religion, and without a conscious spiritual practice or theory.

JEWS WITH MONEY

By the beginning of the 1990s, what might be called the "century of Jewish socialism" was over. The money in Jewish pockets and the ideas about money in Jewish heads had been transformed. Indeed, as we look around at the Jewish world in the 1990s, we see that something strange—almost astounding—has happened.

For generations and millennia, the Jewish people has been a poverty-stricken, marginal, oppressed, victimized community, sometimes enslaved, sometimes massacred. Only two generations ago, Jews suffered the Nazi Holocaust, one of the deepest moments of oppression in all of human history. It confirmed the sense of victimization that went back to the archetypal slavery in Egypt and to the shattering of the Jewish communities in the Land of Israel by Assyria, Babylon, and Rome.

And yet within the lifetimes of survivors of the Holocaust, the Jewish people has become one of the more economically comfortable and politically well-defended small communities in the world, and the tenor of Jewish ideas about money has changed. No longer does the ultimate vision of socialism act as a magnet in Jewish life as it did in the beginning of the twentieth century.

How did this happen?

First of all, socialist organizing brought about an unexpected and ironic effect. Strong labor unions and substantial backing for social welfare programs (including that of the heavily Jewish unions and most of the Jewish voting population) changed capitalism without ending it. They created welfare capitalism, not democratic socialism. They paved the way for broad-based personal and communal prosperity—including a wave of Jewish upward mobility—without socialism.

After World War II, the realistic choices in the world seemed to be between welfare capitalism and the Soviet version of undemocratic socialism. Welfare capitalism flourished in the West for fifty years after the Great Depression. The Soviet

Union was the largest society that called itself socialist (though many socialists said it was not socialist at all); and the Soviet Union fell behind economically, parodied democracy, shattered human rights, and often adopted anti-Semitic and anti-Israel policies. Though many Jews felt sympathy for efforts like those in Czechoslovakia and Chile to create "socialism with a human face," these efforts were quickly destroyed by the contending great powers.

More and more Jews concluded that capitalism—with measures that safeguarded human rights and religious freedom and provided education, health care, and jobs for almost everybody—not only was the best practical alternative for themselves and most people, but also came closest to the search for social justice that Jewish culture and religion commanded.

This emerging worldview converged with a shift in the social and economic lives of many Jews in Western countries. Jews were unusually well prepared to enter the new welfare-capitalist economies that they had helped fight for. Many of them were trained to seek more formal education and became skilled individual entrepreneurs, yet had the collective support of their Jewish communities, including the ability to borrow money from *landsmannschaften* and similar groups. This was a perfect mix of preparation for the economy after World War II, when the leading edge of the economy was not railroad building or steel production but a great expansion of academic institutions, research, social welfare jobs, the health industry, the "law industry," and communications industries like film and television.

In addition, the long Western tradition of anti-Semitism was profoundly weakened by the West's horror at the Nazi Holocaust. So the conventional barriers to Jewish entry into crucial sections of Western economies were much lower than before.

Large numbers of Jews sought and found jobs in the expanding public or semi-public sector—as teachers, social workers, physicians, lawyers. For these Jews, the theory of welfare capitalism, their surviving sense of Jewish commitment to social justice, and their own jobs cohered.

What has this meant in the real lives of large Jewish communities?

- Israel became an economically and technologically advanced society, though by no means as prosperous as countries like Sweden. Though it is burdened by the danger of war and though there is an economic gap between Jews of Western and Eastern origins, its Jewish community as a whole is not economically marginal, especially when compared with that of the Israeli Arabs and Palestinians who are part of the same economic system.
- In the United States, the Jewish community has become broadly affluent (though still with pockets of the poor—especially among the elderly, divorced

and widowed women, some recent immigrants, and recently, younger people who cannot find jobs commensurate with their educations). Indeed, in the last twenty years a sizable class of American Jews with great wealth and power has emerged. An even larger number of Jewish lawyers and doctors and real estate developers and other business people have amassed enough wealth that their children will be financially secure.

- In the countries that used to be the Soviet Union, people as a whole are suddenly much poorer than they used to be, including the Jews. If Russia and Ukraine do not recover economically, a classic victimization scenario might be played out against the Jews. But the Jewish community is not, for the moment at least, more deprived than other Russians or Ukrainians.

- Most members of the smaller Jewish communities around the world, as in England, France, Canada, Brazil, Argentina, South Africa, and Australia, are at least as well off as the average citizen—and often better off.

All these developments pose some deeply puzzling questions to Jewish thoughts and practices about money, and indeed present a challenge to the Jewish people's most basic assumptions about its place in the world.

Remember: Generation after generation, millennium after millennium, the Jewish people has said to itself, "We are a band of runaway slaves, banded together in a journey toward the world of freedom, serving a God Who seeks justice and freedom. We are the generous poor, we are the justice-seeking strangers, we are the courageous oppressed, we are a people always on a journey, never well fed and never satisfied. We are joyful, yes!—for we take joy in our struggle to turn the world around—but satisfied? Never."

Now imagine that same people when it has become affluent and well defended.

Who are we? If we are no longer runaways, exiles, victims, do we need to turn the world around? If we are comfortable and well protected, do we *want* to turn the world around? If not, what is our purpose? Is there indeed a "we," a band of us, at all?

These are the questions that now face the Jewish people, questions for which "money" is both a central issue and a broader metaphor.

MEANWHILE

The first responses to these questions might be called "meanwhile" responses. That is, they are ad hoc, provisional, and aimed at dealing with bits and pieces of the new reality. Some few individuals and groups may begin to put forward a whole new worldview, or several competing ones, but the community as a whole is more likely to try a bit of this...and that...and the other...meanwhile.

The big Jewish institutions are probably the last to realize that the old ways are not working. It is individuals, families, the young who drop out. At first they are written off as oddballs. Only as the dropout numbers grow, only as the official institutions of the community find their own functioning disturbed, do they begin to notice and then respond.

What do they notice?

In Israel, more and more young Jews shrug off Zionism. They see it either as a past dream already fulfilled or, if it continues at all, only as an irrelevant idealism, not connected to their daily lives.

In America, young Jews shrug off Judaism, the Jewish community, and even the Jewish household, as boring and irrelevant. Intermarriage rates rise, contributions to Jewish organizations drop.

Without the élan of an oppressed yet striving community, what is the point of being Jewish?

In America, when large official institutions (especially the fund-raising federations) noticed that the next generation of Jews might not connect, they began to scramble to create programs that might help protect "Jewish continuity": Send young Jews to Israel for a year. Or at least for a monthlong trip to Auschwitz and then Israel. Or at least to the Holocaust Museum in Washington, D.C. Or at least to the movie *Schindler's List.*

In other words, try to reawaken the memory and the passion of Jews as runaway slaves. But this effort does not yet address defining a new purpose for the Jewish people, one that would have to incorporate a new attitude toward money, and power, and exile, and justice, and comfort.

The Jewish community could respond by emphasizing not overall issues of Jewish identity and purpose, but specific issues of money, power, exile, justice, and comfort—and work out new Jewish approaches to these issues. And indeed, as the political changes of the last fifty years have sunk in, several new approaches to the Jewish politics of money have emerged. Some efforts to create substitutes for the "century of Jewish socialism" have been made.

I. One reaction is not really new at all, and is not really based on any new thinking: American Jews vote about thirty percentage points more "progressively" or "pro-outsider" for many candidates and economic issues than people of the same wealth and income in other ethnic groups. This might be taken as evidence that Jews have not really changed very much. Instead of outright socialism, they espouse a progressivism that is about three steps short. On the other hand, these same voters put very little energy into pressing for new programs or approaches, and there are few Jewish organizations, old or new, that take the lead in pressing for new economic programs of a progressive bent.

Some individual Jews and Jewish organizations have been in the vanguard of such "social" issues as feminism, gay rights, and the environment. The "social" label obscures the truth that all these issues have a great deal to do with economics. But this very fact is an index of the new reality: It is these issues, not economics and money as traditionally understood, that are capturing Jewish attention and energy.

2. Another reaction—"Is it good for the Jews?"—is to redefine Jewish values as wholly concerned with protecting the new wealth and political power of the Jewish community, with little concern for social justice and economic equality for the public as a whole.

Thus a minority of the American Jewish community have created a network of neo-conservatives. They are "neo"—that is, different from traditional American conservatives—mainly in that they are much readier to support military intervention overseas, most were socialists of one kind or another in their youth, and most are Jews. On economic questions, they are much more critical of government spending for the poor, and much more supportive of government spending for the military, than practically any Jews of past generations.

In Israel, some political parties take a similar stance against government spending, on the grounds that Labor economics has been suffocating the overall Israeli economy in order to protect existing jobs in particular industries.

3. Some Jews—again, a minority, but a fervent one—have combined feeling like victims with acting like victors. For some, this arises out of a deep and fearful conviction that Jews can easily be victimized again unless they master all possible opponents in advance. For others, this feeling is rooted in a fear that when those at the very bottom of the ladder try to climb up, they may not only shake Jews' precarious hold on the ladder, but even the ladder itself. Some Jews who feel these fears then seek to use their newfound wealth and power to dominate others.

These different feelings become especially apparent when Jews confront anti-Semitism in the African-American community.

—Those Jews who still identify with being a band of runaway slaves are likely to adopt a strategy of changing the basic situation that offers anti-Semitism a breeding swamp. They might, for instance, focus on supporting the comparatively numerous African-American groups that are struggling toward building their own economic base without attacking Jews or whites.

—Other Jews who fear any changes in the status quo confront the same anti-Semitism by directly counterattacking the comparatively small African-American groups in which it appears.

4. A few small groups of Jews warn that the last fifty years during which welfare capitalism has flourished represent only a temporary phenomenon. They predict that the crisis of world markets, declining wages and employment in the richest countries, environmental degradation, huge governmental deficits in the United States, all presage a major economic crisis. This argument runs that wages for many people in the first and second worlds may drop toward third world levels, welfare payments may become unbearable to middle-class taxpayers, and even public-sector high-education jobs where Jews have a major stake may dwindle.

Then Jews may not only be economically damaged but may also be socially and politically scapegoated. So, to forestall this danger as well as the danger to the larger social fabric, Jews should vigorously seek strong government intervention to create jobs, rebuild cities, and strengthen social insurance, and should seek allies among those communities already hurt by unemployment and urban decay.

It is important to note that all four responses focus on what the government should do or not do. In that sense they are all heirs of the socialist assumption that what the government does about money is by far the only important question.

Few efforts have been made to invent analogs of the *landsmannschaft* or the kibbutz for the next generation of Jews: that is, face-to-face organizations that treat money in some collective Jewish way. Today the only structure that even approximates face-to-face decision-making about money is the synagogue. Money is contributed by people who choose to join, and they elect the board that chooses how to spend it—almost always for operation of the synagogue itself, rather than for other social purposes. Rarely does the synagogue become the basis for change in the broader society, or for economic development of its members, or for the political or economic protection of the wider Jewish community.

In our generation, the most characteristic Jewish organizations for dealing collectively with money have been:

—in Israel, the government itself and such quasi-governmental organizations as the Jewish Agency and the Jewish National Fund;

—in America, large professional philanthropies in which there is little or no direct, face-to-face involvement by most of those who give the money. These so-called official philanthropies—called Jewish federations, funds, appeals, or alliances—exist in practically all Jewish communities. Their boards are made up mostly of rich or very rich people who hire professionally trained fund-raisers. This staff also becomes responsible for deciding where the money should go, within the guidelines set by the board. The leaders in the twenty or so largest Jewish communities get together to make strong recommendations to their funds about national and international needs.

The result is that between two fifths and one half of the money goes to large quasi-governmental institutions in Israel, including agencies that help resettle Jews from Russia or other countries in Israel. The rest of the money goes to large local social welfare institutions in America (like hospitals, nursing homes, social work agencies, immigrant resettlement agencies); Jewish newspapers that often act partly as fund-raising cheerleaders rather than independent community reporters and critics; some Jewish day schools; and a few national community relations agencies, especially those focused on issues of anti-Semitism.

Practically none of this money ends up going to small, avant-garde, or experimental Jewish projects, whether in Israel, America, or Russia. And practically none of it goes to helping the non-Jewish poor or dealing with general social issues.

However, in the last decade, some new Jewish funds have been established. One, the New Israel Fund, gives money to voluntarist, nongovernmental, independent, and experimental projects in Israel. Several—Mazon, the Jewish Fund for Justice, American Jewish World Service—channel explicitly Jewish funds in grants to the (mostly) non-Jewish poor in America or around the world; and The Shefa Fund concentrates on raising loan money from Jewish federations and similar groups for community-development purposes in American cities. These new groups, while much smaller than the federations, operate in basically the same way, with the result that small or medium-size donors have little impact on where they spend their money. So none of them acts like the kibbutz or the *landsmannschaft* in the sense of direct democratic face-to-face control of money.

Where does all this leave the Jewish community today?

It is no longer possible simply to return to the Rabbinic model in which Jews were a community separate from the rest of the world, in which their decisions about money affected only themselves, and in which their own identity as a band of runaway slaves was secure.

And it is no longer possible to reassert Jewish socialism as it was, since it was based on the confluence of the Jewish values of protecting the poor with the Jewish reality of being the poor.

There are four underlying issues that the Jewish community now needs to face and to provide answers for:

1. Can any worldview replace "Jewish socialism" as an overall guide to Jewish practice about money and related matters?
2. Do we need a substitute for the kibbutz or *landsmannschaft* as a face-to-face community of money—and if so, what will it be?
   a. Is it possible to create kibbutzim outside Israel, perhaps based on Jewish religious and spiritual practice rather than on nationality?
   b. If the world does face some shattering ecological crises in the form of

famines, droughts, escalating cancer rates, climatic shifts, are Jews ready to create communal organizations that can not only care for people in emergencies but meet their economic, political, and spiritual needs?

3. Can a sense of spirituality and holiness reemerge in the Jewish use of money?
4. For what purposes should Jews work together with other Jews on money questions, and for what purposes with the public at large?

Only if there are coherent answers to these questions can the worldwide Jewish community become renewed with élan and purpose.

So here we are—here I am—moving from remembering my grandparents to imagining my grandchildren. Imagining. That is what this chapter will be, imaginings of the future, with all the limitations and all the possibilities of such images.

The Rabbis taught that what images we see on coins—on money—is a central issue. On ordinary money, they said, the emperor stamps his image—and every coin is identical. But when the Ruler Who rules over all rulers puts the Divine Image on a "coin"—on every human being, says the Torah, there is the *tzelem Elohim*, the Divine Image—then every such coin is unique. For us, their sharp distinction between coin and person may be too sharp; for money is work frozen, the efforts of these human beings held suspended for a time. For us, the question is how to make sure that the Image itself remains visible on the money, not hidden by the faces of those with wealth and power.

The more I try to imagine a Jewish outlook on money that may be useful to my grandchildren and the future beyond them, the more I find myself concerned about issues that do not at first glance seem to be about money: Will there be ozone and water, plankton and forests to share life with them? Will there be a lively Jewish community to share spiritual sustenance with them?

Then, close behind, come images that are about money—not if my own grandchildren will have enough money to live on (which is what my grandparents chiefly worried about), but if others around them will: How thick will be the crowds of homeless, desperate people in their cities? Will their hospital emergency rooms be full of people who cannot afford to go anywhere else to get routine care? Will their government be spending ten times as much for prisons as for schools?

And, paradoxical as it may seem, the deeper I look into the twenty-first century the more I find myself looking back to the distant Jewish past.

Long ago, I keep remembering, the shepherds and farmers of ancient Israel were very conscious that what they did for economic reasons—the number of sheep and goats they pastured on a mountainside; the barley, figs, and grapes they grew around a village; if they annulled debts every seven years and shared the land every fifty years—evoked responses from the rain, the soil, the trees, the land around them. And that the responses of this earth—flourishing if well rested and renewed, languishing if overworked—then made a difference to the Israelite economy.

In the Modern Age, in my parents' and grandparents' generation, money and technology seemed to take the place of land. Many of us forgot this intertwining of earth and economics. The power of our technology grew so quickly that it seemed we could find air, water, oil, productive minerals, and fertile soil, for billions of humans at very little cost. Our work became so powerful and so productive that it seemed a waste of time for us to rest. Debt became a powerful incentive to work harder, produce more.

The planet seemed infinite; the frontier stretched out forever.

But the irony is that this expansive technology was itself magnifying—not eliminating!—the impact human beings have on the earth as a whole—and the planet is not, after all, infinite.

Where once a careless goatherd might denude one mountainside of trees, now a massive global corporation can wipe out whole tropical forests, thereby causing a major effect on the balance of oxygen and carbon dioxide in the worldwide atmosphere. And that change may in turn have an enormous effect on many species in the web of life, on patterns of climate and levels of the seas, and thus on the global economy of the human race.

ॐ

For all of human history, technology has been our genie in the bottle. We could call it forth to do our work and will. Suddenly the genie has grown so big that the bottle is on the verge of bursting.

Since the use of money is exactly the process by which human beings work with the earth in order to make a living, the present fragility of that earth is forcing us to reexamine how we use our money.

Let us recall once more the Torah's commands to reserve the gleanings of a field and the fruit of its corners for the poor, to let the earth rest and to annul debts, to free indentured servants, to redistribute land once a generation.

Till now, we have looked at these rules mostly as an internal matter of the Israelites' social system. Their aim was to intertwine and balance the values of entrepreneurship and equality; to recycle wealth and power, talent and imagination; to unblock hardened social arteries. However, these rules were aimed at creating not only a new kind of relationship among human beings, within society, but also a new kind of relationship between human beings and the earth. By requiring rest and putting limits on material rewards for hard work, the rules created incentives to let the earth itself rest.

Just as the Torah's commands affirm that only the Holy One rules over human society, they affirm that only the Holy One is Owner of the earth.

What would it mean to renew this outlook and extend it, not just to a single country but to our entire planet? What would it mean to shape our systems of controlling money—taxation, ownership, profits, loans, wages—so as to encourage not incessant exploitation of the earth but its rhythmic renewal? So as to foster not hopeless, rage-filled, isolated individualism, but loving families, neighborhoods, communities?

Can we translate the ancient rules about the land into rules about the use of money and of "technological capital"? What does it mean to "glean" money? How does money get to "rest"?

For example: If it is important for the earth to rest, then perhaps it is important to invest our money in businesses that help the earth to rest. Perhaps we should be consciously investing in businesses that reforest the earth instead of in businesses that cut down huge forests.

Or suppose the investment capital that goes into speeding up the technology that slashes the rain forest went instead into supporting a year-long "Shabbat" on that kind of technology? Suppose we set aside one year of every seven as a time of moratorium, a Shabbat, on technological development? A time of "resting," meditating, reflecting? Perhaps that money could help engineers, artists, philosophers, musicians, scientists, teachers, religious and spiritual adepts join the rest of us in neighborhood folk festivals and town meetings where we can reflect on what technology is sacred, and what technology is catastrophic.

One principle we could use to begin answering some of the questions we face: Make *Shabbos!* A very Jewish approach.

IS THIS A JEWISH ISSUE?

If the protection of the earth is now a global matter, does it still make sense for the Jewish people as one small culture to bring its own ancient wisdom, focused on its own land and its own community, to bear on these questions? Is this a *Jewish* issue?

It seems to me that it is. The protection extended by an effective and renewed Jewish community and culture—along with that of the Navajo community, the Buddhist community, the Amish community, the Andean and Amazonian, Cambodian and Xhosa, Basque and Bosnian people—is necessary to prevent the destructive triumph of a destructive technology. Only such communities, not isolated individuals, can stand up to the all-devouring global technology and economy that threaten to damage life on Planet Earth. Only such communities can point the way to an alternative.

Indeed, the weakening of small traditions and communities is both one of the causes and one of the results of technology run amok. There is a vicious cycle:

The new global technology weakens the traditional communal cultures. The weakened cultures find it easier to meet their urgent needs by using the global technology, thus further strengthening what has weakened them, and enfeebling themselves.

How does this work? First, traditional cultures, both physically and in their social structure, get in the way of a "universal" bureaucracy, economy, and technology.

- Physically, most of the traditional communities are closely connected with a piece of earth, and over the centuries have worked out a way, a path of living with that piece of earth sustainably. The global economy seeks to integrate this small ecosystem and economy into itself, wrecking the old life patterns in the process. Often the people are forced to move—whether they are Jews in the Land of Israel two thousand years ago, or British farmers two hundred years ago, or Native Americans a century ago, or Tibetans forty years ago.
- Socially, the patterns of face-to-face communal life get in the way of industrial and political bureaucracies that need to conscript soldiers, organize factory workers, and fill new territories.
- Once the old patterns have been disrupted, people must quickly find some new way to feed, house, educate, and develop themselves. Their easiest alternative is often the global technology and economy. So the global systems then grasp more power to push aside indigenous communities.
- As the global systems learn to automate not only the production of material goods but the production of information and knowledge, they increasingly divide workers into the Disemployed and Overworked. Increasing productivity is not channeled into more leisure, more community, more family, more "Shabbat" but into more exhausting brainwork for longer hours on the one hand, and involuntary idleness, homelessness, crime, and prison on the other. Enormous profits go to a few.
- Exhausted or impoverished, most of the Disemployed and the Overworked give up on community, spirituality, family, or active citizenship. They resort to the mass media, which teach material advancement. The global systems grasp still more power.

The process is much like the annihilation of species. Modern techno-industrialism remakes huge areas of the earth in order to make more money or power; the variegated local species die as their ecosystems disappear; the species that survive are those most able to live on a leveled, homogenized earth—*Homo sapiens*, the sparrow, and the cockroach, for example.

Why do I say that communities can resist and reshape the world when isolated individuals will fail? Because in my experience, communities can generate the spiritual power that makes it possible for individuals to choose *being* more instead of *having* more. If we are spiritually starving, we are more likely to gobble up the earth. If we are spiritually well fed, we can afford to live more simply and let the earth rest in its necessary rhythm.

What does it mean to be spiritually well fed? It means that with the most ancient ceremonies and with new ones, with chanted words and dancing gestures, with special clothes and feasts and fasts, we celebrate together the life-cycle ceremonies of birth and adolescence, adulthood and eldering and death; the earth-connected ceremonies of seed and sprout and flower and fruit; the historical path of liberation, covenant, journey, polity, exile; the spiritual spiral of emergence, encounter, fulfillment, retreat, and renewal. If we do this well, we will find more joy in the sharing of pain, love, and struggle; less need to swallow up the earth by amassing the idols of the mall.

Our most profound decisions about the earth and economics are spiritual ones: Do we view ourselves as owners of the earth, as stewards of the earth, or as participants in the earth? Are we creators of wealth or part of the Creation through which wealth flows? Only out of our answers to these basic questions come economic, technological, and political decisions. Viable visions and plans for a replenished earth will come from communities of spiritual renewal—the same communities that are most endangered by the systems that devour the earth.

Communities: plural. No one culture is sufficient, precisely because each is different from the other. The face of the One becomes apparent through diversity; obscuring any facet of God's Image may darken the Infinite Face. Genetically, the loss of a single species may weaken the whole web of life. Culturally, the loss of any one community may deprive the world of a wisdom that is crucial to the survival of all. Here means become ends, and ends become means. Each species, each culture, in its uniqueness is both itself a sacred end and at the same time a means of safeguarding the sacred diversity that is God's end.

The Jewish people is one of the endangered cultures, and it is one that can provide an alternative rooted in its spiritual practice.

The modern world calls us to extend the wisdom of Torah to the earth as a whole. And the modern world gives us new reasons to renew the strength of Jewish culture and community, not just with gifts of money or debits on a faceless electronic system, but with songs of prayer and celebration, with pages of ancient Torah and modern poetry. Face-to-face, house-to-house, wherever possible, and also with E-mail and CD-ROM, with new technology shaped to the needs of "neighborhood" and "shtetl."

If the earth is spirit, the pocketbook is prayer.

All of this is theory, imagining. In the everyday life of the down-to-earth Jew, how will these issues arise? How can we turn our pocketbooks to prayer?

DOES THE JEWISH PEOPLE HAVE A PURPOSE?

One way of approaching these issues is to start from the bottom up. Look at the small steps that have already been taken toward new ways of addressing money matters Jewishly, and we can imagine the other small steps. The other way is to start from the grand vision: What do we hope the Jewish people will be, and how would that affect our actions in the sphere of money?

Both ways are useful, and we should follow both, letting each have an impact on the other.

I believe that the Jewish people has a purpose in the world. I believe that from generation to generation, from era to era, that purpose unfolds as the world changes and our understanding of ourselves deepens.

For what is unique in the Jewish purpose, I look to the meaning of Shabbat. Shabbat, says the Voice at Sinai, is the sign of the covenant between God and the People Israel. And when I listen to the Ten Sayings that were uttered at Sinai, it is Shabbat that is for me the most unexpected. The rest: Don't kill, don't steal, honor your parents, all these seem the threads that any community would have to weave. Shabbat? Now that's peculiar. That call to a constant practice of a rhythm— work and rest, action and reflection, doing and being—is unique. Unique, not in the sense that only we as a people should live the practice, but that on us is the burden of understanding and teaching its meaning.

What is the meaning of Shabbat? *Two* meanings. As with many issues in Jewish thought, there is "On the one hand..." and "On the other hand..."—and both are true.

- Shabbat marks the cosmic rhythm of rest and renewal in which is rooted the health of all the earth; for God fulfilled the creating of the world by making a day of not-creating. (So says the Book of Exodus.)
- Shabbat marks the liberation of slaves—not only of Israelites from their Egyptian masters, but also of all who work for Israelites and might become their slaves if there were no Shabbat. (So says the Book of Deuteronomy.)

Later in this book we will learn more about the history and meaning of Shabbat. Here I need to say only this: That in our generation, I believe that the world needs three things from the Jewish people:

1. To seek the healing of our earthy planet—especially by making a Shabbat from the last five centuries of unremitting technological inventiveness;

2. To strengthen grass-roots communities and enterprises of work and celebration—both by recycling the investment capital necessary for workers and the poor to build a new economic future for themselves, and by sharing restful "Shabbat" time—time that we all have free from unending toil and tension, and from involuntary idleness, time free to think, reflect, celebrate, strengthen families, neighborhoods, and our own civic organizations;

3. To bear witness that these actions are testimonies to the Presence of God in the world.

All of these have implications for the small steps we must take to deal with money. Now let us look at what such small steps might be.

TZEDAKAH COLLECTIVES

The disappearance of *landsmannschaften* and the flattening out of the kibbutz movement have left the Jewish community almost bereft of face-to-face sharing of money and decisions about money. Even in the arena of *tzedakah* (translated as "charity," but rooted in the Hebrew word for justice), most giving is organized like a modern corporation.

Yet there are a few groups that may point the way to a renewed and revitalized process of pooling money and deciding together how to spend it, in the light of Jewish values.

In the past, the giving of *tzedakah* was a face-to-face action. Groups, called in Yiddish *chevre kaddishes* (holy fellowships), would gather within a congregation to visit the sick, bury the dead, or gather money for the poor.

In the late 1960s and early 1970s in North America, people who were dissatisfied with synagogues and other Jewish organizations began to form *havurot* (small, intimate, egalitarian, and participatory fellowships for prayer and Torah study). Then in the mid-seventies, some of these *havurot* encouraged the creation of *tzedakah* collectives, intended to bring to charitable money-giving the same kind of intimacy, participation, and equality.

These groups meet together, face-to-face, to discuss possible recipients of *tzedakah*. The participants agree in advance on what proportion of their incomes they will give—typically about 2 percent—and on a more or less collective process for deciding how to give it. The group may, for example, agree to vote on a list of acceptable recipients, and then permit individuals to give as much as they choose out of their overall donation to whichever groups they choose from the agreed-upon list. Or they may vote on collective amounts to be given from a general pool of all the donated money, leaving no funds for purely individual decision. Or they may balance the two modes, using the one and the other for different categories of giving.

Typically, the participants divide up responsibility for checking on projects that could be *tzedakah* recipients, and reporting their findings to the group as a whole. One member or another will lead a group discussion of a Jewish text or teaching about *tzedakah,* and then the group will discuss how to apply these teachings to the choices before them. The ambience is very different from writing checks to a national *tzedakah* organization such as the United Jewish Appeal or the Jewish Fund for Justice. Most of the participants plunge much deeper into learning both about the social problems that call for help through *tzedakah,* and what Jewish tradition teaches on *tzedakah.*

For some *tzedakah* collectives, sharing goes beyond money and Torah study. It might, for example, include decisions on time that members might spend working to assist groups that are healing the world.

For example, to deal with the problem of homelessness, the group might decide to give money to homeless beggars on the street, or volunteer together to help out at a local soup kitchen, or invite the homeless into their synagogue, or organize to create publicly subsidized housing, or join in building new houses with Habitat for Humanity, or support groups of squatters in moving into abandoned housing.

Participants in these *tzedakah* collectives report that their involvement feels inspiring and their field results seem good. Yet the number of collectives still appears to be much lower than the number of *havurot.* What would be ways of encouraging this process?

In American Jewish life (and perhaps among Americans generally) there seems to be a very strong taboo against the frank and open discussion of how much money people have, how much they make, how much they want to give to charity, and so on. If those with more and with less money try to talk together, strong suspicions and resentments come to the surface. The rich feel concerned that those with less money will resent them and/or hit them up; the poor feel embarrassed and humiliated, or angry and rebellious. At this historical moment, the taboo on talking about one's money is as strong as—perhaps stronger than—the taboo on talking about one's sexual life.

If money is to be part of a sacred and communal path of life, this taboo has to be ended. Only if people can talk about and celebrate together the important aspects of their lives can they become a community, or infuse those aspects with spiritual meaning. Indeed, turning a hidden secret into a communal ceremony is one of the most powerful spiritual events.

Breaking down the taboo on money talk becomes much easier if the participants have experienced sharing in other areas. People who pray together or who together study Torah in an engaged and passionate way are more likely to trust each other enough to talk freely about money.

So efforts to create *tzedakah* collectives are probably best advised to bring together households that have already been Jewishly involved together.

One of the sharpest and most difficult challenges to sharing the *tzedakah* process is that the membership of many Jewish groups may cut across lines of wealth and income. It would not be surprising, for example, for a group made up of Jewish feminists to include a single mother in her late thirties with two children, who has been struggling to keep afloat on a social worker's salary and has just lost her job because the state budget has been slashed; a prosperous professor or physician or lawyer; and a woman who has just inherited seven million dollars from a father who has done extremely well in real estate. Such gaps between the rich and the middle class, and between the middle class and the poor, often make it very hard to move beyond shame, guilt, fear, and rage. Even simple ignorance of what life is like for other people in different economic circumstances makes it difficult to have an honest discussion about what to do with money.

Out of these painful discoveries, some Jewish women's groups (borrowing from the Movement for a New Society) have developed an approach to dialogue about money that may offer new possibilities for defining *tzedakah* and organizing *tzedakah* collectives. Their approach emerged out of questions about how to pay for small conferences of Jewish women. Should everyone be charged the same official amount, and the poor secretly negotiate to pay less? What about the rich? Should there be a formal sliding scale? Would some people feel so shamed by this process as not to attend at all?

Since this issue felt real and face-to-face, rather than abstract or "macro-social," since the groups' members shared a vision of shaping a new kind of Jewish community, and since they had come to know each other well and strongly valued dialogue and openness, they decided to explore a process of "cost-sharing," which required go-round dialogues to help each member decide what she could afford to pay.

As described by one of its initiators, Felice Yeskel, the process included a series of discussions. Some were conducted in a large group that looked at the social and economic contexts of members' differences, the overall needs of the conference, and similar comparatively cerebral issues; some were held in groups of two or four, in which the members discussed their own life situations, made init.al judgments of what they could afford to contribute, and then reexamined their own situations in the light of others' pledges. The result, Yeskel reports, was not only a broad agreement on a fair way to pay the necessary conference costs, the participants had a much clearer understanding of their own financial situations and those of others and of society as a whole, as well as a strong sense of community.

The success of cost-sharing in these groups is probably based on two important elements: the overall sense of communal commitment that motivated the groups to explore this process in the first place, and the carefully worked-out details of how they did it. Where commitment already exists, or can be encouraged into being, in many different sorts of Jewish groups, it is important to take great care with the details of the process. The result could be a deepening of the sense of Jewish community and a greater willingness to see the *tzedakah* process as a part of spiritual growth.

Two additional steps would also encourage direct involvement in *tzedakah*:

- One is face-to-face organizing by rabbis, Jewish educators, social workers, and similar Jewish community workers, to encourage groups of families to do *tzedakah*
- The other is providing these groups with information not only on *tzedakah* decisions that similar groups are making, but also on Jewish aspects of the everyday use of money for non-*tzedakah* purposes: for example, the eco-kosher use of money for investment, purchasing, taxes, and the workplace. If a packet of informational newsletters were made available every month or two, sent first to rabbis and other key organizers for distribution to "*tzedakah* activists" and then to "*tzedakah* collectives, the chances would be much greater that Jewish values would be consciously applied to the use of money in many aspects of life.

SHAILAS AND TSHUVAS

Let us now look at how Jewish tradition might be applied to other money issues. Why look at such specifics? When the Rabbis made decisions, they insisted that only real cases, real people, come before them. Real *shailas*—queries—led to real *tshuvas*—responses. General principles mattered, but they could never be applied in the abstract. For us today, the deepest issues arose out of specific situations:

- Should Jews who are teachers, real estate brokers, doctors, architects, bankers, and psychotherapists urge their professional associations or unions to adopt codes of ethics about how to treat the earth? Should they form explicitly Jewish caucuses or networks in such unions? Should they draw on explicitly Jewish practices and teachings, like Shabbat, the Jubilee, the Ark of Noah, in which all species found a refuge from the disaster that human misdeeds brought on the earth?

- Should Jews and the organized Jewish community help create and support consumer co-ops? Should these co-ops be made up of Jews, or be open to the whole public? Are there values rooted in Judaism that such co-ops should pursue whether they are Jewishly focused or not? For example, should Jewishly sponsored co-ops commit themselves to strengthen the collective market for organic foods, reusable packaging, renewable energy?

- Where should Jews and Jewish organizations invest their money when they are hoping for a profitable return? Is maximizing profit the one correct concern, or should Jews apply Jewish values of social responsibility to when they make investment choices. Should Jews avoid investing in companies that exploit workers, red-line poor neighborhoods, or pollute the earth? Should Jews and Jewish organizations take an active hand in creating investment funds to support grass-roots economic development in communities of the poor and the excluded?

- What about purchases Jews make? What is the relationship between "having" and "being"? How much material ownership is "enough"? Are intangible purchases like education and psychotherapy different from tangible items like cars and houses? Should we avoid buying from companies that abuse the earth, and buy instead from companies that are making the strongest efforts to heal the earth?

- Are there ways in which Jewish values and precepts can help people settle disputes over money without going to court? Should we be proactively encouraging the use of rabbis as arbitrators? Should we encourage the use of Torah in filing *amicus curiae* briefs? Should we go beyond "friend of the court" status to bring our own lawsuits on behalf of the poor and the voiceless and on behalf of the redwoods, the grizzly, the frog, the rivers of water and air that cannot speak?

- Since a synagogue, a Jewish community center, a nursing home, a federation building, is a pool of money and mortar as well as people, should the board of each one determine how much to spend on pesticides to keep the lawn pretty or on oil to keep the air warm? Should it urge members to car-pool and help plan the linkages that make that possible? Should it offer ceramic cups for wine or coffee instead of paper or plastic? Should the synagogue bookstore/gift shop offer energy-saving light bulbs and water-saving shower heads for sale as sacred objects alongside prayer shawls and *dreidls*?

For thousands of years, the Rabbis dealt with similar questions by convening a *beit din* (house of rigorous judgment) to make rulings after consulting previous Jewish case law and the general principles of Torah. For us today, some of the process as well as the content might be different. In the realm of content, a principle like the equality of women might for us be considered newly discovered Torah, even though it was not by the Rabbis.

Even more deeply, we might seek some fusion of the communal rules and individual choice as a guide to action. Since the Jewish communities we live in are voluntary, not compulsory, and since in the Modern Age we prize the individual's struggle to work out his or her own life-path, we might seek not a *beit din* but a *beit chesed* (house of nurturing love) or a *beit seichel* (house of prudence). Such a convocation would issue loving, knowledgeable advice, not strict rulings. Those who are informed in economics, ecology, and interpersonal relationships at work and home would be asked to become members of the *beit chesed* along with rabbis.

In the most basic sense, we would actually be acting a good deal like the earlier Rabbis. We, too, would need to move back and forth from general principles to specific situations. In the process we would be creating a "whole-earth Judaism," the successor both to Modernity and to the Rabbinic Judaism that preceded it.

Of course, we can still learn a great deal from our forebears. For example—a major example—there is a Rabbinic teaching that "to kill one human being is to kill the whole world." (The Rabbis explain that God intended to teach this lesson by starting the human race with just one person.) This teaching treats destruction of the whole world as the worst possibility: What could be worse than that?

Precisely. For the Rabbis, this teaching was a rhetorical flourish. No human being was in a position to destroy the whole world.

For us, however, it is a sober possibility, not a piece of rhetoric.

If we want to work out some tentative answers or approaches by which to begin answering questions about money that we have just asked, let us imagine a set of basic principles:

1. Actions that bear a considerable risk (even less than a fifty-fifty chance) of bringing about the destruction of an ecosystem or the death of a large number of species are absolutely prohibited.
2. Actions that are likely to bring about the death of a single species or to destroy distinctive human cultures or communities are prohibited.
3. Actions that protect ecosystems and preserve a life species are strongly encouraged and rewarded.
4. All proposed economic actions over a certain dollar amount or that have a ripple effect must pass an environmental-impact assessment before being carried out.
5. Collective financial support must be provided for human communities that might otherwise suffer economically from implementation of these actions.
6. Celebrations must periodically and rhythmically be held to reconnect all communities with these principles.

7. Arrangements must be made to permit the regions and districts of the earth to "rest," that is, be periodically withdrawn from productive economic use.

ULTIMATE CASES

Now let us explore how Jews might apply these principles in an ultimate case, one in which global survival might be at stake.

In the early 1980s, most of the American Jewish community believed that the world was facing the danger of a nuclear holocaust. Large parts of the community called for the American and Soviet governments to agree to halt all further production of nuclear weapons. Besides calling for an important change in public policy, would there have been any role for the Jewish community to play? If this were happening today, could the community as a whole, drawing on its spiritual and religious tradition, speak directly to individual Jews about how to act?

For example, let us look at the area of *work*. Should Jewish engineers, secretaries, scientists, public relations experts, nurses ask whether their jobs contribute to or reduce the danger of a nuclear holocaust?

In the Summer 1984 issue of *Reform Judaism*, Rabbi Laurence K. Milder raised the question "If the Scientists Said No." He described a Boston conference on "The Faith Community and the Defense Industry Employee," in which engineers and scientists examined how various religious and ethical systems might deal with work on nuclear questions. Said Milder:

> Can Jews afford to be disinterested regarding nuclear weapons research? Until now, the Reform movement has been outspoken in its opposition to the arms race. Yet the question remains to be addressed whether the same religious convictions ought to prohibit one from working on the construction of those weapons whose deployment we oppose. Being disproportionately represented in the sciences and high-tech industries, we can be sure that the question would have far-reaching impact. A decision to refrain from such work would be a serious blow to the nuclear weapons industry. Any decision at all would be better than silence, which suggests that Judaism stops at the doors of one's workplace. Congregations can provide a forum for this kind of dialogue, in which Jewish scientists and engineers can talk about their concerns, to one another, and to fellow Jews.

Suppose the Jewish community had studied the question and publicly declared that no job that helped to produce or deploy additional nuclear weapons was "eco-kosher"? Should and could the community have then provided financial help—temporary grants, low-interest loans, and so forth—to Jews who decided to leave such jobs for reasons of Torah and conscience? Should organizing such a fund have been a goal of the Jewish community?

Should the same approach then have applied to investments in companies that were making additional nuclear weapons, or to purchases of other products from such companies?

- Would Jewish institutions, as well as individuals, have divested money they had lent to such companies?
- Would the Jewish community have encouraged alternative investments, or encouraged its members to invest in "socially responsible" funds that excluded nuclear weapons makers from their portfolios?
- Would the community have advised individual Jews not to buy consumer goods from specific companies that were producing new nuclear weapons? Would it have organized a boycott of those companies?

These questions focus on the use of voluntary action in a voluntary society. Let us now direct our questions to areas that are not usually considered "voluntary." If the Jewish community had concluded that there was a clear and present danger of a globally destructive nuclear holocaust, would it then have challenged the use of tax money to carry on such activities? Remember, the Talmudic Rabbis ruled that the Roman occupation of the Land of Israel was illegitimate, and therefore certain taxes imposed by the Roman empire were not binding on Jews. What weight should the modern Jewish community give to the degree of democratic decision-making by elected representatives in setting taxes and government expenditures, even if the expenditures threaten planetary destruction? Under such circumstances, could challenges to such taxes be restricted to lawsuits, or would it be appropriate to conduct public protests or even refuse to pay the taxes?

Do such questions sound astonishing, frightening, hair-raising? They are not unprecedented, especially in regard to other religious communities, other than the Jews, that is. In the United States in the last two decades, the Roman Catholic Church has been asking itself such questions in regard to the issue of abortion. The Amish have had to face such issues, even in America. For most of Diaspora history, most Jews have felt it was too dangerous to confront most governments in these ways. Yet in Czarist Russia, as we have seen, many Jews became socialists, opposing with all their might the unjust actions and structures of a government that was both anti-Semitic and antidemocratic. So in ultimate situations, the Jewish community of the future might bring its concerns into unusual action.

PLANS FOR CHANGE

Having looked at the grand vision and at some specific steps, we can now explore the middle level of Jewish action: some overarching plans for change.

Suppose we were to agree with the three goals on page 218 above: that in our time, the most important things Jews can do with money are to use it to protect the web of life through which the earth creates prosperity; to make sure that communities are not trapped as "slaves" in hopeless poverty and oppression or endless high-stress work; and to imbue action on these questions with a holy sense of God's Presence. What would it mean to do this?

First, if the Jewish people were to see itself as a worldwide transgenerational movement to prevent environmental disasters and protect the earth, then several strategic and structural actions might follow:

- *Every* Jewish organization, large or small, religious or secular, might set up an environment committee. The committee would deal with internal "household" issues like the use of paper, energy, insulation, food, room and building design, and transport, all with an eye to minimizing pressures on the earth. It would make sure that all rituals and ceremonials included some specific focus on healing the earth—not only in the formal prayer services, holy day celebrations, and life-cycle ceremonies of the synagogue, but also the less formal rituals with which most groups greet new members or workers, celebrate retirement, and so forth. The environment committee would plan to educate children and adults about these questions. And it would also organize social action to address major public policy issues that affect the environment.

  Why set up a special environment committee instead of depending on the various committees that in one respect or another deal with the issue at present?

  For one thing, because that would both give the issue a high priority and visibility, and give the committee much more clout to get things done. And also, because intrinsically this issue operates in the most close-in and the most far-out aspects of our lives. It concerns what we eat, how we talk to the U.S. Congress, *and* even how we talk to God. It is about the content of three-thousand-year-old Torah texts, as well as about the source of the very paper upon which today's guide to Torah study is written.

- All major Jewish organizations would declare it the policy of the Jewish people to protect biodiversity; to prevent the extinction of species or the disruption of major elements of the earth (such as the ozone layer or the proportion of "greenhouse gases" in the atmosphere); to protect rare ecosystems from destruction; and to require that all plans (public or private) for large-scale actions that might endanger the environment pass an environmental-impact review before being carried out.

Second, what if the Jewish people also took as its purpose the second aspect of the sabbatical year/Jubilee year cycle, the recycling of economic and political power within the community? (There is a third aspect—restfulness and reflective time for the whole community. We will address that in Part Four of this book, "Rest.")

How would we transfer to our modern world the logic of leaving the corners of the field for the poor to glean, annulling debts every seven years, and restoring every family to its equal share of the land every fifty years?

I think the Torah's idea is that in urgent need, the poor have the absolute right to a "job"—that is, to the food that comes from their own work in gleaning the fields. In the longer run, they have the absolute right to "investment capital"—that is, cancellation of their debts and reassertion of their control over the land that produces food. It is not enough to share the food itself; it is necessary to share what makes it possible to grow food: jobs and capital.

In our world, that would mean:

- First, providing decently paid jobs as everyone's guaranteed right—if possible from private companies but, if necessary, on government projects like building subways, teaching school, learning new skills, and rearing children. (Scholarships at colleges and trade schools could be redefined as salaries that are paid for the job of attending and studying.) Jobs without delay and without equivocation. Not since the Great Depression has the government made this commitment. As Carl Sandburg wrote, "Stocks are property, yes/Bonds are property, yes/Jobs are property/No, nix, nah nah."

- Second, providing investment capital to grass-roots co-ops and businesses in communities whose average income and wealth fall below some cut-off point. Scattered across America, there are small community banks and community-focused credit unions and loan funds that receive deposits and borrow money at low interest rates from committed citizens (often religious organizations and communities), then lend it, along with serious technical aid and oversight, to enterprises of the poor: apartment houses, shopping centers, bike shops. The Jewish community has only begun to take part in these ventures. It could be doing much more, both on its own and by urging various levels of government to enter this investment opportunity.

- Third, recycling investment capital and control over it by funneling money out of the oldest and largest banks and conglomerates, through a special "capital recycling tax," into community-oriented investment institutions.

۞

Returning to the basic question of how a community that is no longer a "band of runaway slaves" is to behave in accord with the values that flowed from the slave experience, it is possible to see various aspects of the sabbatical/Jubilee year cycle as the ancient answer to that question. The sabbatical/Jubilee cycle was the direct way that the people of Israel, having become landholders instead of slaves, could make sure that slavery did not return: neither the enslavement of Israelites, nor the enslavement of others, "sojourners," who lived in the land.

So it makes sense today to go back to that model now that we are property holders in prosperous societies. Our goal: to prevent the reemergence of a slave society, no matter who would be the slaveholders and who the slaves.

WOMEN, MEN, AND MONEY

Up to this point, I have drawn almost entirely on existing Jewish tradition, especially Biblical, about how to treat money and the earth from which money emerges. I have been especially attentive to the Biblical tradition because it was much closer to the earth than Rabbinic or modern Judaism. Now I think we need to look at how one new development—the emergence of women as full and equal partners in shaping Jewish thought and practice—may affect what Jews should do about money.

It may even be that in the deepest roots of Jewish peoplehood there were women and legends of women that did give some subterranean direction to Israelite practice: Sarah, Rebekah, Rachel, Leah, Tamar, Miriam, and perhaps the author as well as the heroine of the Song of Songs. The Song of Songs especially preserves an outlook on sexuality and on the relationship of human beings to the earth that may owe much to women's consciousness and outlook.

Today we find ourselves in a new situation. In some ways, the modern economy had pushed women further away from wealth and power even while it brought women into the labor force. For Modernity drastically weakened the economic importance of the family, in which women had a strong though private presence. In royal families, even kings could not easily ignore the concerns of queens and princesses; in banking families, the women who brokered alliances with other bankers could not be ignored; in Rabbinical families, the wives who worked in the marketplace to support their husbands so they could study Torah could not be ignored.

But in the great bureaucratic governments and corporations of the Modern Age, it was nepotism, corruption, to treat the family as a serious economic force. Orders came from above, and flowed through hierarchies shaped by males, with males at their head. Women entered at the bottom, to buy and to work. Even the right to vote, for which feminists valiantly struggled, was in some ways "entry level" power, a token of "lowest common denominator equality." It was not until strong mass organizations of women gave some shape and content to the vote that it began to make a difference in women's and men's lives.

The realization that even under modern categories of "equality" women were being kept from bringing their values into the public sphere and from seriously sharing power made a difference. Within the past generation, that realization has brought forth a surge of women into the public arena, carrying the values and spiritual life experience that many of them had learned from being isolated in the family and neighborhood: the values of nurturance, peacemaking, and community. Indeed, one of the earliest waves of this new feminist energy was the creation of Women Strike for Peace in the late 1950s in the United States, which focused on protecting children and the earth against fallout from nuclear weapons tests.

Not all women, of course, held or embodied those values; and we do not know whether women will choose to emphasize them once they have an equal share in shaping society and their own lives in it. But for the present and the immediate future, most women have learned these values in private space, and most are bringing them into public space.

In the Jewish community, this new wave of women had by 1990 gone far to guarantee that in almost all arenas of Jewish life, it was not legitimate for women to be treated unequally (though actual behavior had not yet shifted as fully as values). And in some arenas, it was beginning to be understood that equality meant not only arithmetic equality within previous parameters of Jewish life, but a reshaping of that life to incorporate the concerns, values, spiritual insights, and symbols women drew from their own life experience.

What connection does this have to money issues? First of all, for many women money has been mainly concerned with nurturing the family and keeping the house, rather than subduing the earth and winning economic victories over other firms or nations.

Second, many feminist scholars have suggested that the very notion of "subduing the earth," treating the earth as an alien to be conquered and exploited, is profoundly connected with men's treatment of women as "Other." Many of the men who have shaped religion and society have seen both the earth and women as sensual, pleasurably seductive, and productive only if subjugated to the will and work of men. "High" religion, an ethereal and transcendent monotheism shaped and studied by men, was counterposed to "popular" religion, more animistic and superstitious, felt and propagated by women. The former pointed to the sky; the latter, to the earth.

If there is some accuracy in the comment that the men who shaped Judaism have often thought of both women and the earth in this way, then there will likely be some change in Jewish attitudes about the earth and money as women take an equal share in shaping Judaism.

Already many newly enfranchised Jewish women have identified with and added to the more "immanent" strands of existing Jewish theology, rather than the more "transcendent" strands. One of these immanent strands is the Hassidic assertion that the world is itself an aspect and emanation of God, rather than simply a creature of God. Another is the Reconstructionist strand that views God as the power within human beings that seeks holiness. The new feminist strand emphasizes God as the interrelational weave of life, the connections and what lies between the connections.

If this approach continues to grow stronger, perhaps not totally eliminating but muting the sense of God as transcendent, then theological viewpoints that repaid human beings as stewards of the earth will increasingly melt into those that see the earth and the human race as intertwined, each affecting the other in a relational flow rather than a hierarchical rule, both bearing some aspect of God's Image.

If Jewish thought continues to change in the same directions, money may eventually be seen differently as well. Perhaps it will be seen less as an instrument of human action upon the earth and more as itself a fluid version of the earth, required therefore to reflect the earth more accurately. For example, in modern economics certain aspects of the earth are monetarized because they are "productive," while others are left out because they are "relational." If these relational aspects get counted, the monetary worth of the ozone layer may outweigh the whole "production" of the planet for the next century. Ten species that are about to become extinct may outweigh the "production" total for the next million years.

This way of thinking could begin to help us see on every coin not simply the image of power and wealth alone, but the Divine Image. Perhaps, if we start looking at money as a fluid version of the earth, we will see that all money bears God's image—because it both conceals and reveals the interplay and interweaving of *adam* and *adamah*.

One of the issues that an emerging whole-earth Judaism will need to face is whether, and how, to affirm holiness and God's Presence in the use of money.

This question is an old one that has become new, because of the life experience of many Jews who grew up in the last generation. The Jewish socialists of the last century, seeking freedom from their bonds, fought against the tight religion of their day, as well as against a constricting politics and economics. They asserted the secularism of explorers. But since the late sixties in North America, this has mostly changed. Instead, many of that era have felt caught in a one-dimensional, disenchanted secular world in which community, spirituality, and ecstasy were missing.

So during the last quarter-century or so, many of those who were most active and creative in renewing Jewish life have sought to celebrate what is holy and Divine in many aspects of their Jewish lives. Some might say that simply using money ethically is itself a holy act; others might say that we need to focus our conscious attention on holiness.

How could we do this? What can we draw on that the Jewish people found useful in the past? If we look at such traditional tools of *kavvanah* (holy intentionality) as blessings, Torah study, ritual or ceremonial action, and sometimes meditation, we find they are rarely used in regard to work and money.

What about blessings, *brakhot*, for example? We have seen that Rabbinic Judaism put blessings before and after every meal, and for many Jews this helped one focus on the holiness in food.

For money? There are no blessings in the tradition. No blessing before giving *tzedakah*, whether 25 cents to a beggar on the street or $250,000 to the United Jewish Appeal. No blessing to begin the day's work—unless it happens to be Torah study. No blessing before spending money, either for a threadbare blanket to warm a child against the icy winter, or for a gossamer luxury. No blessing for saving money, investing money, wasting money, receiving money, grasping money.

As far as Torah study is concerned, two texts are traditionally read that concern money for the communal funds. They are the Torah passage (Ex. 30:11–16) about the half-shekel tax paid by every Israelite male when the Wilderness Shrine was being built, and the prophetic passage (II Kings 11:11-12; 17) about the creation of a chest to receive donations for the repair of the Temple.

The Temple-repair chest was instituted because individual priests were keeping contributions for themselves instead of using them to keep the Temple in good repair. So the two passages are amusingly appropriate together; the one reminding us what we owe the public funds, the other reminding us that officials can become corrupt. These two passages were assigned to be read on the Shabbat two weeks before Purim (six weeks before Pesach), partly because Purim is a day of giving gifts to the poor and partly because the Temple tax was part of the process leading up to the celebration of Pesach.

Two Talmud texts that focused on *tzedakah* and other acts of loving-kindness (Mishnah Peah I:I and Shabbat 127a) were assigned to be read at every morning service, not specifically at times of giving *tzedakah*. One of the texts begins, "For these deeds there is no prescribed limit: [leaving food for the poor in] the corners of the field...." The point may have been not only to remind everyone on every morning that *every* day was one for giving *tzedakah*, but also that there could be no specific blessing for every specific act of giving because there was no way to tell when *tzedakah* was "enough."

Except for the special *shofar* blast on Yom Kippur that signaled the beginning of the Jubilee year of redistributing land and releasing all slaves, there was no traditional ritual action in regard to transformations of work and money.

At this point, I now propose several scenarios through which decisions about work and money might be infused with a sense of holiness.

Let us begin with work.

Perhaps you have begun a job search, or perhaps you have been offered a job, or perhaps you are beginning to address these issues because soon you expect to finish school or training that is intended to prepare you for a job. You gather a group of friends. Together you say: "Let us bless the One Who makes the world a Unity, and who teaches us to connect the strands of Unity by uniting with each other to study the wisdom that can unite us. *Baruch attah YHWH eloheynu ruach ha'olam asher kidshanu b'mitzvot vitzivanu la'asok b'divrei Torah.*" Then you read together a few passages of Torah (the following, for example), in order to begin the discussion:

Rabbi Hana the Moneychanger said: "Bar Nappaha asked to borrow from my banker's bench a Gordian *dinar*, to measure a crack [in an animal's skull, to ascertain whether it was kosher]. When I tried to stand up to honor him, he would not let me, saying: 'Sit down, sit down, my boy; workers involved in their work need stand for no one, not even students of the Holy Wisdom.'" (T.B. Hullin 54b)

The world cannot stand without perfumers and tanners; but happy is the one whose craft is perfuming, and alas for the one whose trade is tanning. (T.B. Kiddushin 82a)

R. Zutra bar Tobiah said in the name of Rav: "The verse 'God has made everything beautiful in its time' [Eccl. 3:1] means that the Holy One made every trade seem beautiful in the eyes of those who work it." (T.B. Brakhot 43b)

When Rav entered among growing ears of grain and saw them swaying in the wind, he said to them: "Sway, sway, as much as you will; turning over merchandise is still more profitable." (T.B. Yevamot 63a)

"Who is wealthy? Whoever is content with his wealth"—so said R. Meir. But R. Tarfon said: "Whoever has one hundred vineyards, one hundred fields, and one hundred slaves working in them." R. Akiba said: "Whoever has a spouse whose beauty shines in deeds [not appearance only]." R. Yose said: "Whoever has an indoor bathroom." (T.B. Shabbat 25b)

Then explore these questions: When I imagine myself doing this work, do I feel like an active arm of God, helping to continue the work of Creation? Is the work more likely to build up the world, or tear it down? Do the particular shapes of my own soul, body, heart, and mind fit this particular work? Does it delight me or repel me? Will it make the earth more fruitful, and will I be paid a reasonable share of that fruitfulness? Will my working at this task bring more vitality and more honor to the Jewish community, or less? Will I have time and space for rest as well as for work, being as well as doing?

And when you are finished discussing these matters, read this passage of summary and wonder:

R. Shezbi said in the name of R. Eleazar ben Azariah: "Providing people with their daily bread is as miraculous as splitting the Red Sea, for the verse 'Who gives bread to all flesh' [Ps. 136: 25] is equal to the verse 'Who tore apart the Red Sea' [Ps. 136: 13]." (T.B. Pesahim 118a)

ॐ

On the day you actually begin a new job, and possibly every day as you begin work, you could say; "Blessed is the One Who makes us holy by connecting us with each other, and teaches us to connect by serving and doing work. *Brucha aht YAHH eloheynu ruach ha'olam asher kidshatnu b'mitzvot vitzivatnu la'avod u'la'asot kol malakha.*"

How to make holy the process of *tzedakah*? Different kinds and degrees of attention to *tzedakah* might begin in different ways. As you meet a beggar on the street, for example, and decide to give him or her a quarter, you might say: "Blessed is the One Who makes us holy by connecting us with each other, and teaches us to connect through sharing what grows from the corners of the field. *Baruch attah YAHH eloheynu ruach ha'olam asher kidshanu b'mitzvot vitzivanu al ha'pe'ah.*"

When a *tzedakah* collective meets, or when family members gather at Purim, Rosh Hashanah, or Hanukkah to decide how much *tzedakah* to give to which groups, it might be appropriate to begin with a blessing that draws on the origins of the word for *tzedakah* in the root *tzedek* (justice), which is repeated with strong purpose in the verse "Justice, justice shall you pursue" (Deut. 16:20). Thus: "Blessed is the One Who makes us holy by connecting us with each other, and teaches us to connect through seeking justice, justice. *Brucha aht YAHH eloheynu ruach ha'olam asher kidshatnu b'mitzvot vitzivatnu tzedek tzedek lirdof.*"

Then before beginning any allocations of funds, probe some of the Jewish values that guide those allocations: how much to give to Jewish and how much to general causes. How much to the immediate neighborhood and how much to global needs. How much directly to those in immediate, desperate need; how much to support institutions that provide jobs and other arrangements so that people can begin meeting their own needs. How much for political action to eliminate inequities and make sure such institutions flourish instead of being marginal. (In the age-old formulation, when to give a fish, when to give a fishing rod. To which we might add, when to help organize a fishers' kibbutz to ensure that all who need them can share in owning fishing rods, and when to restrict the use of huge fishnets so that the fish and the fishers can continue to sustain each other through many generations.)

One of the classic delineations of *tzedakah*, by Maimonides, urges that it be given and received anonymously, to prevent shame on the one side and tyranny on the other. Some contemporary practitioners—notably Jeffrey Dekro of The Shefa Fund—have raised the question whether sometimes it is even more important for donors and recipients to meet together to plan the use of the money. The idea of "maximum feasible participation" by the poor in deciding how best to use *tzedakah* money looks beyond shame to creating a base of political power and therefore of human dignity for the poor. In the New Israel Fund, for example, recipient organizations in Israel sit on decision-making councils along with (mostly North American) philanthropists, not only to allocate money but to plan for the further growth and empowerment of the recipient groups. When to apply the one rule and when the other is an important element in allocating *tzedakah*.

All these arrangements would be ways for society as a whole to teach that producing, inventing, doing, consuming, making, are not the only point to life, that these modes of living can be surrounded and infused with a sense of quiet, celebration, reflection, being still. They are a way of asserting that the economy is not an end in itself; that the process of making and using money is a sacred process, to be filled with love and awe.

Part Three

SEX

XXI. AND HE SHALL RULE OVER YOU

In our generation, issues of sexual ethics have taken on an aura of enormous anxiety. For women and for men, for heterosexuals and for homosexuals, definitions of what is permissible, what is honorable, what is hurtful, what is criminal have all been changing with great speed among some people—and among others, not at all.

One response has been "Make up your own mind," that is, individual choice rather than a communal ethic. But since sexuality is par excellence about relationships between people, this response is for most people, unstable. Not even a "couple's ethic"—"Make up your own *two* minds"—can settle most of the issues, even at a purely secular and practical level. Even more, for people who draw their spirituality, sacredness, from a sense of communal wholeness and of sharing in the web of life, sheer privacy in sexual decision-making often seems a rejection of the sacred.

And yet—how to create a communal sexual ethic, even one with a great deal of elasticity and pluralism, that *would* honor sexuality as sacred? For many of our generation, the various religious traditions have not seemed very useful sources for a healing, sacred sexual mode of behavior. Indeed, even those Jews who have wrestled and danced with Jewish tradition in many other areas of their lives have often felt that in the sexual arena traditional rules did not make a sacred path possible. Yet those same Jews, like many others in modern society, have found few resources from which to shape a coherent, communally shared ethic of sexuality.

Result: anxiety.

Ironically, if we examine the ancient spiritual teachings of the Jewish people about sexuality, we find that they, too, are suffused with feelings of anxiety. The anxious tone focuses on or flows from different doubts, different fears, different hopes from those that cause sexual anxiety today. But the tone is similar.

For the Biblical Israelites, there were three major aspects of sexuality:

- Control by men over women. Sex was one of the major arenas in which men ruled over women, and through which women affirmed their caring-obedience.
- Control by the present over the future. Without sex, there would be no children. And with sex came intense desires that could break down the bound-

aries between the Israelite people and other peoples—so that children might
end up not being Israelites.

• Control over the uncanny overtones of the boundaries between life and death.
With sex came fluids and issues, particularly of blood and semen, that seemed
uncanny, eerie, murky.

Sex as part of a broader practice of intimate companionship in a family setting
does *not* seem to have been a major Biblical concern.

All three efforts at control led to a sense of unease. What if these controls were
to break down?

During the rest of this chapter, we will look more closely at the efforts of men
to control women. It is the most basic of the three aspects of sexuality, in that it
shaped the way Israelite society dealt with the other two. Israelite society, like all
the societies around it at that time, was based on the assumption that men in
general ruled over women in general—that is, men made decisions for and shaped
the culture of the whole society. What the code of sexual ethics was, what stories
of sexual relationships would enter and remain in the sacred literature, even what
part of human life was considered to be sexuality, were decided ultimately by men.
Perhaps in the process these men had listened to some women's voices, but women
and men did not decide together, as equal partners.

For our generation, of course, this casts great doubt on all the patterns of Jewish
sexual life that have come down to us. Most of us welcome the emergence of the
equality of women and men, including an equal share in deciding what sexual
relationships should be like. Therefore, we could ask ourselves three and four times
about every detail of the past sexual ethics and rituals: If women and men were
now to work out their sexual practices together, as equals, is this what they would
be creating?

Our very questions may originate in a different strand of Israelite thought, a
kind of subversive literature that seems to challenge dominion by men and that
offers hints of different ways of thinking and acting about sexuality that may have
sprung from women. Given that men were in charge, women do not seem to have
been utterly voiceless, though we must also keep in mind that when they speak,
their words were probably edited and authorized by men.

The largely male Israelite outlook on sex seem to have been that sexuality in
general, and marriage even more strongly, were defined by a particular man's being
in control of a particular woman; that by far the most important function of sex
was procreation; that sexual relations between an Israelite and someone of another
people were problematic, especially since the children might not end up as part of
the community of Israelites; and that seminal emissions and menstrual blood bore

a potent taboo that interfered with direct contact with God and such sacred spaces as the Wilderness Shrine, the Altar, and the Temple.

It is important to note, however, that sometimes these different aspects of the Israelite outlook on sex collided with each other. The desire to protect male control over sexual relationships, or the desire to keep all sexual relationships inside the Israelite community, might collide with the desire to multiply children.

We should also be conscious that much of the material on sexuality from this period comes not from a broad segment of the male population, but from the small group of men of the priestly caste who gave form to the priestly sections of the Bible. The priests, unlike the prophetic, historical, and literary writers of other parts of the Bible, were men chosen by and for their bodies. Chosen by heredity, chosen for the absence of a mar or blemish in their bodies, chosen to celebrate the bodily aspects of God's universe—food, earth, smoke, flame. They were not selected for their ethical sensitivity or their ability to turn history into great literature or their ability to stir the masses or charm the rulers.

The concern of the priests was the rhythmic life of the society in its passages through the year and the life cycle, the intertwining of the human community with the earth, the moon, the sun, the vegetation, the animals. So it should not surprise us that they took over the realm of sexuality as their own. Since their role and status depended so wholly on heredity and birth and on the "perfection" of their bodies, it is also not surprising that they felt great anxiety about many aspects of sexuality.

We are not used to shaping our own culture in this fashion—as if, say, the great athletes of our time, and their children and grandchildren, were in charge of deciding rules of sexuality. So there may be both something we can learn, and something we must question, from a Torah of sex shaped in this way.

For the priests, these "body-Israelites," what were the issues?

- Must their own heredity be unblemished, "pure"? Then they worried about whether official fathers were the real ones, whether women were truly and truthfully transmitting the priestly inheritance to future generations.
- Would the biological cycles of humanity as well as those of animals and vegetation, continue into future generations? Then they worried about how to guarantee the bearing and rearing of children.
- Could the celebration of YHWH, their special province, be kept unsullied by the alluring practices of other priests who served local gods? Then they worried about the powerful tugs of sexual attraction across ethnic and spiritual boundaries.
- Was it their specific task in Israelite society to help the common folk navigate the awesome moments of the beginning and the end of life? Then they worried

especially about the sexual rhythms and expressions that might bring life into existence, but might also cast life potential away, bringing about a kind of eerie half-death where life had not yet fully taken hold.

THE RULE OF MEN

It is then not surprising that the sexual ethic these priestly Israelite men created was based on the premise that not only did men in general rule over women in general, but also that particular husbands ruled over their particular wives.

This power relationship included sexual relations, but was not limited to sex alone. Property holding, for example, was normally limited to men, though exceptional situations arose (like the death of a father who left only daughters but no sons to inherit the property) in which women might hold land. The authority to transmit religious teaching that would ring across the centuries was mostly (though not absolutely) limited to men.

And men were in charge of sexual relationships between men and women. Not that they could do whatever they liked—there were limits. Most of the limits were aimed at men. The Torah assumed men had power, and then put limits on their power. By far the worst violations of the law occurred when men violated another man's sexual authority over a woman, not when they violated women sexually who were not attached to other men.

According to the Torah's Creation story, this unequal relationship between women and men is not the ideal, but it is the "reality" of history. Just as the story of Eden, the Garden of Delight, distinguishes the ideal life of the human earthling in relation to the earth from real life, so it distinguishes the ideal and real-life versions of relationships between men and women.

The story of Eden suggests that the ideal earth-earthling relationship was one of playful, joyful mutual nurturance, shattered by the "misdone" eating so that it turned into a thorny, sweaty battle. Similarly, the story suggests that the ideal relationship between women and men was the comradeship of counterparts, but the mis-done eating and its chain of blame shattered that comradeship. "Toward your husband will be your desire/lust, and he will rule over you," says God to Eve as life in the Garden of Delight draws to a close.

If this is the Torah's underlying assumption about the nature of history and society, why did the Israelites feel some anxiety about this regime?

First and most important, the very fact that the deepest and highest Edenic vision is of comrades and counterparts, a vision where *Ish* and *Isha*, Man and Woman, see each other as "bone of my bone, flesh of my flesh," where Woman

has power to take independent action and initiate human history, all this subverts
a history of male dominion.

Second, the description of post-Edenic life in which men will rule is oddly
asymmetrical. Not "You will obey your husband, and he will rule over you." Not
"Your desire will be toward your husband, and his toward you"—or even "and he
will shun you." For one partner, the relationship is power, for the other one, it is
sexual desire. Does this suggest that men will not feel desire for women in general,
or for their wives? An unlikely unrealism for the Torah!

What seems more likely is that the Torah is expressing something between an
observation and an anxious intention: that wives must feel desire *for their husbands*—
and no one else. There is no symmetric reciprocity because there is no intention
to assert that men will or must feel desire for their wives alone.

Third and far more explicit than this passage from the Eden story, there is the
Torah's rule for a case in which, indeed, a man becomes consumed with anxiety
and jealousy that his wife desires another man. The Torah here expresses concern
for a situation where there is no tangible evidence of adultery, nothing at all that
can be brought to a court of law. All there is, is a feeling: the husband's jealousy.

What to do? The Torah prescribes an awesome ritual ordeal, the "Bitter Waters," that the wife must undergo, not the husband. The ordeal is intended to single
out the innocent and the guilty—still without presenting evidence that any human
court could weigh. If the ordeal shows the wife to be guilty, she becomes sick, and
unable to conceive children. If she is shown to be innocent, the husband is expected
to be so awed by the result that his jealousy vanishes.

This is the only nonrational or nonempirical ordeal prescribed by the Torah to
settle any dispute or problem, under any circumstance. It is not prescribed for
jealous wives—as if they never felt jealousy, or as if their jealousy were not entitled
to serious adjudication. This bespeaks both male anxiety, and the insistence of men
that their anxiety be assuaged.

We should also note that even this assuaging of male anxiety, despite bearing
heavily on the woman, offers some evidence of limits that Israelite men accepted
upon their own power. For if the Torah had seen marriage as an absolute monarchy,
it could have provided that any man who was convinced of his wife's adultery,
with or without evidence, could have punished her or killed her. If the ordeal of
the Bitter Waters was intended to act like a lie detector test, affirming innocence
as well as discerning guilt, then it might have functioned as a way of protecting
wives.

As for cases where there is in fact evidence sufficient to convince a court that
a married or espoused woman has voluntarily had sex with a man other than her
spouse, the Torah condemns her to death, along with the man (Lev. 20:10). (The
Rabbis later ruled that this, like other capital punishments required by the written

Torah, could not be enforced unless two witnesses were actually present and warned the perpetrators that they were committing a capital offense. It does not seem likely that this was often the case in matters of adultery. It is not clear how early on the Jewish community observed this way of radically reducing capital punishment.)

A girl who is still under her father's authority is prohibited from having sex with a man, or at least from marrying some other man and pretending to be a virgin—on pain of death if she is later found to have misrepresented herself as a virgin. A woman who is mature—twelve and a half years old—and is not espoused, or a woman who is a widow or a divorcee, may have sex as she chooses, though if she later marries, her bride-price will be lower. Women (like men) are prohibited from having sex with an animal (Lev. 18:23); they are not explicitly prohibited from having sex with other women, unlike men, who may not have sex with other men (Lev. 18:22).

The power of the fear of adultery in Israelite culture is indicated by the way several of the Prophets used adultery as a metaphor to challenge Israel's disobedience to God. Hosea, Ezekiel, and Jeremiah see, and smell, the People Israel as a wanton woman, caressing not God but other gods as a married woman might caress other, forbidden men.

The metaphor assumes not only that women are and should be subordinate to men in sexual relationships (as Israel is subordinate to God), but also that men are afraid that women might rebel. For unless these Prophets expected their nightmarishly intense images to ring true, they would not have used them as tools to transform Israelite society. Thus the images might seem to represent a deep fear of women, even misogyny. Hosea cites his own life, venting rage at his wife, Gomer, whom he perceives to be adulterous, so as to make the image more than a metaphor.

On the other hand, Hosea then proceeds to imagine a transformed future in which God no longer wants Israel to see God as Master but as an equal partner in their marriage, espousing Israel in love, trust, and justice. This metaphor could only have worked if Hosea expected his audience to greet with joy the possibility of such marriages on earth—marriages that stretch the mind because they would be quite different from those the Israelites were used to.

Yet we should be aware of the limits on this mind-stretching. Hosea does not describe such an earthy marriage with the strong and vivid imagery with which he attacks Gomer. The notion of an egalitarian marriage is left as just a notion. And perhaps more basic: Even in Hosea's best vision, the dominant partner—God—gets to define what equality is, and how the marriage will be structured. There is no suggestion that Israel, or Gomer, will be able to work out a covenant with her husband. The metaphor is one of equality as it is defined by men. A stretch, but with limits.

Within a single person and within society as a whole, these images bespeak a tension between hope and fear. It is easy to imagine that in a society that is either experiencing or imagining the breakdown of a system of stable inequality, one response could be a nightmarish fear: that people who used to take orders (i.e., women) could kick up their heels and destroy all order and stability. The other possibility, barely glimpsed, is that the only cure for repression and rebellion is for society to go forward to a new order based on equality and justice. But then, for some, this image itself stimulates different fears—for such a new Eden, Eden as it should have been, may seem a disaster for those who would lose power over others.

Perhaps Hosea was embodying in his own person and his own message the conflicting fears and hopes of Israelite men in general, in a time when broad social upheaval might have been intertwined with doubts about the stability of sexual relationships. If so, our own generation—more, precisely, the men—might hear these ancient struggles and anxieties as akin to their own.

Finally, let us note that when a Prophet like Hosea treats as a metaphor one element of the priestly arena, the result may be a subtle blend of undermining and affirming the priestly path. What the priests are doing is shaping rituals and laws that mark body boundaries in space and the life cycle of the body in time. What might have been only the unending circle of birth, sex, death, only the unending rules of sexual relationships, may become socially and psychologically more fluid, more questionable, when they are used as metaphor.

Let us now return to the priestly outlook in the Book of Leviticus. It adds to the general fear of adultery some more specific fears of where a man's sexual desire might lead him, and lists more precise prohibitions:

- It lists the nearby relatives for whom it expects men may feel desire, and forbids sexual relations with them. These relatives are mother, sister or half sister, granddaughter, daughter-in-law, aunt, niece, sister-in-law. Men are also forbidden to have sex with two closely related women, such as sisters or a woman and her daughter or granddaughter. In almost all of these cases, the reason given for the prohibition is that having sex with them would be "uncovering the nakedness" of the men who can legitimately have sex with them. Perhaps there were two reasons for prohibiting these relationships: They would disrupt the authority of specific men; and by crisscrossing the lines of family intimacy ("nakedness"), they might disrupt the family patterns in which it was safe and stable to raise children.

- It does not explicitly forbid sex with a daughter. The Rabbis ruled that the inclusion of daughters was implied; but it is not clear what the actual limits were in the Biblical period. Some scholars think that indeed, at least in principle if rarely in fact, fathers were viewed as owners of their daughters' sexuality until the daughters were espoused. But the mandated death penalty for women who were discovered not to be virgins when they got married does not seem compatible with the notion that it was expected or allowed that fathers have sex with their daughters—and perhaps that is part of the reason why the Rabbis concluded that sex with daughters was also prohibited.

It may be that between the earlier legal and moral codes of Leviticus and the period shortly before the destruction of the First Temple, which is when Deuteronomy was probably written (or composed, rewritten, and reshaped from older traditions), the temper of Israelite law on these questions changed. It may be that originally fathers were allowed the power of life-or-death and sexual domination over their daughters, and that by the time of Deuteronomy they were not.

• Men were prohibited from "lying with a man as with a woman." The exact intention of this prohibition is hotly debated today: Was it aimed at what Israelites thought was a pagan religious practice? Did the Israelites have any idea that two men could create a loving and stable sexual union, or was this verse aimed at outlawing sporadic relationships within a household or clan, as a sort of broad-gauged definition of incest involving men? Is the basic premise that since men are in charge of their own sexuality—unlike women, whose sexuality is controlled by men—for two men to have sexual relations means that one is being controlled "as if" he was a woman, an unacceptable or unfathomable arrangement?

This last suggestion accords with a broader sense that Biblical society did not expect, understand, or in some sense even allow sexual relationships to be fully mutual and egalitarian. It is always the man who took a woman in marriage, and a man who gave a divorce. The woman's consent was necessary, but she was the passive partner.

If we follow out this last suggestion, it also suggests that there is no explicit Biblical prohibition of lesbianism because to the Biblical mind this was not sex at all. If sex required one male actor in control of the situation, then two women could not be having sex; and two men might be having sex, but only in such a way as to twist it on its head, beyond all social understanding.

One could even imagine that if two men were having sex in a mutually loving relationship and not in such a way that one was subordinated "like a woman"— say, David, the aspiring King, and Jonathan, the prince of the House of Saul— then in the Biblical view this would not have been a real sexual relationship, any more than a similar egalitarian relationship between a man and woman would have been understood as a marriage.

To return to the arenas of male sexual desire over which the Torah seeks control, what did the Israelites consider rape?

- If a man forces or cajoles an unespoused woman to have sex, he must pay her father fifty silver shekels and marry her. He can never divorce her. The Torah does not explicitly address her own sense of loss, humiliation, or rage, or whether she would want to be in his household (though the Rabbis later specified that she must also be paid damages for her humiliation). It assumes that she has lost chiefly social status, and that status can be restored through marriage with the man.
- If a man forces sex on a woman who is espoused but not yet married, this is even worse than adultery. It is like murder, and he is executed.
- The Torah expects that in wartime, some men will want to rape the enemy's women. To check this tendency, the Torah prescribes an elaborate process by which the captive women must be given time to mourn their dead and defeated menfolk (and in the mourning process, to come to look undesirable), and then they must be offered marriage.

In regard to prostitution, the ancient Israelites were far more concerned with the threat this might pose to the authority of a particular male than any intrinsic immorality of trading sex for money. Biblical texts do not criminalize or cast contempt on prostitution by women who are not under a husband's or father's authority; but they do express anger and horror at the possibility that a woman who owed allegiance to some man, a father or a husband, might become a prostitute or (as Dina's brothers said of her [Gen. 34:31]), be treated like a prostitute. In ways that are most surprising to modern understanding, prostitution per se, by women who had no contrary obligations, may not have felt like sexuality to the Biblical Israelites any more than did lesbianism, because it stood outside the structures of male control over sex.

The Biblical tradition also describes—but only glancingly, with little exploration of its law or custom—a relationship between men and women that is not marriage and not casual or commercial. It was called *pilegesh*, usually translated as "concubine." In King David's and King Solomon's households, there were many such women; but this was not an arrangement for royal households alone.

The *pilegesh* seems to have had somewhat lower prestige and less claim on property or income than a formal wife, but she had more sexual freedom. Evidently, she could leave the relationship on her own, not requiring a *get* (bill of divorce) in order to be free to marry. As a corollary, she might not be entitled to a financial settlement if the man sent her away, but Abraham is described as giving gifts to the children of his *pilagshim* while he made a fuller provision for Isaac. In a sense, the *pilegesh* traded one aspect of self-protection under male control for another form of female freedom.

There are several Biblical tales in which a son had sex with his father's *pilegesh*, evidently in order to assert some political power and usurp his father's governing control. In one of these stories, Reuben slept with Bilhah, at this moment in time described as the *pilegesh* of his father and clan leader, Jacob/Israel. Saul's general, Abner, slept with Rizpah, Saul's *pilegesh*; David's son Absalom slept with his father's *pilagshim*. This behavior was condemned, but not treated as an act of adultery or incest, which it would have been had the *pilegesh* been a formal wife. There is no suggestion that the son is raping the *pilegesh*. So from her standpoint, perhaps she is trying to take a hand in shaping the power patterns of the future, establishing her own role in the clan or the palace. On the other hand, each of these men was trying to assert future power over the household or the nation; so the *pilagshim* may have felt cowed into submission.

Within the general pattern of male control, the *pilegesh* relationship may have been an escape valve of sorts—very much "of sorts"—for anyone who wanted a sexual relationship that was not based on male dominance, and perhaps there was also some financial advantage in the arrangement. Something between an evasion and a subversion of the general rule.

If lesbianism is not addressed by Israelite law or custom because it did not enter the categories of male-controlled sexuality, we might see both prostitution by an adult unmarried woman and the *pilegesh* relationship as gray areas of behavior that are only loosely and vaguely defined by a code of sexual conduct, because these relationships have a little—but only a little—tinge of male control.

· As we have seen, the assumptions of male dominance over society in general, over the sexual code in particular, and over the sexual lives of specific women deeply affected practically every aspect of Israelite thought and action about sex. This may make it especially hard for us to learn from the Biblical patterns, since most of our generation are moving toward the equality of women and men in shaping the society as a whole, the Jewish community, and the patterns of sexual relationships.

We will look at these new possibilities in more detail later. For now, we should note that there are many levels of meaning to the different kinds of men-women relationships that our society is exploring. There are changes in power relationships inside the home; in the broader society, and therefore in how women and men move into and out of the household; and in cultural affirmations of how worthy it is to act "like a man" and "like a woman." Even in our psyche, the assumption that there is such a thing as "acting like a man" or "acting like a woman" comes into question.

These emerging patterns are so different from the Biblical patterns that it may be hard to "listen" to the one if we are trying to explore the other. Indeed, many of us may poignantly feel that some aspects of our current sexual relationships that we are struggling to change may stem precisely from the roots of Biblical culture and from the male domination that shaped it. Harder still to listen then!

Is there anything at all we can learn from the Biblical patterns? Several possibilities occur to me:

First of all, many women and men today may feel—as the men of the Biblical era did—a deep anxiety over aspects of sexuality that are swiftly changing. Perhaps we have something to learn about anxiety itself, and how to cope with it. For example, the ritual of the Bitter Waters was, within ancient Israel, an effort to let anxiety and jealousy, the "shadow side" of change, be transmuted into a healing ritual rather than into destructive fear and rage. How could our own generation create rituals for discharging sexual anxiety—rituals that can heal because they lay anxiety bare for all to see and ultimately laugh at?

Second, we also need to watch for those aspects of Biblical culture that were subversive of the official male-dominant mode and subversive of sexual anxiety itself—some more so than others. We have already noted Hosea's partial subversion of male-dominant marriage. Among others are:

- In the "founding families" of the Jewish people, the Matriarchs—Sarah, Rebekah, Rachel, and Leah—are described as sharing in or even making crucial decisions for the future of the people. Sarah demands and receives the expulsion of Hagar and Ishmael; Rebekah has a much more explicit relationship with God than her husband, Isaac, and she reverses Isaac's intention about which of their children is to receive the paternal and Divine blessing; Rachel and Leah have a sisterly "Godwrestle" before their husband Jacob, facing his brother Esau, learns to wrestle with God. It is clear that in their families of origin, all these women had great stature and independence. One modern commentator, Savina Teubal, has even suggested that they were highly respected priestesses in a woman-centered culture, whose role was diminished when patriarchal men edited the stories and shaped the Torah. If so, the editors nevertheless left enough of the original atmosphere to undermine their own patriarchal values. How subversive! In the Torah's most important families, it was vital that the women be equals of the men.
- The Scroll of Esther tells of a king who begins by deposing a queen lest all women learn from her example to take control over their husbands, and thereby sets in motion a train of events that ends by his slavishly obeying the desires of his new queen.
- In the Song of Songs, the woman singer seems at least as strong and self-confident as the man. She (and more important, the writer or editor) bring

what may be a woman's experience of flowing, fluid spirituality into a Biblical culture that was deeply different. And in the Song the anxiety of men who cannot control the sexual vitality of a woman becomes faintly comical and utterly ineffectual.

- The sage of David, the great Biblical hero, recounts sexual relationships that were not only numerous but enormously varied—with remarkably different kinds of women and, possibly, one man—and rarely colored with anxiety.
- And perhaps the *pilegesh* relationship.

We will look at some of these subversions more deeply in a later chapter.

XXII. BE FRUITFUL AND FILL UP THE EARTH

Now let us turn to the second major focus of the Torah's rules about sexuality: the relationship between sex and procreation. When I said earlier that not from sex came children, but that "without sex, there would be no children," I chose this phrasing because throughout the Bible there is a sense that having children is not easy. Always there is danger. Somewhere, sometime, there was carved deep into Israelite consciousness the fear that there might be no next generation.

According to the Biblical stories, this fear goes back to the very origins of Israelite identity, with the saga of Abraham and Sarah. Although God covenants with Abraham (whose name is still "Avram") that his offspring will be as numerous as the dust of the earth (Gen. 13:16) and the stars of the sky (Gen. 15:5), by the age of eighty-five Avram and his wife (still named Sarai) have had no children. She is so profoundly troubled by this childlessness that she urges him to take her handmaid Hagar (whose name means "the sojourner" or "the live-in") as an additional wife. With Hagar Avram has one son, Ishmael.

Thirteen years later, God gives Abraham and Sarah their full names, adding the Hebrew letter "*hey*" to each of their names—the letter that appears twice in God's Name, that mimics an in-breath or out-breath. God explains that this renaming is a sign that they will have a child of their own, and that their offspring will become many, fruitful, and prosperous. God introduces ritual circumcision, the hallowing of the male genitals from which many nations are to spring, for Abraham as an adult, Ishmael as a thirteen-year-old, and Abraham's soon-to-be-born son Isaac (and all future male descendants) when he turns eight days old.

The story then recounts that not till Abraham is one hundred years old and Sarah but a few years younger do they have Isaac. And when Isaac grows up, he and his wife, Rebekah, also have trouble conceiving. The problem continues even into the third generation. When their son Jacob grows up, one of his original wives has great difficulty and the other some difficulty in conceiving, enough that they, too, urge him to take their handmaids as additional wives. Only after these difficulties and from a variety of wives does Jacob have the twelve sons that in the Biblical mind mark a viable and successful nation.

So the saga of Patriarchs and Matriarchs makes clear that for Israel, procreation is not the easy, flowing process it seems to be for many peoples. It is a struggle.

PRUNING THE FRUITFUL TREE

Beginning with the story of Abraham's two families, Israelite culture connected anxiety over procreation with the ritual of circumcision, and connected circumcision with the "everlasting covenant" of successful procreation. Indeed, circumcision points even beyond the very next generation, toward the more distant future, for circumcision of a son focuses on the genitals that will help create *his* children—the generation of the grandchildren.

Anxiety over procreation became the most powerful and perduring of Israelite and Jewish fears, and circumcision became the most powerful and perduring of Israelite and Jewish rituals.

Other aspects of Biblical culture echo circumcision as an "opening" for fruitfulness. Howard Eilberg-Schwartz (whom we have already met in our discussion of the meanings of the Biblical code of kosher food) has pointed out, removal of the *arelah*, or foreskin, is echoed by the practice of *orlah* (from the same root), in which a fruit tree must be three years old (plus a year of dedication to God) before its fruit can be eaten. Through this pause, its temporal "tree-skin" is removed and its fruitfulness enhanced. The Torah also speaks about God's removing the "foreskin of the human heart," that is, cutting away the hard-hearted outer shell in order to soften the heart, make it more fully and spiritually fruitful.

What else are we to make of this ceremony? It certainly focuses on male "covenanting" with God and on male anxieties about fruitfulness as if it is the male, not the female, genitals that are at fault in barrenness and need in some sense to be "opened." Some have suggested that circumcision may betoken a male imitation of menstruation: Men learn from women that blood from the genitals is crucial to the cycling of life. Others have pointed to the later story in which Abraham, preparing to offer Isaac as a sacrifice to God, substitutes instead a ram that is caught in the thicket—and suggest that the foreskin may be a kind of ram, acting as a substitute for what would be a tragic bind wherein the father feels that to guarantee his own fruitfulness he must sacrifice his firstborn son. Perhaps the Abraham-Isaac story points also to the possibility that some fathers who fear being displaced by their sons may want to kill them, and must learn both to express and to control that urge by killing a ram instead or by delicately "opening" the genitals toward the future generations instead of castrating them.

We might also say that because the cutting of the foreskin necessarily engendered deep anxiety—in fathers, if not in their infant sons—the act of circumcision fully embodied in one stark moment all the different anxieties about sexuality felt by the Israelite men who shaped sexual conduct.

These ways of understanding circumcision take some strength from the story of the return of Moses to Egypt after his experience of the Burning Bush (Ex. 4:18–26). God has just commissioned Moses to become the liberator of the Israelites, and has threatened that if Pharaoh resists, God will kill Pharaoh's firstborn son and honor the people of Israel as God's firstborn. Suddenly God threatens to kill Moses' own firstborn son (or Moses himself), until Moses' wife, Tzipporah, circumcises the child.

This story stuns the reader with its swift and utterly unexpected interruption of what seems the orderly saga of the liberator Moses. So we pay attention all the more: Could the crucial ritual of circumcision be intruding on the crucial saga of liberation because it betokens a whole community's rebirth and fruitfulness? In this moment of crisis, when we already know that women—two midwives, Miriam, and Pharaoh's daughter—have made freedom and rebirth possible, are we being told that circumcision also owes something to a woman's wisdom? And does this story, following that of Abraham, strengthen the possibility that circumcision is a way of redeeming firstborns from sacrifice and death and their fathers from profound anxiety?

As the tale of Moses as an individual becomes intertwined with the story of the entire Israelite people struggling toward its own birth, the theme of difficult procreation is even more striking. The Torah emphasizes that the entire people in their ordeal of slavery in Egypt stand under threat of the destruction of their children. Where one might imagine that the description of slavery would emphasize the exploitation, torture, imprisonment, and despair of adult Israelites, instead the story focuses most attention on Pharaoh's effort to kill all male babies. The first act of resistance to Pharaoh was not about overwork or underfeeding, but about this infanticidal decree and the refusal of midwives to obey it.

One way to understand the story of the Exodus itself is that the entire people is a child whose birth is difficult. "Israel is my firstborn," says God, reversing the normal pattern of history, since Israel is not the oldest, richest, or strongest among peoples. Instead, the newest, poorest, and weakest of the peoples becomes God's "firstborn," preferred, just as the younger brothers and sisters in Genesis became "firstborns."

But this firstborn has no easy birthing. *Mitzrai'im*, the Hebrew word for the geographically and politically narrow land of Egypt, literally means "the Narrows." If Egypt, Mitzrai'im, was a narrow birth canal for God's firstborn, the splitting of the Red Sea was the breaking of the waters. What could be described as the contractions and pangs of normal labor were the plagues and disasters caused by the obduracy of Pharaoh. God becomes both Midwife and (like Tzipporah) Circumcisor, releasing the blood of a substitute—lambs and Egyptian firstborns—in order to permit and affirm the birth of Israel, and keep this endangered child alive.

THE SEED OF DAVID

In the political and religious life of the People Israel, when large parts of the Torah were probably being shaped into present-day form, the royal House of David—especially its ability to produce an acceptable royal heir—was central to the people's self-understanding. It is especially interesting to note that the Torah describes a serious crisis of procreation in the life of the forebear of David's tribe, the major southern tribe of Judah, Yehudah.

Yehudah is described as having three sons, each of whom fails to have children. It is only when Tamar, a woman who came from outside the Israelite community, tricks Yehudah into sleeping with her by disguising herself as a prostitute that he is able to create the line of descendants that leads to his tribe's ascendancy in King David.

Indeed, the echo of Yehudah's difficulty into David's life is powerful in itself. Though David has many children, there is a striking problem in his life: Will he be able to produce a fit heir to the throne? God has promised that his offspring will rule, but this seems as hard to bring about as it was for Abraham to fulfill God's promise that his seed would populate the earth.

For David, the easiest way to creating an heir would have been to have a son with his consort, Michal, for she was a daughter of King Saul. A son of hers and David's could have united all the factions of Israel behind him. But Michal laughed scornfully at David when he danced ecstatically before the Holy Ark when it was first brought into Jerusalem, dishonoring himself, she said, by "revealing himself" even to lowly maidservants. He responded by cursing her with barrenness—saying that he would rather "get himself honor" with those same maidservants than with Michal.

At the most explicit level, perhaps the tale is saying that Michal's prudery stirred up in David a sexual aversion that left her childless. The story may even be a counterpoint to another tale, one in which the opposite of prudery in a woman stirs in David a lust so undisciplined that it leads to murder—and also stultifies fertility, though in a different way from the childlessness of Michal.

David sees the beautiful Bathsheba bathing on a housetop. He commits adultery with her, and covers up the crime by ordering Bathsheba's husband to his death in battle. Their child dies in infancy. Only after a series of fraternal wars and incestuous rape have soiled the royal household is a son born to David and Bathsheba who can ascend to kingship: Solomon.

Surely there is more to both stories than the sexual dynamic. The dynastic tangles of Saul's house cloud David's relationship with Michal as they do his relationship with her brother Jonathan. (With both, the love they bear David comes to a barren end.) David's crime with Bathsheba is even more about the corruption of power and the act of murder than about sexual license and adultery. But the tales of Michal and Bathsheba carry opposite valences. In the one, David uses sex as a tool to further his royal ambition and pride. In the other, he uses his royal power to pursue his sexual desires. The first leads to utter barrenness; the second, to death and a series of ugly conflicts, but also at last to the successful peacemaking king "Shlomo," the "shalom-one," Solomon. For David, even murder as a tool of sexual passion is more successful than sexuality as a tool of power.

These stories, along with other aspects of David's sexual life, suggest that the Bible is sketching another outlook on sex beside the priestly and prophetic one. Where the priests focused on sexual rules that would transmit bodily purity and the Prophets emphasized rules that would preserve social justice and interpersonal ethics, the royal outlook focused on something more majestic, more charismatic, more esthetic. Fierce pleasure in beauty, fierce joy in dancing are parts of the sexual ethics of the king—bound to subvert the standard regulations. (This king, remember, was also a great poet and guitarist: subversive callings that rarely ascend to rulership!)

Although most of the Biblical tradition handed on to later Judaism a strong suspicion of what kings who cared only for their own majesty might do to their subjects, Biblical culture seems to have been fascinated by the royal life-path. Even the Rabbis take David as the model for the Messiah—someday. The sexuality of sensuality, beauty, and pleasure is also given a voice, though a muted one, in the tradition. As in other arenas, so in this one: Torah does not speak in a single voice or see a simple vision. Biblical as well as later Judaisms take their revealing power from seeing that the One God wears many faces.

These stories of the House of David are especially important because much of the Torah as we know it today was probably shaped in the era of David and Solomon. So the traumatic struggles for legitimate inheritance within the royal house may have lit up in an intense glare the earlier stories of problematic procreation in the House of Abraham—just as these older tales may have predisposed later Israelite culture to give a brighter salience to any problems encountered in procreation.

Whether all these accounts of difficulty in begetting and bearing children are historically accurate or represent a powerful cultural tradition, they bespeak traumatic fear. As the Israelites gathered, selected, embellished, and focused the stories of their peoplehood, events in their lives led them to make this theme a central one.

Hence it is not surprising that as Israelites told the cosmic history of the universe and the human race, the theme of children became crucial. The first words from God to the first human male and female (Gen. 1:28) were, "Be fruitful, and multiply, and fill the earth, and subdue it."

When we examine the legal and ethical systems that spring from this cultural directive, we see that sexuality is supposed to focus on procreation. There is only one text in the whole of the Bible in which sex is favorably described as pleasurable, joyful, and loving for its own sake—and that text, the Song of Songs, seems a "countertext" in many important ways to much of Israelite culture.

In the Biblical understanding, sexual expression is most approved when it not only procreates but occurs in a family context where children can be most protectively reared to adulthood. Homosexuality is forbidden; masturbation and contraception are condemned; marital sex is prohibited during the menstrual period, and therefore skewed toward the time of highest fertility. Women who do not conceive are seen as barren (*akarah*, literally a "hardened root"). Marriage of a man to more than one woman, which is likely to multiply offspring, is approved. Marriage of a woman to more than one husband—which is not likely to lead to more procreation—is not approved.

Men are prohibited from having sex with women who are married or who are family members, for in these situations sexual relations would tend to confuse parental ties and disrupt the family units in which children were being raised. The one exception to these rules against incest concerns the special situation when a man has died, leaving no offspring. In that case, his brother and his widow are obligated to marry—in a special ceremony and arrangement called "levirate marriage"—for the specific purpose of "raising up children" in the dead brother's name.

Did the Biblical tradition ever approve violations of these rules? Yes—when having children was at stake. There are several interwoven, multilevel, and multigenerational Torah stories that, for the sake of procreation, approve what would otherwise have been transgressions against the usual rules of sexual behavior.

It is the Book of Ruth that weaves these stories together. Ruth's husband has died, leaving her no children. According to the rules of levirate marriage, she would be entitled and obligated to marry his brother, so as to raise a child in his name. But his brother has also died, and Ruth's rights remain unfulfilled. Under her mother-in-law Naomi's instructions, she attracts her husband's kinsman Boaz. When Boaz gets drunk celebrating the harvest at threshing time, Ruth breaks the rules by "uncovering Boaz's feet" (a Biblical euphemism for engaging in sex). They get married and have a child who becomes the forebear of King David.

This forward look to the begetting of Israel's model king effectively affirms and celebrates this particular case of breaking the sexual rules. But the story reinforces the point by connecting both Boaz and Ruth with two unconventional ancestors.

For in a very similar way, Boaz's ancestor Tamar has suffered the death of her husband, the death of his brother, and then her father-in-law Yehudah's refusal to let her marry a third brother in accord with the levirate rule. She breaks the rules by pretending to be a prostitute, tricking Yehudah into having sex with her. When she reveals the trick, Yehudah admits, "She is more righteous than I." More important, her "transgression," like Ruth's, is blessed with a child who becomes Boaz's progenitor and therefore King David's also (Gen. 38).

The story in the Book of Ruth even hints at the still more scandalous tale of Ruth's ancestor Moab, who is the child of Lot after he is seduced by his own daughter (Gen. 19:30–38). The daughter is convinced, after Sodom and Gomorra go up in flames, that there are no men left in the world whom she can marry, and with whom she can have children. So she gets her father Lot drunk and sleeps with him—in order to have a child. She names her son Moab, which according to the Bible's folk etymology means literally "from Daddy."

The force of these three interlocking tales is enormous. In all three, women who are explicitly or implicitly denied the marriages and children to which they are entitled are then healed by unconventional versions of a levirate "husband"—a father, a father-in-law, a distant cousin. Against all the rules of correct sexual behavior, these three women, who are being denied the possibility of having children, act—and have them. Not just any children, but the forebears of the central figure of Israelite history, King David. It may even be that for the author of the Book of Ruth, these earlier stories were hinting at the emergence of the Messiah from the House of David. (Certainly the Rabbis saw King David, and therefore Ruth and Boaz, Tamar, and Lot's daughter in this way.)

There could hardly be a stronger assertion that the main point of Biblical sexual ethics is procreating and rearing children—and that if the usual ethics get in the way, then the usual ethics can be transcended.

For many in our generation, this emphasis on begetting, bearing, and rearing children may seem double-edged. On the one hand, human beings have created the technologies that give them far more control over whether to use sex chiefly for procreation or chiefly for pleasure and joy. The same technological leaps have filled the earth with far more children, have damaged and poisoned the earth, and have undermined the old ways of creating stable families and communities.

Today some may look to the Bible to teach them how to provide a stable framework for having and rearing children. Others—or even sometimes the same people at a different time in their lives—may feel that a sexual ethic that is aimed only at begetting children is not what they or the world as a whole need at this moment of history. Now that we can not only imagine but act upon a sexual ethic and practice that are not centered on children, can we learn to shape that kind of sexuality as a sacred path?

THE SEDUCTIVE FOREIGNER

Meanwhile, one level deeper beneath the surface of these stories about Tamar and Ruth, there is a suggestion that non-Israelite women who take the sexual initiative are very attractive. In certain circumstances this can be extremely dangerous: Moabite women, according to a Wilderness tale (Num. 25), invite Israelite men both to have sex and to worship their god Ba'al. The men partake, and the God of Israel threatens death to the leaders of the people without regard to individual guilt, perhaps on the theory that they have all failed in their duty of supervision.

Moses limits the command to those who are personally involved in the worship of Ba'al. Before the death sentences can be carried out, an Israelite leader brings a Midianite princess to his bed. A member of Aaron's priestly family spears the two of them in the very act of intercourse; their death acts as a ransom for all the guilty.

This story expresses the intense anxiety that some Israelites felt about a back-and-forth flow between a fluid sexuality and a fluid spirituality that frightened and angered them. Several of the Biblical Prophets, especially Hosea (2:4–25), Jeremiah (2:20–25), and Ezekiel (23:36–49), use vividly sexual language in accusing the Israelites of whoring after foreign gods. This language compares an unfaithful Israel to unfaithful wives or to sexually voracious women—never to sexually voracious or unfaithful men.

There are several ways to understand these diatribes.

• One is that Israelite women were, or these particular Prophets thought they were, using sexual promiscuity deliberately in service of pagan gods who wanted orgies as a form of worship, calling forth the fertility of the earth and its animals by acting out fertility through the sexual act. On this understanding, the Prophets were making the analogy between sexually promiscuous women and religiously promiscuous Israel because they saw the connection as a literal fact.

Perhaps influenced by this reading of these Prophets, many nineteenth-and twentieth-century Biblical scholars concluded that when the Bible mentions and criticizes the k'deshim and k'deshot of Ba'al and other gods and goddesses of the neighboring peoples, these words meant "cult prostitutes," either male or female. However, the words themselves mean only "holy men" and "holy women," that is, priests. Perhaps priests of a secondary or subordinate status, as Levites were secondary to *kohanim* in the Israelite priestly system.

Perhaps the reference to holy women or to women as priests boggled that generation of Bible scholars, who could imagine women as priestesses only if they were using their sexuality to serve the gods.

- There is a whole alternative way of understanding these passages from the Prophets that has been put forward by a newer generation of Bible scholars (like Tikva Frymer-Kensky): to interpret the diatribes as purely metaphorical attacks on the whole People Israel (not just its women) for *collectively* and metaphorically acting toward God the way a promiscuous wife acts toward the husband to whom she presumably owes singular sexual allegiance, by rebelling, departing, sharing of her self with others.

This alternate way of understanding these prophetic passages also undermines the imagery of a surrounding set of fertility rituals and sexual celebrations. The *k'deshim* and *k'deshot* become merely male and female priests of the non-Israelite communities. On this basis, prohibiting (Deut. 23:18) the sons and daughters of Israel from becoming *k'deshim* or *k'deshot* means simply that they not become religious functionaries of other religious communities. The next verse, forbidding us to bring "the hire of a whore or the price of a dog" into God's house, may mean exactly what it says about ordinary prostitution, not cultic or sacred prostitution. Indeed, the scholars of our own generation, looking at the archeological and anthropological evidence of ancient Canaan, have found little evidence of sexual fertility rituals or of sacred prostitution.

If this second view is accurate, however, it still leaves unanswered a question: Why was the metaphor of promiscuous women so powerful, why was the possibility of promiscuous women so dreadful for Hosea, Jeremiah, and Ezekiel?

At one level, the intensity of fear and anger might have been rooted in the initial anxiety we noted earlier, the anxiety of men who were in charge of the social system (including sexuality), and who were anxious about the possibility of socially, religiously, and sexually wayward women.

Yet perhaps there is more. Trying to put myself in the situation of these "sexually anxious Prophets," this is what I imagine:

Around me—not only among the "Canaanite" peoples who are not Israelites, but among the Israelites as well—there are many who celebrate and worship earthly spirits, *ba'alim*, gods and goddesses of the cycles of the year, as well as YHWH, the Breath of Life, who sometimes seems to unite all their aspects but sometimes leaves them out. As for me, I am trying with all my might to teach the people that all these aspects simply reflect the One Great Unity.

In my attempt to do this, I am speaking out of and toward the life experience of only part of the People Israel. I and my brother Prophets—at least those of us whose works are canonized, protected, and thus kept alive for the future—have little feel for the life experience of women. For few women are named as Prophets and the messages of even these few are mostly lost. The persons and the works that are canonized as "Prophets" and "prophetic" are overwhelmingly male. I—the Seer who gets to be canonized as Prophet—am not nearly as open and effective in bringing women's diverse spiritual experiences into the celebration of YHWH as I am at bringing men's diverse experience into that Unity.

So women continue to celebrate what is left out of my unified YHWH. The power of their rituals that celebrate these other Divine energies become, for me, intertwined with their sexual attractiveness and energy.

Some of the women who seem both sexually powerful and spiritually "outsiders" are clearly not Israelites; they come from other tribes and ethnic communities. And some are in fact daughters, sisters, mothers of men whom I regard as "Israelites." With respect to both, I *identify* their spiritual waywardness with their sexual attractiveness, and I am suffused with sexual anxiety as I respond, attracted and repelled at the same time.

Those women who are not Israelites I imagine use their sexual attractiveness to seduce Israelite men, including me, into worshiping their gods. And for sure, when I hear that some Israelite men are attracted to them, I am convinced that the men are going to adopt rituals and ceremonies that seem devoted to their "foreign" gods. From this to fusing images of sexual promiscuity with images of spiritual deviance may be only a short step of imagination or polemic.

Those Israelite women whose ways of celebrating YHWH deviate from the covenant that to my mind binds the People Israel together, in some metaphoric sense seem "adulterous." What is more, since I experience these women, too, as sexually alluring, I feel that their spiritual deviance is an "adultery" against the people—perhaps even an invitation to men of other, non-Israelite communities.*

In either case, the tension over the sexuality and the spirituality of these women invokes the emotionally charged question of whether the Israelite community will have a "next generation." That is, will the children of these two sets of sexually attractive women end up as Israelites if the mothers do not exclusively worship YHWH?

So the conflation of spiritual risk with sexual risk intensifies the need of these men (and perhaps also the women who agree with them) to control sexuality so that it produces not only biological children but children who will be raised as

---

*Please keep in mind that the "I" of this passage has been my role play of an ancient Prophet—not my real "I."

Israelites—devoted to YHWH alone. The relationship between controlled sexuality and controlled child-rearing is strengthened.

Viewed from this angle, the stories of Tamar and Ruth can seem like counter-traditions that challenge and transcend the fear that foreign women will seduce Israel into worshiping foreign gods. Tamar and Ruth, two women who were both ethnic outsiders and sexual risk-takers, gave children to the Jewish people, not to some other community, and to the covenant of YHWH, not to the celebration of other gods.

Let me repeat that all this has been an exercise of the imagination. The historical documents that might prove such a train of thought among the male Israelite Prophets do not exist. Whether it seems a reasonable way to explain both the literary Biblical texts and the archaeological evidence must remain the decision of each reader.

ISSUES OF LIFE AND DEATH

Finally, there is the anxiety that emanates from the knowledge that sexuality stands at the lip of life and death, and the flow of sexual fluids represent precisely this fluid, uncertain boundary. The blood of menstruation and of childbirth comes leaking, flowing, when there is no wound, no sharp and certain slash—and it comes when it pleases, cannot be defined in time. Spurts of semen may seem more controllable, but even they occur sometimes at night, without conscious decision.

And in both cases, the possibility of life can turn to death. With menstruation, the uterus sheds its skin and an egg of potential life. With an emission of semen, thousands of sperm die; one, or none, goes on to make a life. Even cultures not so anxious about procreation as Israelite society take these flows seriously.

In the life-path of Biblical Israel, any sexual encounter between a man and woman that included a seminal emission made both the man and woman *tamei*. They remained *tamei* until the following evening, and then had to bathe in *mai'im chai'im* (living waters) to put an end to their special status. Then they became *tahor*.

How to translate and interpret the concepts of *tamei* and *tahor* is open to debate. Conventionally, *tamei* is translated "impure" or "unclean"; *tahor*, "pure." But these words seem to denigrate the status of *tumah* (the noun of which *tamei* is the adjective) in a way that does not fit its use very well. *Tumah* resulted, for instance, not only from sexual relations and their fluids but also from contact with a corpse, certain skin eruptions, mildew on buildings or clothes, and—especially surprising in this list—childbirth. Some have suggested that translating *tamei* as "taboo," "uncanny," "eerie," perhaps even "murky"—and *tahor* as "clear"—would come closer to the Bible's intention.

Individuals who were *tamei* could not enter the Shrine of God's Presence or, later, the Temple in Jerusalem. Indeed, for almost all purposes the entire status of *tumah* went into abeyance when the Temple was destroyed. Later we will examine the one aspect of *tumah*—the menstrual taboo, *Niddah*—that survived after the Temple was destroyed.

In addition to sexual relations, seminal emissions of any sort made a man *tamei*.

Menstruation made women *tamei* for seven days. Any man who had sexual relations with her became *tamei* for seven days.

Men and women who had unusual genital discharges (not semen and not menstrual blood) became *tamei* for a week. Their *tamei* status was ended when they bathed in *mai'im chai'im*. (The Biblical passages specify this for men and not for women, but by the Second Temple period at the latest, there is evidence that women as well as men were ending *tumah* by bathing in the *mikveh*, a ritual bath.)

Different aspects of *tumah* had different effects beyond the person who became *tamei*. In regard to seminal emissions, *tumah* was transmitted to cloth or leather on which semen fell. Those who became *tamei* as a result of menstruation or discharge from the genitals transmitted their *tumah* to other people whom they touched, to bedding, to chairs on which they sat, and to vessels that they used. Anyone who touched these secondary recipients of *tumah* became *tamei*, but did not further transmit *tumah* to other persons or objects.

Join all these specific rules to the Torah's statement that, at the foot of Mount Sinai, Moses ordered all the men of Israel to separate themselves from their wives for three days in order to prepare for the Revelation of the Ten Words, the central crystal of Torah. It is hard to escape the feeling that for the men who shaped Israelite culture and society, sexual intercourse and its fluids created an anxious distance from God.

True, God was the Source of all procreation and birth. But perhaps for that very reason, the people that had just become God's newborn, the "firstborn," that had struggled strongly in the womb, and that with God's help had just succeeded in being born, needed to make a separation between physical procreation and their covenant with God.

We should take care to note that at Sinai, as with *tumah* at the Shrine and Temple, the distancing was temporary. With time (and ritual immersion), *tumah* vanished. Priests and others with close-in sacred tasks were not only not required to be celibate, it was almost unheard of that they would be. So the pause between a sexual flow and direct contact with God acted rather like the eight-day pause between birth and circumcision, or the three-year pause before eating fruit from an "uncircumcised" tree. Sexuality and fertility were acts that called for covenanting—but only after a pause.

EDEN ONCE AGAIN

In the midst of a long and multigenerational literature that is filled with sexual anxieties, there are two major texts of the Bible that bespeak a much more joyous, flowing sense of sexuality. Both challenge the assumptions of a sexuality carefully ordered in time and focus. One of them comes from a male standpoint, and assumes the continuation of male dominance; the other, probably deriving from a woman's standpoint, contains more radical challenge to Biblical assumptions about the nature of sex.

The first of these texts is the saga of David. He, and he alone throughout the Bible, is presented as a strongly sensual hero. He is as erotic a lover as he is melodious a singer, caring a shepherd, bold a guerrilla, and adept a king. His wives are many and varied—from the haughty Michal to the earthy Abigail to the passionate Bathsheba to the comforting Abishag. And his relationship with Jonathan is presented in such a way as to invite the speculation that it was not only erotically charged but also physically sexual: "Wonderful was your love to me, more than the love of women!" (I Sam. 18:1–4, and 20:1–42; II Sam. 1:26).

The second great text of joyful, flowing sexuality is the Song of Songs. The Song is quite unlike any other book or passage of the Bible. It never mentions God's Name, and barely mentions the people of Israel. It focuses almost entirely on the tastes and smells and sights and songs of earth, and on the delights of love and sex. Alone in all the Bible it celebrates the throat and breasts and thighs of a woman, the brow and chest and legs of a man. Even more astonishing—alone in all the Bible it offers a dialogue, or many dialogues, in which a man and woman praise each other as sexual beings.

Most astonishing of all, the Song of Songs does not describe a world ruled by men, though it mentions men who try to rule the world. Nor does it describe a sexual relationship that is governed by men, or a man. The woman who leads the story—or if one believes the book to be a collection of songs and poems, the women who take the lead in most of them—seems to be shaping her own reality, sexual and otherwise. The Song is the easiest book of the Bible to imagine having been written or edited by a woman.

The only anxieties put forward in the Song are those arising in and from the men who try to control or forbid the sexual expressions of the woman who is the leading figure.

There are no anxieties over procreation: For the Song, children are not the main point of sex. Loving, joyous pleasure is the point. Or rather, the process, for the Song does not arrive at any climax, any point.

There are no anxieties over the flow of sexual fluids. Instead, the Song takes joy in the flow and fluidity of love itself and of love's story. Is there a single story, or is it a gathering of tales and poems? We cannot tell; the Song wants not to tell us; the story gushes, trickles, vanishes, wells up again. It flows, and no one needs to call, "*Tamei!*"

"Do not rouse or wake love until it please" is a recurring refrain, surely a departure from a tradition that speaks over and over about when sex is permissible and on what time schedule it must be redeemed from *tumah*. Indeed, the Song's sense of time is fluid and interpersonal not only when it comes to sex, but in the whole life-path of the Song, in its telling of the relationships of human beings with each other and with the earth,

Some scholars believe that the Song entered Israelite culture from a Canaanite context, either as the celebratory text for a *hieros gamos*, or "sacred wedding," of a god and goddess, or a king and goddess, or an earthly king and queen representing a god and goddess. Other scholars believe the book was a collection of songs and poems to celebrate "ordinary" weddings of the ordinary folk. In any case, the Song seems to be celebrating sexual union as a spiritual process.

When the Rabbis faced the question of whether to include the Song in the canonical literature, they justified doing so basically by reading it as a purely spiritual and allegorical text, not physically erotic at all. We will take a look at how this approach fit into the Rabbinic mind-set, and later also look at how a contemporary Jewish community might read the Song as an erotic poem that has much to say to us today about sexual ethics.

Now, as we close our exploration of the Biblical life-path of sexuality, let us take a moment to experience this remarkable text. As the Bible opens with the alluring and painful story of the Garden of Delight, so late in the Bible appears this midrash, this commentary on the Garden.

A Garden, now, for grown-ups.

No longer children bursting into rebellious adolescence and resisting Papa/Mama/God, no longer at war with the earth, no longer at war with each other—a woman and a man who now are grown-ups.

The Name of God no longer outside them but integrated wholly within, holy within.

The Bible's last word on sexuality and spirituality.

The cultural and military triumph of Hellenistic civilization shattered the life-path of Biblical Israel. After a period of internal struggle and exploration, most Jews settled into following the Rabbis who encoded their new version of Judaism, the Judaism of Diaspora, into the Talmud.

The outlooks of Rabbinic Judaism on issues of food and money were relatively stable, even though Rabbinic civilization was stretched to great length in three dimensions. In time, it lasted about 1,800 years; in space, it reached such distant points as Spain, England, Poland, Egypt, Babylonia, and even beyond; in culture, it existed alongside Hellenistic, Zoroastrian, Christian, and Muslim civilizations. When it came to sexual issues, this multidimensional stretch helped create a much wider spectrum of Rabbinic opinion and Jewish practice than it ever had about food or money.

> The Rabbis of Babylonia seem to have differed in their sexual lives from the Rabbis in the Land of Israel.
> The Rabbis expected sexual behavior among themselves to be different from that expected of other Jews.
> During the 1,800 years or so of Rabbinic leadership, there were deep changes in attitudes toward sex.
> Responding to Christian practice moved Jews in different directions from responding to Muslim practice.

Yet it is possible to talk about some overall approaches to sexuality during the Rabbinic era, so long as we keep in mind that there was also great diversity within the Jewish outlook.

As we focus our attention on the Rabbis' attitudes toward sexuality, it is perhaps even more important than it was in regard to money and food to keep in mind that all, or practically all, the Rabbis were men. Unlike the male priests who were responsible for shaping daily practice in the Biblical period, they were men defined not by bodily descent, or by perfect bodies, or by making physical offerings of food to God, but they were chosen for their verbal skills, for their ability to argue with wit and wisdom in reinterpreting passages of Torah to meet the social needs of their day.

There were two clusters of Rabbis who had a long-term effect on Jewish practice. One group lived in the Land of Israel, from about the beginning of the Common Era to about the fifth century. Their work was codified first into the Mishnah and then into the *Talmud Yerushalmi* (*Jerusalem Talmud*, or *Talmud of the Land of Israel*). The second group, which drew heavily on the work of the first, lived from about the third to fifth centuries C.E. in Babylonia, where the majority religion was Zoroastrian. They developed the *Talmud Bavli*, or "Babylonian Talmud."

It was the Babylonian Talmud that formed the seedbed for Rabbinic Judaism— but sometimes its mind-set can be understood more clearly by comparing it with its *Yerushalmi* brother. For example, in our own day the scholar Daniel Boyarin concludes that the Rabbis of the Land of Israel were more open to women studying Torah than were the Rabbis of Babylonia. Ultimately, the great flow of Rabbinic culture and practice followed the direction of the *Bavli*, not the *Yerushalmi*.

It was the editors of the Babylonian Talmud who provided the skeleton of Rabbinic Judaism for more than a millennium to come. Why do I specify the editors rather than the individual Rabbis whom they quoted? Because it was the editors who framed the questions, shaped the lines of argument, rejected or preserved or for that matter perhaps invented the debates and tales they reported and ascribed to individual Rabbis. This fact is important to keep in mind in order not to get hooked on one story or one dictum as the meaning and intention of the Talmud, but to keep in mind the broader weave of argument, including self-critique and self-subversion.

Faced with sexual attitudes in the world-sweeping Hellenistic civilization that differed radically from Biblical attitudes, what were the Rabbis to do? Sometimes, adherents of Judaism, Christianity, Hellenism, or modernism have described what happened as a head-on ideological war in which the Jewish, Hellenistic, and Christian positions became clear-cut and oppositional, or perhaps more like a guerrilla war in which one or the other side subverted each other's official territory.

The relationship was more complicated than that. In the whole Hellenistic world and in all its subcommunities, similar currents of thought were swirling. People in each community were searching for a new spiritual outlook on sex, and were listening to, learning from, and disagreeing with each other in the process. Ultimately, there was some sorting out and "Response A" became more characteristic of one community, "Response B" of another. Even then, the subcommunities sometimes drew on and sometimes resisted the sexual outlooks and practices around them. And even when they resisted, it often appears that their resistance itself took into account the cultures they were resisting.

EARTHY WOMAN, SPIRITUAL MAN

The Rabbis inherited from Biblical culture several dominant streams of thought and practice about sex:

- Men were in charge of society as a whole and of shaping sexual practice in particular, and specific men were in charge of specific women in specific marriages.
- Within that constraint, begetting, bearing, and rearing children within a stable family framework was a high priority.
- Within those constraints, the sensual pleasures of sex were a blessing, and not themselves a sign of sin or brokenness in the world.
- Yet between sensual pleasures of sex and the spiritual connection with God, there was a gap. This gap was a result not of the demonic nature of sex, but rather of the "hypererotic" nature of contact with God. This Divine erotic intensity did not require a rejection of earthly sexuality, only a separation in time between both forms of eros—so that after a sexual expression there needed to be a temporary withdrawal from direct contact with the Divine.

As we have seen, there were minority and subversive strands in Biblical culture—exemplified by the hint of a woman's viewpoint in the Song of Songs, by Hosea's prophetic hope, and by the stories of King David—that might have affected Rabbinic practice. The Rabbis might imaginably have moved in these specific directions. But they had to cope with a Hellenistic civilization that affected their thoughts deeply and their material life situation greatly.

The dominant voices of Hellenism did not reinforce—rather, they worked against—the more subversive voices of Biblical culture. Their impact on Judaism over the long haul was doubled by the fact that there were two waves of Hellenistic influence on Rabbinic culture: one when the Talmud was being formulated as Rome ruled the world, and another about one thousand years later when Jewish, Muslim, and Christian thinkers all rediscovered and absorbed many half-forgotten Greek philosophers.

Both the military and the philosophical power of Hellenism seem to have had an impact on Rabbinic attitudes toward sex:

- Hellenistic armies made the Jewish community feel much more fragile and its future more precarious in its widely scattered settlements than it had felt even in its precarious geopolitical slice of land between the great powers of Egypt and Babylonia. For this reason, for the Rabbis the Biblical concern about having children in order to secure the communal future became even more urgent.

- Many Hellenistic thinkers viewed women as "them"—"Other," different from the men who were in charge of shaping Jewish culture—in a much more radical way than Biblical culture had viewed women (whom Biblical men saw mostly as "bone of my bone, flesh of my flesh").
- At least among Hellenistic men, the idea gained currency that women represented what was earthy and material, men what was intellectual and spiritual, and sexual expression what was earthy and unspiritual. This set of notions was quite different from most Biblical attitudes toward women, men, and sex. Yet it too connected with the basic Biblical assumption that men were to rule and women to be ruled both in society at large and in particular marriages.

Among Jews and non-Jews in the Hellenistic world, there were several possible responses to these new ideas.

1. One was to encourage men to have sex with each other when they wanted to unify physical and spiritual joy.
2. Another was to separate the two worlds by encouraging men to pursue sexual pleasure with women who did not "count" intellectually, spiritually, or as family members, while pursuing the spiritual world with men.
3. Still another was for men to avoid both women and the pleasures of sex as antispiritual.

Especially because the Rabbis cared so much about procreation, they did not pursue the first or second possibilities, though some Hellenists did. The fullest achievement of the third approach might be celibacy, at least for spiritual adepts. And indeed, among those Jews and non-Jews who became Christians (and perhaps for some Jews of the Dead Sea sects), the ideal came to be celibacy for men and women, though it was considered impractical for most people.

Although the Rabbis rejected this ultimate version of the third approach, once again, probably out of the concern for procreation, they were clearly drawn to some aspects of it.

- For many of the Rabbis, the study of Torah in an all-male community became so erotically charged that they felt it more delightful than spending time with their wives. Some of them, therefore, felt strongly tugged toward long separations from home and sex.

- Along with this physical and emotional distancing went an intellectual distancing, in which women were assessed not only as subordinate to but profoundly different from men, and this created a much greater distinction in their life roles than had existed in the Biblical culture.
- Some of the Rabbis not only saw women as different from men in that they were earth-oriented but viewed them as therefore *anti*spiritual, an opening to evil. The main line of Rabbinic thought rejected this view (which was more prevalent among more Hellenized Jews, like Philo, and among Christians). But even the Rabbinic definition of Woman as "different" opened the way to the later denigrations and even demonizations of women and sexuality in medieval Judaism.
- Although the Rabbis' attraction to Torah and their distancing of women as "Other" might have logically fulfilled itself through celibacy, they strongly and unanimously affirmed marriage not only for Jews in general but for themselves as well.
- One of the major reasons for this promarriage stance was the Rabbis' strong insistence that procreation was crucial to a holy life. Some of them also asserted that joining the quite different male and female aspects of humanity was a necessary aspect of holiness.
- Many of the Rabbis, therefore, felt sexual relations with their wives to be more a duty than a delight, and procreation more a Divine command than a Divine blessing.

In seeking to regulate and institutionalize this basic outlook, the Rabbis took certain steps that made the new Jewish sexual code quite distinct from that of Biblical society. The areas in which they did this were:

- The introduction of high erotic tension into the arena of Divinity, in the female "Persons" of the Torah, the Shekhinah, and Shabbat.
- The practically total exclusion of women from Torah study.
- The extension of *niddah*, the ritual menstrual taboo, to half the month.
- The detailed regulation of marriage—how to enter it, how to conduct it, and how to leave it.
- The detailed regulation of sexual relationships within marriage.

And, let me say it clearly as we enter into this way of seeing the world, among the Rabbis as well as within the Bible, there were critical and independent voices. Voices that questioned and subverted the dominant views about men, and women, and sexuality, even if they could not overturn those views. Independent voices that we can still hear today, and can learn from, because the final editors of both

Talmuds thought it was important to preserve many of them, since the God they worshiped was a God full of contradictions, surprises, and dialectic.

Many of the Rabbis felt torn and divided within themselves as individuals, about the tug of sexuality. They also clearly understood that between them were deep disagreements. So they described "the [sexual] urge" as itself internally and intensely dialectical.

What was this urge? In Hebrew it was called the *yetzer,* a word taken from the vocabulary of the craft of shaping pottery. *Yotzer* was the word for the potter and for God as Creator, Shaper, the One who shaped Adam, the earthling, from *adamah,* the earth, as the potter shapes the pot from clay. From the same root, *yetzer* meant the imagination, the impulse, the urge that impelled the potter toward making a given shape of pottery.

For the Rabbis, the *yetzer* in human beings became the impulse—in general, sexual/erotic—that impelled human beings toward not only a specific act of creation or procreation but also toward creativity and procreativity themselves. The impulse could become *yetzer hara,* the urge toward evil, or *yetzer hatov,* the urge toward good. Even more deeply, this urge was not only poised to choose between good and evil, but was already and always, in its deepest nature, both good and evil. The Rabbis must have felt constantly challenged to choose between good and evil in their own sexual behavior, and simultaneously to experience the presence of good and evil within themselves, their sexual urges, and their community.

The Rabbis encapsulated this view of sexuality in a tale of the urge toward evil: The Jews who returned from Exile in Babylon were able to capture and imprison the *yetzer* toward idolatry that had brought about the destruction of the First Temple. Emboldened by their triumph, they sought to capture the urge toward [sexual] evil as well:

> He was handed over to them. But he [or perhaps He, God] said to them, "Realize that if you kill him, the world goes down." They imprisoned him for three days, then looked through the whole Land of Israel for a new-laid egg—and could not find one. So they said, "What shall we do now? Shall we pray for 'half-mercy' [so that the urge toward life-giving sexuality survives but its temptations toward evil, destructive forms of sexuality cease]? But Heaven does not grant prayers for half-measures." So they put out his eyes and let him go. It helped somewhat, for he no longer entices men to commit incest.

And with other tales, the Talmud teaches that the urge toward evil is a necessary and life-giving, as well as a dangerous, element of life.

LOVERS OF THE TORAH

How then to turn the urge toward evil in the direction of life and holiness?

For most of the Rabbis, the process of studying Torah was the most fulfilling way of being in touch with God. To this they brought the passion of their urge toward evil. More than prayer (which they occasionally forgot to do at the correct time because they were so deep in Torah study), more than meditation, or resistance to Roman tyranny, or acts of loving-kindness, or walking in the fields, or making love, or even bringing offerings to the Temple while it still stood, it was Torah study that let them touch the Holy One.

It is true that for the sake of the Jewish community as a whole, they taught that after the destruction of the Temple (where the Altar had been the public communal dinner table) the dinner tables of every Jewish home became the Altar. When it came to their own lives, however, they acted as if the Houses of Study everywhere were really replacements for God's Sacred House in Jerusalem.

As our own contemporary Talmud scholar and midrashic novelist Ari Elon has shown, some of the Rabbis in Babylonia imagined the Torah as *ayelet ha'shachar*, "the gazelle of dawn." Why this image? The morning star, named for Ishtar/Venus—a goddess, let us note! indeed, the goddess of love—was called the gazelle of dawn. The Rabbis compared the morning star Ishtar to Esther, whose name mimicked her goddess-name and whose radiant beauty like hers came at first dawning in a tiny spark of light, light that grew and grew to full resplendence. And they compared the redemption of Israel to the gazelle of morning for the same reason: a tiny hint at first, then more light and more light until . . . a great sunburst.

But the Torah resembled a gazelle of morning for still another reason: The gazelle, according to the Rabbis, had a "tight womb" so that its mate felt, coupling after coupling, as if it were still as tight and sensually stimulating as when they had first mated. Just so, they said, was the Torah—as full of grace and beauty, as quick to satisfy, the millionth time the Rabbis turned to her beloved words and letters as when they came to her the first time.

The danger, says Elon, was that some of the Rabbis might have turned, or did turn, the Torah into an idol-goddess, an idol not because she was female but because she was split off from the world of change and politics and striving toward truth and trustworthiness. Fall in love with Torah alone, and your burst of redemption has already come, you need no longer work to bring the rule of Heaven through a world of peace and justice.

Indeed, it is not only the span of justice in the world that you might forget. If you are making love to a supernal goddess-woman, why would you remember to make love to your own wife? And so the Rabbis tell a set of stories in each of which a Rabbi does indeed, in the flush of passion with the Torah forget to go home to his wife.

The stories are cautionary tales. In one the wife goes out on the road to watch for her husband on the day before Yom Kippur, the only day in all the year when he returns to her. "Now he comes," she says; "Now he comes!" But he does not come. She cries one tear, and instantly her Rabbi husband falls off the roof of the House of Study and is killed. In another tale, the Rabbi is bested and humiliated by the Torah knowledge of his own son, who has been taught by someone else—perhaps his mother?—because he, the father, has not been home for many years to do his duty.

These tales are the Rabbis' warning to themselves, or more precisely, the warning some of them gave others. In the same breath, they report how erotically drawn some of the great Rabbis were to Torah—and how dangerous that tug could be.

There were other dangers. The more intense this erotic weave of Torah, the more anxiety that within the weave of scholars there might be a prohibited sexual expression. There are two stories that point toward—not directly at—such dangers.

One of the great learned teachers of his generation was the beardless Rabbi Yochanan the Beautiful. He was so beautiful that if you brought a silver cup still ruddy from the forge, filled it with red pomegranate seeds, put rose petals around its lip, and let it sit at dawn to catch the first fiery rays of the dawning sun, its beauty could not match that of Yochanan! So beautiful was he that he used to stand outside the *mikveh* so that women returning from the postmenstrual ritual bath to make love with their husbands would first see his face and thus conceive children full of beauty. That very same Yochanan was swimming one day in the Jordan River. The swordsman Resh Lakish, a robber and a gladiator in the Roman games, took him for a woman and leaped into the water.

Yochanan cast one look of admiration at the swordsman's muscles and shouted, "Your strength should be for Torah study!" To which Resh Lakish answered, "Your beauty should be for women!" Together they worked out that Resh Lakish would marry Yochanan's sister, and Yochanan would teach Torah to Resh Lakish.

The story barely conceals what the relationship itself barely concealed—the intensity of the erotic tug between the two, in which Yochanan's sister acted as a kind of screen and Torah study as a form of play. The story darkens when they insult each other and, as in a love story gone wrong, the agony of their separation brings both to deep depression and at last to death.

In this story, one can see both a celebration and a warning about the quality of the two young men's relationship with God: a cautionary tale about how the eros of Torah could spill over into jealousy and death.

In the other story, a woman who was studying Torah with the great Rabbi

Me'ir stayed so late as to miss the Shabbat candle lighting with her husband. He became so jealous that he ordered her to spit in her teacher's face. For weeks she hovered, helpless, caught between her desire for harmony at home and her love and respect for Torah and her teacher. Finally, Me'ir divined her trouble and concocted a ruse to have her spit seven times into his eye. When his other students protested, he said that just as God had ordained the ordeal of the Bitter Waters as a way of restoring harmony between a jealous husband and his wife, so he, Me'ir, could allow the bitter water of her spitting to restore her household harmony.

This cautionary tale is from *Talmud Yerushalmi*, and forms part of Boyarin's evidence that in the Land of Israel, women were much more welcome to study Torah than in Babylon (*Talmud Bavli*). The anxiety it hints at is more about the dangers that intense devotion to study may pose to family life than it is about the dangers of a woman's studying. Of course, this danger arises when she is just a few hours late for Shabbat, whereas the stories about dangerous male devotion are about years of separation. Perhaps there is a special concern about women after all.

We should also notice that the Talmud does not report even a challenge to Me'ir's assumption that the Bitter Waters was not an ordeal to threaten women but God's trick to protect them. Perhaps Me'ir was deliberately closing the circle of an earlier discussion of the relationship between the Bitter Waters and Torah study by women:

One of the Rabbis says that knowledge of Torah carries so much merit that it would absolve a woman from failing the ordeal of Bitter Waters; so, he says, teach them! Others respond: In that case, don't teach them! For then Torah will become a tool of women's lewdness. (Mishnah Sotah 3:4)

Perhaps Me'ir (whose wife, B'ruriah, was one of the tiny number of women known to be deeply learned) is saying: Look, this woman with a jealous husband is learning Torah, and for this merit God has already released her from the danger of failing the Bitter Waters ordeal. But since her husband is so jealous, let her subject *me* to this ordeal.

Which is more worthy—to protect women or to punish adultery? And which process is more worthy—to welcome women into Torah study or forbid them? Despite Me'ir and B'ruriah, it would seem that the Talmud as a whole (especially *Bavli*) answers both questions in such a way as to keep women in their place—both sexually and in the matter of Torah study.

And yet, and yet...Oddly enough, by the time these conversations had been held, according to the Mishnah, the great Rabbi Yochanan ben Zakkai had already ruled that the Bitter Waters ordeal could no longer be administered to anyone. Why? Because adultery had become so widespread, among men as well as women, that God would no longer single out uncertain cases to be punished (Mishnah Sotah 9:9).

This ruling by Yochanan ben Zakkai is one of the first in a long string of Rabbinic decisions that increase the de facto legal status of women in marriage and divorce beyond the Biblical norm. And this process went forward even while— or perhaps because—Rabbinic culture viewed women as more "Other" than the Bible had.

THE SONG: AN ALLEGORY?

One of the best indications of how the Rabbis reworked Biblical approaches to sexuality is in their reinterpretation of the Song of Songs. They turned it almost upside down. This most passionately earthy and explicitly sexual book of Biblical poetry, one of only two Biblical books in which God is never mentioned and the only one in which the People Israel is barely mentioned, was transformed by the Rabbis into an allegory of the love between the people of Israel and God.

How did the Rabbis do this? First of all, there was an intense battle over whether to include the Song among the literary works that had been touched by the Ru'ach HaKodesh, the Holy Spirit, and therefore belonged in the canon of the Bible. The Rabbis actually voted, one by one, on this group of literary works, which also included Kohelet (Ecclesiastes), Esther, and Ruth.

The day on which this disagreement was resolved was perhaps the most remarkable in the history of the Sanhedrin, the highest Jewish legislative-judicial body. It was approximately the year 90 c.e. Early in the day, the president of the Sanhedrin, Rabban Gamaliel, had once again displayed enormous arrogance toward one of its most respected and popular members, Joshua ben Hananiah—forcing Joshua to remain standing while Gamaliel, seated, poured contempt on Joshua's interpretation of a point of law.

The members of the Sanhedrin rebelled. They chanted "Stop!" until the proceedings were forced to come to a halt, and they decided to depose Gamaliel as president and appoint a new one.

The new president permitted several hundred students of Torah to enter the House of Study who had been barred by Gamaliel because he deemed them insufficiently learned.

That day became so memorable to the Rabbis that the Talmud says, "Whenever the expression 'On that day' appears, it means *that* day"—the one on which Gamaliel was deposed.

On that day, the Sanhedrin decided that members of the proscribed tribe of Ammonites could marry Jews because the tribes that had been proscribed by the

Torah had been mixed up beyond analysis by the Assyrian invasions five hundred years earlier. And on that day, after hot debate the Sanhedrin voted to include both Kohelet and the Song of Songs in what is now called the Bible.

In the dispute over the Song, it was Rabbi Akiba who carried the day. He had the reputation of a poor illiterate shepherd who had become a great scholar and had safely experienced a mystical entry into the Garden, or Paradise, while his companions in that experience lost their lives, their religious faith, or their sanity. Later he endorsed the Bar Kokhba revolt against Rome by affirming that its leader was the Messiah. Ultimately he was condemned by the Romans for teaching Torah, and tortured to death.

What did Akiba say? First of all, he attacked the customary use of the Song as an erotic ballad: "Whoever trills and sings the Song of Songs in taverns and banquet halls has no share in the World to Come." Then he asserted, "The whole world is not worth the day on which the Song of Songs was given to Israel. All the Writings are holy, but the Song of Songs is the Holy of Holies [using the phrase for the innermost and most sacred room of the Holy Temple]." (See Mishnah Yadai'im 3:5; T.B. B'rakhot 27b–28a; Tosefta Sanhedrin 12:10.)

Judging from later explication, Akiba probably defined the Song as an allegory about the love between God and Israel, in which the woman who sings to her evanescent lover is Israel seeking God. This understanding evidently made the Song acceptable to a generation of Jews who were unable to treat it as sacred if it were about the joys and pleasures of earth and eros. And in the generations that followed, there was an elaboration of this allegory so that, for example, the two breasts of the playful shepherdess were interpreted as Moses and Aaron, reaching out to God before the rest of Israel.

In this way, the Rabbis lifted erotic joy to a purely spiritual experience, mirroring their own experience of the erotic joys of Torah study. Just as the sense of playful, joyful intertwining with the earth retreated when Jews no longer had a connection with the Land of Israel, so the play and joy of sex retreated into Heaven. Left behind, the body's sexuality became more focused on obligation, duty: the duties of marriage and of procreation.

Procreative marriage was central to the Rabbis' views of Jewish sexuality. Let us look at how they defined such a marriage: how it was to begin, to be conducted, and to end.

The Mishnah provided for three different ways for a man and a woman to establish a marriage: by acquisition (that is, the transfer of property), writing (a formal contract), and by "coming" (*biyah*), or sexual relations. Each step had to be preceded with a public declaration by the man and a public but tacit consent by the woman that this act was for the purpose of marriage.

By the time (three centuries later) the Gemara was encoded, the second two methods had been abandoned as separate possibilities, and were in some sense incorporated into ceremonies that surrounded the first method—"acquisition."

At that point, three legal stages were defined for accomplishing a marriage.

First of all, a couple (or their families, if the male was younger than thirteen or the female younger than twelve and a half) would agree to what we might call an engagement or betrothal, a *shiddukhin*. This would not change the legal status or sexual relationship of the parties, but it would make promises about when a marriage would take place and especially about the financial arrangements. These clauses were called *tenna'im*, or "conditions," and often the whole process was known as *tenna'im*. Since no marriage could occur without the consent of both parties, the *shiddukhin* could be broken if either party refused to go through with the wedding. In that case, financial penalties stipulated in the *tenna'im* would go into effect.

Often, this agreement became the focus of a celebration. A plate would be broken as a symbol of contract (and perhaps as a foretaste of the broken glass at the wedding).

Second came the ceremony called *erusin* (espousal) or *kiddushin* (separation or consecration). For centuries, this ceremony took place about a year before the final wedding; but for about the last thousand years, it has been directly connected with the wedding and takes place just before it, under the *chuppah* (wedding canopy).

Erusin did change both the legal and sexual status of the parties. Once it was complete, the woman was forbidden to have sex with anyone—including her intended

husband—and the espousal could only be dissolved by a *get,* a formal divorce.
Erusin was carried out with the following rites:

> Two blessings were said: one over wine, and one specifying the new sexual
> status of the couple: "Blessed are You, YHWH our God, Ruler of the
> universe, Who makes us holy by Your *mitzvot* and has given us *mitzvot* about
> forbidden sexual relations; Who has forbidden to us the one now betrothed
> and permitted [only when the wedding is completed] the one whom we will
> wed through the *chuppah* for marriage."
>
> In the presence of two witnesses, the groom gave to the bride some piece
> of property that was his own, worth at least two *p'rutot* (coins of very small
> value), and said to her aloud: *"Harei aht m'kedushet li b'taba'at zo k'dat Moshe
> v'Yisrael.* Behold!—You are separated/consecrated to me by this property, in
> accord with the law of Moses and Israel." In most communities, it became
> customary to use a ring for this property.

The third ceremony was *nissuin,* or marriage proper, after which the couple was permitted and expected to have a sexual relationship. These were the rites of *nissuin:*

- The groom accepted the obligations of the written marriage contract or *ketubah.*
  This he did by a traditional symbolic act of acquisition: Before two male
  witnesses, he took a handkerchief from the hands of the *m'sader* (literally,
  "coordinator"—that is, the officiating rabbi or other learned Jew). He lifted
  the handkerchief and returned it. Then the *ketubah* was signed by the witnesses.
- Under a *chuppah* (originally, the canopy over the actual bridal chamber; later,
  a canopy symbolizing the new joint household of the couple), and in the
  presence of a *minyan* of at least ten men, the *m'sader* led in chanting seven
  blessings (*sheva b'rakhot*) that began with the blessing over wine. The other six
  blessings celebrated God:
    Who created all for Your radiant glory;
    Who shapes humankind;
    Who shaped humanity in Your image and likeness [that is, echoing the
    text of Genesis I, male and female], and made for humans an internal process
    through which they became self-perpetuating forever [that is, sexuality for
    procreation];
    Who makes Zion joyful through her children, though she had been a barren
    mother;
    Who makes bride and groom rejoice as did the beloved companions in
    the Garden of Eden;

Who created joy and gladness, groom and bride, mirth and delight, love and fellowship—may You bring again into the cities of Judah and the streets of Jerusalem songs, weddings, and gladness!—and Who makes the groom rejoice with the bride.

The seven blessings ended with the drinking of a cup of wine.

Then the couple would retire within the bridal chamber, actually to have their first sexual fulfillment. More recently, the relationship has been symbolized by a brief withdrawal for "unification" (*yichud*) into a private room guarded by members of the community.

In Talmudic times, several Rabbis smashed a wine cup to remind the assemblage to limit their celebration—perhaps in memory of the destroyed Temple. In its beginnings, this act occurred during the festive celebration; later, it became the last ceremony carried out under the *chuppah*.

During the centuries since the Rabbis codified this marriage procedure, a number of changes have been made in the ceremonies. Perhaps the most important, legally, was that which occurred slightly before the year 1000 C.E., when one of the great Rabbis of the generation, Rabbenu Gershom, "Light of the Exile," forbade polygamy to Jews who lived in the Christian sphere of the world. Since the Biblical authorization of polygamy was so clear, Gershom felt it was impossible to assert this was an absolute law, and announced it instead as a *takkanah* (prudential repair) to protect Jewish communal honor in areas where the surrounding culture viewed polygamy with contempt. His *takkanah* did not, therefore, apply to Jews in Muslim countries where polygamy was honored. He restricted the *takkanah* in time as well as in space, presumably expecting that social conditions might change even in Christian Europe, after one thousand years.

Aside from its effect on the prestige of the Jewish community, the importance of the *takkanah* was that it tended to protect women (who had never been permitted to have more than one husband) from the diminution in power and prestige within the household that often arose when their husbands took another wife.

Another important change in defining marriage was putting an end to the period of sexual limbo originally created by *erusin*, by bringing it together with *nissuin* under the *chuppah*.

Let us step back for a moment to assess and understand all the aspects of these arrangements for initiating a marriage. Together, they intertwine a legal commitment with a set of theological assertions. Legally, the groom acquired the right to sexual relationship and other comforts with and from his wife, in exchange for making available to her his own sexuality, supporting her financially, and protecting her against the financial dangers of his own death or divorce. As a contract, the marriage required witnesses who could if necessary testify in court. The wife's consent was necessary, but it was understood from her presence and her silence, the absence of any objection from her. For other contracts, silence might not have been sufficient; in the marriage contract, the framework of acquisition considered the wife partly as property, partly as person. In a sense, she was both the object of the contract and one of its subjects: the seller (perhaps along with her father), as well as what was being sold.

It is this ambiguity that today makes the underlying theory of Rabbinic marriage unappetizing to the great majority of the Jewish community—to the extent that we know what the ritual forms of celebration symbolize. It raises for most of us the question of how to draw on our Jewish past without being imprisoned by it; in this case, how to draw on and reshape the rituals while giving them new meaning.

We should notice that even for the Rabbis, the wedding and the marriage contract were already something more than a simple contract. Business contracts did not require a blessing. Marriage did. Entering it was no less a sacred act than eating a meal, studying Torah, or witnessing a rainbow. All these required blessings to affirm that they were moments of obeying and thanking God. Although no blessing was set aside for each specific act of sexual union, the seven blessings under the *chuppah* covered them all.

Although the seven blessings seem much like those said over bread or candles, they went much further to encode a theology of the behavior they were honoring. They celebrated three circles of sexuality: the universally biological, the generically human, and the specifically Jewish. They interwove hints of the joy of sexuality with explicit celebration of the joys of rearing children. And for all these they focused attention upon God.

AFTER THE *CHUPPAH*

Marriage began at the *chuppah*, but Rabbinic regulation of it did not end there. The Rabbis examined in great detail what the marriage meant in sexual terms. They were not prudish; even at their most ascetic, they discussed the issues with frankness, sometimes with bawdiness. Let us look at five examples of their frankness, starting at the most ascetic end of the spectrum:

They asked Imma Shalom, the wife of Rabbi Eliezer, "Why do you have such beautiful children?" She said to them, "He does not have intercourse with me at the beginning of the night, nor at the end of the night, but at midnight, and when he has intercourse with me he unveils an inch and veils it again, and appears as if driven by a demon."

When Rabbi Eliezer is asked why he behaves this way, he does not answer that he fears or dislikes sex, but rather

"In order that I not imagine another woman, and the children will come to be bastards." (T.B. Nedarim 20a–20b)

He knows that he owes his wife undivided attention and devotion, and that this will lead to having beautiful children, even though he evidently finds it hard to keep his mind on her. Why he feels driven to imagine another woman remains a secret of their marriage bed, but we should note that elsewhere the Talmud pours scorn on the practice of having sex while clothed (T.B. Ketubot 48a), and that even Eliezer and Imma Shalom have no problem discussing their sexual lives with the other Rabbis. Even if they, or he, tend toward the ascetic, they are not prudish.

There are limits, however, to public disclosure:

Rav Kahana came in and lay down beneath the bed of Rav. He heard him talking [about sex] and laughing and having sex. He said, "The mouth of [Rav] seems as if he has never tasted this dish." [Rav] said, "Kahana—get out! This is not proper behavior!" [Kahana] said, "It is Torah, and I must learn it." (T.B. B'rakhot 62a)

The Talmud proceeds to reject Kahana's intrusion, and affirms that sexual relations should be private. But in the meantime, it has actually made Rav's lusty behavior public, and affirms that sexual talk between a couple is desirable in order to arouse sexual desire.

Sometimes the Rabbis' own sexual conversation seems more for fun and ribaldry than to understand the meaning of marriage. For example:

Said Rabbi Yochanan, "Rabbi Ishmael ben Yose's member was like a wineskin of nine *kav*; Rabbi Elazar ben Rabbi Shimon's member, like a wineskin of seven *kav*." [And the discussion of the sizes of the penises of various Rabbis continues.]

And another example:

A certain matron said to [two fat Rabbis]: "Your children are not yours." They answered, "Theirs [our wives'] are even bigger than ours!" She said, "If that is so, all the more so!" Some say that they said to her, "As the man, so his virility." Some say they said to her, "Love compresses the flesh."

Daniel Boyarin in *Carnal Israel,* his study of sexuality in the Talmud, explains
that the woman is saying that these Rabbis' bellies are so big that they could not
have sex—or at least, procreative sex. The two Rabbis thought that she meant
their penises were too big for intercourse, so they explained that their wives' genitals
were big enough to make sex work. Then she thinks they are talking about their
wives' bellies, and concludes that if their wives are as fat as they are, for sure they
can't have sex together. The Rabbis finally get it, and perhaps explain that with
love all things are possible—even a good tight squeeze.

Do we take this seriously as a practical medical report? Or do we see it as a
bawdy joke from the stand-up Catskill comics of their day? If the conversation
itself is meant to be a mirror of its subject—their verbal intercourse is as mixed
up as the sexual intercourse they are talking about; at first the woman and the men
can't connect with each other, but at last they do—then these are really brilliant
stand-up comics. In any case, such a Talmud is certainly not prudish.

And finally, over the edge:

> If a woman sees a snake and does not know whether it has turned its
> attention to her or not, let her remove her clothes and throw them in front
> of it. If it winds itself around them, its mind is upon her.... How can she
> fix this up? She should have sex in front of it. Others say that will even
> strengthen its urge. Rather she should take some of her hair and nails and
> throw them at it and say, "I am taboo [through menstruation]."
>
> If a snake enters a woman, let her spread her legs and place them on two
> barrels. Fat meat must be brought and thrown on burning coals; and a basket
> of cress brought together with fragrant wine and placed there, and well beaten
> [to bring out its fragrance]. They should be ready with a pair of tongs in
> hand, for when it smells the fragrance it will come out, so it can be seized
> and burnt in the fire, as otherwise it will reenter her. (T.B. Shabbat 110a)

I find it hard to take this seriously, or to believe that the Rabbis took it seriously,
as medical or zoological lore. What was it then for them? A male sexual fantasy—
perhaps what we might call a pornographic fantasy? The expression of a fear of
grotesque invasion—a kind of "Night of the Body-Snatchers"? An eruption of
subterranean fears about their own sexual attractiveness to their wives—whom they
sometimes abandoned for the sake of their beloved Torah?

In any case, for sure, it was not prudery.

What, then, do the Rabbis think the sexual relationship within marriage should be?

- They passionately affirm procreation as the root goal of sexual relations, but
  explicitly permit married couples to have forms of sex—oral and anal, for

example—that are not procreative. One rabbi asserts that erotic practices like genital kissing, pillow talk, nakedness, or variant sexual positions will lead to lame, deaf, mute, or blind children; but the other Rabbis dismiss this assertion as bad science and worse Torah. Instead, they say that sexual practices are like eating: As long as the food is kosher, a couple can cook it any way they please—roasted, broiled, braised.

- They affirm that wives are entitled both to have (a reasonable amount of) sexual relationship with their husbands, and absolutely to refuse a specific sexual encounter that they do not want. If the husband coerces a sexual act, that is rape.

- They decide that what is a "reasonable amount" of sex depends chiefly on the husband's vocation. Since, for example, camel-drivers who carry goods across a desert may have to be away from home for as long as a month, and sailors for as long as six months at sea, they are permitted long gaps between having sex with their wives. About Torah scholars, the Rabbis vacillate: Ideally, they should have sex with their wives once a week, and at minimum they must return home from study at least once a month. But later, absences of several years are condoned—with the warning that they may lead to disaster. Ordinary laborers owe sexual intercourse to their wives twice a week; donkey drivers, once a week; men of leisured wealth, once a day.

Note that all these pronouncements are phrased in terms of the wives' needs and desires: Is this because as the less powerful parties the wives needed more protection? Because the Talmud was, as almost always, addressing men and assumed that they would look out for their own desires but had to be cautioned to remember the desires of women? Because the Rabbis thought women were more sexually desirous than men? Because it was easier for men to satisfy themselves with additional wives or other women? Or because the Rabbis preferred to talk about women's desires as a cover story for their own? It is not clear.

- The Rabbis forbid husbands to have sex with their wives while fantasizing about other women. More broadly, they show great concern for the emotional relationship within which sex occurs, on the grounds that children will be born damaged if they are conceived from angry, fearful, or even merely chilly, alienated sexual relations ("when he has divorced his wife in his heart" or when his wife is asleep). Note that their worry about the effect of emotional trouble on children is diametrically opposed to their lack of worry about specific erotic practices.

Although most of these passages and comments seem to affirm the sensual and emotional pleasures of sexuality aside from the goal of procreation, it remains true that for the Rabbis, sex was by far most fulfilling when it led to having children, and that the main benefit of sensual and emotional pleasure in sex was that it would create healthier children.

The Rabbis (who often used food as a metaphor for sex) looked on sensual pleasures in sex much as they looked on taste in food. The main reason for eating was to support life and health in the individual body, but that did not mean one was forbidden to take joy in the taste of food, or forbidden to eat something delicious but nutritionally unnecessary (so long as it was kosher). So, too, with sex: Its main purpose was to support living continuity for all species, for the human race, and for the Jewish people—but that did not mean it was forbidden to enjoy sex when intending to procreate, to have additional nonprocreative sex as well, or to have sex when no children could be expected.

There were several ways in which the Rabbis strongly pointed sex in the direction of procreation. The most important was their expansion of the Biblically defined period of menstrual taboo when sex was proscribed, from five days a month to twelve.

THE MENSTRUAL TABOO

As we know, the Torah described as *tamei* or taboo a number of bodily states that concerned the boundaries and issues of the body: that is, certain skin infections (inaccurately translated "leprosy"), seminal emissions, menstrual flows, genital discharges, childbirth, human corpses, some animal carcasses and, in some cases, physical contact with people who were already *tamei* for one of these reasons.

What was the practical effect of being *tamei*? Persons who were *tamei* could not enter the Temple precincts until they had taken part in a ritual of clarification and had waited certain specified periods of time.

With the destruction of the Temple, therefore, the practical effect of all these taboo states disappeared, and the rituals for clarifying and ending taboo status disappeared—except for one.

That one was *niddah*, the menstrual taboo. And in that one single case, the taboo status not only did not vanish, it was intensified by the interpretations of the Rabbis.

In the absence of the Temple, what became the practical effect of *niddah*? It resulted in husbands and wives not being allowed to have sex, or even to touch each other, for an extended period of time each month. That time coincided with the period in which a woman was least likely to be capable of conceiving.

Why did this one aspect of *tumah* survive when the others did not?

When the Mishnah was edited, it included many detailed examinations of how

Jewish practice of the Temple offerings, tithings, and pilgrimages had been carried out—even though the Temple had been destroyed more than a century before. (Perhaps its restoration in the near future seemed reasonably possible.) In the section Taharot of the Mishnah, there were detailed law codes elaborating all the Biblical traditions of *tumah*/taboo/uncanniness as they bore on ritual clarification before visits to the Temple. *Niddah* was dealt with in as much detail as all the others.

But three centuries later, when the rest of the Talmud was edited, there was no Gemara commentary on any part of Taharot, except for the section Niddah. All the taboos had come to seem irrelevant, except for the menstrual taboo. Isidore Epstein, the editor-in-chief of the Soncino translation of the Talmud, points out that other sections of the Mishnah that concerned Temple practice did receive Talmudic commentary; only the passages on taboo and clarification did not. Epstein says the reason is that the Rabbis looked forward to the restoration of Temple offerings when the Messiah came, but they did not look forward to the restoration of taboos. For, Epstein adds, Messiah's very advent would bring purity and clarity (*tahor*) to all life. All that was taboo, all uncanniness, all murkiness, would disappear.

But *niddah* did survive. The Rabbis picked up on two special notations about this in the Torah text. One was that a man who had sex with a woman in *niddah* would himself become *tamei* for seven days. If someone simply touched her while she was *tamei*, that person also would become *tamei*, but only till the evening and after a ritual immersion (Lev. 19:24). Alone among the rules of various taboos, this one singles out a sexual relationship with the *tamei* person for unique effects. (Sex with a person who has a taboo skin infection is not singled out, for example.)

Moreover, the prohibition on sex during *niddah* appears not only in the Torah passage on taboo (Lev. 15:19–31), but also in the lists of prohibited sexual relations (Lev. 18:19 and 20:18), and is said to be subject to the Divine punishment of being "cut off" from the people. (This punishment, *karet*, is left entirely to God. The Rabbis concluded that this meant the punishment of an early death.)

The double placement of the Biblical prohibition on sex with a menstruating woman indicates a special sensibility. It seems likely—especially since the Rabbis actually expanded the prohibited period—that they were not only responding to the Biblical text but themselves shared, and perhaps felt even more strongly, the Biblical mind-set about menstruation.

That mind-set seems to have been one in which the taboos about blood, the sense of sacred power in sexuality, and the desire for procreation all came together and intensified each other. Also, the Rabbis' sense of women as profoundly "Other" may have been strongest as they contemplated the monthly recurrence of menstruation. Since it was men and only men who were writing the rules, they had no internal experience of what it meant to menstruate: a distancing that could easily have become a sense of eeriness, uncanniness, about menstruation.

Without any explicit evidence, we can imagine that menstruation may have seemed especially strange to men who spent a great deal of time away from their wives and whose most erotic experience was Torah study. If these same men were more than willing to reduce the time for sexual relationships with their wives and were especially focused on procreation, expanding the period of menstrual taboo may have had a deep appeal. Result: Even for the Rabbis, who were much more "word-Jews" and much less "body-Jews" than the Biblical priests, this aspect of the body had great power.

Over the centuries as Rabbinic Judaism evolved, the regulations governing *niddah* tended (at least till the twentieth century) to become more and more strict. A growing fear or disdain of women, especially encouraged by a new wave of Greek thought introduced into Jewish life by medieval Jewish philosophers, may have had something to do with this. But even when the greatest of these philosophers, Maimonides (himself hostile to women), criticized some new restrictions of women in *niddah*, the (male) public tended to adopt them.

As the rules governing *niddah* developed, these restrictions became the norm (as described in the *Shulchan Aruch*, the most recent major and authoritative code of Jewish law):

- Women were obligated to ascertain when their menstrual periods ordinarily began. This could be established by noting three regular recurrences of the flow: The periods began on the same day of a (lunar) month; or they began a regular number of days after the end of the previous menstrual flow; or they regularly began after some perceptible physical symptoms appeared. Women whose periods came irregularly were obligated to examine themselves and their clothes before joining in sexual intercourse.
- The "beginning" of a menstrual flow was defined as the appearance of any spot of blood "as large as a mustard seed" on a woman's body or clothes in a place where it would probably have come from her genitals. Even if this blood did not appear in her regular menstrual period and seemed likely to be a nonmenstrual discharge (as long as it was not from an actual wound), the entire sequence of the *niddah* ritual was followed.
- At least twelve hours and preferably twenty-four hours before a woman expected her menstrual period to begin, she and her husband began refraining from sexual intercourse and any other physical contact. They slept in separate beds, and the husband could not hand her any object, hold her hand, or even do things—like sending her a cup of wine—that would communicate such intimacy and caring that sexual desire might be aroused.
- This separation continued for a minimum of twelve additional days. Beginning with the first spot of blood, the woman counted five full days (including the one

on which the blood appeared) as the days of her period. If by the end of that time no more blood appeared, she put on clean white underclothes, spread clean white sheets on her bed, and began to count seven additional days.

- During these seven days she examined herself twice a day, even inserting a soft white woolen cloth, to see whether there was any further discharge of blood. If there was, her menstrual period was not considered ended until this blood no longer appeared, and she began to count seven days again from this time.
- When these seven "white" days ended successfully (that is, no blood appeared), the woman washed herself thoroughly, washed and loosened her hair, pared her nails, cleaned her teeth, and then proceeded in privacy (after sundown) to the *mikveh*, or ritual bath.
- At the *mikveh* she removed any item on her body—clothing, jewelry, even caked dough from baking—that might prevent the water from covering her entirely and throughout.
- She immersed her entire body (including her hair), letting the water wash over every inch, and recited the blessing "Blessed are You, YHWH our God, Ruler of the universe, Who has made us holy through His commandments and commanded us concerning immersion. *Baruch attah YHWH eloheynu melekh ha'olam asher kidshanu b'mitzvotav vitzivanu al t'vilah.*" In many communities, the woman then immersed herself again, from one to three times, or even more if she were praying for a specific healing—for example, to have a child. (This is one of the few cases when the usual sequence—blessing first, action afterward—is reversed. Why? Perhaps because it was considered better to say the blessing after one had lifted the state of taboo.)
- We should note that the *mikveh* (which must come from *mai'im chai'im*, "living waters," such as rain, a natural spring, a lake, and so forth) is a miniature version of the ocean from which all life came and an enlarged version of the womb from which all human life comes. The *mikveh* also figures in the ceremony of conversion to Judaism—representing a kind of rebirth—and some communities utilize the *mikveh* for spiritual rebirth before Shabbat and Yom Kippur. Its use in ending *niddah* is especially poignant, since the taboo that springs from a woman's womb is thus ended by her symbolically entering into a larger womb—the womb of all life.
- And after the *mikveh*, the woman returned home to make love with her husband.

As Judith Romney Wagner points out in her analysis of the gender politics of the Mishnah, this whole process of *niddah* delivers a double message. Although the Mishnaic Rabbis were most concerned that women in *niddah* might obscure the ritual clarity of men so that they could not enter the Temple, the Rabbis left the decision about announcing the onset of *niddah* in women's hands and eyes. In one sense, women were a means to an end beyond themselves; in another sense, they were themselves ends, since they were treated as responsible persons, trusted to use their own knowledge, judgment, and moral sense.

BE FRUITFUL AND MULTIPLY

One of the effects of the twelve-day suspension of sexual relations was to shift all intercourse toward the time when a woman was likeliest to conceive a child. During the whole of Rabbinic Judaism, procreation became not only one of the hopes and joys of marriage but its greatest goal and legal obligation.

Where the heart of Biblical Israel was full of anxiety lest there not be children and a next generation, the mind of Rabbinic Judaism was full of determination to make sure that there would be children and a next generation.

Why and how did this change come? The Biblical mood bespoke a sense of external fate, danger, and blessing; the Rabbinic mood, a sense that procreation was up to the Jews themselves. In the Bible, God over and over offers to the animals, to all humans (in the person of the original Human and then in the persons of all the descendants of Noah), and again to Abraham and his descendants, the blessing "Be fruitful and multiply," with several variations. The Rabbis turned this universal blessing into a particular command: a command to the Jewish people to procreate, and to each Jewish married couple in particular.

Jeremy Cohen, examining the three-thousand-year career of the Biblical blessing, suggests that this change met the Rabbis' need to define Jewish destiny as distinct from that of the other peoples. For them the covenant with God had become increasingly centered on the Jews and their special tasks, even though they also elaborated on the seven commands that God had given to all the descendants of Noah. Procreation, in the Rabbinic mind, was not one of these seven.

Why such a shift in thought?

1. At a philosophical level, the original command to all humanity—"Be fruitful and multiply, fill up the earth and rule it"—put the human race, as Cohen points out, on the cosmic boundary between the animal ability to have sex and multiply, and the Divine ability to rule. As the Rabbis conceived the Jewish mission, it was the need to synthesize these capacities.
2. At the social and political level, the Roman empire was demanding that its subjects multiply. The Jewish leadership may have both copied the imperial mode and felt it necessary (especially after the decimation of the Jewish community following the Bar Kokhba revolt) to insist that Jews increase their numbers.

3. In addition, some of the Rabbis hinted that there was in Heaven a storehouse of souls waiting to be embodied, and that Messiah could come only when all the stored-up souls had accomplished their bodily destiny. The more children there were, the more quickly it would be done.

To whom, then, was the command directed? Chiefly to Jewish men, though through the centuries, some Rabbinic commentators puzzled over this singling out of one gender for a responsibility that in fact could be accomplished only by both. In light of the fact that the Rabbis generally thought of men as the social universe to which all their decisions were directed, the singling-out is not so surprising.

The characterization of men as the body politic may also have had deeper reverberations: If women were defined as nurturers of the home and family, the Rabbis may have assumed, and it may have been true, that almost all women sought to have children so as to lead a fulfilling life. Men who were focused on the public sphere, however, may have needed a command to pursue the begetting of children, just as some of the Rabbis needed to be reminded to visit their wives.

What degree of procreation satisfied the command? After debate, the Rabbis concluded that two children were necessary, and if one of them was a boy that was sufficient. (Certain of the Rabbis thought both children must be boys.) In principle, they believed that the obligated partner—the husband—should end a marriage that after ten years had not produced two children, and should seek another wife. In practice, however, many of the Rabbis over the generations did not pursue the issue.

In line with their strong desire for procreation, the Rabbis were in general hostile to most forms of preventing conception, though they left some methods open.

For men, they left no openings at all, citing God's death sentence on Onan (Gen. 38:8–10), who spilled his seed uselessly in order explicitly to prevent his levirate wife Tamar from bearing a child who would have been raised as his dead brother's heir. In later Rabbinic and mystical thought, male masturbation, seminal emissions, *coitus interruptus,* and other ways of preventing semen from reaching the ova came to be considered among the worst of sins, worse even than simple murder, because they murdered many souls. Men were haunted by nightmarish visions that Lilith, demon of the night and the archetype of a rebellious woman, would couple with the wasted semen and would then give birth to thousands of demons, which would strengthen the dark Other Side of the Cosmos and reverse any efforts to heal and hallow the world.

However, the Rabbis permitted young girls, pregnant women, and nursing mothers, to use an inserted absorbent cloth—essentially a tampon—to prevent a new pregnancy from endangering their lives or the lives of their children. (It was believed that a new pregnancy could occur on top of an existing one and could deform the first fetus.) In addition, women who were likely to be endangered by pregnancy could take an oral contraceptive—a "cup of roots"—especially if they had fulfilled the obligation to have two children. But under most circumstances, contraception was strongly discouraged.

THE PROCESS OF DIVORCE

Just as marriage begins with an active deed by the groom and a tacit consent of the bride, so divorce requires initiation by the husband and tacit consent by the wife. Under some very limited circumstances, a Rabbinical court acting at the request of the wife could require the husband to give a divorce; otherwise only the husband could initiate the proceedings, and in any case, without the husband's formal act of divorcement, no divorce could happen. Since about the year 1000 of the Common Era, by decree of the same Rabbenu Gershom who prohibited polygamy, no divorce has been valid without the consent of the wife (or, in extremely rare circumstances, the consent of one hundred Rabbis).

The Rabbis frowned on divorce and tried to minimize it, in the spirit of Rabbi Eleazar: "If a man divorces his first wife, even the Altar sheds tears." But in responding to the three-way debate in the Mishnah among Akiba and the Houses of Shammai and Hillel, the Rabbis followed Akiba's ruling that any dissatisfaction (on the part of the husband) could be grounds for release. Once it became clear that the wife's consent was necessary, the door was opened partway to what we might call today "mutual consent" and "no fault" divorce.

Among the reasons that Rabbinical courts would press an unwilling party to agree to a divorce were (1) either party's unwillingness or inability to have sexual relations, and (2) diseases that were contagious, dangerous, and inspired revulsion in the other party so that sexual relationships came to an end.

The act of divorce itself was surrounded by the strongest safeguards against mistakes or fraud. The verbal content of the *get* was totally formulaic except for the date and the names of the parties, and the wording could not be altered at all. It was framed as a statement from the husband to the wife, and climaxed in "Thou art permitted to every man."

Although the written content was the same for every divorce, the entire document had to be handwritten specifically for precisely the two divorcing parties—there were no preprinted forms with blanks to be filled in. The writing instruments had to be owned by the husband (who was usually given them as a gift by the scribe), and the scribe had to have great knowledge and skill, to make sure that no error whatsoever was made. The husband then tossed the *get* directly into the hands of the wife, or under some circumstances he might send it to her through an agent. By accepting it, she signified her consent.

In Rabbinic lore, the care taken over the *get* was seen as a protection for the woman, who without a valid *get* would become an adulteress if she remarried or if she had a sexual relationship without marrying. In either situation, any children she might have would become *mamzerim*—a special category of stigmatized Jews who could marry only others in the same situation.* Under these conditions, procreation—usually so passionately desired—was viewed by the Rabbis as a deep flaw in history and the Cosmos. Therefore, a valid *get* prevented dire results.

But beneath the most immediate understanding of the care taken for a valid *get*, it is obvious that in all of this, the wife had no possibility of taking the initiative to divorce her husband, except in the most extreme circumstances and then by convincing a Rabbinical court to intervene. In cases where a husband disappeared and there was no proof of death, or, in more recent times, the man refused to give his wife a *get* and could not be coerced by Rabbinical courts because they no longer had the power to punish people, the wife could become an *agunah*, forever anchored to her absent husband, debarred from remarrying under traditional Jewish law and auspices.

In those situations the law of divorce and the requirement of a valid *get* did not protect the woman. Seen in this light, the Rabbinic provisions for divorce mainly protect the basic system in which marriage was seen as a relationship between a dominant man and a subordinate woman. The prohibition on polygamy and the requirement that a woman consent to the divorce mitigated but did not eliminate this underlying fact.

Therefore, even in its provisions for ending marriage, the Rabbinic culture tried to safeguard its underlying intention: to focus as much sexuality as possible in a male-dominated marriage so as to maximize the procreation of children, who would then be reared in a stable hierarchy that they could reproduce in the next generation.

---

*The *mamzer* category in Rabbinic law applies to children conceived from a sexual relationship that is intrinsically forbidden—forbidden whether or not the parents have gone through a wedding ceremony. The main examples are sexual unions that are adulterous or incestuous under Jewish law, or unions between a *mamzer* and a non-*mamzer*. The category does not apply to children born to unmarried people who could have contracted a legal marriage if they had chosen, or to children born to a Jew and non-Jew who could, if the non-Jew had converted, have contracted a legal marriage.

Over the 1,500 years during which Rabbinic Judaism dominated Jewish life, procreative marriage was the main arena for sexual expression, but not the only one. Through that long era, some proposals and experiments were put forward that were more ascetic than procreative marriage, and some that were more erotic.

There is no way to cover the history of Jewish sexual practice through these 1,500 years in the same depth and detail that I have given to the sexual images, ethics, and practices of Biblical and early Rabbinic cultures, and still stay inside one book. In some ways, it is not necessary. For most of this time, the assumptions underlying Rabbinic Judaism remained in place. What we need to look at with special care is those moments when some other approach to human sexuality came to the surface, or when Rabbinic thought went in an unexpected direction.

There were two periods of major change in Jewish thought and practice about sex: one from the tenth to the thirteenth centuries of the Common Era, in which changes came basically within the Rabbinic model; and one from the nineteenth century to the present, in which Modernity challenged some of the basic Rabbinic assumptions.

In the Middle Ages, three major new approaches to sexual expression had a strong impact on the way Rabbinic Judaism dealt with sex. All three had some of their roots in the Jewish community of Spain, which in this period was mostly under Muslim rule, and when there existed an atmosphere of open dialogue among Muslim, Christian, and Jewish intellectuals and courtiers.

- The earliest was the evolution of courtly love as a practice and as literature among the noble families of Muslim-ruled Spain during the tenth and eleventh centuries. The male Jewish courtiers of that time and place—the "Golden Age," as it is known among Jews—joined with their Muslim counterparts in creating an atmosphere of erotic love, directed both to men and women, that was profoundly different from the official strictures of Rabbinic Judaism.
- Yet these men were not "secular Jews," alienated from community life or from prayer and Torah. Indeed, many of them were writing poems addressed to God that the Rabbis of that time eagerly introduced into the prayer book,

where many of them are still found today. We certainly need to explore this at greater depth.

- The second was the emergence of "Jewish philosophy," a school of thought that drew heavily on the ideas of ancient Greek philosophy. Maimonides, who grew up in Spain before leaving for North Africa, was its most influential exponent.

ð

These medieval Jewish philosophers also brought into Jewish thought another influence, the Greek outlook on sexuality, especially the tendency to the "Otherization" of women, and asceticism, the taming of sexual desire.

- The third was Kabbalah, a mystical approach to the meaning of Torah that had some roots in early Rabbinic thought but flowered in new ways in the Middle Ages, especially in the *Zohar*, a book of Kabbalah, mystical midrash, written in Spain in the thirteenth century. Some of the Kabbalists focused so strongly on sexual metaphors within the Godhead that they urged that human sexual expression be intensified in order to bring on and strengthen the sexual union of the Feminine and Masculine aspects of God.

THE EROTIC POETS

Let us first look at the more erotic and ascetic departures-from-the-norm that emerged in late medieval Judaism.

In the tenth and eleventh centuries, the country now called Spain was divided into a number of principalities, mostly ruled by Muslims, in many of which a Jewish community flourished alongside Muslims and Christians. The leaders of these Jewish communities were often socially and politically well connected, and served as military, diplomatic, financial, and political advisers to the Muslim rulers. They took a full part in the social life of the courts. And at the same time they took a full part in the religious and political life of the Jewish community.

In the courts of Granada, Seville, Saragossa, and Toledo, a full life evidently included a sexual life, a love life, that was not restricted to marriage, one in which both men and women might be the beloveds of the great statesmen, generals, poets, halakhic interpreters, and midrash-makers who served in these courts.

This approach to life entered into the stream of Jewish literature and culture through the poetry of a series of remarkable men of the Golden Age in Spain.

Let us begin with Samuel HaNagid, who lived from 953 to 1056 and became a very important statesman in the Muslim kingdom of Granada. He was known from birth as Ismail ibn Nagrela (note the Arabic form of his name), and he was called HaNagid—the President—after being chosen by the Spanish Jewish community to be *nagid,* or president.

This recognition from the Jewish community paralleled his rising career in Granada. He became its vizier—in effect, prime minister—and for eighteen years he commanded Granada's army in almost constant warfare. During the same period he wrote a major work of halakhic summary and interpretation, recognized by his contemporaries as the first major attempt by any European Jew to bring the halakhic authorities of Persia into a thoroughly European context.

And—Samuel HaNagid wrote poetry. Let us listen to the translations by Jerome Rothenberg and Harris Lenowitz:

> I'd sell my soul for that fawn
> of a boy nightwalker
> to sound of the 'ud and flute playing
> who saw the glass in my hand said
> "drink the wine from between my lips"
> and the moon was a *yod* drawn on
> the cover of dawn—in gold ink . . .

And

> . . . that boy who told me: pass
> some honey from your hive
> I answered: give me some back
> on your tongue
> & he got angry, yelled:
> shall we two sin against the living God?
> I answered let your sin,
> sweet master,
> be with me.

❧

And . . . a poem built on the misspeaking of many Spanish Jews of a guttural *g* for the Hebrew guttural *r* sound—a misspeaking turned into a poetic pun, as translated by Norman Roth:

Where is the stuttering boy, where has he gone?—
Gazelle perfumed: pure myrrh and frankincense.

. . .

He meant to say "bad" (*ra*) and said to me "touch" (*ga*);
I touched him as his tongue declared.
He meant to say "go" (*surah*) and said "belly" (*sugah*);
I hastened to his belly, fenced with roses.

❧

What is one to make of this halakhic master who jokes about the sin of having sex with men, who plays with Hebrew sounds and letters and draws on references to the Bible for his gay love poetry? Echoes of King David, the warrior/poet/lover!

Many readers and translators of Samuel HaNagid's love poetry, and that of the other poet-statesmen of the Golden Age, have tried to argue away the aura of homosexual eros.

Some have asserted that these poems addressed to men were a cover story for love poems aimed at women; but why "cover" one sin with another that was far worse in the eyes of *halakha?*

Some have said that the poems are merely literary fictions, not at all reflective of real life. Even if that were so, what an astonishing thumb in the eye for conventional Jewish sexual ethics! But more and more, historians of the Golden Age are saying that there is little or no evidence to back up this assumption—and that moreover these poets and their poems were not living or writing in a literary ghetto but were deeply involved in Jewish life.

❧

One of the greatest Jewish poets of the Golden Age was Moses ibn Ezra, who lived from 1055 to about 1135. He grew up in Granada but was forced into exile in the Christian-ruled areas of Spain after a new militant Muslim religious movement captured Granada from its previous Muslim rulers. Among his great poems were hymns of repentance, forgiveness, and reconciliation with God, written for the High Holy Days of Awe and Turning. He was called by his generation HaSallach, the writer of *slichot* or "forgiveness-poems." Some of his poems remain in the prayer book to this day.

And Ibn Ezra also wrote poems like these, translated by Raymond P. Scheindlin:

Caress a lovely woman's breast by night,
And kiss some beauty's lips by morning light.
This is the joy of life, so take your due.
You too deserve a portion of the Ram
Of Consecration, like your people's chiefs.
To suck the juice of lips do not be shy,
But take what's rightly yours—the breast and thigh!

The joy of my eyes and my heart's delight—
A fawn at my left and a cup in my right!
Many men fault me, but I don't mind.
Come, watch me crush them, beautiful hind.
Old age consume them! Death to their kind!
Come, my gazelle, give me something to eat;
The mead of your lips makes our banquet complete.
Why do they want to discourage me, why?
What in the world is the sin if I
Thrill to your beauty? *There's* Adonai!
Pay them no heed, and in their despite,
Come and caress me, stubborn wight.
He listened, and let me come home with him.
He did what I wanted, obeyed every whim.
By day and by night we dallied within.
I took off his clothes and he took off mine,
He offered his lips and I drank of their wine.

ð

In the first poem, Ibn Ezra is playing with the Biblical wave-offering of the breast and heave-offering of the thigh of the sacrifice by which Aaron was conse- crated to the priesthood. In the second poem, this profoundly religious poet turns on its head the name that is traditionally used as a substitute for the Name of God, and applies it to the very lover who is specially forbidden to him by this same God.

The two poets whose works we have quoted were by no means the only erotic writers of this period. Solomon ibn Gabirol, one of the greatest of Jewish liturgical poets, also wrote love poems to boys and men; so too did Yehudah HaLevi, famous for his religious dialogue *The Kuzari* and for many religious and nationalistic poems. There were many of less fame but great artistry who similarly took a major part in Jewish religious and communal life while celebrating what today is called a gay lifestyle. And we are talking not about a few unusual poems but about hundreds of different poems in the same vein.

What can we make of this—we, who have grown up assuming that all committed traditional Jews viewed homosexuality with abhorrence? To my mind, what makes all this instructive is not necessarily the actual lifestyles of these men. There is some evidence that the youths with whom they were making love and to whom they were writing these poems were very young, and that the disparities in power between the older and the younger lovers were very great. The Rabbi-poets seem to have taken for granted the great imbalance in power between men and women in a sexual relationship, and then applied these same ethical standards to relationships between men and men. What I learn from the poems is not to affirm their specific sexual ethics but to apply my understanding of a Jewish sexual ethics to same-sex as well as different-sex relationships, despite the fact that the Torah forbids between men that which it affirms between men and women.

So for me, it is not so much the behavior of these men and their poems but who and what they were that is important. These were Rabbinic and communal leaders who never blinked away the contradiction between traditional Jewish sexual ethics and their lives, but rather used that contradiction as one aspect of their poetry, an element not of angst but of humor and play. These poets of the Golden Age break down stereotypes of what is possible for Jews who care about God, Torah, and a strong Jewish community. I believe these poets are beckoning us toward the possibility of rethinking how committed Jews can choose to live, not necessarily just as they did, but how to bring present-day ethical considerations to bear upon such choices.

What is more, the literature these poets left behind may be useful in our own liturgies, our own creation of an ongoing Jewish culture. Imagine using these poems as a kind of Haftarah, a prophetic commentary, when in every yearly cycle we come to the reading of the Torah passage from Leviticus that rejects all male homosexuality as an abomination. Imagine the impact on our communities of reopening a window to these centuries in Spain, a window to these desires in ourselves.

In 1492, a triumphant Spanish Catholic monarchy expelled all Jews from Spain and thus utterly shattered the world of the Golden Age. But it was we ourselves, the Jewish people ourselves, who then expelled from our own midst the memory of these poets, or rather, the memory of who they truly were and what they truly wrote. In our own day, ten Jubilee cycles later, the government of Spain has repented of its act and has welcomed Jews once more to Spanish soil. Perhaps this is also the moment for us to welcome back into our communities our expelled truths.

THE ASCETIC PHILOSOPHER

The cosmopolitan atmosphere of Muslim Spain, with its open dialogues across all communal boundaries, certainly helped create a soil fruitful for erotic poetry. But Spanish soil, and the dialogues between the religious communities, brought forth other fruit as well. Muslims, Jews, and Christians together rediscovered and discussed Greek philosophy—a discussion that gave birth to the new "Jewish philosophers." And what the Jewish philosophers learned from the Greeks pointed strongly away from eros, toward an ascetic outlook on sexual expression.

Perhaps the most extreme presentation of the ascetic view came from Maimonides (called in traditional Jewish circles Rambam from the acrostic of his name, Rabbi Moshe ben Maimon). Rambam was born in 1135 in Spain, lived and taught in Morocco and then in Egypt, where around the year 1200 he wrote and published his major philosophical work, *Guide of the Perplexed*. He died in 1204.

Rambam was the greatest of the Jewish philosophers and the one whose synthesis of Aristotle and Judaism won both the most intense hostility and the deepest respect. The respect won out, and over the centuries Rambam came to have a profound impact on Rabbinic thought and Jewish teaching.

His basic approach to the Divine was that God is Ultimate Mind, the highest of all Ideas, and that human beings most closely approach and understand God through acts of supreme intellect, of which prophecy is the highest. From this perspective, the emotions and, even more, the body are at best troublesome, at worst dangerous; the sense of touch is shameful and sex, disgusting.

Indeed, Rambam's outlook on sex was shaped in part by Aristotle's contempt for the sense of touch in general:

A person must fulfill the following conditions before becoming a prophet... There must be an absence of the lower desires and appetites, of the seeking after pleasure in eating, drinking, and cohabitation; and, in short, every pleasure connected with the sense of touch. Aristotle correctly says that this sense is a disgrace to us, since we possess it only by virtue of being animals; and it does not include any specifically human element, whilst enjoyments connected with other senses... though likewise of a material nature, may sometimes include [intellectual] pleasure, appealing to the human being as a human being, according to Aristotle. (*Guide of the Perplexed*, II:36)

Rambam then explains that although many great sages have clearly been filled with desire for the pleasures of touch, that is one reason they have not reached the rung of prophecy.

Beneath this disgust with the sense of touch lay Rambam's agreement with the Greek philosophers that "all corruption, destruction, or defect, comes from matter. ... Eating, drinking, sexual intercourse, excessive lust, passion, and all vices have their origin in the substance of [the human] body." He goes on to assert that "no excuse whatever should induce us to mention or speak of [sexual intercourse]." (*Guide*, III:8)

Although Greek philosophy was the intellectual source of Rambam's teaching, these Aristotelian ideas probably did not appeal to him for intellectual reasons alone. In the chapter of his *Guide of the Perplexed* from which I just quoted, he discusses sexuality and sexual language at a length that he himself finds surprising, and for which he finds it necessary to apologize: "We have made in the greater part of this chapter," he notes, "a digression from the theme of this treatise."

Even this small but revealing bit of evidence suggests what makes sense on other grounds: Rambam's own willingness to accept Aristotelian formulations, as well as the willingness of other Jews in the Middle Ages and since to accept his views about sexuality, probably had as much to do with his own body and feelings and those of the society around them as with sheer intellectual conviction.

Rambam finally teaches: "We ought to limit sexual intercourse altogether, hold it in contempt, and desire it only rarely." The prohibitions on incest and even on mating two different species of animals with each other or allowing them to plow together were, he argues, attempts to make sure that Jews would find few occasions even to think about sexual desire, and thus would reduce it to an absolute minimum.

Indeed, Rambam caps his critique of sexual desire and pleasure by asserting that one reason for the command of circumcision was to reduce sexual pleasure and thereby improve the moral sense. "There is no doubt," he claims, "that circumcision weakens the power of sexual excitement, and sometimes lessens the natural enjoyment. The organ necessarily becomes weak when it loses blood and is deprived of its covering from the beginning."

Although some commentators assume that Rambam is talking about the reduction of male pleasure in intercourse, Rambam himself goes on to say, "Our sages [Bereshit Rabbah, Chapter 80:11] say distinctly: 'It is hard for a woman with whom an uncircumcised man had sexual intercourse to separate from him.'" In other words, Rambam seems to be saying that the "weakening" of the male organ that results from circumcision is a weakening in its appeal to women. He adds, "This is the best reason for the commandment concerning circumcision."

WALKING THE TIGHTROPE: EROTIC/ ASCETIC MYSTICS

Rambam's views did not by any means go unchallenged among Jews of the Middle Ages. One of the most powerful critiques came in an essay called *Iggeret HaKodesh*, "The Holy Letter." *Iggeret HaKodesh* was probably written between 1290 and 1310, perhaps by the Spanish Kabbalist Joseph ibn Gikatilla, and certainly by a similar Kabbalist.

Scholars of our generation disagree whether *Iggeret HaKodesh* was intended to teach Kabbalah by using the metaphor of bodily sexual intercourse, or was intended to teach how to have sexual intercourse in a holy way by drawing on Kabbalah. In either case, it affirmed sexuality:

> No one should think that sexual intercourse is ugly and loathsome, God forbid! ... The matter is not as Rambam (be his memory for blessing) said. ... He was incorrect in praising Aristotle for stating that the sense of touch is shameful for us, Heaven forbid. The assertion whispers heresy, for if the accursed Greek believed the world was created purposefully, he would not have said this.
>
> We who possess the holy Torah affirm that the Holy Blessed One created all, and did not create anything ugly or repulsive. For if sexual intercourse were repulsive, then the reproductive organs would also be repulsive.
>
> If the reproductive organs are repulsive, how did the Creator fashion something blemished? If that were so, we would find that His deeds were not perfect; yet behold, Moses, the great master of prophecy, proclaimed, "The Rock Whose work is perfect."

Iggeret HaKodesh then makes an analogy between the inner reality of God and human sexual experience:

> Know that the male is the mystery of Wisdom [*Chochma*, one of the higher aspects or emanations of God called the *s'phirot*] and the female is the mystery of Discernment [*Binah*, another of the *s'phirot*]. And when they make a pure sexual connection, that is the mystery of Knowledge [*Da'at*]. Such is the mystery of man and woman in the esoteric tradition. ... Even greater than this is the mystery of the Divine Chariots [that is, the sacred entities on which the Holy Spirit rides] when they unite in the manner of male and female.

In what way should human beings have sexual intercourse so as best to encourage the Divine "sexual" unification?

The *Iggeret* teaches what times, foods, thoughts, and words will be best. It says, for example, that an ancient instruction to place the bed "between north and south" was not really about spatial orientation—that would have been foolish, says *Iggeret*. It really means to place the body's internal organs (especially the kidneys) "between cold and hot," that is, neither chilled by hunger nor overheated by much food: therefore at midnight, when food has been well digested. "Then [a man's] organs will not be at heat, and he will not ejaculate quickly. So the woman will become excited and have her emission beforehand."

This, it hinted, would stimulate the Shekhinah—the Divine Feminine Who is in exile here on earth "beneath"—to an initial arousal that would then bring on the overflowing love of the Divine Masculine "above." Thus Her exile would for at least a moment end, the two would be united in joy, and their fulfillment would fill the earth with abundance.

Iggeret HaKodesh hints at what is said boldly and distinctly by the Zohar, the preeminent text of Kabbalah by Moses de Leon, which was published in Spain during the same generation. The Zohar explicitly celebrates a complex set of internal sexual dynamics within the Godhead, carried on by the *s'phirot*, which are emanations or aspects of God.

Applying its understanding of the *s'phirot* to bodily human sexual intercourse, the Zohar walks a precise tightrope between the ascetic and the erotic. For, it says, sexual union undertaken in a holy frame of mind, focused on the sexual union of the Masculine and Feminine aspects of God, will bring intense ecstasy to the couple and the conception of devout and prosperous children. But intercourse carried on with only physical pleasure in mind, particularly when the husband is thinking of some other woman than his wife, will invite into the marriage bed Lilith, a whorish and destructive demon who is the dark side of the Shekhinah—"another woman," so to speak. The result will be perverse and rebellious children.

Let us taste just a bit of the poetic symbolism of the Zohar when it talks of both human and Divine sexuality:

> Sons of the most high, celestial holy ones, the choicest of the world, the kernel of the nut [that is, the mystics] assemble together to gain knowledge: See, the bird [the Shekhinah] descends every day [from the *s'phirot* into the world]. She is aroused in the Garden; there is a flame of fire in her wings, and in her hands are three spikes sharper than a sword [the three *s'phirot* that partake of fiery judgment], and the keys to the treasuries [of blessing and abundance] in her right hand. She cries out in terror and says, "If any of you [the mystics] have a resplendent face; if you have entered and emerged [both

the mystical Paradise and the sexual place] and grasped the Tree of Life [the central male *s'phira* and, probably, the male genitals], if you have touched its branches, reached its roots, and eaten its fruit, which is sweeter than honey, and gives life to the soul and healing to the bones, then beware of evil thoughts that are false to the Tree of Life, defile the stream and the river, the source of Israel, and bring death to the soul and destruction to the bones; for there is no life in it at all.

A thought that defiles its source produces a tree of deceit [an unholy child], because that thought ascends and changes soul for soul. . . . He has no branches, he never sees good; he is dry . . . his fruit is bitter as wormwood. . . . A good thought, however, climbs to the upper world, holds fast to the Tree of Life, grasps its branches, eats its fruit, and it produces every blessing and every kind of holiness, giving life to the soul and healing to the bones. (Zohar I, 154b–155b, Sitrei Torah)

ॐ

The Zohar also gives birth to a notion about the effects of male masturbation or spontaneous seminal emission that continues in Kabbalistic and later in Hassidic thought: that these seemingly "unproductive" emissions actually provide semen with which the demon Lilith can conceive thousands upon thousands of new demons.

Thus every male orgasm, in and out of licit connection with a woman, is fraught with enormous consequences. On the one hand, utter sweetness; on the other, utter destruction. A recipe for intense sexual anxiety but also, given what we know about the relationship between tight restraints and explosive release, quite possibly a recipe for intense sexual pleasure as well.

These Kabbalistic images of the Shekhinah as the Divine Feminine and of a balance between female and male aspects of God in the *s'phirot* opened up some new doors toward imagining equality between actual women and actual men. The doorways were not necessarily easy to enter. For one thing, many of the images of the Shekhinah saw Her not as an equal part of the Divine but only as a consort to the King—and may therefore have partly blocked the door to women as well as partly opening it.

In the outburst of Messianic hope that centered on the false Messiah Sabbatai Zevi in the 1660s, there were elements both of sexual liberation and the equality of women. One of the major components of Sabbatianism was Messianic release from Jewish law: The commandments "engraved" (*charut*) upon the Sinai tablets would become "liberated" (*cherut*) instead.

In the context of traditional Jewish law, it was perhaps not easy, either for traditional Jews or for Sabbatian messianists, to distinguish innovations that treated women as equals from those that dissolved all rules of sexual behavior. It is plain that Sabbatai Zevi saw women as participants in the religious life of the community in heretofore unknown ways. Thus on the climactic day in Smyrna in December 1665 when Sabbatai Zevi and his followers entered the regular synagogue to transform the service, he called out the "true" Name of God in the blessings (rather than the euphemism "Adonai"), refused to distinguish between Kohanim (those descended from the hereditary priests), Levites, and ordinary "Israelites" in calling people up to read from the Torah; then he called women up to read from the Torah as well!

With regard to sexual liberation, it is hard to disentangle what the Sabbatians themselves said as theory; what they actually did; what they were accused of by their opponents, especially after the Messianic bubble burst; and what was said and done by a later Messianic claimant, Jacob Frank, and then read back into the Sabbatian movement.

What is clear is that some Sabbatians asserted that Sabbatai Zevi's advent as Messiah would free the sense of touch—especially sexual touch—from the shamefulness ascribed to it by Rambam. It is also clear that he proclaimed a blessing over "the One Who frees the bound" while eating some forbidden fats from a (kosher) animal, which some considered to be a violation also of traditional sexual regulations (since these were considered in the same halakhic category). The Sabbatians were accused of holding sexual celebrations at the end of Passover. A Messianic movement might conceivably have adopted this practice to honor the tradition of reading the Song of Songs at Passover. But on the other hand this was precisely the kind of charge often falsely flung at radical religious movements.

The issue is further confused by the way in which Rabbinic Judaism conflated its commitment to male dominance in society with its belief in the need for constraints on women's sexuality. For some of Sabbatai Zevi's contemporaries, his meeting with women in private without chaperones, sharing with them at a banquet (today this might simply be considered treating them as equals) seemed sexually provocative, licentious behavior. Rumors that his wife, Sarah, had been orphaned in the pogroms of 1648 and had made her own way in the world, been a servant in a beggars' hospice, traveled on her own from town to town turned into rumors that she was a prostitute, and that he had married her deliberately to imitate the Prophet Hosea, who said his wife, Gomer, became a prostitute.

Sabbatianism may have continued to affect Jewish gender roles and sexual ethics underground as a movement of radical Kabbalah that survived the downfall of Sabbatai Zevi himself. Indeed, Gershom Scholem, the twentieth-century historian who has written the most detailed studies of the Sabbatians, has suggested that their proclamation of the end of traditional Jewish law may have prepared the soil in parts of Europe for Jews to welcome Modernity.

THE *PILEGESH* TRADITION

Before exploring how Modernity affected Jewish attitudes toward gender roles and sexual ethics, we should look at another strand of Jewish thought that stood outside the mainstream commitment to procreative marriage, a strand that can be identified most clearly in two far-distant Rabbinic responses to questions of acceptable practice.

The first came from Nachmanides, or "Ramban" (an acrostic from his name, Rabbi Moshe ben Nachman) who in Catalonia and then the Land of Israel during the thirteenth century became a great halakhic scholar and rule maker as well as a great Torah commentator. Ramban was asked whether a sexual relationship outside of marriage was permitted. He answered:

> I do not know why there is any cause for doubt, for of course she is
> permitted to him since she lives with him. Non-marital sex was prohibited to
> Israel only by the teaching of Rabbi Eliezer ben Yaakov, who warned: "One
> should not live with one woman in this land and with another woman in a
> second land, lest their offspring unknowingly marry, and brother thus marry
> sister." But if she comes into his house openly and is known to live with him,
> she is permitted. (Responsa, No. 2)

Ramban connects this question with the Biblical *pilegesh* tradition (*Pilegesh* is usually translated "concubine," which itself comes from Latin roots meaning "one who shares a room." Gideon, Caleb, David, and Solomon are all described as having *pilegesh* relationships with one or more women.) Ramban explains that neither in the Bible nor the Talmud is there any suggestion that a king may have a *pilegesh* but a commoner may not. Moreover, he says, there is no evidence that this relationship was outlawed by any Rabbinical court after the Biblical period.

In the eighteenth century, Rabbi Jacob Emden, an outstanding Talmud scholar in central Europe and a bitter enemy of the remaining underground Sabbatians, was asked to rule on nonmarital sexual relationships. Some halakhists had ruled against them on the ground that women in such relationships might forgo the obligatory *mikveh* after their menstrual periods, in order to avoid being embarrassed in front of the married women of their community. But, said Emden,

> She should feel no more ashamed of immersing herself at the proper times
> than her married sisters.... Those who prefer the *pilegesh* relationship may
> certainly do so ... for perhaps the woman wishes to be able to leave imme-

diately without any divorce proceedings if she is mistreated, or perhaps either party is unprepared for the heavy responsibilities of marital obligations....
The Torah offered the option of the *pilegesh* relationship, which is mutually initiated orally and terminated orally. (Shailos Yavetz, Vol. II, No. 15)

Although most of the official codes of Jewish law looked with scorn upon the *pilegesh* possibility, it remained an option for the bold of heart. Women who accepted this arrangement would have fewer legal protections, more legal freedoms, and probably less communal approval. If they began with independent wealth or prestige of their own, it might conceivably work to their advantage; otherwise, the risks would be great.

As Rabbis responded to specific situations that more or less fit the *pilegesh* model, some rules became clear:

- Children born of a *pilegesh* relationship had all the rights to inherit property as did children born "under the *chuppah*."
- Women were not committing adultery if they had sex with a man other than their *pilegesh* partner, and their children out of such relationships were not stigmatized as *mamzerim*.
- The women did not have the right to a financial settlement in case of separation.

ॐ

Although one might have imagined that the *pilegesh* arrangement would come into its own under the conditions of Modernity, in fact it remained almost unused in most Jewish communities.

THE BEGINNINGS OF MODERNITY

Throughout the nineteenth century, Modernity brought hurricanes of change into Rabbinic Jewish communities throughout Europe. Among the elements of the tradition that were profoundly weakened were its assumptions about women and sexuality.

New economic and social realities spurred many men to leave their wives (or delay marriage) for many years, to make more money in America or some other far-off land. Women were hired for new industrial jobs without regard to their family relationships. Personhood was defined more by individuality, less by family or communal relationships. Assumptions about matchmaking, arranged marriages, permanent marriages, village gossip as a way of controlling sexual adventurism, all dissolved.

Meanwhile, contacts with Western culture and society were also undermining old strictures about the value of words and study over physical and sexual expression. Currents of modern nationalism were swirling their way into the Jewish community, bringing with them images of bold, muscular, athletic men and women. By the early twentieth century, some Zionist thinkers were connecting three forms of redemptive physicality: the redemption of the oppressed Jewish "body politic" through free nationhood and manual labor on its own soil, the redemption of the (they thought) abandoned Land of Israel through a spiritual commitment to "make the desert bloom," and the psychological redemption of "repressed" Jewish individuals through the liberation of women and men into freer erotic relationships.

As in other arenas of life, the challenge of Modernity to Rabbinic Judaism was analogous to the challenge Hellenistic culture posed to Biblical Judaism. In the arena of sexuality, however, Hellenism had put women at a greater distance from men (though with some additional legal status) and had denigrated sex more than previous Jewish norms. Modernity treated women as both more similar to men and more equal in obligations as well as rights, and celebrated sexuality more than previous Jewish norms.

XXVI. TOWARD A NEW JEWISH SEXUAL ETHIC

Today the Jewish people stands on the verge of shaping Judaism anew for the generations and centuries ahead, and on the verge of deciding what the place of sexual expression will be in that future Jewish life. There are four significant new factors that will be affecting these decisions.

One is that throughout Modern society, women are moving toward sharing fully and equally with men in shaping the future. Within Jewish life, that means more and more women are sharing more and more fully, not only in private, small-scale ways but in the broadest public forums, in defining what Judaism as a whole, and Jewish sexual ethics, should become. There is practically no precedent for this development.

The second factor is that as a result of explosions of technology and population, the human race in general is feeling much less urgency to produce more children, and in fact is moving toward a new ethic of stabilizing or reducing its numbers on the planet. Many Jews feel that change as well. If the command to "be fruitful and multiply, fill up the earth and subdue it" has been "fulfilled," what are the implications for Jewish sexual ethics?

Third, the Modern world has taught us that a whole community should, in principle, be democratically involved in shaping communal values and laws, and it has also taught us the values of a voluntary community/culture that is not controlled by the state and does not control a state of its own (in other words, the two related values that in America we call "the consent of the governed" and "freedom of religion"). On the one hand, this means that Jewish practice is shaped not by a small elite of rabbis alone and not by the past alone, but by a much larger body of all who are in covenant with each other, with the past and future, and with the Divine. On the other hand, it means a deeper respect for individual conscience and individual practice within a voluntary Jewish community, rather than automatic and universal obedience to *halakha*. Since sexuality is felt more intensely and is more individually variable than most other aspects of life, and has been more profoundly affected by social upheaval, the growth of democracy and voluntarism in shaping Judaism is likely to make great changes also in Jewish sexual ethics.

The fourth is a change in spiritual metaphor and rhetoric in which (just as visible human power is no longer in the hands of kings or Rabbis who are "up there" and much more in the community and the self "in here") God is less and less imagined as "Up There," "Beyond," and more and more as "In Here," "Between," "Within." This fourth factor may influence sexual ethics because it tends to soften the distance between "spiritual eros" and "physical sexuality." In Up There theology, the more erotically the Rabbis described their love affair with Torah, the less they made love with their wives. The more joyfully they defined the Song of Songs as a spiritual love poem between Israel Below and God Above, the more they insisted it was absolutely *not* an erotic poem for women and men. The more the Kabbalists celebrated the sexual union of the Holy One and the Shekhinah, the more narrowly they defined sacred sexuality. So a theology that sees God as more fully "in-the-world" might reject this dichotomy and view eros toward God and sexuality toward human beings as a flowing whole, not separate and contradictory.

These four changes are not all having the same impact at the same time on all parts of the worldwide Jewish community. For some, Rabbinic Judaism continues to be viable and attractive. Some may keep on finding this true over the long haul. Others, as time goes on, may want to make perhaps gentle changes and perhaps more basic ones. Still others will seek to create an entirely new gestalt or paradigm of Jewish life.

THE GRANDDAUGHTERS OF MIRIAM AND B'RURIAH

If women are becoming equal in defining Jewish culture, what difference will that make? Won't it just be the same Jewish culture, only now with women as rabbis, family breadwinners, federation presidents, playwrights, politicians, and so on?

It could, but I don't think that it is likely. It would be the same as saying that when Jews entered more fully what was once a strongly Christian American culture and politics, nothing changed except that Jews, too, became senators. But in fact, to take just one example, as Jews became full citizens in the United States, the fact that the government had been sponsoring Christian religious observances became much more visible. American society responded not by endorsing Judaism too, but by putting new limits on government's power to define, control, sponsor, and impose religion of any sort. If Jews were half the society, as women are, American culture and politics would have changed even more.

I think there will probably be three levels of changes as women bring their own life experiences to bear on defining Judaism. One level has to do with power, one with social and cultural roles, and one with biology:

1. The generation that crosses the Red Sea from slavery to freedom—in our day, this generation of women—usually wants to empower all who have been excluded before (just as the Israelites who never forgot they were a band of runaway slaves proclaimed a Torah that put drastic limits on slavery, included foreigners in the society, and periodically annulled all debts).
2. The fact that women have been socially defined into certain specific roles (nurturers and child-rearers) and defined out of certain others (students of Torah, expounders of Jewish law, and charismatic rebbes) means that they will probably bring the previously submerged aspects of Jewish life to bear in new ways on public and visible Jewish decision-making.
3. Women will now bring into Jewish sexual ethics and life-celebration their sense of their own distinctive biology in sexual expression and procreation.

Since these changes in the direction of women's full equality are so far only partway realized, we can see only dimly what may be emerging.

The most obvious change that newly empowered women have already wrought in Jewish sexual culture is the development of special rituals to observe life-cycle events that are unique to women's bodies: pregnancy, labor, and giving birth; weaning; the onset of menstruation in adolescent girls; and the cessation of menstruation in older women. Women for whom menstruation is recurrent and familiar may sense and celebrate its eeriness on the edge of life and death, but assuredly in ways quite different from those legislated by men.

Beyond these obvious changes in liturgy and celebration, the most likely possibility—and I think it can be seen already—is that just as the men who dominated Biblical Jewish culture as a whole defined specific sexual relationships as those in which specific men dominated specific women, so women and men who are sharing equally the power to shape the future of their society will want to define specific sexual relationships as those in which the participants are equal.

Indeed, it seems to me that Jewish women and men are both moving toward asserting that *real* sexuality exists only if the parties involved are reasonably equal in power.

Notice that such a definition would be almost the reverse of the Biblical assumption that real sexuality required a relationship between a dominant man and a subordinate woman. In the Biblical model, even if there were a genital or other physical sexual expression between two people, if the man was not dominant and the woman subordinate, then the relationship was something else—trivial, or abominable, or friendly, but not sexual. If I am right that what is emerging today is an egalitarian image of sexuality, then in the new sexual ethic, relationships will probably not be treated in law or lore or liturgy as sexual if there is a large imbalance in power between the people involved. Such relationships may instead be treated as varieties of rape, or abuse, or harassment, or prostitution, or even more neutrally as political or business arrangements, but not what society wants to affirm, celebrate, and guide under the category of sexuality.

What makes me think that this change is already under way? For example, sexual relationships between rabbis and members of their congregations, even where they seem to be consensual, are now often considered disgraceful on the grounds that the power imbalance is so great that the sex is in actuality coerced.

The other side of this coin is that in large parts of the Jewish community, the wedding ceremony has become egalitarian. Rings are exchanged rather than given only from one party to the other; both parties rather than just one formally speak aloud the statements of commitment; and new versions of the *ketubah*, egalitarian and often specific to the couple, are written. Similarly, versions of the text and ceremony of Jewish divorce are now in use in which either party may initiate the divorce and neither can block it from being completed.

Where halakhically committed Jews have warned that these innovations may threaten the validity of the marriage or the divorce in Jewish law, larger and larger numbers of Jews have replied that these innovations are a new expression of Jewish law. Some have even suggested that they have increasing doubts about the validity of marriages and divorces that are not egalitarian.

Another change that seems to be taking place, partly as a result of the redefinition of sexuality as egalitarian, is that part of the reason that male homosexuality was felt to be abominable is disappearing. (We will return to this question later in this chapter.)

The equality of women and men has only begun to have an impact on how Jewish life is led. For four thousand years, Jewish culture has been shaped by men. We should not be surprised to see the new reality shaping a new Judaism—nor to see that the reshaping may take generations.

There are also other changes that are having important effects on sexual ethics and behavior. Three examples:

I. In Modern societies, people tend to marry much later than in premodern societies, long after they reach puberty and sexual awareness. Their identities are often more fluid and change much more during their life spans, because they experience many different cultures, jobs, and places. What are the implications of these changes for sexual expressiveness by people who are not married, and for the stability and longevity of marriages?

2. Modern technology has made it easier to prevent conception and birth from any given sexual encounter, thus making a human ethical choice out of what was once only a Divine power. The "godliness" of this power (and also of the power to bring about conception and birth where it was before impossible) beckons us to see an aspect of God in ourselves that was once beyond us.

3. In Modern societies, widely scattered cultures and populations come into contact with each other much more easily and quickly than ever before. This has had a biological as well as a cultural impact: Diseases are far more easily exchanged, and sexual contact comes far more easily.

These two facts are powerful enough where they exist only side by side, or are loosely intertwined. But where the connection is very close—for example, when sexual contact is the main factor in conveying diseases like syphilis and AIDS—the impact on sexual imagery, ethics, and ceremony is likely to be very strong. Shadow areas that blend life (sex) and death (disease) often give rise to strong feelings of uncanniness, eeriness, taboo.

As a result, many contemporary Jews are exploring, with doubt and trembling as well as with excitement and joy, some possible changes in sexual ethics. Sometimes excitement and doubt are expressed in public questioning, sometimes in quiet practice and experiment. Among the areas of doubt are:

—sexual activity by unmarried people;
—sexual activity between people of the same gender;
—sexual monogamy in marriage; and
—the breadth of acceptable sexual practice in any kind of relationship.

We will look at each of these doubtful categories in some detail, but first let us explore why traditional sexual ethics in these areas seem out of tune, or questionable.

For most of Jewish tradition, the link between sex and procreation was very strong, though not absolute. This connection strongly influenced Rabbinic attitudes toward masturbation, homosexuality, contraception, abortion, and marriage. The Rabbis paid great homage to what they considered the first of all the commandments: "Be fruitful and multiply, and fill up the earth and subdue it."

In our generation, however, it is possible to argue that the commandment has been so thoroughly fulfilled by the human race as a whole that it no longer needs to be obeyed by all human beings as individuals. Not only is the earth "filled up" with human beings; with the advent of the H-bomb and other planet-changing technologies it has been "subdued." We have achieved the ability to destroy most or all of life, to change the chemistry of the oceans and the atmosphere, to change the planetary climate, to extinguish species and to bioengineer new species into existence.

So the human race and the Jewish people could say to God: We have done Your bidding, we have mastered this planet. What comes next? We have achieved the powers of adulthood; now what is the behavior that befits an adult?

EDEN FOR GROWN-UPS

Since the command "Be fruitful and multiply" comes at the outset of the Garden of Eden and controls all human history from Eden on, perhaps what we are ready for now is Eden for grown-ups—the Garden of the Song of Songs.

In Biblical culture, as we have seen, the Song of Songs spoke of a submerged and subversive alternative to male domination of sexual relations, and even to marriage and procreation. The sexual ethic of the Song of Songs is focused not on children, marriage, or commitment, but on sensual pleasure and loving companionship.

As we have also seen, the Rabbis' transformation of the Song into a spiritualized allegory of the love between Israel and God was a touchstone of important changes in Jewish sexual ethics under Rabbinic leadership. Precisely because they said the Song was *not* about sex, it shaped Jewish sexuality in new ways: "upward" toward joy and pleasure, toward God and Torah, rather than toward women and men.

So there would be a kind of spiritual symmetry, as well as irony, if the Song became an important teaching of sexual ethics and practice with new music, a teaching in which pleasure and joy were earthy and spiritual at the same time. One in which the explicit mention of God's Name is absent, but instead we are invited to sense God's Presence throughout the Song, in every breath of its music, in all its form and all its content.

For indeed the absence of the mention of God is one reason we can think of the Song as a Garden of Eden for grown-ups. In Eden, Adam and Eve are children moving into adolescence. Hearing the Ultimate Parent give orders, and rebelling against those orders. Feeling embarrassed and ashamed by their emerging sexuality. Facing the necessity of an adulthood in which they must work with the sweat pouring down their faces in order to get enough to eat; an adulthood in which men will rule over women, and procreation will be painful.

In the Song of Songs, the Divine Parent is gone. Adam and Eve are grown up now, and the Parent has been absorbed into their own identities. What is more, they are no longer focused on their own parenthood, nor on wringing from the earth just enough food to keep themselves and their family alive. In the Song, their relationship with the earth is as fluid, playful, loving, and pleasurable as their relationship with each other.

What if we were to take this as a teaching for our epoch? What if we were to look at the whole human race as if it had reached that period of maturity that a happily married couple enter when they no longer need or want to have more children? When they no longer need or want to toil the earth? When they no longer need or want to do everything according to the clock or calendar, but can live more fluidly, more attuned to their internal rhythms?

As in the Song of Songs these grown-ups connect sexually for the sake of pleasure and love, so could the human race, or the Jewish people. Without denigrating the forms of sexuality that focus on children and family, we might find that forms of sexuality that are centered on pleasure are more legitimate at this moment in history than ever before.

With this broader understanding in mind, let us turn to the specific areas in which ethical doubts and questions have arisen.

BEFORE THE *CHUPPAH*

First, in regard to sexual activity by unmarried people, most Jews today do not get married at sixteen or eighteen, or even by twenty-one or twenty-five. And in most countries, many Jews get divorced while they are still sexually alert and involved. So at any given time there is a large pool of adult Jews who are not married. Many of them, probably most, do not refrain from sexual relationships until they do get married.

According to most streams of Rabbinic Judaism, for an unmarried person to carry on a sexual relationship violated the norms of a Torah-oriented community, even if it did not violate specific laws of Torah. As we know, some Rabbis appealed more to the lenient letter of the law; but most mainstream Rabbis condemned unmarried sexual relationships, few condoned them, and hardly any celebrated them.

There are several conceivable responses to our present-day life:

I. Accept that the Rabbis were right and Jews today are doing wrong according to the laws of Torah, but keep right on violating Torah because it is unbearable to live any other way.

Problem: A large number of Jews live in a clouded consciousness that they are alienated from their community and tradition, and are guilty of betraying God and Torah in a very important part of their lives. This will probably not heal or strengthen either individual Jews or the Jewish community as a whole.

2. Reverse the basic situation and restore the kind of society in which early marriage was possible because life patterns were set close to the onset of puberty and did not change much.

Problem: Except for some Hassidic and other ultra-Orthodox communities, few American Jews believe this can be, or should be, done. For few American Jews believe that we can leave or get rid of our complex society, where personalities, careers, and life-paths almost never jell in the teens and often not till the mid-thirties, sometimes come unjelled during the forties and fifties, and usually change again with long retirements beginning in the sixties or seventies. It is hard enough to make stable lifelong marriages when one partner is changing in this way; when both are doing so, it is extremely difficult.

3. Practice celibacy for long periods of unmarried time. This is the solution that the great majority of American Jews have rejected in their own lives. It is also, however, the solution that many of them identify as the "official" position of Jewish tradition and religious authority.

Problem: This chasm between practice and understanding of the tradition may be one of the most powerful elements driving most Jews away from Jewish life in their premarried and "postmarried" sexually active years. Who wants to be part of an institution that looks with hostility or contempt on the source of much of one's most intense pleasure, joy, and fulfillment?

Only in the mid-1990s have a few religious authorities asserted publicly that the requirement of celibacy for the unmarried is not the only permissible Jewish view. In 1994, for example, a commission of the Conservative rabbinate asserted that under certain ethical conditions, it was possible for unmarried people to create a degree of holiness in sexual relationships. This assertion moves in the direction of the approach described on page 341.

4. Make marriage and divorce a great deal easier and "lighter." Expect almost everyone to live through several marriages in one lifetime because almost everyone's life patterns will change several times. Redefine marriage so that it carries fewer financial and emotional burdens and other involvements. In other words, make it easy for sexually active people from puberty on to enter and leave marriage.

Rabbinic Judaism did occasionally hint at approaches like this. The Talmud, for example (Yebamot 37b), mentions that a few of the Rabbis, when they went on what we would call lecture tours, would marry a woman one night and divorce her the next morning. In that period, of course, men were permitted polygamy. So the same men who were involved in "light" marriages could be involved in "heavy" marriages at the same time. Women, of course, could not do this. In a Modern society where women and men intend to be equal, to use this Talmudic way out, would require relegitimizing polygamy for men and women.

Problem: Marriages that are redefined this way are probably not likely to provide a good environment in which to raise children or to explore the emotional depth that two people can create together over a long, committed, caring time.

5. Accept the fact that many unmarried people are sexually active—without creating standards of ethical behavior for unmarried sexual relationships or creating ceremonial or legal definitions of them. In many Jewish singles groups and *havurot*, this pattern has been generally accepted.

Problem: Absent any agreed ethical standards or ceremonies for celebrating change and healing loss, the group as a whole cannot deal effectively with problems of jealousy and other painful emotional experiences. Individuals are on their own except for help from close friends or outside psychotherapists.

6. Create new Jewishly affirmed forms of sexual relationship other than marriage, that are defined with certain standards and can be honored ceremonially. Some Conservative rabbis have taken a few steps in laying out guidelines for ethical unmarried sexual relationships, but so far these rabbis have urged that the Jewish community not celebrate or honor such relationships publicly. The ancient tradition of the *pilegesh* relationship might, however, be drawn on in shaping and celebrating such new relationships.

Problem: This approach requires a more explicit effort at change, rather than simply ignoring traditional and halakhic categories. For some, the name and ancient content of the *pilegesh* may contaminate this approach with its background of imbalance in power and wealth between the parties. But new content could be poured into this halakhic category, and perhaps we need to seek a new name for this sort of sexual relationship. For the moment, I suggest we use *ben* or *bat zug* (masculine and feminine of "member of a couple") as a formal name, since it evokes not only contemporary Israeli Hebrew usage but also the tradition of *bar* or *bat mitzvah*.

Now that we have looked at a range of possibilities and seen their benefits and dangers, how do we choose among them? If we wish to make these choices based on Jewish spirituality, wisdom, and community, if we think there was some measure of wisdom in the Jewish past along with some outlooks that raise deep ethical and spiritual problems, then we need to have a way of drawing on Torah. One way, of course, is simply to bow to the authority of the past and of those who today repeat the content of its decisions. Another path is to try to look into the deeper structure, the deeper intent, of the wisdom of the past. We would have to choose in the name of the deeper intent of Torah, as the Rabbis did when they evaded the sabbatical year's annulment of debts in the name of the deeper needs of the poor.

For me, that deeper intent includes a sense of the great spirals of human and Jewish history as part of the great spirals of the earth. The Torah points explicitly to spirals of every seven days, seven months, seven years, and seven year-cycles— climaxing in the rhythm of fifty years. That is the largest rhythm Torah knows, though Kabbalists divined within its hidden spaces a teaching of much larger spirals of seven thousand years.

The Torah's written text could hardly have pointed to thousand-year spirals, because a community needs to live through several turns of any spiral before understanding that it is a spiral. Now that we have entered another great turn in the spiral of Jewish history, it is easier to see the shift from Bible to Talmud not as a one-time earthquake but as the first turning in what may be a longer series than most of us (except for the Kabbalists) could have imagined.

From that place, we ask ourselves what serves the needs and celebrates the joys of the great life cycle of the human race and Planet Earth. We ask this question because the Torah teaches it by teaching the smaller spirals that we understood already.

So I find myself wanting to honor and celebrate a new version of the human life spiral, one that is shaped in different ways precisely because we live in a new part of the great life spiral of our species and our planet. When I search for ways to affirm and shape this new pattern, it is in the deeper teachings of ancient Torah that with joy I find the deeper wisdom of the spirals.

THE NEW LIFE CYCLE

In the new life cycle, I do not think the various possibilities will turn out to be mutually exclusive. We could imagine, in the famed formulation of Kohelet (Ecclesiastes), "There is a time for *chuppah*, and a time for *zug*." That is, Judaism can affirm that at different times of life, it is possible for individuals reasonably to pursue different basic sexual relationships:

- Times of great fluidity, when the community affirms and insists that sexual relationships be carried on with a serious concern for each partner's physical health so as to prevent sexually transmitted diseases, with honesty about degrees of emotional involvement and about other sexual relationships, and without coercion or the use of superior power. In this mode, the Jewish community would not expect the partners to be monogamous or emotionally intimate, or expect them to share their property or income. There might be a public ceremony to welcome a person into this general period of life (like the time of becoming *bar* and *bat mitzvah*); but there would be no formal celebration or definition of the particular relationships.
- Times of commitment without great permanence, when a specific *zug* relationship is announced to a face-to-face Jewish community made up of friends, a congregation, a *havurah*, but not to the state. Each particular *zug* relationship

would be defined by the people entering it (explicitly monogamous or not, living together or not, sharing some financial arrangements or not). The community would join in honoring, acting in accord with, and celebrating such arrangements, and provide an easy semipublic ceremony in which either of the parties may dissolve the relationship.

* Times of marriage, which may also be partly defined by the couple through the *ketubah*, but which are expected to be more long-lasting. These relationships would include the sharing of property and income, would be considered essential for child-rearing (though would not exclude couples who do not expect to have children), and could be dissolved only by joint agreement of the couple and by the serious participation of the Jewish community as well as civil authorities in arranging the terms of separation.

It seems to me that this approach of "a time for this, a time for that" takes the complexity of our present situation and the resources of Jewish tradition most fully into account. But it would take more than a piece of paper announcing the category of *zug* for this approach to begin functioning. In the next chapter, we will look in greater depth at how this approach might look in actual practice.

THE GAY POSSIBILITIES

During the last twenty-some years, there have been major changes in the attitudes and behavior of the organized Jewish world toward sexual relationships between men and between women.

Most major Jewish organizations, including the Reform and Conservative denominations and evidently most individual American Jews, support guarantees for the civil rights and employment rights of gays and lesbians.

The large Reform and much smaller Reconstructionist denominations, as well as many independent *havurot*, have affirmed that a gay or lesbian life-path can be as fully and authentically Jewish as a heterosexual one. What makes all these paths Jewish and sacred is their effort to adhere to Jewish ethics, ritual, Godwrestling, and reaching toward holiness—rather than their sexual orientation.

These groups have encouraged gay and lesbian synagogues and *havurot* to become affiliates, and have also begun to urge their mainstream, broad-spectrum synagogues to welcome gay and lesbian members and enable them to be public about the nature of their relationships. The number of synagogues that have achieved the level of fullest affirmation—celebrating weddings of gay and lesbian Jews, hiring out-of-the-closet gay and lesbian Jews as rabbis, electing them to congregational leadership—is small, though growing.

Various Orthodox Jewish groups and some segments of the Conservative denomination have adhered much more closely to the Rabbinic view of homosexuality: It is not only forbidden but an abomination, and its actual expression cannot be tolerated.

In some Conservative circles, there has been a reexamination of the *halakha* on these questions and an intense debate on whether to ordain gay and lesbian Jews as rabbis. The Rabbinical Assembly (Conservative) has urged that congregations welcome individual gay and lesbian Jews as members.

I have suggested that the Biblical and Rabbinic unfavorable outlooks on male homosexuality may have been rooted in two values: a strong assumption that all real sexuality is carried on between a dominant male and a subordinate female, and an intense desire to multiply children. If these were the concerns that underlay the traditional view, then many Jews may view the issue differently today.

On the question of dominance in a sexual relationship, today many Jews urge that sexual relationships be built on equality or something close to it, not on dominance. For that reason, a sexual relationship between two men does not automatically connote an abominable confusion of two dominants.

As for children, we too, in the era of the H-bomb, ozone depletion, and global warming, are concerned over whether there will be a next generation. But we live also in the era of population explosion. Too few children does not seem to be the problem. It is clear that the human race as a whole has much more to fear from violence and environmental destruction as a threat to its children than from the failure of biological reproduction.

It is true that the Jewish people is not experiencing a population explosion. But the great threat to Jewish continuity seems to be a failure of cultural transmission, the failure to convince children born to Jews that Judaism will be a vital and meaningful path of life for them.

It seems to me the answer to that challenge is not to denigrate gay Jews, who are unlikely to be coerced into biological reproduction anyway. Rather, the answer seems to be the renewal of Jewish life and the recognition that Jewish numbers will depend on the conscious choosing of Judaism—both by those born in Jewish homes and those who are not. Indeed, the rearing of children into Judaism is far less likely to happen simply through their being born into a hereditary Jewish household, and far more likely to result from conscious efforts to involve them in shaping a Judaism that meets their needs. This may be much easier to do with two children than with six or twelve. That is why it seems much more important to involve all Jews of all sexual orientations in teaching a living Judaism to the next generation, than to exclude gay and lesbian Jews from the community.

Indeed, as parts of the Jewish community have in the last generation become more open to gay participation, some gay and lesbian Jews have themselves been deciding to have children and rear them Jewishly.

For all these reasons then, concerns about biological reproduction are not nearly so central in attitudes toward homosexual practice as they once were.

As I have suggested, it is possible that the ethic of sexual pleasure and love celebrated by the Song of Songs, will come into its own alongside the ethic of family. It may seem ironic that the Song, one of the greatest celebrations of heterosexual sexuality in all of literature, could also affirm the homosexual community's bent toward sex as pleasurable and loving rather than as procreative. Sometimes ironies bear truth.

In our epoch, if any community of Jews has embodied the values of the Song of Songs (taken literally, not allegorically), it is gay and lesbian Jews. Perhaps in our epoch, then, the gay subcommunity that was despised and rejected will turn out to be the unexpected bearer of a newly important teaching. As the tradition teaches, sometimes the stone that the builders rejected becomes the cornerstone of the Temple.

In this light, it is especially poignant that the sexual ethics of commitment and family have taken on new seriousness within the gay community. This seems to be happening partly as a result of the impact of AIDS and partly because society as a whole, by moving toward legitimating and celebrating gay families, is making such relationships possible. Since a gay family is perforce more visible than a gay individual, so long as the wider society used violence, economic threats, and legal sanctions against homosexuality, even gay people who would have liked to create gay families took greater risks than those who avoided committed relationships.

It is as if the two ethics which had been ghettoized, each embodied in a separate community, have now begun to be intertwined, sharing a more holistic vision of a sexual ethic that can incorporate the values of family, commitment, procreation, sensual pleasure, and loving companionship.

If another of the ancient Jewish objections to homosexuality was the belief that it was connected with idolatry or Hellenistic philosophy, today gay and lesbian Jews live along the same range of dedication to and rejection of honesty, modesty, fidelity, intimacy, spiritual searching, holiness and God as do heterosexuals.

If Jews once objected to homosexuality as they observed it in other cultures because it seemed to divorce sex from affection and fidelity, then today there is a wide variety of ways in which homosexuality can be connected with or divorced from continuing and committed relationships. If certain specific gay male subcultures of extremely multiple sexual partnerships seem contradictory to most Jewish values, then care must be taken to avoid blanketing all homosexuality into those subcultures and to note that there are also similar heterosexual subcultures in our society.

In other words, if the basic value at stake is stability and focus in sexual relationships, then it ought to be affirmed without regard to the gender of the partners; and then it is also important to be clear about whether we respect a "time of fluidity" in sexual practice.

Even aside from the shift in the whole framework of sexual ethics from male dominance to egalitarianism, three additional factors have recently come into play that have their own specific connections to the Torah of gay sexuality.

One is the argument that for a large number of gay men and a (perhaps smaller) proportion of lesbians, homosexuality may not be a matter of choice, but of identity set either genetically or very early in life. Rabbi Hershel Matt was the first to point out that when this is true, it calls into practice the halakhic principle that absolves of "sin" those who act under compulsion.

At a more "aggadic" or symbolic level, this relatively new argument raises the question whether a community that has celebrated the Song of Songs as "the Holy of Holies," imagined its own relationship with God as that of spouse and lover, and refused to make a virtue of heterosexual celibacy, ought to insist that someone who cannot experience sexual pleasure with a partner of the other gender should have to choose between celibacy or privatized, stifled sexuality rather than publicly affirm his or her homosexuality.

On the other hand, a few proponents of gay liberation have argued (as do their opponents) that some gay people, especially some lesbians, do choose their sexual orientation and could change it if they wished during their lifetimes. A few people have said that this means that Jews who feel tugs toward homosexuality should clearly choose to abide by the ancient strictures of Torah. For other people, it means that adult Jews should be free to express their sexuality toward each other in an ethical and celebrative way, with their conduct being judged and celebrated by the same standards regardless of the gender of their chosen partner.

Others have also argued that in a broader sense, the sexuality of every individual is shaped by social definitions of sexuality. For example, some individuals may have homosexual experiences or heterosexual ones without either act becoming a "tag" for their own identities. For example, men who live for long periods of time with other men aboard ship, in prison, or in boarding schools and who focus their sexuality on other men during those times are not usually type-cast as "gay." Even in earlier, more censorious times, specific sexual acts under these conditions were not stigmatized as intensely as the same acts were under other conditions.

All this has led some Jews to argue that the Jewish community should make decisions about sexual ethics not on the basis of what might or might not be genetic or early-childhood identity, but on broader ethical and ceremonial principles that would apply to Jews of all sexual orientations, however arrived at.

Another new factor is a semiexplicit identification of gay men and lesbians as an oppressed community. Esther Ticktin has explicitly connected the oppression of gay people as fellow-victims of Nazism with the Torah command to love and protect the stranger "For you were strangers in the land of Egypt/the Narrow Place." Less explicitly, other Jews of any generation may view gay and lesbian people as oppressed because they were victims (though not in the same way) of the Nazis. And there are other overtones of the Jewish experience with anti-Semitism. For many Jews, the fact that gay and lesbian relationships have been stigmatized as immoral by various religious groups awakens echoes of centuries of the Christian stigmatization of Jews. The response of many Jews (often not with words but in the *kishkes,* at gut level) has been that gays should be treated as the Torah commands that all strangers, the excluded and oppressed, be treated: with love, respect, and equality.

Once we have noted that the Torah demands that the stranger be treated with justice and love, we should also note that it may be precisely the "strangeness" of gayness that is at the root of the fear and hatred it arouses. Perhaps it is not only the desire for children, not only the hatred of idolatry that have been at the root of the rejection of homosexuals, but the fear of what is different, strange, queer. ("What do they do in bed, anyway?")

The argument has also been advanced that this deep fear of what is strange and queer is embedded in the deep fear that "I myself" am somewhat strange, queer, different from the person I have advertised myself to be. That when I take a close look at the strange face of the stranger, it will look a great deal like the strange face in my own mirror.

The Torah repeats the command to love and respect the stranger thirty-six times—a hint that this command was not so easy to obey, whether it applied to separate peoples or to individuals who were strangers, or to what is strange within ourselves. Ultimately, how we deal with this piece of Torah may turn out to be a more solid grounding than ever-changing scientific research for our decisions how to deal with different sexual expressions.

A third new factor is that as more and more gay and lesbian individuals are invited to make their sexual orientation and relationships public, more and more members of the Jewish community who assumed and accepted that homosexuality was an "abomination" now find that beloved friends or members of their families are gay or lesbian. Standing face-to-face with real live people whose persons and actions do not seem abominable, many who were formerly ready to ban homosexuality as an abstract category now accept it as an aspect of the variousness created by an Infinite God.

In some ways, this discovery bears out the wisdom of the Jewish legal tradition that a Rabbinical court never decides an abstract hypothetical case, but only one involving real people, and only after examining the specific situation.

Some reinterpreters of religious practice have suggested, with conscious irony, that the Biblical command that "a male shall not lie with a male as with a woman" could be understood midrashically to mean, "A man shall not have sex with a man *as if* it were with a woman—shall not pretend that it is with a woman." In other words, shall "come out of the closet."

In the light of all these values, the present-day Jewish community might reexamine its attitudes toward gay, lesbian, bisexual, and heterosexual Jews.

- How can we reaffirm the importance of raising the next generation of Jewish children without denigrating homosexual practice, indeed by affirming the right, the ability, and the duty of all Jews, regardless of sexual orientation, to join in teaching the children of that community?
- How can we affirm the Jewishness of new family constellations—gay parents, single parents, adopted children, couples without children, single people living alone, extended families based on or not based on blood relationships—not only in rhetoric but in the actual behavior of synagogues, social agencies, and other institutions?
- How can the Jewish passion for social justice and for freedom for outsiders and cultural minorities be utilized in preventing discrimination based on sexual orientation?
- How can we develop an ethic of sexual relationships that takes into account gay and lesbian as well as heterosexual relationships, while the ethic itself addresses the quality of relationship, not the gender of the partners?
- How can we celebrate God as Lover and Spouse with images that work for Jews of all sexual orientations?

If this is the path we take, we will need to work out ways for congregations and communities to open up prayer, life-cycle celebration, *tzedakah, shalom bayit,* and other aspects of Jewish life to full and public participation by gay, lesbian, bisexual, and heterosexual Jews. No matter what ethic we develop about the nature, techniques, and celebration of different forms of sexual relationships, it could be applied equally to sexual partnerships regardless of gender. Homosexual marriages, homosexual *pilegesh* relationships, homosexual "fluid" time could all be treated in the same way as their heterosexual equivalents.

THE MEANING OF MARRIAGE

What sexual ethic should operate within a marriage is another arena in which there are some doubts.

Concerning, for example, the inequality or equality of partners within a marriage, there has been a strong shift toward equality in almost all segments of the Jewish community. In many circles, the marriage ceremony and the arrangements for divorce have been modified to reduce or eliminate forms that bespeak inequality, and even where the old forms are retained, the marriage itself is generally expected to be egalitarian. Where traditional forms of Jewish divorce are adhered to, however (as in most Conservative and Orthodox communities), this assumption of equality can come to a swift and volcanic end when the marriage itself ends, and the ancient context of male dominance may reassert itself in very troubling and damaging ways.

Among some parts of the Reconstructionist and Reform denominations and within the loose networks of the movement for Jewish renewal, marriages, or analogous "commitment ceremonies" or "covenant ceremonies," have begun to be celebrated for gay and lesbian couples.

With respect to marital sexual fidelity and adultery, among the Jews of today there has been a great deal of private and secretive agony, though little public discussion. Indeed, some Jewish circles might condemn even the discussion presented here as itself a weakening of traditional norms and an invitation to the shattering of marriage. In my own view, when private pain grows as widespread as are the pains of both monogamy and infidelity in contemporary Jewish life, there is a great deal more danger in keeping the pain secret than there is in raising questions about how to address it.

Once a marriage or covenanted partnership has begun, the great majority of Jews assert the norm of sexual monogamy and fidelity for the married or covenanted couple. But a sizable number violate this norm in practice, and the community is certainly unclear what sanctions to apply.

Should known adulterers be expelled from congregations? denied leadership offices? denied honors such as being called up to read Torah? admonished privately? treated as if their sexual behavior were irrelevant to the Jewish community—to its sense of holiness, its communal coherence, or its public legitimacy?

The question gets more complicated when some argue that the norm is disobeyed in practice not because people are perverse, but because the norm is untenable—at least for many couples. Should couples then make their own decisions whether their particular *ketubah* requires monogamy? Is sexual relationship outside marriage adultery only if the partners entered a commitment to monogamy, and one then betrays the commitment? Or does the community as a whole have a stake in affirming that a marriage should be monogamous?

A very few voices have suggested addressing the question by drawing on one of the oldest strands of Jewish sexual ethics—the openness to certain forms of polygamy. Until a thousand years ago among European Jews, and until a few years ago among Jews in Muslim countries, it was legitimate, though unusual, for men to have more than one wife. Was there any wisdom in allowing this possibility?

One of the main reasons that polygamy was proscribed was to protect women who were in a deeply unequal status. Does this reason for the prohibition of polygamy still hold for our generation, or does the changed status of women suggest ending the prohibition and also permitting a woman to take several husbands? (For those who would like to avoid a radical break from traditional *halakha*, the latter decision would be a great deal harder to accomplish.)

Since the other main reason that polygamy was forbidden to Western Jews was that it exposed them to contempt in Christian eyes, does the incredulity or ridicule that the notion of polygamy still sometimes provokes suggest that it is still viewed with contempt in the West and so should still be avoided, that de facto adultery is less dangerous than de jure polygamy?

To point out how hard some of the questions about what constitutes "adultery" can be, consider the following hypothetical case: A well-known leader of the Jewish community approaches his rabbi and the lay leaders of his synagogue. He has been lovingly married for many years. His wife has for several years been institutionalized with a debilitating and disabling but not fatal illness. He has cared for her with love and devoted attentiveness. Her illness has now been diagnosed as incurable. He does not wish to divorce her, for that would damage her both financially and emotionally. Yet he cannot bear to live forever lonely. He has come to love another woman, and wants her to live with him and be his sexual and emotional partner. What is the view of the congregation?

Should the Jewish community forbid him to carry on an additional sexual relationship, on the clear and simple ground that adultery is forbidden and it would endanger others as well as himself? If he insists, should he be forced to retire rather than allowed such a relationship, considering his high visibility in Jewish and public life? Should the community tolerate his life-path, provided he leads it in secret? Should it insist that he divorce his wife? Should it view this case as grounds for an exception to Rabbenu Gershom's prohibition of polygamy, and allow him to marry the other woman? Should it also affirm his choices as Jewishly best under the circumstances? Or should it perhaps refuse to decide at all, and leave the whole matter to individual conscience?

And finally, would the answers to any of these questions be different if the genders were reversed and the leader were a woman, her beloved a man? Or if the bereft leader's new beloved were of the same gender as himself or herself?

To take a very different case, rooted not in agonized difficulty but in deliberate choices aimed at achieving what the participants hope to be greater marital joy: Small groups of people, including some committed to Jewish life and practice, have privately agreed to enter what they call commitments of "polyfidelity": that is, sexual relationships among more than two people who agree to restrict their sexual relations to members of the group (not necessarily in all possible directions, but only those specifically agreed on). Sexual relationships outside the group are forbidden.

The participants call this a "polycentric marriage," or perhaps a *zug* in the sense we have discussed. They have entered it with full knowledge, loving commitments to each other, the desire to create a sacred space among themselves, and without coercion or commercial intent.

By traditional Jewish law, this would probably be adultery—at least, if women in the group were having sex with more than one man. (If it were the other way around, this arrangement might be not much different from those of King David's court or Abraham's tent.)

How should the Jewish community respond? Can this group authentically use Jewish rituals to honor their agreement?

I have set forth these hypothetical cases only in order to show some of the problems we now face (though both of them are based on real situations). I do not suggest that anyone try to "resolve" or "decide" such cases without having a real live situation before them.

Why does community discussion or agreement matter? Why not just leave these issues to the people who want to carve out new life-paths, or live by old ones? Aside from the values of community, of sharing ideas and friendships and rhythms of life, the individuals themselves, whether seeking old or new paths, cannot walk them alone. For example, a couple decides to be monogamous. But others who share neither that value nor a commitment to support people in their own paths act seductively, invite sexual relationships, make it hard to preserve the covenant. Or when one or both of the committed couple seek emotional intimacy with others than their marriage partners, but exclude a sexual relationship as part of the intimacy, both they themselves and their friends will find it hard to draw the lines.

YOUR BED IS TORAH

Finally, there is doubt about specific sexual practices in any relationship, without regard to who the partner is. Most Jews today use or support forms of contraception that were forbidden by Rabbinic law, and most use contraception at times when the Rabbinic codes would have opposed it. Many argue that families with

large numbers of children are no longer the most effective way to celebrate the
Jewish covenant with God, and that families with fewer children who educate them
in Judaism at much greater depth (a costly process in the Modern world) are
fulfilling the covenant in a way that is at least as sacred.

Most contemporary Jews reject the practice of *niddah.* Many believe that it den-
igrates femaleness, in that it rejects menstruation as an "unclean" time and process.
Not all feminists have taken that view. Some have argued that it is a valuable way
of rhythmically separating and reconnecting two sexual partners, particularly helpful
for women who are under sexual pressure from their husbands or are being treated
as sexual objects. The feminist theologian Rachel Adler at first explained *niddah* as
a way of honoring the uncanny edge of life-and-death that is involved in menstruation's casting off of a viable egg cell, but later concluded that its overtones of
misogyny were too strong for her to affirm its value.

Debates over *niddah* have turned up suggestions of how to affirm some of these
values without denigrating women. One couple who were in deep disagreement
over the question asked for help from Phyllis Berman, a feminist leader of the
movement for Jewish renewal. The husband wanted some time for sexual separation;
the wife felt that the rules of *niddah* denigrated menstruation and women. Berman
suggested that they explore separating sexually for the days of Rosh Chodesh—
the New Moon—rather than at the time of menstruation. In this way they could
experience the rhythm of separation and return without focusing on menstruation.
Others have suggested refraining from sex for just a day or two of the menstrual
cycle, thus honoring its uncanniness without defining it as unclean.

THE MEANING OF DIVORCE

What does it mean for Jews who live in Modern societies to end marriages and
committed relationships? What should be the role of the Jewish community? Is
divorce a purely legal matter, or also a spiritual separation? How might we deal
with the emotional charge involved in divorce?

Practically all Modern societies have defined divorce as a matter to be addressed
by secular civil authorities, which regard themselves as responsible to deal with
issues of property and the custody of children. Where does this leave the Jewish
community and Rabbinic law and culture?

Some communities—especially those now defined as Orthodox and Conservative—have adhered to the traditional Rabbinic law of divorce. Many of them have,
however, decided that under the new conditions of Modern society, some new
elements must be introduced.

One of the most serious problems, in the eyes of such communities, is that under Modern conditions, the problem of the *agunah* or "anchored" woman has become greater. For it has become much easier for men to receive a civil divorce and to refuse to give their wives a Jewish divorce. Under traditional law, their wives cannot remarry without committing what under Jewish law would be adultery, and thus bringing on the danger that any children from the second marriage would be *mamzerim*. Some men have refused to give the traditional *get* out of dislike for Jewish law; others as a way of blackmailing wives who wanted to continue their involvement in traditional Jewish life. Since in most Modern societies the Jewish communities and the Rabbinate cannot use legal punishments to enforce decisions, it has been hard for Rabbis to insist on giving a *get*.

As this danger grew, some Conservative (and a few Orthodox) authorities decided to introduce new conditions to be attached to the wedding *ketubah*. In general, these conditions have provided for ways to end or annul the marriage if it collapsed and a husband refused to give a *get* under specified conditions.

A second response to the new conditions of Modernity was the decision by the Reform Jewish community to abolish both the need for a divorce under Jewish auspices and the category of the *mamzer* (since they found it ethically offensive to punish children for the deeds of their parents). This left divorce to the civil authorities, and thus Jews could remarry without fear that the Reform community would regard children of the new marriage as *mamzerim*.

Newer currents in Jewish life—particularly the Reconstructionist denomination and some formal and informal groups committed to Jewish renewal—have moved in another direction. They have developed an egalitarian procedure, in which each party provides a *get* to the other, or either party to a marriage can dissolve it by initiating a *get* if the marriage has already been dissolved under civil law.

Most of these newer communities do not recognize the *mamzer* tradition as valid in Jewish law. Their main reason to develop the egalitarian *get* has been a sense that a marriage or covenanted relationship initiated under Jewish spiritual auspices should be ended the same way, rather than by secular authorities. They have argued that ending a marriage or covenanted partnership raises not just legal issues, but also emotional and spiritual issues that are just as powerful as those that are involved at the beginning of the marriage. Not dealing with matters of the heart and spirit are liable to leave festering sores for either or both parties.

For that reason, the efforts to create an egalitarian *get* have been accompanied by attempts to make the ceremony of Jewish divorce more emotionally and spiritually fulfilling, with a real sense of dignity and closure for both parties.

- Some rabbis, teachers, counselors, and spiritual guides have asked those who expect to divorce to meet with them for prayer and counseling about the issues between them, just as many officiants do when couples plan to get married.

- Rabbi Max Ticktin has asked divorcing parties to exchange private and personal letters as well as the impersonal and formulaic *get*. Some counselors have choreographed the ceremony to include each partner's carefully looking the other in the eye. Ticktin has also suggested that friends and close co-congregants of each of the divorcing parties might gather to share love, support, and prayer.

THE HOUSE OF LOVING COUNSEL

These efforts to create an emotional and spiritual Jewish presence before and at divorce are only a special case of broader efforts to draw on Jewish values and symbols to deal with sexual relationships. What processes should our generation use to do this?

Berman's response to the couple's question about *niddah* discussed earlier did not arise out of a sense of being judgmental. It came, rather, from a place of nurturing wisdom, seeking to reconcile deeply held values that are not necessarily contradictory and to draw on Jewish tradition without rigidly obeying the strictures of the past.

In a sense, Berman responded to the question not as someone would in Rabbinical court or *beit din*—"house of rigorous judgment," but as in a *beit chesed*— "house of nurturing love."

It was no accident that this *beit chesed* approach arose precisely over an issue of sexual ethics and ceremony, and over a collision between the Rabbinic code and a woman's rethinking of sexuality in "post-Rabbinic" marriage that was striving toward an egalitarian relationship. No accident, because the issues of sexual behavior are among those in which individual values and differences most strongly coexist with the desire to create a strong community. It is an area in which the rulings of a *beit din* seemed least appropriate, and those of conciliation and advice most sensible.

We might well imagine that this change in process from rule-making to relational weaving is one of the more implicit and osmosislike results of women's new role in shaping of the Jewish future. It is an example of how women, previously isolated in relational roles in the family, can now bring those ways of thinking into new places outside the family, in public Jewish life.

We might even consider making it a matter of communal ethical agreement and obligation that before undertaking a major change in sexual relationships, members of a given community were required, not simply encouraged, to consult with such a *beit chesed*. Whether they followed its recommendations or not would be up to them. That would be one way to resolve the tug between individual and communal desires.

Pursuing this approach to sexual ethics could be one of the most important steps that Jewish communities and congregations could take. Imagine how different attitudes toward the rich fabric of Jewish thought and practice might become, and how unnecessary the desperate loneliness of people now faced with decisions they see as utterly individual, if every synagogue and havurah were to create a panel of women and men noted for their practical *chesed* and *seichel* (prudence), from whom a person or a couple in an agony of doubt and pain over sexual issues could choose one or a few people with whom to counsel.

Imagining a new Jewish sexual ethic takes place in the World of Mind (*Briyah*). That leaves the other three worlds of Jewish mysticism—Body, Feelings, and Spirit—to explore. What new forms of Jewish celebration might we create for the fusion of body and spirit in sexual expression?

The simplest way may be to walk through a "typical" lifetime of sexual expression as a Jew of our generation might walk through it, drawing on the ethical considerations already sketched. What follows are, of course, suggestions in the mood of a *beit chesed* rather than new rules.

UNLOCKING THE DOOR

Traditionally, Jewish boys (and more recently girls) have celebrated the onset of puberty by reading from the Torah and prophetic Haftarah passages shortly after their thirteenth (or for girls in some congregations, twelfth) birthday.

Why these particular birthdays, and why these ceremonies? The Talmud names these birthdays as the times of obligation to observe *mitzvot*, the acts of connection with God and the community that are commanded by the Torah. Since one of these *mitzvot* is taking part in the communal worship that includes reading the Torah, and since no one can lead the community in this process who is not himself or herself obligated to take part in it, the ceremony arose of marking the onset of obligation by leading the congregation.

These ceremonies have rarely acknowledged that they have anything to do with puberty. When we look at the Talmudic passages that specify the ages of obligation, however, they say that obligation begins when several pubic hairs appear on the body. But, adds the Talmud, since it would lead to embarrassment to examine each boy or girl individually, we agree on these birthdays for everyone.

So the moment of becoming *bar* or *bat mitzvah* is, in principle, the moment in which a young Jew becomes a potentially sexual being. Does it make sense to restore this meaning to the moment?

In the last decade, women have begun bringing their daughters to a celebration of their first menstrual period. Typically, a group of women meets together, some-times at the first New Moon or Full Moon after the menarche, sometimes at a body of water. Often included are the friends of the mother and those of the young woman. The women share whatever Torah has spoken powerfully to them about becoming a woman ("Torah" either in the sense of Jewish tradition or in the broader sense of general wisdom). They bestow on the young woman whatever blessings seem appropriate.

The ceremony complements the *bat mitzvah* ceremony in a synagogue or *havurah* without replacing or competing with it. Many women have been finding that for their own sakes as well their daughters', it is important to replace the shame that used to accompany menstruation with a spiritual celebration of new possibilities as well as practical guidance.

This menarche ceremony was introduced by women who were conscious of the shame and fear that had marked their own first menstruations, which in some sense had contaminated their lives long after, and who wanted to make sure their daugh-ters did not begin womanhood in the same mood. Perhaps because most men have not had the same feelings of shame about their male sexuality, no such ceremonies have yet been created by fathers for their sons to celebrate, perhaps, their first seminal emission. Yet increasing numbers of men have been influenced by the "mythopoeic men's movement" to explore the vision quest or similar experiences as ways of coming into their maleness.

It might make sense for groups of young men and young women separately to undertake a "vision quest" just before the synagogue *bar* and *bat mitzvah* ceremony. This quest might be based on the Israelites' path of the Exodus from slavery in Egypt, which was also an archetypal birthing of the people through the "Narrow Place," a birth canal, through the breaking of the Red Sea waters, and into the open space of Sacred Encounter to receive the Sacred Wisdom at Mount Sinai.

If groups of age-mates made this journey together, men and women of the age of their parents and their grandparents could act as mentors and guides for initiating them into the experience of manhood and womanhood, including imparting the secret wisdom about sexuality that is rarely communicated across the generations. In this way, the Jewish "head trip" of the present *bar/bat mitzvah* ceremony might be combined with a "body trip" that could make puberty and sexual awakening into Jewish events.

In many Israeli kibbutzim, the traditional religious *bar/bat mitzvah* ceremony has been replaced by a purely secular joint project in which twelve-year-olds spend the year before their thirteenth birthdays taking communal responsibility through social action and deeds of loving-kindness with the sick and the poor. This approach is based on the desire of many adolescents to serve others, and is itself a way of giving new focus to the onset of puberty. I am not proposing to replace the traditional ceremony focused on Torah, but to add to it both the more physical-spiritual exercise of the vision quest and the more communal-spiritual exercise of communal service.

In short, the growth of these youngsters into their own sexual lives should be integrated with, not separated from, their growth into Torah study, communal service, and prayer.

For many young people, the first intense sexual experience is masturbation. It used to be regarded by Jewish law, and especially by mystics, as among the worst of sins—expiated only through guilt and multiple acts of *tshuvah* (repentance). In a new Jewish spiritual and ethical sexuality, masturbation could instead be seen as desirable, especially for men and women who have no sexual partner. It might greatly encourage teenagers to realize that the Jewish community affirms their learning their way into the process of sexual warm-up and orgasm *without* the added complexity of a partner.

As with women's transformation of menstruation, it could be spiritually important for masturbation not just to have the shame removed from it through a "scientific" and "practical" explanation of the physiology of orgasm, but to have that information connected with a celebration of sex as a marker of the Divine.

How can masturbation be seen this way—especially since it does not seem to be the kind of I-Thou interpersonal relationship that much contemporary Jewish theology (based on Martin Buber) says is a way of connecting with God?

Masturbation is more like the mystics' experience of *Echad*, the deep Unity in which God is not a One Who is separate from us, but The One who includes us. So the aspect of God that may come to us in masturbation is aloneness-dissolving-into-the-universe. Are young people who are first exploring sex on their own likely to connect their pleasure with the mystical vision of the One? Will older people who have had partners but now are alone make this connection? I don't know. What seems likely is that some will, some won't; and that the community would gain from opening up the possibilities, perhaps on the pre-*mitzvah* all-boy and all-girl vision quests that I have suggested earlier in this section.

OPENING THE DOOR

As teenagers grow into their sexuality and begin to express it with other people, a Jewish community should want them not only to know the physiology of procreation and contraception, to know how to prevent sexually transmitted diseases, but also to learn with their peers how the intensity of sexuality can lead to emotional joys and tangles, to fears and jealousies, to compassion and connection.

They need to learn—and the community should want to teach—how to assess their own emerging diverse sexual orientations, and how these are partly shaped by society and how they can help shape society's definitions of sexuality.

They need to learn the broad spectrum of outlooks on sexuality available in Torah, in Talmud, in Jewish poetry, in the legal responses of the Rabbis, in current ethical and liturgical writing.

They need to learn—and the community should want to teach—how a sexual act can either be part of an I-It event, an objectification of the other person, or an I-Thou experience, in which a moment of love is present and the barriers between human beings fall. And they need to learn that not every sexual act can be or perhaps should be an I-Thou event, even in the most deeply loving relationship. Sometimes, for even the best of reasons (such as planning and acting to conceive, or not to conceive, a child), there may be an element of the instrumental.

And they need to learn—and the community should want to teach—that in the I-Thouing between two humans, the Eternal I-Thou also becomes present; that in the I-It there can appear also the Creator, the Doer God.

For all these reasons, it might make sense for a congregation to gather those whom they want to prepare for sexual relationships. For example, the group might be composed of those who are approaching or are in their seventeenth year; or it might be made up of people a year or so younger. The community will have to choose between acting sooner, thus making relatively sure that almost everyone takes part in the preparation before actually undertaking a sexual relationship, and waiting longer—thus signaling its desire that the young be more experienced in life before they enter into sexual relationships with other people.

The congregation might then invite the younger community to take part in informal study groups where there are no tests and no grades, for discussion and sharing of all these levels of understanding.

As the teenagers complete such a year of learning together and look toward the time when many of them will leave home, they might be invited to stand before the congregation as a group, not individually, to be welcomed into the world of interrelational sexuality. For them, it may well be a world of "fluidity" in which no one expects or even desires them to undertake committed relationships until they understand their own emotional, sexual, and spiritual makeup more deeply.

What should be the content, the Torah, of such an event? The members of the group could choose passages on sexuality from the broadest range of Jewish tradition and culture, and present these together with their own midrashim on these passages—in stories, short dramas or monologues, paintings, or videotapes. In this way, from year to year the ceremony would vary in accord with the individuals and the generational outlooks of each year; and yet the framework would remain the same. The medium itself would be a rich evocation of both the individuality and the communality of the next generation of the Jewish people.

And then the congregation could—with a mixture of pride, awe, perhaps some fearful trembling, and love—say explicitly that it sends them forth both to explore and to control their own sexual selves, in relation to other people. That it welcomes them into the making of their own responsible decisions—possibly to abstain from sexual relationships with others, rather than to enter them out of fear of ridicule or greed for power; possibly to contribute through sexuality to the great rhythms that make love and change possible, in which lonely human beings connect, cling, separate, and reconnect in new patterns; the great rhythms of the Cosmos and the planet, in which species differentiate, find their niche, serve each other's needs, disappear into seed, and reemerge; the rhythm in which an infinitesimal Unity may explode and dissolve, fragments may reconnect and fuse again into new unities, and separate again into new identities.

At some point in their lives after this, most of the group that has newly come of age may actually begin to have sex with someone else. Most will experience the relationship as experimental, through which they learn much more about themselves and their way of relating to others. Here we might ask: How can these temporary partners conduct their relationships with a measure of holiness?

Before we explore this question in detail, I need to make clear what relationship I see among the four "life-aspects" or "life-phases" of sexual relationships sketched in this chapter:

—single sexuality, alone and unrelated
—temporary relationships
—a focused *zug* or couple
—covenanted marriage or commitment

I do not see these four aspects or phases marching in single file, in a straight and simple chronological line: first have sex alone, then experiment with other partners, then focus with one partner on creating a *zug*, finally get married or "covenant-committed."

- For some people, one or another of these relationships may never happen.
- For some others, they may overlap. For them, an "experimental" relationship may in fact be an experiment in creating a *zug*, with many *zug* qualities to it; for others, a *zug* may partake of the qualities of marriage.
- And for many, these four life-aspects may not come in the order presented there. For example, someone may get married early in life, the marriage may break up, and then s/he will begin exploring in the "experimental" mode. Or someone may go through the sequence in order. Then after a divorce, they might have a period of living alone, then go onward to a *zug* relationship.

Why then distinguish between these life-phases and describe them in a sequence at all? Because I do see them in a sequence that is spiritual, not chronological: Each focuses on a domain of space and time that can be made holy, and from the first to the fourth phase, this sphere of potential holiness expands.

In the domain of space, the single person may legitimately focus on his or her own body; partners in an experimental sexual relationship may legitimately focus on the shared bed—the sexual encounter itself; the *zug* may focus on the household—the broader relationship between them; the married/committed couple looks both deeper within, into their own intimacy and spiritual growth, and outward, either to children, or to others and the broader world.

In the domain of time, a person whose sexual experience takes place alone may focus on the "now" of the orgasm; partners in an experimental relationship in principle see it as short-lived precisely because it is experimental; partners in a *zug* leave its duration undetermined; and in marriage or a committed relationship, the couple affirms that they intend it to be a lifelong covenant.

In any one of these relational forms, the partners might choose to look beyond the space-time spheres. But they should not be held responsible to do so. In short, these levels of concern should be seen as a minimum in each form, not a maximum.

Before we look at the four life-phases in more detail, let me suggest a language for charting the directions of spiritual growth. In traditional halakhic language, there were two categories. One obeyed God's commands by doing a *mitzvah*, or one "crossed over" (transgressed) the line drawn by God by performing an *aveirah*. Now I suggest categories that would be different in several ways: There would be three of them, rather than two (thus asserting that the world is more a continuum than a Yes/No, On/Off system); the categories see God as considerably more within the world, connecting us, rather than beyond the world, commanding us; and they reflect a moving spiritual target—moving as we change from one life-phase to another.

First, let us take the word *mitzvah* to mean "connection" rather than "command"—drawing on several Semitic tongues in which the root-verb *tzivui* means "connect." Doing a *mitzvah* means maintaining the sacred connections that hold the world together.

Second, we might use the word *sh'virah*, which means "break" or "shatter," for the act of breaking the sacred connections, thus shattering the Divine vessel.

Third, the word *m'chayeh*, "act of giving life," could be used to describe going beyond maintaining connection to deepening the life process.

- For a single person, viewing her or his own sexual experience with self-contempt, guilt, or shame would be a *sh'virah*, or breaking the weave of life that expresses God in the world; imbuing the experience with holiness would be a *mitzvah*, or maintaining sacred connections in the world; devoting it to learning how to connect with another person would be a *m'chayeh*.

- For one partner in a temporary relationship, ignoring the holiness of the sexual relationship, looking only within the self, would be a *sh'virah*; enhancing the holiness of the couple's bed would be a *mitzvah*; looking beyond the bed at their broader relationship would be a *m'chayeh*.
- For the *zug*, making only the bed holy would be a *sh'virah*; making the household holy, a *mitzvah*; making the world holy, a *m'chayeh*.
- For the married couple, making only the household holy but not the future or the wider world would be, sadly a *sh'virah*; creating holiness into the future and the outside world, a *mitzvah*; and by extension, reaching beyond death to hallow eternity—a *m'chayeh*.

It is possible to create holiness at every level. None of these levels should, for its own sake, be thought of as sinful. Only sexual expressions rooted in coercion, dishonesty, violence, hatred of self or other, are *ipso facto* sinful. Taking on responsibility for any one of these spheres of sexuality, from the smallest to the largest, and then reneging on it—that is a misdeed.

Now, let us return to how partners in a sexual relationship that both consider to be experimental can fill that experiment with holiness.

On the physical level, each partner can make sure that each is willing to take the most effective precautions to protect themselves against sexually transmitted diseases. They can make sure that they are effectively preventing the conception of a child, explicitly acknowledge that any heterosexual coitus might result in conception anyway, and agree that if that were to happen, they would come to agreement or consult a *beit chesed* on what to do—all this in an atmosphere of sacred contemplation. They can join in reading, watching, and talking about the best of the instructive guides to the physicality of sex and to the sensual pleasures of various erotic practices.

On the emotional level, the most important requirement at this level of relationship is simple honesty. The partners can be clear at the beginning about the degree and the limits of their connection to each other, and can also be clear as these change during the relationship. They can talk through together whether either or both intend to be monogamous during the time of their relationship or not, and they can commit themselves to being honest about entering other relationships, even if that honesty might threaten or disrupt their own relationship.

If and when one or both of them decides it is time to part, they can do that clearly, without evasions or pretenses but with gentleness, naming explicitly what they have learned, each accepting responsibility for entering and ending the relationship rather than taking credit for what has been joyful or blaming the other partner for whatever has gone wrong. If the partners decide to move their relationship to a different level, more focused and less fluid, they should do that too with clarity and deliberately mark the new decision, for themselves and their friends.

Intellectually, the partners can explore their own philosophies and understandings of what sex means to them and in the world. They can draw on the whole range of Jewish tradition and culture and, especially if one of them is not Jewish, other religious or cultural traditions as well—and on the array of Modern thought. They can find out where they agree and disagree, not necessarily with the intention of fusing their different outlooks into one but with the hope of clarifying their own beliefs.

Spiritually, they can find what each or both of them can do to affirm the holiness of each sexual encounter between them. They might use the Jewish pattern of blessings over food: first a blessing, then eating and becoming satisfied, then once more giving a blessing.

> For example, they might begin each encounter by pausing to look carefully at each other, to acknowledge the Face of God glowing in the other person's face, to give a blessing to each other in whatever words come simply and honestly. "I love you" may be a lie (or maybe not), but "I wish for you that..." can always be completed with a truth. They might read or recite to each other the passages of the Song of Songs that praise the bodies of a man and of a woman. And then after being with each other they might say a blessing together: "Blessed are You, YAHH our God, Breath of Life, Who has shaped every human being in Your image, male and female. *Baruch attah [Brucha aht] YAHH eloheynu ru'ach ha'olam, asher yatzar et-ha'adam b'tzelem elohim, zachar u'nekevah.*" Or each partner could simply, in his or her own words, praise God, or the Breath of Life, or whatever metaphor of Wholeness they felt most expressed their own selves.

In suggesting ways of affirming the holiness of each sexual encounter, I am trying to achieve two things:

First, it is important consciously to erase the sense of shame and guilt or of estrangement from religious communities and traditions that has often shadowed nonmarital sexual relationships, shame and guilt so strong that the last thing many people wanted was to bring God into the bedroom.

And second, by clearly affirming that each sexual act is sacred, I hope to encourage a change in the quality of those acts; encourage honesty, caring, equality, and conscious choice rather than manipulation, coercion, and automatism in sexual relationships. Affirming that sex is holy may make it possible for sex to become more holy.

BEDECKING THE CHAMBER

At some point in sexual growth, most people are likely to want to enter a more focused relationship with one other person, perhaps one that will not merge their lives as fully as a marriage, but one that they view as more than experimental.

As we have seen, for some people there may be no absolute dividing line between this type of relationship and the kind we call "experimental." For some experimental relationships, the "experiment" may be to discern whether the partner is one with whom one wants to create a more focused relationship. In that case, some of the aspects of the process and practice of a *zug* (or couple) may be appropriate in the beginning, as two people try to find out whether they belong together.

Yet even if the boundary lines of day-to-day behavior are fuzzy, it is useful to keep a clear boundary line of conscious decision. Members of a *zug* take on new responsibilities toward each other, and even if they have already been acting as if they felt responsible toward each other, accepting that this is no longer "as if" is an important step.

In the pattern we are imagining, this decision to become a *ben zug* or *bat zug* (member of a couple) could be marked by a small face-to-face community made up of the couple's intimate friends.

If the couple has decided to live together, the ceremony for acknowledging the *zug* might include the ceremony of dedicating a home, *chanukat ha'ba'yit*, in which a *mezuzah*, a small case enclosing a tiny scroll of quotations from the Torah, is affixed on the main doorpost and other doorways of their dwelling.

Whether they plan to live together or not, the couple could recite appropriate passages from the Song of Songs or from Jewish gay love poetry modeled on the Song of Songs, as well as other writings that feel sacred to them. They could say in their own words what the relationship means to them—what specific connections, obligations, and freedoms they are affirming. They could state in a general way that it is temporary but open-ended, or they could name a time during which they intend for it to last, after which they might extend, end, or change the relationship. They should make clear that either of them can end it without the consent of the other, the community, or the state, and in other ways distinguish it from a marriage. They could ask their friends' support and help in carrying out their commitments, and in preserving the areas of freedom they have reserved.

Since the arena of their relationship has broadened, the "zone of blessing" for the *zug* ought to be broader than that expected of the experimental sexual relationship. Where before I have suggested a rather narrow focus on the sexual encounter itself in order to address the Four Worlds of Body, Feelings, Mind, and Spirit, for the *zug* these four issues should address the wider relationship. (As I pointed out above, some people who are still in an "experimental" mode may find these suggestions useful as well, especially if they are considering turning their relationship into a *zug.*)

Physically, the couple could reflect on and share with each other what they have learned about their own sexual expression during previous relationships. Some sex counselors have suggested that each partner literally make three lists of their own sexual patterns: what they most powerfully desire, what they cannot abide, and what they are open to exploring—and then share these lists with each other. The couple could at each sexual encounter use the same blessings that I have suggested above for more experimental relationships. In addition, they could address not only the issues arising directly from their sexual encounters but also broader concerns about their bodies and health. How do they choose when, what, and how to eat; how much bodywork and bodyplay to do (and of what kind); how, when, and where to sleep.

Emotionally, they might share how their family histories have affected their own sexual and emotional lives; how they look upon money, and what it will mean to share household expenses, entertainment and vacation costs, and perhaps such items as *tzedakah*; how they feel about sharing household space with guests, tenants, and each other; how they plan to deal with old possessions and with placing furniture, and so on.

Intellectually, the couple might explore what ideas shape their lives. What sort of relationship does each feel to the Jewish people and Judaism? If their two approaches are dissimilar, how will they deal with that? Does one of them have roots in another religious community? If so, how will they approach, separately or together, the times and places and words and persons sacred to their different traditions? What aspects of Jewish tradition and culture and spirituality speak to them with power—positively and negatively? What other life-paths—spiritual, ethnic, centered on profession or vocation or on a political vision, guided by the mass media or by some subculture—are an intrinsic part of their own selves? Can they shape these different life-paths into one that both can share? If different paths feel desirable to them, can they walk together nonetheless? How?

Spiritually, they might explore how they see the relationship between their *zug* and the wholeness of the world. Do they see the exchange of energy between them as a microcosm of the exchange of energies in the planet and the Cosmos? Do they experience moments of love as moments when they are being loved by that wholeness? Do they feel that what they do with each other and in the world helps to heal the broken places of the universe or, sometimes, shatter them still more? Do they seek to change the hurtful things they do, do they seek forgiveness for them, do they extend forgiveness to each other? Do they feel commanded by some Deeper Power to act in decent ways?

INNER SPACE

At some point, many people who have entered into a *zug* (and probably some who have not) may decide that they want a deeply committed relationship. Just as the ceremonies and legal structures of betrothal, espousal, and marriage changed over Biblical and Rabbinic history, so these arrangements are in flux today:

- Many couples will probably choose a form that closely tracks the Rabbinic symbols and practices of marriage, with perhaps some modifications.
- Others may want a strongly modified version of the ceremonies and patterns of marriage.
- Still others may create new forms of "commitment ceremonies" or "covenant ceremonies." This is especially likely to happen with gay couples who cannot yet legally contract governmentally accepted marriages in most countries, and who are only beginning to have Jewish wedding ceremonies and Jewish legal protections available to them.
- Couples in which one partner is Jewish and the other not, and in which neither is prepared to convert, may find it necessary to explore new types of wedding ceremonies. Many rabbis and other knowledgeable Jews are not willing to officiate at a wedding under these conditions. Some are, but may insist on using a ceremonial form that is distinct from the traditional Jewish form, or even from anything that echoes it.

❧

Many couples have made changes in the Rabbinic wedding ceremony that affirm equality of the spouses, or affirm the possibility of gay and lesbian marriages, or otherwise respond to new sexual practices. These changes may range from recognizing both women and men as fully legitimate witnesses to the marriage, to instituting an exchange rather than a one-way delivery of rings, to changing the words of the blessings and the formal espousal, to changing the body language of the ceremony.

- Some couples have decided to set aside a time and ceremony to reflect on, mourn, and let pass any previous sexual connections.

- Some have decided that both partners will go to a clarifying *mikveh* immediately before the wedding or commitment day (rather than just the bride, as in Rabbinic practice).
- Some couples have decided that both partners rather than just one should recite the *"Harei aht..."* pledge, suitably changed according to gender. (The pledge to a man: *"Harei attah m'kudash li b'taba'at zo, k'dat Moshe v'Yisrael."*)
- Some have changed the words of this pledge to reflect the deeper changes in their understanding of Judaism, saying, for example, *"... k'dat dorot Yisrael—* according to the law of the generations of Israel," rather than *"...* the law of Moses and Israel."
- Some have dropped the *"Harei aht"* altogether or have added a sentence about *brit chuppah,* or "the covenant of marriage," to affirm marriage as a covenant rather than an "acquisition," as in the Rabbinic model.
- Some have introduced passages from the Song of Songs or from Hosea's vision of a betrothal in justice without mastery.
- Some have changed the *erusin* blessing that explicitly forbids sexual relationships other than marriage.
- Some couples have replaced the traditional seven circling dances of the bride around the groom to one in which each partner dances three times around the other, ending with a double twirl around each other.
- Some couples join in breaking the traditional glass instead of having it done by one partner only.

In certain cases, gay couples have asserted their right to stand under a broadened version of the *chuppah.* Others, speaking for deeper change in the pattern of committed relationships, have created new ceremonies in that vein. Some heterosexual couples have done the same, and others have, as part of their own wedding ceremonies, publicly urged that the Jewish community and the general society affirm the rights of gay as well as heterosexual couples to both civil and sacred marriage.

Not only ceremonial forms but the *ketubah* or commitment agreement has also taken on new forms. The traditional Rabbinic *ketubah* dealt with such specifics as marriage settlements and divorce indemnities, but gradually these became formulas centered on the husband's livelihood. In reaction, some contemporary couples have opted for new *ketubot,* or have written their own, that in general terms assert their loving commitment to each other as equals, but omit practical issues of home, job, finances, children, or politics.

More recently, couples have begun to wrestle with those practical issues, especially those ones they find hardest to agree on, and have begun writing individual *ketubot* that bespeak their own ideas and decisions. Along these lines, couples could address a number of questions that they might want to answer not in the publicly read *ketubah* but in a private addendum to it:

- whether they are committing themselves to sexual monogamy;
- whether they want to create a rhythm of sexual connection and separation based on *niddah* or on any other rhythmic calendar;
- whether there are any specific erotic practices that are important to them either "in" or "out" of their marriage;
- whether they wish to share all their financial assets, only income, or only part of their expenditures;
- whether their political views are similar enough that they can work together for *tikkun olam*;
- whether they wish to have children, and if so whether they share a basic approach to child-rearing;
- how they want to deal with children either partner may have from a previous partnership, and how they expect to deal with the parents of either partner;
- how they plan to deal with tugs in different geographic directions;
- how they intend to deal with renewing and deepening the emotional intimacy between them—by setting aside special weekly times for intimate talk, by reviewing their relationship during the ten days between Rosh Hashanah and Yom Kippur, or by periodically consulting an emotional counselor;
- what spiritual and religious and Jewish practices they intend to observe;
- whether they will keep their previous names or change them.

ঔ

Increasingly, couples who affirm an egalitarian version of marriage also formally agree in advance that either party may initiate a divorce, and arrange to prevent a widowed or abandoned wife from becoming an *agunah*, as she might under Rabbinic law.

Either in the initial *ketubah* or in the process of their marriage, the couple may agree to review their life-path in a regular rhythm.

On their anniversary, they might bring out the handful of shattered glass that they broke under the *chuppah*, and ask themselves: What is shattered between us? What will repair it? Then they might bring out the wine cup from which they drank the joy of loving celebration, look carefully at its glowing wholeness, and perhaps drink from it again, asking, "What is whole and sweet between us, and how can we enhance it?"

In the seventh year, they might review their entire *ketubah* together, see if they need to change some of those agreements, and if whole new areas of concern have arisen so that they need to write a new agreement. And they might take some special time together to rejoice as well as to reflect. In some communities, groups of couples in their seventh years of marriage or commitment join together for a public renewal of their covenants.

Every Shabbat, a couple may take the time to renew the moment of their joining. In Rabbinic tradition, on Friday evening husbands bless their wives with the recitation of the "Woman of Valor" passage from Proverbs. This does not, however, sit well in a post-Rabbinic household where partners are equal. Some egalitarian couples have introduced a new custom to express Shabbat renewal:

> Since Jewish tradition teaches that the ritual washing of hands before a meal should be done with the fingers naked of any ornament, it is customary to remove all rings—including wedding rings—for this washing. On Friday evening, as the Shabbat meal begins and the mood becomes one of loving celebration, after a couple has removed their rings, washed their hands, and said the blessing over the bread, there comes a moment of great emotional and spiritual power when they put the wedding ring back upon each other's finger, repeating the words *"Harei aht . . . /Harei attah . . ."* they had said beneath the *chuppah*.

ð

Why is it that in focusing on the married or committed couple, as distinct from the *zug*, I suggest setting aside conscious moments for reflection, renewal, and rejoicing?

The covenanted couple, simply by desiring to make its covenant lifelong, creates for itself the need for conscious self-transformation, which requires self-reflection. And this sense of an extended future means that the covenant has committed the couple to creating something beyond themselves. This may or may not be children; but whether it is or not, the wisest of married couples might examine, in each of the Four Worlds, what they are doing to reach beyond themselves.

- Are their bodies helping to birth or heal other bodies—through begetting, birthing, or adopting children, through hands-on healing of the sick, bringing food directly to the hungry, seeding one specific piece of earth?
- Is their love helping to create wider circles of love and justice, peace and ecological balance?
- As they grow in knowledge and wisdom, are they teaching what they have learned to others, especially to the young?

• As they achieve a sense of spiritual center, are they making themselves available to others as a focus of calm and openness?

AND BEYOND

The traditional markers of a Jewish life all come at crucial moments of change: birth, puberty, marriage, divorce, death. In recent years, Jews have begun to develop ceremonial markers for a time of midlife transformation in which bodily, social, psychological, and cultural changes are intertwined in complex ways.

Some of these emerging ceremonial markers are also connected with some bodily change, particularly, for women, the end of menstruation. For men, hormonal changes are usually much vaguer and the ability to beget children lasts much longer than women's ability to bear them. For both women and men, midlife changes may not involve changes in sexual desire, or only mild changes. Some women and some men report that at some point, their pleasure in sex remains undiminished but the intensity or frequency of their desire for it is less.

Other changes of daily life may have more effect than changes in one's sex drive. For example, the creation of relationships with grandchildren; feeling drawn to passing on one's knowledge and wisdom to the next generation in a vocation or profession; changing one's own vocation; changing one's *zug* or covenanted partnership; or turning to more spiritual explorations.

The work of mapping out these mostly unknown territories of a Jewish life-path has only just begun. Menopause ceremonies have appeared. So have *bar yovel* and *bat yovel* ceremonies at age fifty, drawing on the Biblical Jubilee (*yovel*) time of rest and renewal for the land, in every fiftieth year. One new ceremony draws on the Torah's description of the "midlife" transformation of Abraham and Sarah when they were in their nineties and Isaac was yet to be born; and it incorporates a ceremony drawn from the "Offering Between the Parts" that Abraham presented God on that occasion.

These and similar ceremonies focus more on peaceful creativity and wisdom than on specific changes in sexual expression. And yet, as the tale of Abraham and Sarah makes clear, at some psychic and cultural archetypal level, there is a symbolic sense in which new kinds of generativity and old uses of the genitals, new forms of creativity and old forms of procreation, are connected.

As the number of people who live into their eighties and beyond increases, there may even be two unmarked life-stages from age fifty to death. As we face these open places in the map, it is appropriate to end not with answers but with a question: How shall we honor these life-stages with Jewish ceremony and with a communal Jewish sense of new obligations and new freedoms?

THE PUBLIC FRAMEWORK

Up to this point, we have treated sexuality as if it were only an internal concern of the Jewish community. In fact, sexuality has become one of the major arenas of debate over public policy. Some religious communities—notably, the Roman Catholic Church—have responded to that reality by entering the public discourse and political process, hoping to affect not only its own membership but also the society as a whole on issues like abortion, birth control, and homosexuality. As the Jewish community evolves its own new approaches to a Jewish sexual ethic, it could also bring its views into the public arena and carry on the struggle to shape the broader society toward a deeper respect for the holiness of sex.

Such an effort would not have to fall into the trap of trying to legislate a Jewish moral stance upon other communities. Cultural and religious pluralism is a strong Jewish value, arising from millennia of experience in being a minority culture and perhaps also from a profound sense that in a world as yet unredeemed, no existing culture is altogether holy—not even our own.

Yet at the same time, the more Jews come to draw their sense of the world, their vision and their passion, from a renewed, revitalized, and reshaped Judaism, the more likely they, we, are to want to bring what wisdom we do have into the public assembly.

The distinction will at some times be easy to make, and sometimes hard.

For instance: Traditional Judaism requires that if the development of a fetus threatens the life of its mother, the fetus *must* be killed to save the mother's life. Catholic law requires that the fetus *must* be protected, even at the cost of the mother's death. Either community could claim that its own morality is universally true, and could try to mobilize the power of government in order to impose its moral code on the other. But practically all Jews would prefer to allow people to choose which moral system seems to them more holy.

For instance: If most of the Jewish community were to conclude that gay and lesbian marriages should be Jewishly celebrated, it would be one thing to try to force other religious communities to do the same thing. It would be quite another to urge the secular society to recognize the same legal rights and responsibilities for all marriage partners, heterosexual and homosexual.

Given the basic approach to sexual life phases that I have sketched in this chapter, the Jewish community could urge that public bodies provide people in different life-phases with different sorts of support. We might, for example, make sexual counseling available at public cost to couples (not just to large classes of individuals, the "lonely crowd") in the first year of an experimental sexual relationship. And we might provide that couples who have been married for seven years or more be covered by special wages-and-hours laws, be offered fewer work hours at the same amount of overall pay, in order to give them more time to strengthen their family relationship at a time when it might be under great strain.

These specific examples are intended only to point the way toward the evolution of a Jewishly rooted public policy on sexual ethics. What is perhaps most important is that the shape of our world will be deeply affected by social and political decisions about sexuality, gender roles, and the emotional relationships of women and men. The Jewish community needs to address these questions in the public arena, where it has had little experience in addressing them, as well as in the communal and religious world where some efforts to do so have at least begun.

Part Four

REST

My friend wisecracks: "Food, money, sex, and...what's this, the *rest* of life? Food, money, sex— *Nu*, what else is there?"

There is resting, which is always the "rest" of life. The "nothing" that gives meaning to everything, as a drum has no beat without its hollow, as the empty Holy of Holies was the defining space of the Holy Temple, as quiet gives form to the music.

Threaded all through the questions we have so far examined is the question of rest: repose, reflection, renewal. When Jews prepared to eat, first they paused to bring an offering or make a blessing, to reflect on the sacred origins of food. When Jews used the land to create wealth, they paused every seventh year to rest and let the land rest, so as to renew their selves, refresh the sacred rhythms of the fruitful earth, and honor the One Owner. When Jews had sex, they paused in a rhythm of connection and withdrawal, to clarify and comb the uncanny fringe of life and death.

Somewhere in this sense of rest, this pause to simply *be*, this pause from a life of making, creating, procreating, was rooted the Jewish sense of holiness. The first use in the Torah of the word *kadosh*—"holy," "unique," "distinctive"—referred to the seventh day, the day of rest, the day of Shabbat—"Pause."

Through moments as brief as the *brakha* before eating, or as long as the seventh year of pausing to renew the land, moments of *shavat va'yinafash*—"pause and catch a breath," as the Torah describes God Doing/Not Doing on the first Shabbat— are at the heart of Jewish spiritual life. From generation to generation and epoch to epoch, the how and when and why of rest have changed without changing, like the shimmer of a sacred diamond turned slowly in the hand. The touchstone of this path of "being" has been Shabbat. Let us now look at how the Jews have preserved Shabbat, transformed it, and renewed it through the millennia—and what we might draw from it today.

I am not suggesting that the only time or form of Jewish repose is the day of Shabbat, though some might say that Jews who push so hard all week to change the world are only kept from frenzy by the practice of Shabbat. What I am saying is that from the image of Shabbat we can learn more deeply how to rest, repose, reflect, renew everything in our lives every day.

In the Biblical traditions of the People Israel, there seem to be two strands of thought about Shabbat. One of these strands sees Shabbat as a reflection and expression of cosmic rhythms of time that are rooted in the process of Creation. The other views Shabbat as an expression of human freedom, justice, equality, and dignity.

The Biblical tradition regards these two strands not as contradictory but as complementary, intertwined and perhaps even isomorphic—an expression of a single truth on two different levels of reality. The second version of Shabbat is probably the Bible's own midrash on the first version. It probably emerged in a period of Israelite history when social conflict between the rich and poor was intense and the desire to see Shabbat as an expression of social justice was strong.

RHYTHMS IN COSMOS AND CREATION

The strand of Cosmos and Creation dominates the view of Shabbat that is expressed in the Books of Genesis and Exodus. Perhaps the focus on birth, Creation, and nourishing emerges from the birth experience of the Jewish people, and the desire of a people, newly a-borning, to understand the birthing of the universe. The second strand is more characteristic of the Books of Deuteronomy and of the Prophets Jeremiah, Ezekiel, and Second Isaiah, all of which seem to be connected with a period of internal social conflict. The two views are most explicitly and effectively intertwined in Leviticus 25–26, which may be from the same period of social upheaval.

The cosmic strand begins with the Biblical story of Creation. God ceased, paused, or rested (*shavat*) on the seventh day from the work of creating, blessed the seventh day, and made it holy (Gen. 1–2:4). This "calling" speaks to the depths of reality, but not yet to human ears. Even the explicit tales of contacts and covenants between God and the world—through Adam and Eve, Noah and his family, the generation of Babel, and Abraham and Sarah and their clan descendants—do not explicitly communicate the holiness of Shabbat. Perhaps this silence should be heard as evidence that Biblical Israel remembered that in its earliest history, Shabbat was not observed among the Israelites or the surrounding peoples.

There is, however, an odd hint at restfulness—not yet Shabbat—in the story of the Flood. In the Rainbow Covenant that follows the destruction of the planet by the Flood, God promises (Gen. 8:21–22) that the great cycles of life will never cease again:

Beyond all days of earth,
Seedtime and harvest,
And cold and heat,
And summer and winter,
And day and night,
Shall not cease.

Here the Hebrew for "cease" is from the same root as Shabbat. The great cycles will never again "make Shabbat." Is there a hint here that what has gone wrong on the earth involves a restlessness, a driven obsession to *make* and *do*, that has canceled out all rest, shattered the great cycles, and thereby brought destruction on the earth? That the great cycles require a rhythm of rest in order for them to be cycles and not straight lines of making, working, that march forward without a pause only to destruction? Is there a hint, almost a joke, that the one thing that must not pause is pausing? That if there is no Shabbat the world itself, all of it, will make a Shabbat by drowning in the waters that gave life?

If so, the hint remains only a hint in the Torah's history of the earth and its earthlings, until the generation and the season of our freedom arise.

The Torah places the first human discovery of Shabbat in the midst of one of the tales of the newly freed rebellious generation in the Wilderness (Ex. 16). Very soon after the liberation from slavery in Mitzrai'im, the Narrows, Egypt, when the Israelites were still running single file into the Wilderness, God sent manna to feed them.

On the sixth day of this free and joyfully received food, twice as much manna appeared as before. Previously, when the Israelites had tried to hoard the manna overnight lest it not be enough for the next day, the manna had turned rotten. But the extra that they gathered on the sixth day did not rot. Even so, on the morning of the seventh day they went out to gather it again. There was none, and Moses explained why: The seventh day was a day of Shabbat, a day for resting and renewal. Not a day for even the gentle gathering of food that came so freely from God's nourishing breast, the breast of earth that feeds and pauses, gives and withholds.

"Let no one leave his place on the seventh day," said Moses. So the people learned to "rest" or "pause" or "remain inactive" (Ex. 16:29–30).

It is only after this direct experience of Shabbat that the Torah describes the formal proclamation of Shabbat at Sinai. At the mountain where the people itself is first able to pause from its headlong flight out of slavery comes the teaching to join in the resting of the Cosmos.

Of the Ten Words proclaimed at Sinai, Shabbat is the longest and the most detailed. "Remember" the day of Shabbat, says the version preserved in Exodus 20. Six days shall you work, and on the seventh rest: all of you, adults and children, women and men, humans and beasts, free and slave, home-born and strangers "within your gates." Why? Because God rested in creating the world, and when you rest, this day becomes a sign, a symbol, of the covenant between your tiny people and the One Who made all earth and heaven.

Thus Exodus sees the seventh-day Shabbat as a cosmic event, created by God and placed within the rhythms of the universe, allowed to emerge from those rhythms just then in the moment of freedom, to become a part of human consciousness. And now, beginning now, it is to be carried out as a symbol and an enactment of that creative cosmic rhythm.

The Covenant at Sinai, with Shabbat as its sign, complements the Covenant of Abraham, for which the sign is circumcision. Circumcision is connected with fertility. By hallowing the male organ of generation, by offering a foreskin instead of a son's life to God, the People Israel begs Divine favor for all future generations. In the covenant at Sinai, the sign is not an offering to the God Who makes life fertile but an imitation of the God Who rests. And what God offers in return is not fertility but the possibility of resting. The mark of a free people, perhaps, but in the words of Exodus, much more the mark of a people in touch with the God of Cosmos, the God of Creation.

This belief that the Cosmos requires rest may not have been unique to the Israelites. Some scholars believe that in Babylonian culture, there was an analogous time of rest called *shappatu*. It, too, came in a seven-day rhythm but it signified a time of danger and fear. On the day of *shappatu*, the king avoided most activity because things would not turn out well.

This atmosphere is quite different from the celebratory mood of the Israelite Shabbat. Yet it may come from the same deep sense of reality, with a vital twist of feeling. Imagine a culture that knows that the universe is so mysterious that human beings experience a time when they do not know what to do next. They stare into the abyss of human limitation, and they draw back. Stay home! Do nothing! Kindle no fires, for the world is dark and we can see no light to clear our path. When the time of dangerous mystery has passed, come out to work once more.

Now imagine a culture that also knows that the universe is so mysterious that human beings do not know what to do next. They stare straight at the Mystery, and laugh in joy. They know that freedom is the knowledge that the future is not absolutely under control, is not certain, is not knowable.

So they celebrate the Mystery. They see it as the fulfillment, not the negation, of the universe and of themselves. They are not frightened. They are glad and joyful to imitate the Mysterious God Who rests—by resting.

SURROUNDING SACRED SPACE IN
SACRED TIME

The cosmic strand of Shabbat connects it closely with God's earthly sanctuary, the portable Shrine of the Indwelling Presence (*Mishkan*, from the same root as Shekhinah). The people build the Mishkan in the Wilderness, under the direction of artists whom Moses has been told by God to select. The Mishkan is a portable platform for the Altar, a sacred table, and a small cube of space, the Holy of Holies. It is a microcosm of the world, a miniature representation of the universe in which God dwells.

According to the Torah, the design of the Mishkan comes directly from God to Moses on the holy mountain. Section by section, God describes in detail what to build. The seventh and last section of the description is, however, a repetition of the command to rest on Shabbat, this time with another command that anyone who violates it shall be put to death. Once again, God explains that the people shall rest as a sign of the covenant between them and the Creator Who rested on the seventh day (Ex. 31:17).

In the literary pattern of the Torah, this description of God's description to Moses of how to build and how to rest is followed at once by the story of how the people, frightened by Moses' absence, make a Golden Calf. The story proceeds with their punishment, God's rage and then forgiveness, and Moses' return first to the mountain and then to the community, bearing a new set of tablets of the covenant.

On Moses' return, the first words he says to the people (Ex. 35:1–3) repeat the command of Shabbat—adding the first specific prohibition on work: The people shall kindle no fire on the day of rest. Only then does he report what God wants the design of the Mishkan to be.

Thus Shabbat is both the end of the blueprint and the beginning of the building of the Shrine of the Indwelling Presence. Moses has heard it last but tells it first. Perhaps he wants to make sure that the people keep it in mind throughout their building.

The Torah text seems to be suggesting strongly an analog between the great Creation and the small creation. Just as God made Shabbat after constructing the macroworld of the universe, and perhaps could complete and fully hallow the building only by an act of not-building, so the People Israel, constructing the microworld of the Mishkan, must hallow the building by pausing for Shabbat.

The cosmic connection between Shabbat and the sanctuary is repeated in

Leviticus 19:30 and 26:2: "You shall keep my Shabbats and revere my Holy Place: I [am] YHWH your God."

The story of the Wilderness trek becomes an arena for describing how to apply the basic command of the Shabbat so as to shape the people's behavior for the future. What the people have heard from Moses is to kindle no fire and to gather no manna on Shabbat. They discover someone gathering firewood on Shabbat (Num. 15:32–36). Either they are not certain whether this activity is proscribed, or they know it is proscribed but are not sure of the punishment. They bring the woodsman before Moses, Aaron, and the whole community. Moses, who is evidently not so certain himself, consults God, Who commands that the woodsman be put to death.

Thus the Torah makes clear that Shabbat rest is not confined to the specific rules originally proclaimed. But what are we to make of such a ruthless punishment? Death for gathering firewood! Other violations of relationship with God rather than the community, such as a violation of Yom Kippur, are left to God to punish with *kareyt*, or "cutting off"—perhaps of the soul, or of the future through childlessness. Only work on Shabbat and sacrifices of children to Moloch are to be punished both by *kareyt* and by death at human hands. It seems that the Torah views violation of Shabbat as a threat to the whole community, not as a rebellion against God alone. Or perhaps the Torah is warning that working on Shabbat brings about an early death, just as, we will see, ignoring the sabbatical year brings about exile and desolation.

Although the cosmic vision of Shabbat dominates the Book of Exodus, in it there is also a hint of Shabbat as a matter of social justice, liberation, and equality. Implicitly, we are shown that the whole process of the unveiling of the cosmic Shabbat comes—when?—in the time of liberation from slavery. There is also a more specific indication: Exodus 23:12 commands rest upon the seventh day "so that your ox and your ass may rest and your servant and the stranger may catch their breath."

The first hints that the rhythm of a seventh sacred cycle applies to cycles other than night and day come in Exodus: The people is to make every seventh year in life upon the land a year of *shmitah* (rest, release, liberation), when the land is not cultivated and the poor have access to its freely growing produce (Ex. 23:10). And those who have been sold into indentured servitude must be freed in the seventh year of their service.

In Leviticus, this hint is made explicit; the seventh cycle of the lunar month and the seventh cycle of the year are explicitly connected with the word and concept of Shabbat.

The seventh month is singled out from its sisters in the lunar rhythm. Four festivals are proclaimed for the seventh month, one each in the four phases of the moon (corresponding to the festivals we now know as Rosh Hashanah, Yom Kippur, Sukkot, and Sh'mini Atzeret). Each is to be observed as a *Shabbaton*. What is more, Yom Kippur is described even more intensely as *shabbat shabbaton* (Lev. 23: 23, 32, 39).

And the *shmitah* of the seventh year is spelled out in far more detail. Leviticus 25 creates an expanding spiral of rhythmic time. In every seventh year, the land itself shall observe a year of Shabbat. It shall have a *shmitah* so as to be free of cultivation or organized harvesting. In the year after the seventh seventh year—the fiftieth year—there shall be a *yovel*, or Jubilee. Once again (twice in a row, the forty-ninth and fiftieth years) the land shall rest, and each piece of it shall be returned to the family or clan that originally lived on it. Why? "For the earth is Mine, and you but visitors and guests with Me," says God.

These levitical provisions reassert that the Creator has imbedded Shabbat in the cosmic rhythms of created time, and the people must honor it in order to recognize and keep their covenant with the Creator. For in the seventh daily spinning of the earth from sunset to sunset, and in the seventh "moonthly" journey of the moon around the earth, and in the seventh yearly circle of the earth around the sun, human beings—who alone among earth's creatures know how to count to seven—mark these cycles of which they are a part.

What if the people refuse to keep this Shabbat covenant with God? Leviticus says (26:33–35, 43):

> Your land shall become a desolation and your cities a ruin. Then shall the land make up for its Shabbat years, through the time that it is desolate and you are in the land of your enemies. Then shall the land make Shabbat-rest and make up for its Shabbat years. All its days of desolation, it shall have Shabbat-rest for the non-Shabbat of the Shabbat years while you were sitting on it.

In other words, the command to let the earth rest is not simply a statement of what is pleasant, gracious, nice. Nor is it even a statement of what is just and equitable. It is a statement of necessity, the law of what just *is*. The earth *will* rest.

The only question is whether human beings and the earth will rest together, in joy and happiness; or the earth, denied rest and worked to exhaustion by humans who think they are its masters, will rest by expelling its human guests and smashing their societies, forcing them to leave the earth alone so it can have a time of peace and quiet.

The same passage of Leviticus that speaks of the earth's right to rhythmic rest weaves the rights of human beings into this cosmic rhythm: the right to freedom and to justice as aspects of the great Shabbat.

Leviticus requires that equality in landholding be renewed every fifty years by restoring to those who have become poor their family's equal share in the land—and conversely, by withdrawing from those who have become wealthy the surplus land that was not originally in their family's possession.

Leviticus provides that whatever else has happened in the lives of slaves—no matter whether they are in the middle of their own seven-year cycles of servitude, or have decided to reject the freedom they were offered in their individual seventh year—all slaves in all Israel are to be freed in the Jubilee year.

RHYTHMS OF FREEDOM AND JUSTICE

This liberating aspect of Shabbat comes front and center in the period when Deuteronomy was written and Jeremiah prophesied that social oppression would result in disaster for the people.

The importance of social justice as a purpose of Shabbat is made clear in the Deuteronomic version of the Ten Sayings at Sinai (Deut. 5:12–15): Shabbat is grounded not in the memory of God's Creation, but in the liberation of the people from slavery under Pharaoh. This was no mere recollection of a transformed past. For God also gives as reason for Shabbat that it will periodically release the Israelites' own slaves from endless drudgery.

In the Sinai passage of Deuteronomy, the Shabbat command does not begin with "*Zachor*, Remember!" (as in Exodus) but with "*Shamor*, Keep!" The first word brings to consciousness the cosmic truth of restful rhythm. The second is a more activist, prophetic call to act, to change society. This, says the author of Deuteronomy, is what it means to honor the covenant with God.

In this text of Deuteronomy, it is easy to hear the voice of a Prophet making a midrash upon the text of Sinai, which was already well known to the Israelites. Not *zachor*, he says, *shamor!* Do not merely remember the God of Creation, act in partnership with God of liberation!

Two specific provisions for social justice appear elsewhere in Deuteronomy:

In the seventh year of the nationwide cycle, the *shmitah* year when all land was released from cultivation, all debts were annulled. Thus those who had fallen into debt, whether through improvidence, bad luck, generosity, or laziness, along with those who through hard work, shrewd bargaining, good luck, or stinginess had become so wealthy that they could lend money to others—all were restored to equal dignity.

In the cycle of individual indenture for those who had become servants, the seventh year of freedom was the time when they would receive severance pay in the form of grain, oil, and sheep or goats.

In the crisis that befell the People Israel beginning just before the destruction of the First Temple and continuing through the Babylonian Exile and the return, this sense of Shabbat as redemptive social force was powerfully expressed by Jeremiah, Ezekiel, Second Isaiah, and Nehemiah.

Jeremiah called for merchants to observe Shabbat by pausing from carrying commercial burdens through the gates of Jerusalem. He promised that if they did refrain, the Davidic kings would be carried freely, in triumph, through those same gates (Jer. 17:21–25). If the people can free themselves from the burdens placed upon them by these merchants, they will be freed from the burden of the fear of foreign conquest. If they will create a deeper Shabbat on the seventh day, a greater Shabbat will be created for them.

By the same token, Jeremiah invoked the Jubilee tradition of the *dror*, or the liberation, of all slaves. During the time of the great, overhanging fear of Babylonian Conquest, Jeremiah called for the Israelites to free their slaves. When the masters first agreed to do this and then reneged, Jeremiah proclaimed on God's behalf a *dror*—a release—to war and famine (Jer. 34:13–22). Now, he announced, Israel is doomed to submit to Babylon. Since the people will not share the land, they will lose it; since they will not free their slaves, they will all become slaves.

The very last chapter of the very last book of the Hebrew Scriptures (II Chron. 36:21) reports that so it was. "To fulfill the word of YHWH by the mouth of Jeremiah," says Chronicles, the Exile lasted "until the land had been repaid its Shabbat-years. For as long as it lay desolate it kept Shabbat, till seventy years were fulfilled."

The prophecy of seventy years of exile does indeed appear in the text of the Book of Jeremiah as it has come down to us. But the Jeremiah texts contain no statement that this period of exile would be a way for the land to win back the years of Shabbat it had been denied. Here Chronicles echoes rather the warning of Leviticus 26, and intertwines it with memories of the Jeremiah who called for a *dror* of sabbatical or Jubilee release, who prophesied exile if there were no *dror*, and who spoke out during the same period in which other prophetic voices were calling for Shabbat to be a beacon of social justice as well as cosmic rest.

Chronicles thus completes the cycle of hope and warning that is encoded from the beginning of the tradition of Shabbat.

Speaking in and from the Exile itself, Ezekiel (20:12–24, 22; 23; 28) connected the desecration of Shabbat with child sacrifice, bribery that led to the death of innocents, the taking of interest, the oppression of the poor. Or, possibly, he equated each of these betrayals with a betrayal of Shabbat, a refusal to rest. In either case, these betrayals—especially the desecration of Shabbat—were what brought on the Exile. And for Ezekiel, a powerful symbol of redemption from exile was that a renewed priesthood would hallow Shabbat in a new way, by bringing a new offering that would vividly represent the rhythm of workdays and rest: six lambs and a ram.

For the Prophet called Second Isaiah, who spoke after the Exile, Shabbat was even more important for the vision of a just and decent society. In his great outcry (Isai. 58) that seems tuned to Yom Kippur and that indeed has for millennia been read in the synagogue on Yom Kippur, this Prophet seems to speak in the idiom of the Jubilee:

> What is the fast that I demand from you? Is it to hang down your head like a bulrush, and then triumphantly ride on earth's high places? No! It is to feed the hungry, clothe the naked, free the prisoner. What is the way to rise in ecstasy? It is first to find a place beside the lowly, the humiliated. And then, together with them, to make a true Shabbat, Renewal-time, that will transcend the busy-busy chatter of ordinary days, make Shabbat a joy in truth—because all My people can take joy in it.

The great Shabbat; the greatest of all possible Shabbats—the Jubilee.

Yom Kippur, the *shabbat shabbaton*, was the day when a Jubilee year was supposed to be proclaimed with a blast of the ram's horn. So the form and content of Second Isaiah's outcry—"Lift up your voice like the ram's horn!"—suggests that perhaps it was indeed a speech he shouted one year as the throng of Temple celebrants on the great fast day grew ever more ecstatic, ever more triumphant, ever more sure that it had already won God's favor and forgiveness.... Only to be challenged by this passionate troublemaker demanding that the Jubilee be truly called.

Certainly in calling for a "year of God's favor" when the oppressed shall hear good tidings and the captives shall go free (Isaiah 61) the Prophet is demanding the Jubilee.

Even a far less visionary man, the practical Nehemiah who led the Israelites back from the Babylonian Exile to rebuild the Temple and their society, spoke with passion for a Shabbat of social meaning. He recites (Neh. 13:15–22), in a moment of spiritual triumph and devotion, his decision to stop the rich and powerful merchants of Jerusalem from bringing grain, wine, grapes, figs, and fish into the city to sell on Shabbat. He warns them that such commercial desecrations were precisely what brought on the Exile.

So we see that the Books of Deuteronomy and Leviticus and the Prophets felt no contradiction between Shabbat as cosmic creation and Shabbat as social recreation; between the theme of equality and justice, and the theme of calm and reflection. Cosmic creation and social re-creation were analogous, each a renewal in two spheres that were so deeply intertwined that neither could be renewed alone.

Modern Jews, for whom the worlds of cosmos and of society are deeply different and separated, may find it hard to understand the profound integration of these worlds that Biblical Israel seems to have felt. Indeed, "integration" as a word and concept may already falsify the Biblical experience. For what we consider to be two worlds was then a single truth, bearing an integrity that did not need integration.

For them, Shabbat, *dror, yovel*—all these words for rest, repose, release, liberation—affirmed the rhythms of the cosmos and the rhythms of society.

In this Biblical outlook, what today we call "social justice" was treated as one aspect of rest, social repose, if you will. "Work" was not just physical labor but the scaffolding of institutional structures of domination and control. These institutions are not work merely because of the economic roles they play, but because domination and control are themselves a kind of "work." The exertion of effort over others that these institutions require is, in the Biblical mind, closely akin to the work of plowing the earth and reaping its produce. So the structures themselves, not merely the physical efforts that they carry on, must be periodically dissolved in order for a true Shabbat to happen. That is why debts must be annulled and land must be redistributed, for the *shmitah* and *yovel* to be carried out.

To "rest," then meant to return to a state of nature, not "nature red in tooth and claw" but nature loving like the Garden of Delight. (Indeed, after two years of uncultivated growth the earth would look unshorn, as Eden did in the beginning.)

In this way of seeing, "nature" is where the earth grows peacefully, without economic coercion, and feeds the earthlings peacefully, without withholding. And "nature" is where the human community grows peacefully in natural clans and families, without institutional distortions and coercions. The land freely feeds the people without sowers, dressers, cultivators, harvesters; the people freely feed the land without owners, masters, creditors, employers.

This is Shabbat. It re-creates the Shabbat of the beginning, the Shabbat that seals Creation, because at that Shabbat all was free, loving, and in a state of plenitude, sharing, and repose. For *adamah* and *adam*, earth and earthlings, to act in this way is most fully to honor and imitate the Creator. And for the Creator to act again in this way—as in the liberation from Egypt and from every time of slavery—is most fully to repeat the act of Creation.

Shabbat emerges from its hidden cosmic place to dwell among the People Israel as the first step in the redemption of the human race from the curse of endless toil that ends the delight of Eden. In the moment just after liberation, there rises up one day that will not be full of toil and agony, one day of rest, of Eden. To begin with, only one day, for only one people. But because Shabbat echoes the fullness of Eden, it also beckons us toward the Messianic day when all days will be fully Shabbat for all peoples.

FORTY LABORS MINUS ONE

In the dispersion of Jewish life from the Land of Israel, the balance of when and how to rest shifted and Shabbat was redefined. The agrarian Shabbat of the *shmitah* and Jubilee years was greatly diminished in force; the prohibitions on work for the seventh-day Shabbat became more detailed and broader.

This shift in emphasis was neither accidental nor deliberately chosen: It flowed from the basic change in the life situation of the Jewish people as it became dispersed in many lands, and lost its authority to shape the economy of the Land of Israel. The less authority Jews had over broad expanses of space and time through and in which they could bring about a sacred rest, the more effort they put into creating forms of sacred rest that could go into effect for short periods of time, like a single day, and tiny spaces, like households and neighborhoods.

As Roman power circumscribed Jewish authority in the Land of Israel, the Rabbis narrowed and restricted the practice of *shmitah* and *dror* in the seventh and fiftieth years. Since Jews neither controlled the economy of the Land of Israel nor shared in setting agricultural or economic policy in the countries where they eventually lived, it became less tenable to celebrate or enforce a yearlong economic pause, rest, and release. So the Rabbis and their successors ruled that debts need no longer be annulled in the seventh year, if the lender and borrower would arrange the loan through a Rabbinical court. The Rabbis and the Jewish people did not carry the practice of leaving land fallow in the seventh year into the Diaspora. The Jubilee was explained away as inoperative when the Jewish people no longer lived in the Land of Israel.

As these macroversions of Shabbat withered, the people focused more and more on expanding and encoding the practice of the Shabbat of the seventh day. Indeed, just as the family dinner table and the House of Torah Study had become miniature replacements for the Holy Temple, so Shabbat became a version of the Temple, inscribed in time rather than space. The patterns of Shabbat observance became as elaborate as the architecture and furnishings of the Temple.

What would these practices be? First and most basic, what kind of work would be prohibited on Shabbat? How would the absence of such work become a definition of rest?

When the Mishnah discusses what work can be permitted on Shabbat, it plays with some interesting underlying ideas. The Mishnah's tractate *Shabbat* opens with a seemingly odd assertion that an act that would be considered work if one person did it, and therefore prohibited on Shabbat, is not work if it is begun by one person and completed by another. The underlying thought seems to be that work is the full accomplishment of a willed act by a single willing soul. Perhaps the sort of act that is only initiated or only completed by a single person is what we would today call "play," and this is permissible on Shabbat.

Since it is this passage that initiates the whole discussion of Shabbat, it may even be hinting that, in the beginning, God's making of the world in the first six days was a fully accomplished act—a piece of work—that could not be continued on Shabbat.

For six chapters, the Mishnah examines and in a workmanlike way settles such issues as whether cloth may be dyed before Shabbat if the colors continue setting into Shabbat, and how the oil may be placed in the Shabbat lamp. Only after this examination is under way does the Mishnah turn—in the seventh chapter!—to take up broader precepts. We can feel the Mishnah itself turning from six units of toilsome, tiresome work to the more open, thoughtful domain of Shabbat.

Following this path of thinking about Shabbat, the Mishnah finds the basic labors that are forbidden on Shabbat. They are cast in a near-poetic or liturgical form, in that the Mishnah tells us there are not a prosaic thirty-nine but:

Main labors: forty minus one.
Sowing, plowing, reaping, binding;
Threshing, winnowing, cleansing, grinding;
Sifting, kneading, baking.

Shearing wool—
And washing, combing, dyeing it;
Spinning, weaving,
  Making two loops,
  Weaving two threads,
  Separating two threads.
Knotting and loosing.
  Stitching two stitches,
  Tearing to stitch two stitches.

Hunting a deer
And slaying, flaying,
salting, curing,
scraping, or cutting up
its skin.

Writing two letters;
Erasing in order to write two letters.

Building
Smashing
Extinguishing
Kindling
Hammering.

Carrying forth
from
domain
to
domain.

Here they are!
Main labors: forty minus one.

The Gemara, responding to the Mishnah, acknowledges that these "forty minus one" main labors are known from the Torah. (T.B. Shabbat 49b) At first the Gemara is not certain why. Do these thirty-nine labors correspond to thirty-nine mentions of the word "labor" in the Torah? The Gemara concludes that they actually correspond to the forms of labor necessary to build the traveling Mishkan in the Wilderness.

Presumably, the Rabbis make this theological leap because of the way in which the vision of the Mishkan is enclosed within two statements of the holiness of Shabbat. In building the Mishkan, says the Talmud, "They sowed, hence you must not sow; they reaped, hence you must not reap; they lifted up the boards from the ground to the cart; hence you must not carry forth from domain to domain."

The Rabbis and their followers deduced many additional forms of prohibited work from the initial "forty minus one." But in principle, from that time on Shabbat rest has consisted of abstaining from the work that built the Shrine of God's Presence on earth. God rested from making the Cosmos, hence the people rested from making its microcosm. They rested from making the microcosm; hence we rest from remaking the Cosmos. The spiral takes a full turn upward, from God's resting to our own. The holiest act of work—even the holiest act, especially the holiest act—is fulfilled only by stopping. Only by recognizing and celebrating its wholeness and its holiness.

In this way, the Shabbat of the seventh day became a liturgical-practical replacement for the Temple and the Land—the depository for sacred rest when the

Temple and the Land could no longer serve this need. More than this, Shabbat *became* the Temple—a time/place in which not only to contemplate God but to heal and renew God's Own Self.

The Rabbis expanded this when they decided what kinds of labor to outlaw on Shabbat. They prohibited some activities (like blowing a *shofar* or throwing an object from one private domain to another) that were called *shevut* ("rest," from the same root as "Shabbat"). The community was told to avoid certain acts on Shabbat, such as handling tools, for fear these acts would encourage people to forget themselves and make Shabbat violations more likely. The Rabbis instituted the Shabbat perimeter, an area, called *t'chum Shabbat*, beyond which one could not travel on Shabbat even if walking.

The Rabbis gave Shabbat a special air of celebration by prescribing special meals, lighting candles before sundown on Friday evening, drinking wine, saying special additional blessings to welcome the day and to celebrate its midpoint, wearing special clothes, sauntering instead of hurrying. They also instituted the practice of reading portions from the Torah in a regular progression, week after week. Even the end of Shabbat became a time of pleasant songs and fragrant spices, joined to blessings that marked the boundary line from rest to everyday.

Among all Jewish communities, it was understood that the whole community was responsible to make sure that each person had the food, wine, shelter, and companionship necessary to celebrate Shabbat with joy rather than in pain. Thus Shabbat became a time to affirm and act out the social equality of all Jews, even though it was for but a moment.

Shabbat became a moment of complete release from work, commerce, and poverty, a release into the realm of song, joy, sharing, prayer, and Torah study. This felt experience lay beneath the Rabbis' comments that Shabbat was a foretaste of the Messianic Age, and that if all Israel kept Shabbat properly just once (or, some said, twice, to prove it was no accident), the Messianic Age would begin.

This connection between Shabbat and the days of the Messiah—days that would be *yom shekulo Shabbat*, "fully and utterly Shabbat"—shows how seriously Shabbat is taken in Jewish tradition. Only Shabbat connects the three supernal moments and the one supernal place in which eternity breaks into history and geography. The three times were (and continue to be, for each is a continuing process) the Creation, the Liberation/Revelation period from the Red Sea to Sinai, and the Messianic redemption. The one supernal place was (and remains, for it too is a continuing process) the Mishkan/Temple in which eternity—*HaMakom*, The Place—breaks its way into geographic space and becomes a microcosmos.

Thus, Shabbat inverts the ordinary four dimensions—three of space, one of time—to be located in three dimensions of time and one of space.

The entrance of Shabbat into human time and space, which was the first step toward curing the post-Edenic wound of painful toil and enmity between human beings and the earth, will be fulfilled when the whole earth can fully celebrate a continuing Shabbat.

SHABBAT AND SHEKHINAH

In our own generation, there are many mythic images, symbols, and ceremonies associated with Shabbat that are astonishingly "new." They were shaped by Jewish mystics between the twelfth and sixteenth centuries—often to the surprise of many Jews who celebrate them today, and who would not consider themselves mystics.

The Kabbalists saw Shabbat in a quite different way from most Jews who preceded them. To them, Shabbat was not only a human practice but also, and more vitally, an aspect of God's Own Self, an aspect of Wholeness through which the alienated and exiled aspects of God are reunited.

Some Kabbalists connected Shabbat as human practice and Shabbat as an aspect of the Godhead: The more fully and deeply human beings observed Shabbat, the more fully the wounded God of an alienated world could be restored to Wholeness. In this way, the flow between Creator and creature becomes a Möbius strip of creative process, in which Shabbat (as the emblem and practice of Wholeness in a not-whole world and a not-whole God) is what curves the Möbius strip into its flow.

Shabbat became a central element in Kabbalistic thinking, beginning with the Zohar, the great book of Jewish mysticism published in the thirteenth century.

By that time, Kabbalists had gone far toward working out the notion of a series of *s'phirot*, dynamic emanations or aspects of God, that bridged the gap from the *Ayin/Eyn Sof* (Nothingness/Utterly Beyond Infinitude) to the world we live in. Neither before the Zohar nor since have all Kabbalists agreed on the theology of the *s'phirot*. Yet a schematic sketch may be useful in order to give a context for the ways in which Shabbat became crucial to Kabbalistic thought.

So—keeping in mind that the theology of the *s'phirot* is a great deal more complex and varied than this outline can be:

There were three triads of *s'phirot* plus a final all-encompassing one—ten altogether. These were seen, through one eye of the mystical beholder, as a "historical" progression within the unfolding Divine, moving one after the other in chronological succession through the creative process; and through the other eye of the beholder, as a pulsating nonchronological system in which all the *s'phirot* are in constant simultaneous dynamic tension and relation with each other in the continuing creative process.

The first triad moved from Infinitude into the World of *Atzilut*, which can be (awkwardly but accurately) translated as "Highest-Level Direct Spiritual Emanation," and then into the World of *Briyah* (Creating, or Divine Mindfulness).

Since *Briyah* represented the very process of Creation of the created world, only after *Briyah* did Creation take on form, and so only after *Briyah* was the world within human abilities to apprehend.

The remaining seven *s'phirot* were, therefore, much more accessible. For many Kabbalists, these became the realm of focus and discussion.

The second triad was in the World of *Yetzirah* (Formation, Shaping, Relation, Emotion).

The third triad was in the World of *Asiyah* (Action, Making, Body).

And the tenth *s'phirah* (the seventh in the more accessible group) is the created world itself, in which all the *s'phirot* are gathered into the spiritual, intellectual, ethical/emotional, and physical reality we know.

For many Kabbalists, the seven more accessible *s'phirot* became identified with the Seven Days of Creation, and the most accessible one with the day of Shabbat. Yet this was never crystal-clear. Indeed, the Zohar made a virtue of this uncertainty by identifying two of the *s'phirot* with Shabbat—one a male and one a female aspect of Shabbat. As support for the notion of two Shabbats, they quoted a Biblical text: "I [God] have given you my Shabbats; revere my Holy Place." They added that the two aspects of Shabbat mentioned in Exodus—"*Zachor*, Remember!" and in Deuteronomy—"*Shamor*, Keep!"—also hinted at these male and female aspects of Shabbat. The male *s'phirah* was called *Yesod* (literally, "Foundation," but meant as "Connection"). The female *s'phirah* was called *Malkhut* (literally, "Rulership," but meant as "All-Encompassing Collectivity").

All the *s'phirot* were symbolized by parts of the human body, as well as by colors, Biblical figures, and other attributes. *Yesod* was symbolized by the male genitals; *Malkhut*, by the female genitals. The Kabbalists saw *Yesod* as the aspect of God that brought the higher Divinity together in an effort to reach out toward the world and impregnate it with the Divine impulse toward life. They saw *Malkhut* as the aspect of God that already lived within the world in order to arouse, welcome, respond to, and quicken the Divine seed into a living universe.

Thus Malkhut was identified with Shekhinah, the Indwelling Divine Presence of Godflow within the physical, ethical, and intellectual universe. Since Shekhinah was the Feminine aspect of God, She was often set forth as a consort of the Divine Masculine. The Kabbalists drew on earlier assertions that She had gone into exile—that is, had been separated from her Divine Husband—when the Temple was destroyed and Israel went into exile.

For the Kabbalists, Shabbat became not only the time when, but also the very fact that, the Masculine and Feminine Divine were reunited in a sexual relationship that gave new life, harmony, and peace to the world. Shabbat/Shekhinah was both the Bride Herself and the union of Bride and Groom. Shabbat was both the process and the product, the medium and the message.

What human beings did could strengthen or weaken this supernal union. In order both to stimulate and to imitate this union in the invisible world above, the Kabbalists urged, it was vital for Jews to make love in the visible world below, during Shabbat. So that the Shekhinah could send forth glowing light in her love-making with the Divine Masculine, wives should light the candles as Shabbat began. When Jews said the Kiddush prayer over wine on the eve of Shabbat, they were saying it not only for themselves but as the wedding blessing for the Divine sexual union.

If the male and female fluids that poured forth were abundant, a flood of love and goodness came into the world through Shabbat. It was so powerful that the influences of the demonic Other Side were weakened, and Jews need not fear demonic threats on this one day. So even prayers for God's protection were changed on this day to express utter confidence and trust.

Even the choice of a time when Jews lit the flame of the Havdalah candle at the end of Shabbat would affect the Divine energies. To light the candles before the end of Shabbat would subject the sufferers in Gehenna, who every week were relieved from punishment for the period of Shabbat, to the immediate rekindling of their own tormenting flames. And to delay the Havdalah lighting was to delay the return of power over the world from God's Own resplendent and lovingly satisfied Self to lesser angels and in some degree to the Other Side.

The Zohar especially expanded and enriched the older notion that on Shabbat an extra soul comes into the human ken, in order to strengthen the ordinary soul.

By the sixteenth century, when an extraordinary group of Kabbalists gathered in the city of Safed, near the Sea of Galilee in northern Israel, these ideas had become widespread and rich enough to build new liturgy from and for them, not only to reinforce existing practice. The ceremony of Kabbalat Shabbat as Shabbat entered, and especially the well-known hymn "L'Cha Dodi," were rooted in the mystical identification of Shabbat with the Shekhinah and with the union of the Divine Male and Female.

What the Kabbalah contributes to our sense of Shabbat and of profound and sacred rest is the belief that human beings can not only imitate God the Creator, God the Liberator, and God the Revealer by resting and musing on God's teachings; can not only reaffirm God's sole ownership of the earth by pausing for Shabbat and *shmitah* from making the earth work; can not only prevent communal and ecological disasters, but can stir the deepest life energies in the universe; can not only imitate God and honor God but also heal God.

SHABBAT AND ALL THE EARTH

As we have seen, the forms of rest in Jewish culture and the emphases of Shabbat have changed several times—from cosmic rhythm to social justice, from the *shmitah/ yovel* cycle to the seventh day—as the community faced profoundly changed circumstances. In our own day, both Judaism and the world have entered another crisis that has begun to affect the shape of rest and the practice of Shabbat.

Two postmodern Jewish thinkers, the theologian Rabbenu Abraham Joshua Heschel and the psychotherapist Erich Fromm, have led the way in reformulating the meaning of Shabbat. In an era of technological triumph, writing in the immediate aftermath of the Nazi Holocaust and the first use of nuclear weapons, they saw Shabbat as an affirmation of values beyond technology.

Said Fromm (in *You Shall Be as Gods*), "Work is any interference by man [sic], be it constructive or destructive, with the physical world. 'Rest' is a state of peace between man and nature." Fromm interprets in this light the seemingly obsessive prohibitions of Jewish tradition upon accomplishing on Shabbat even the slightest, least effortful changes of ownership or place of objects in the world. So Shabbat becomes for him an actual (though brief) transformation of the human path into a real experience of Messianic harmony and peace.

For Heschel, Shabbat is an affirmation that holiness is borne more by the flow and rhythm of time than by objects in space, and he too sees Shabbat as a challenge to a "technical civilization" obsessed by the conquest of space and the improvement of objects:

To set apart one day a week for freedom, a day on which we would not use the instruments which have been so easily turned into weapons of destruction, a day of detachment from the vulgar, of independence of external obligations, a day on which we stop worshipping the idols of technical civilization, a day on which we use no money, a day of armistice in the economic struggle with our fellow men [sic] and the forces of nature—is there any institution that holds out a greater hope for man's progress than the Sabbath? (Heschel, *The Sabbath*, p. 28)

Perhaps for the first time in Jewish history, Fromm and Heschel suggested that the practice of Shabbat in some form might be profoundly important to the entire human race—not to the Jewish people alone—in redeeming the world from the threat of technology run amok. Until this generation, Jews had assumed that Shabbat was the sign of the Sinai covenant between God and the Jewish people, and therefore of consequence to Jews alone.

There may be ways to affirm both these views without rejecting either. The observance of Shabbat in the myriad specific ways in which Jewish tradition has developed it may reasonably be seen as uniquely Jewish, while the well of wisdom at the heart of Shabbat and some of the most salient aspects of its observance might give new life and new forms of rest to other peoples as well as other species.

We have already looked at how this might be done when we thought about applying the sabbatical and Jubilee years in our generation.

For example: Could the world celebrate a "techno-*shmitah*" by saying that every seventh year engineers and scientists would suspend work (except for work on mortal diseases) for a year while they rested, reflected, celebrated, reconsidered and reevaluated their efforts, and prepared to take a new look at how to shape the world's technologies in more humane and more holy directions?

Or, if this would be too difficult, could businesses decide that every seventh year, they would introduce no new products or services and provide only the old ones, thus giving themselves and the world a breather from the treadmill of speed-up?

What if every seventh day became a Shabbat, observed throughout the world with minimum use of fossil fuels like gasoline and coal, so that the earth's atmosphere could rest from being drenched in carbon dioxide?

What if every nation set aside the seventh month as a time for holding neighborhood folk festivals, town meetings, crafts fairs, and similar celebrations close to home?

What if workers were to receive a year of paid vacation in the middle of their working lives (trading it for retiring one year later), a year of reassessment, recreation, renewal?

What if the Jewish community organized efforts for a major reduction in the hours of work, with no reduction in total wages and salaries? Till now, the new productivity of high-tech machines has led to frantic labor by those with jobs, coerced idleness by the unemployed, and less free time for everyone. Why not allow the new leisure to provide more time for reflection and for community service rather than waste it in the despair, rage, and violence of permanent unemployment?

All these might be seen as "fringes (*tzitzit*) of Shabbat," observances of Shabbat by all the nations that will help shape a sacred rhythm of work and rest without replacing the internal Jewish definitions of Shabbat.

SHABBAT FOR EVE AND ADAM

The current crisis created by Modernity and technology seems to be connected with another crisis: the earthquake of remaking the relationships of women and men. In intimate as well as profound ways, this upheaval is moving us to reexamine our assumptions about rest, reflection, and repose.

Let us look at Shabbat itself as it has affected women. The traditional practice of Shabbat (and also the deeper assumptions about what "work" was) neither required nor encouraged women who were sustaining a home, nurturing a family, and rearing children to rest on Shabbat.

Unlike making money or moving objects from one household to a public place, these activities were simply not considered "work." Indeed, they were often unconsciously treated as if they were already part of Shabbat. Those who did what it took to keep home, community, and family going—feeding people, cleaning floors and tables, moving the furniture, calming fights, laughing and singing—did not get "time off" for Shabbat. Both men and women did the sorts of work that did end for Shabbat, but women did most of the work that did not end on Shabbat because no one (except perhaps women!) considered it to be work.

Now, therefore, we face what it would mean to shape a Shabbat in which the women's work gets recognized as work, and in which they too, get a chance to rest. If this kind of "work" cannot stop on Shabbat because the nurturing of community is exactly what we want to encourage on Shabbat, then how can we do this without burdening one part of the community while letting others rest?

For many households today, it is worse torment and harder work to prepare for and celebrate Shabbat than to let it go. Just as Jewish communities have always made sure that the poor had a communal place to pray and a household where they could eat, sleep, visit, and sing on Shabbat, so communities should meet analogous needs today.

So, here are some thoughts:

- Every Thursday evening, a community center or synagogue offers overburdened households a variety of help in preparing for Shabbat. Every member has a time credit and a time obligation: On seven Thursday evenings a year, I will be available to help someone cook, clean, care for children; and in exchange, on other Thursdays I am entitled to have others help me. To the extent possible, we do this work in a communal place; if not the synagogue, then a friendly neighborhood co-op store or Laundromat. For whatever needs to be done at home, that evening's co-op volunteers go to someone's home to do.

- Every Shabbat afternoon, every community offers parents time and space to bring their children to a communal center—ideally, the synagogue—and stay with them, or if they prefer go walking, napping, studying Torah, dancing, singing.

- In households that do not need outside help, women and men explicitly agree that they will share in preparing and celebrating Shabbat, and will periodically reshuffle the tasks so that no one person gets locked into one role.

- If someone in the household is habitually the child-care person during the week, that task switches around for Shabbat. In households without children, whatever is the major chore that cannot be done before or after Shabbat is similarly switched around.

Ending the rigidities of the roles assigned to women and men should not be narrowly confined to the twenty-five hours of Shabbat. For that slice of time speaks to the larger question of what we think is work and what we think is rest throughout the week, the month, the year. And it speaks to the even larger question of the roles assigned to women—a question that goes back to the primordial march from Eden, out of the Garden of Delight.

For let us remember that just as the Torah describes the end of Eden and the beginning of history as the eruption of war between human beings and the earth, so it describes that moment as one of alienation between women and men and the subjugation of women to men. In the realm of work and the relationship between *adam* and *adamah*, earthling and earth, Shabbat represents the first taste of a future in which the human race can create a higher version of Eden. Not a womb for unconscious children but a conscious Eden for grown-ups.

What about this second realm of Eden and the march from Eden? In that second realm, relationship and alienation between men and women, what are the implications of Shabbat? If Shabbat were to represent more fully the foretaste of a Messianic future, should not this element of Messianic change be part of what we taste? Should not Shabbat then include a new, freer, more fluid relationship within the human race as well as between humans and the earth?

Why is this all coming into question now? Just as tension between human beings and the earth has risen to a new pitch, as dangers to the weave of life around the planet have arisen, so the tension between the old and rigid roles of women and men has risen to a new pitch because the roles have become even more harsh and isolated.

The crisis we now face in the change or the collapse of conventional gender roles may be rooted in the rigidification of these roles themselves. Perhaps, when men were assigned chiefly to action and "work" while women were assigned chiefly to nurturing and "rest" or "Shabbat," a rough balance was struck between the two modes of being that met the needs of the world. In that world, the two modes were not totally isolated from each other. Families that included women were intimately involved in all public doings throughout the world: Royal and aristocratic families ruled politics, business families ruled the economy, in Jewish life the Rabbis who led religious life at least had wives to respond to. So women were not totally isolated from public action, or "work," nor men from shaping community, or "Shabbat."

In the modern world of huge and highly structured bureaucracies, women were almost totally excluded from having some effect on public action. Their assignment to caring for the family and nurturing the community became more and more ghettoized inside the home. And the home became weaker. In shaping community, just as bureaucratic structures like public education and the mass media got stronger, so the families in which women had a voice became weaker and weaker and their voices, too, became weaker.

Now new and energetic movements have emerged in which women have asserted a role in public life, calling for a rebalancing of the roles of public action and caring for community. They have also called for a reopening of the flow within each human being of the roles of action and community, I-It and I-Thou, work and repose that have been rigidified by assigning one role to men and one to women.

Here the two mythic issues that emerge from Eden—the relationship of Eve and Adam and the relationship of *adamah* and *adam*—make contact with each other. For there is a close connection between the concern that many men and women have that the new gigantic bureaucracies despoil the earth, and the concern that women (and some men) have that they and their nurturing roles have been consigned to insignificance. Might bringing nurturance into public action—making such "work" more like Shabbat—help to heal the clash between earth and its earthlings?

All this suggests that we are at the threshold of a new great transformation of Shabbat and of Jewish patterns of rest. In the Deuteronomic-Prophetic period, Israelites unveiled the cosmic theme of Shabbat and discovered within it the theme of social justice and liberation. Today we take another spiral turn as we look even deeper into Shabbat and see it as a protection for Creation. The theme of liberation need not be lost, any more than the original theme of cosmic rhythm was lost. Justice and freedom for human beings, especially but not only for the female half of the human race, may be intimately connected with considering ourselves as earthlings who are intertwined with other aspects of the earth.

Certainly Shabbat should be a time when Jews gather to contemplate the restful wholeness of "being" rather than "doing." A time for Jews not to scan hurriedly but to pause and meditate with care on the second paragraph of the Sh'ma that says that if we make our actions in the world a part of the great weave of life as Torah teaches, the rains will fall, the rivers will run, the earth will bloom, and all earthlings will eat; but that if we turn away from that Unity to become addicted to something that is only a part of the whole, if we crack the harmony, then the broken harmony will crack us: The rain will turn to poison, the rivers will fail, the earth will turn barren, and we will starve.

Could Shabbat become once more not only a time of meditation on the truth of Wholeness, but also a time to practice it? Many synagogues decided that under Modern life conditions, it was necessary to use gasoline for transport and electricity for light on Shabbat. Could they now reexamine whether, for the sake of truly remembering the restful seal of God's Creation, it would be wise to minimize the use of gasoline and oil and electricity on Shabbat? Not necessarily to eliminate them utterly, but, for example, to provide a van or bus or strongly urge car-pooling to bring congregants to synagogue on Shabbat rather than encourage each family to use its own car? To turn down the electric lights so that people can still see their way and their prayer books, but in a gentle glow more like the light of candles? To turn down the heat and encourage congregants to wear sweaters? To urge that families apply similar standards to their own use of energy at home? To redefine as sacred Jewish practice the habit of letting the earth, along with its earthlings, rest on Shabbat?

There is a deep connection between what we have learned about rest and what we have learned about food, money, and sex. The Kabbalists taught that Shabbat, the Day of Rest, was itself the Divine Wellspring from which all *shefa*, the entire stream of Divine abundance, flowed forth into the world. In our own day, we can see that it is Rest that renews and makes possible the continuing flow of food, money, and sexuality, the great flows of abundance in our earthly, earthy lives. If we are so thirsty to create more abundance for ourselves that we refuse to rest, we poison and choke the flow of earthy abundance. The spiritual insights of our greatest mystics and the practical teachings of wisest scientists fuse into one.

At the end of an epoch in which the human race has gained enormous knowledge and great mastery, Shabbat remains the emblem and the practice of Mystery. When we realize that we do not always know exactly what to do next, instead of moving instantly to conquer our ignorance—

We may pause.

We may catch our breaths.

We may, in a Shabbat mode, acknowledge that we do not know.

We may celebrate the fruitful truth that there is in the world not merely ignorance, but Mystery.

the gentle friends, the blessings to awaken in the morning, the nap, the sauntering afternoon. The resting.

Here and here and here, what we do on Shabbat that is not-doing. That is being, not doing. Some of these can be not-done when you have a day, a week, a month, a year. Some can be not-done, just snatches of Shabbat, at any moment.

Rest. Reflect. Renew. Return. Rest. Reflect. Renew. Return.

GO AND STUDY, GO AND DO

Once a cluster of Rabbis debated, "Which is greater, knowledge or action?"

This was no academic question. At the time, the Rabbis were hidden in an attic, trying to avoid arrest by the Roman army, which had outlawed both Torah study—knowledge—and the performance of specific Jewish precepts—action. Which, the Rabbis wondered, would be more crucial to pursue anyway, even outside the law, if Judaism were to be preserved?

And they were also asking something else, even more basic: If all that the Jewish people held in its hands at that moment was the power to study, could knowledge prevail against the power of Rome—the imperial power to act? Did the political situation control knowledge, or could knowledge transform the political situation?

Said Akiba, "Which is greater? Knowledge—if it leads to action." The other sages agreed with him.

This book is intended to bring together knowledge that can lead to action. Knowledge that can help us, if we choose, to transform the worlds we live in—our households, our friendships, our kitchens, our banks, our beds, and the wider worlds of all the earth.

The Hebrew word for "knowledge" that the Rabbis used was also the word for "making love." The kind of knowledge that they were discussing was not "objective," objectifying, the study of cold facts—but learning with hot facts. Knowledge that we become intertwined with; knowledge that we are changing while it changes us.

This book was woven out of many strands of that kind of knowledge. Some of the strands were conversations with a person; others, conversations with a book or article or even an organization. All of them would repay further exploration by those who are intrigued by this book.

As I wrestled with this book, I was also able to wrestle and to dance with some extraordinary people whose wisdom found its way into my heart and sometimes explicitly into these pages: my friend, my lover, my *bashert*, my beloved, and my wife, Phyllis Ocean Berman; my brother and sister, Howard Waskow and Grey Wolfe; my children, David Waskow, Shoshana Waskow, Michael Slater, Joshua Sher, and Morissa Sher; and my friends, colleagues, and teachers, Rabbi Zalman Schachter-Shalomi, Rabbi Max Ticktin, Esther Ticktin, Judith Plaskow, Rabbi

Laura Geller, Professor Ari Elon, Jeffrey Dekro, Rabbi Brian Walt, Rabbi Mordechai Liebling, Rabbi Jeff Roth, Rabbi Joanna Katz, Rabbi Goldie Milgram, Barbara Breitman, Rabbi Julie Greenberg, Marion Katz Jahn, Christie Balka, Rebecca Subar, Rabbi Marcia Prager, Rabbi Devora Bartnoff, Cantor Chaim Rothstein, Susan Saxe, Shefa Gold, Rabbi Marshall Meyer (whose memory is a blessing), Michael Lerner, Sidney Shapiro, Mitch Marcus, and Susie Marcus.

When I got mired in the writing of this book, it was Phyllis Berman who suggested that I write a preface about how hard it was to write the book, and why. As she wisely knew it would, that released me to write it—and then all along the way she gave me cogent suggestions for how to write it better. When I had finished a second draft, Rabbi Max Ticktin read the entire manuscript and gave me the most extraordinarily detailed, thoughtful, knowledgeable, and wise suggestions and criticisms. My editor, Zack Schisgal, and my copy editor, Sonia Greenbaum, also read the whole manuscript, and with patience and persistence showed me how to tighten and sharpen what I had to say.

Rabbi Zalman Schachter-Shalomi, Rabbi Caryn Broitman, Vivienne Cato, Jeffrey Dekro, Rabbi Tzvi Blanchard, Judith Plaskow, and Shoshi Larkey read large parts of the manuscript and gave me the benefit of their knowledge and experience toward improving it.

My brother Howard and my agent, Sydelle Kramer, each gave me some crucial advice at critical moments in the writing.

Long ago, in the early days of the movement for Jewish renewal, Rob Agus proposed the creation of a "new holistic Jewish lifestyle" as our goal. That vision has beckoned me toward this book, though its content at this point is different from what he—or I—would have imagined, in those days.

My friend Ira Silverman—supporter, teacher, guide, defender; founding chair of The Shalom Center and transformative president of the Reconstructionist Rabbinical College; above all, *mentsh*—died when this book had been conceived but was still in the womb of time. I honor all that he gave and long for all that he would have given me, the Jewish people, and the world.

Two others of my teachers died while I was finishing this book: Rabbi Shlomo Carlebach, who took my hand just after I crossed the threshold of Jewish life and led me in his paths of music, joy, and ecstasy; and Ann Sara Weiss, founding cochair of ALEPH: Alliance for Jewish Renewal, who taught me the Torah of steadfast, gentle, practical leadership dedicated to children—the world's children, to be kept safe from a nuclear holocaust or other environmental disaster; the children of the Jewish people, to be handed a Judaism full of life and value; her own children, to be nurtured even in the very moments of her own dying.

Many of the issues I explore in this book are being addressed by ALEPH: Alliance for Jewish Renewal, 6711 Lincoln Drive, Philadelphia, PA 19119, which has appointed me one of its Pathfinders, and by its journal, *New Menorah*, which I edit. I hope people will get in touch with us to raise questions, share insights, and make connections toward the revitalization of down-to-earth Judaism: infusing all our life work with the Breath of Life.

Three previous works of my own—*Godwrestling* (Schocken, 1978, republished with major revisions as *Godwrestling, Round Two* by Jewish Lights, 1995); *These Holy Sparks* (Harper & Row, 1983); and *Seasons of Our Joy* (Bantam, 1982; second edition, Beacon, 1990)—address other aspects of Jewish renewal: The first deals with how we can learn from reading Torah together in new, open-ended ways; the second, how the contemporary movement for Jewish renewal emerged over the last generation; the third, how we can make the Jewish festivals into a spiritual path.

In weaving my own approach to "down-to-earth Judaism," I have drawn especially on four strands of Jewish thought-practice:

- Spiritually, a renewed and transformed version of Hassidism and its joyful sense of God's Presence in the world, through the work of Martin Buber, Rabbenu Abraham Joshua Heschel, and especially in my own life, Rabbi Zalman Schachter-Shalomi, who has helped me "rename" and "re-imagine" God embodied as the Breath of Life, the Four Worlds and the Ten S'phirot of Kabbalah embodied in the human psyche, and the Divine life cycle embodied in the great transformations and eras of history;
- Intellectually, that aspect of Mordecai Kaplan's work which focused on how the Jewish people has over and over reshaped Judaism as a religion of ethical nationhood;
- In the world of relational community, the remarkable interwoven Jewish-renewal community that is itself one strand of the Mount Airy neighborhood in Philadelphia, and the feminist Judaisms that are appearing, especially in the work of Rabbi Laura Geller, Rabbi Sue Levi Elwell, Susannah Heschel, Rachel Adler, Esther Broner, Marcia Falk, Marge Piercy, Shefa Gold, and Judith Plaskow; and
- In the realm of active change, my direct experience of Jewish commitment to the pursuit of peace and social justice, in the practice of Hannah Waskow, Henry Waskow, Marcus Raskin, Paul Goodman, Paul Jacobs, and Bella Abzug, and in the theory as well as the practice of Martin Buber, Rabbenu Heschel, Rabbi Everett Gendler, Rabbi Marshall Meyer, Rabbi Gerald Serotta, Rabbi David Saperstein, Rabbi Rebecca Alpert, Jeffrey Dekro, and Michael Lerner.

I especially recommend for serious study Plaskow's book *Standing Again at Sinai* (HarperSanFrancisco, 1990), Piercy's novel *He, She and It* (Knopf, 1991), Schachter-Shalomi's *Paradigm Shift* (Jason Aronson, 1993), Gold's audiotape "Chants Encounters," and Lerner's *Jewish Renewal* (Putnam, 1994).

My work at The Shalom Center and ALEPH has made it possible for me to do parallel work on this book. So I thank contributors to The Shalom Center and ALEPH, including the Albert A. List Foundation, the Nathan Cummings Foundation, the Max and Anna Levinson Foundation, the Rita Poretsky Fund, the Ploughshares Fund, the Reiss Family Fund, the Edgar Stern Family Fund, The Shefa Fund, and the Emet Foundation; the Coolidge Colloquium of the Association for Religion and Intellectual Life; and many synagogues, colleges, and other centers that have invited me to speak on these themes.

I have noted below the people with whom and works with which I had useful conversations as I wrote this book, divided into the four sections of *Down-to-Earth Judaism*.

FOOD

It was Barbara Breitman, reporting a child's insight, who taught me the difference between "grown-ups" and "blown-ups." I first heard the joke about Moses, God, milk, and meat from Chava Weissler. Debbie Zucker suggested that I think about the spiritual roots of eating disorders. Shefa Gold pointed out that the Talmud begins by connecting food with the affirmation of the Sh'ma.

For key guides to and encouragements of public observance: Isaac Klein, *A Guide to Jewish Religious Practice* (Jewish Theological Seminary, 1979); Hyman E. Goldin, translator, *Code of Jewish Law (Kitzur Shulhan Aruch)*, edited by Solomon Ganzfried (Hebrew Publishing Company, 1961); Josh Heckelman and Sue Levi Elwell, "Hallah," in *The Jewish Catalog*, edited by Richard Siegel, Michael Strassfeld, and Sharon Strassfeld (Jewish Publication Society, 1974); Ronald Androphy, "Shehita," in *The Third Jewish Catalog*, edited by Sharon Strassfeld and Michael Strassfeld (Jewish Publication Society, 1980).

For scholarly analyses of the various issues of offerings and food in the Torah, see Baruch A. Levine, "Excursus 2," in *The JPS Torah Commentary: Leviticus* (Jewish Publication Society, 1989), pp. 241–42; Jacob Milgrom, "Excursuses 41, 42, 43, 46," in *The JPS Torah Commentary: Numbers* (Jewish Publication Society, 1990); and entries under "Sacrifice," "Dietary Laws," "Tithe," "Cooking," "Milk," "Hallah," "Fasting and Fast Days," "Grace After Meals," in *Encyclopedia Judaica*.

For anthropological approaches to issues of *kashrut*, see Howard Eilberg-Schwartz, *The Savage in Judaism* (Indiana University Press, 1990), and Mary Douglas,

Purity and Danger (Routledge and Kegan Paul, 1966). Late in my writing, two books appeared that bear on these issues in important ways: Gillian Feeley-Harnik, *The Lord's Table: The Meaning of Food in Early Judaism and Christianity* (Smithsonian, 1994), and Leon R. Kass, *The Hungry Soul* (Free Press, 1994).

For the ways in which Kabbalah addressed food, see Miles Krassen, "Trees of Beauty Below, the Tree of Life Above" [translation of *Peri 'Ez Hadar*], in *New Menorah* (Chanukah 5751/December 1990), pp. 7–8; Moshe Idel, *Kabbalah: New Perspectives* (Yale University Press, 1988); Gershom Scholem, *Kabbalah* (Quadrangle, 1974); Lawrence Fine, "The Contemplative Practice of Yihudim in Lurianic Kabbalah," in Arthur Green, editor, *Jewish Spirituality* (Crossroad, 1986–87); Louis Jacobs, "The Uplifting of Sparks in Later Jewish Mysticism," in Arthur Green, editor, ibid.

For changes among Reform and Reconstructionist Jews in dealing with food issues, see Michael A. Meyer, *Response to Modernity* (Oxford, 1988); *Gates of Mitzvah* (Central Conference of American Rabbis, 1979); Walter Jacobs, *Responsa . . .* ; Gunther Plaut, sources on Reform Judaism, 2 volumes; Mordecai M. Kaplan, *The Future of the American Jew* (Macmillan, 1948), and *A Guide to Jewish Ritual* (Reconstructionist Press, 1962).

For the practice of traditional Eastern European Jews, see Mark Zborowski and Elizabeth Herzog, *Life Is with People* (International Universities Press, 1952), and Chava Weissler, "The Traditional Piety of Ashkenazic Women," in Arthur Green, editor, op. cit.

One approach to creating new blessings over food can be found in Marcia Falk, *The Book of Blessings* (HarperSanFrancisco, 1995).

On vegetarianism, see Richard H. Schwartz, *Jewish Vegetarianism*, and Jewish Vegetarians of North America, 6938 Reliance Road, Federalsburg, MD 21632.

M O N E Y

For details on some specific issues, see entries on "Hafkaat She'arim," "Taxation," "Onaah," "Labor," "Socialism," "Socialism, Jewish," "Bund," "Holiness Code," "Leviticus," "Tithes," "Taxes" "Poor, Provisions for the," "Shekalim," in *Encyclopedia Judaica*.

For the philosophy and internal dynamics of the kibbutz, see Martin Buber, *Paths in Utopia* (Beacon, 1949), and Dan Leon, *The Kibbutz* (Israel Horizons, 1964).

On the role of Mishnaic women in economic life, see Judith Romney Wegner, *Chattel or Person? The Status of Women in the Mishnah* (Oxford University Press, 1988).

On Judaism and the environment, see especially two useful handbooks: *To Till and to Tend*, published by the Coalition on the Environment and Jewish Life, 443 Park Avenue South, 11th Floor, New York, NY, 10016; and *The Green Shalom*

Guide, published by Shomrei Adamah of Washington, D.C., 706 Erie Avenue, Takoma Park, MD 20912. For more philosophic and midrashic discussions, see Arthur Waskow, *Seasons of Our Joy* (Bantam, 1982; second edition, Beacon, 1990); Arthur Waskow and Ari Elon, editors, *The Tu B'Shvat Anthology* (Jewish Publication Society, 1996); back issues of *The Shalom Report* and *New Menorah* from ALEPH, 7318 Germantown Avenue, Philadelphia, PA 19119; *Melton Journal* (Spring 1991 and Spring 1992); *Conservative Judaism* (Fall 1991); Richard H. Schwartz, *Judaism and Global Survival* (Atara, 1987); Elisheva Kaufman, *Shorashim: Earth Roots/Jewish Roots/Roots of Being: Exploring the Jewish Roots of Ecology with Children* (5 North Street, Montpelier, VT 05602); many works by Ellen Bernstein, especially *Judaism and Ecology* (written with Dan Fink and published by Hadassah in cooperation with Shomrei Adamah, 1993); David E. Stein, *A Garden of Choice Fruits* (Shomrei Adamah, 1991).

Environmental organizations: Shomrei Adamah at Surprise Lake, 50 W. 17th Street, New York, NY 10011; The Shalom Center, 7318 Germantown Avenue, Philadelphia, PA 19119; Coalition on Environment and Jewish Life, c/o NJCRAC, 443 Park Avenue South, New York, NY 10016; Israel Union for Environmental Defense (*Adam Teva vaDin*), 317 HaYarkon, Tel Aviv; Society for the Protection of Nature in Israel (*Haganat HaTeva*), 3/4 HaShfela Street, Tel Aviv; Abraham Joshua Heschel Center for Nature Studies, 9/6 Bar Giora Street, Tel Aviv.

On the sabbatical year and Jubilee cycle, see Arthur Waskow, "Beyond Marx and Buddha: The Jubilee," in *Godwrestling* (Schocken, 1978; second edition, Jewish Lights, 1995), pp. 110–17 in first edition, and "From Compassion to Jubilee," *Tikkun* (March–April 1990), pp. 78–81.

For information on *tzedakah,* see Jacob Neusner, *Tzedakah* (Rossel, 1982); Betsy Tessler and Jeffrey Dekro, *Building Community, Creating Justice: A Guide for Organizing Tzedakah Funds* (The Shefa Fund, Philadelphia, 1994); Mazon, 2940 Westwood Boulevard, Suite 7, Los Angeles, CA 90064; American Jewish World Service, 15 West 26th Street, New York, NY 10010; Jewish Fund for Justice, 920 Broadway, number 605, New York, NY 10010; The Shefa Fund, 7318 Germantown Avenue, Philadelphia, PA 19119; Ziv Tzedakah Fund, 263 Congressional Lane, number 708, Rockville, MD 20852; Council of Jewish Federations, 730 Broadway, New York, NY 10003; New Israel Fund, 1101 15th Street, NW, number 304, Washington, DC 20005.

On the Jewish roots of socially responsible investment, see especially the pathbreaking work of Lawrence Bush and Jeffrey Dekro, *Jews, Money and Social Responsibility* (The Shefa Fund, 1993). Two such investment funds are: Calvert Funds, 4550 Montgomery Avenue, 1000N, Bethesda, MD 20814; Working Assets, 230 California Street, San Francisco, CA 94111.

On Judaism and business ethics, see Wayne Dosick, *The Business Bible* (Morrow, 1993), and Meir Tamari, *With All Your Possessions* (Free Press, 1987). For cost-sharing and the philosophy behind it, see Felice Yeskel, "Coming Out About Money," *Bridges* (Spring–Summer 1992), pp. 102–12.

Information on the relative average affluence of the American Jewish community is rooted in the research of Gerald Bubis and Gerald Krefetz, as reported by The Shefa Fund. My thoughts on how the new Jewish affluence may change Jewish approaches to social justice and social responsibility have been sharpened by the insights of Rachel Adler and of Jeffrey Dekro.

S E X

In my explorations in issues of sexuality, I am especially indebted to conversations with Barbara Breitman and Judith Plaskow.

On a number of specific questions, see entries under "Concubine," "Mamzer," "Prostitution," "Purity and Impurity, Ritual," "Niddah," "Onanism," in *Encyclopedia Judaica.*

A quite remarkable "school" of scholars of the history of Jewish sexuality and the body has emerged in the San Francisco Bay Area. Among its important works are Daniel Boyarin, *Carnal Israel* (University of California Press, 1993); David Biale, *Eros and the Jews* (Basic Books, 1992); Howard Eilberg-Schwartz, *The Savage in Judaism* (Indiana University Press, 1990) and *God's Phallus* (Beacon, 1994); Howard Eilberg-Schwartz, editor, *People of the Body* (State University of New York Press, 1992).

For the Biblical history of sexuality, see especially Tikva Frymer-Kensky, *In the Wake of the Goddesses* (Free Press, 1992), and Jeremy Cohen, *"Be Fertile and Increase, Fill the Earth and Master It": The Ancient and Medieval Career of a Biblical Text* (Cornell University Press, 1989). My thoughts on the nature of *tumah* have been strongly influenced by the work of Rachel Adler. For me, the power of the Song of Songs has been enormously enhanced by Marcia Falk's stunning translation, *The Song of Songs* (HarperSanFrancisco, 1990).

As I sought to understand the outlook of the Rabbis of the Talmud on their own work and on sexuality, my most important guide was Ari Elon, from whom I learned to explore the Talmud in new ways. See especially Alon's "The Torah as Love Goddess," in Michael Chernick, *Essential Papers on the Talmud* (NYU Press, 1994), pp. 463–76.

See also Judith Romney Wegner, *Chattel or Person? The Status of Women in the Mishnah* (Oxford University Press, 1988).

The text and translation of *Iggeret HaKodesh* is presented in Seymour J. Cohen, *The Holy Letter* (Jason Aronson, 1993).

The Kabbalistic and Sabbatian views of sexuality are discussed by Isaiah Tishby, "Conjugal Life," in *The Wisdom of the Zohar*, Volume III (Oxford University Press,

1989), pp. 1355–1407, and Gershom Scholem, *Sabbatai Sevi* (Princeton University Press, 1973).

For information on the Rabbinic outlook on the sexual expression of unmarried Jews, see Gershon Winkler, "Sex and Religion: Friend, or Foe," in *New Menorah* (Second Series: Number 7), pp. 1–3, and Lakme Batya Elior, "Pilegesh Relationships—A Responsa," *Pumbedissa* (March–April 1994), pp. 10–11.

On the gay Jewish poets of the Golden Age in Spain, see Raymond P. Scheindlin, "A Miniature Anthology of Medieval Hebrew Love Poems," *Prooftexts #5* (1985), pp. 105–35, and Scheindlin's book *Wine, Women, and Death* (Jewish Publication Society, 1986), pp. 77–134; Norman Roth, " 'Deal Gently with the Young Man': Love of Boys in Medieval Hebrew Poetry of Spain," *Speculum* (January 1982), pp. 20–51; Jerome Rothenberg with Harris Lenowitz and Charles Doria, editors, *A Big Jewish Book* (Doubleday Anchor, 1978), pp. 516–17.

Two early examinations of Jewish-renewal approaches to sexual ethics are Arthur Green's "A Contemporary Approach to Jewish Sexuality," in *The Second Jewish Catalog*, Sharon Strassfeld and Michael Strassfeld, editors (Jewish Publication Society, 1976), pp. 96–99, and Arthur Waskow, "Torah of the Heart and Innards: Body," in *Godwrestling* (op. cit.), pp. 96–109.

In regard to the emerging discussion on and new outlooks toward homosexuality and other contemporary Jewish sexual ethics, see the classic, dialogue-opening article by Hershel J. Matt, "Sin, Crime, Sickness, or Alternative Life Style?: A Jewish Approach to Homosexuality," *Judaism* (Winter 1978), pp. 13–24; Elliot Dorff, " 'This Is My Beloved, This Is My Friend': A Jewish Pastoral Letter on Human Sexuality" (Commission on Human Sexuality, Rabbinical Assembly, April 1994); *New Menorah*, Special Issue on "Celebrating Gay and Lesbian Awareness," Pesach 5751; Sara Paasche, David Rosen, and J. B. Sacks, *Ka'Afikim BaNegev: A Manual for Rabbis to Engage Their Communities in Embracing Lesbian and Gay Jews* (Rabbinical Assembly/Commission on Human Sexuality); Susan Weidman Schneider, *Jewish and Female* (Simon and Schuster, 1984); Christi Balka and Andy Rose, *Twice Blessed* (Beacon, 1992), and the ongoing work of Rabbi Rebecca Alpert, Martha Ackelsberg, and Judith Plaskow.

Two rabbinical students, Toba Spitzer and Shawn Israel Zevit, have written an excellent ritual for sanctifying sex and sensuality, *Kiddush Ta'avat Min* (Creative Liturgy Center, Reconstructionist Rabbinical College, 1995).

To these should be added Peter Pitzele's exploration of a postpatriarchal Judaism in *Our Father's Wells* (HarperSanFrancisco, 1995).

R E S T

On the Biblical issues of Shabbat, see Baruch A. Levine, "Excursuses 10 and 11," in *The JPS Torah Commentary: Leviticus* (Jewish Publication Society, 1989), pp. 270–81.

For the Kabbalah concerning Shabbat, see Isaiah Tishby, "Sabbath and Festivals," in *The Wisdom of the Zohar*, Volume III (Oxford University Press, 1989), pp. 1216–80, and Elliot Ginsburg, *The Sabbath in the Classical Kabbalah* (SUNY Press, 1989).

Crucial new approaches to Shabbat were set forth by Abraham Joshua Heschel, *The Sabbath* (Farrar, Straus, and Giroux, 1951), and Erich Fromm, *The Forgotten Language* (Holt, Rinehart, and Winston, 1951), pp. 241 ff., later elaborated by Fromm in *You Shall Be as Gods* (Holt, Rinehart, and Winston, 1966).

For a renewed Kabbalistic/Hassidic view of Shabbat, see Zalman Schachter, *Fragments of a Future Scroll* (Leaves of Grass Press, 1975), pp. 45–48, 137–48, and Zalman Schachter-Shalomi, *Paradigm Shift* (Jason Aronson, 1993).

On how to infuse modern societies with more equality, broader community, and deeper spirituality through shorter work weeks and more widespread community service, see Jeremy Rifkin, *The End of Work* (Putnam, 1995).

ॐ

Traditionally, just as we begin the exploration of Torah with a blessing, so we end with a special Kaddish to lift high the Great Name that includes all the names of those who learn together, in all times and places. Once again, as at the beginning of this book, I want to say this in a renewed form:

May the Godwrestling people Israel—
May all who wrestle in the dance of life—
May our teachers and their students and the students of their students—
May we ourselves and all whom we go forth to teach—
May all those everywhere who aim toward wisdom—
Be blessed with love and peace,
With a harmonious livelihood from working in harmony with earth,
With awareness that all these blessings come not from lonely effort
But from our efforts woven in the web of Unity.

Dear Reader: If this book has stirred in you further questions or thoughts about "down-to-earth Judaism," an interest in the process of Jewish renewal, or ideas that you think might be woven into a future edition of this book, please write me. The journal *New Menorah*, which I edit, deals with these questions. You can use this page to subscribe. I look forward to connecting with you.—AW

TO: Arthur Waskow
    Shalom Center/ALEPH
    6711 Lincoln Drive
    Philadelphia, PA 19119
    OR By E-mail: Malkhut@aol.com

Dear Arthur Waskow,
    My question, comment, or suggestion is

    Please enter my subscription to *New Menorah*. My check for $36 is enclosed.

Name _____

Address _____

_____

Phone/s _____

FAX _____

E-mail _____

INDEX

Aaron, 20, 299

Abigail, 267

Abishag, 267

Abortion, 348

Abraham, 18, 21, 86, 251, 255–256, 257, 356; clan of, 27, 258, 259

Absalom, 252

Adam. *See* Garden of Eden

Adler, Rachel, 329

Adultery, 247–248, 249, 251, 277–278, 326–328, 330; and ordeal of bitter waters, 247, 253, 277

African Americans, 208

Aggadah (extralegal code), 122–123

Agriculture (agrarianism), 5, 41–42; in biblical era, 5, 20–21, 27, 46, 147, 148, 149, 364; and drought, 21, 92–93; gardening and, 132; hydroponics and, 81; Israeli exports of, 80; modern practices of, 15–16, 43, 119, 121, 136; pesticide use in, 16, 118, 137; Talmud and, 61; Torah and, 80–81

Ahaz, King, 149

AIDs, 154, 314, 322

Akiba, Rabbi, 42, 50, 279

ALEPH: Alliance for Jewish Renewal, 121–122, 126–129, 385

American Jewish World Service, 210

American Jewry, 113, 194–195, 200–202, 204–205, 207, 311–312. *See also* United States

Anarchism, 198

Animals, 17, 34, 121; blood of, 74; domesticated, 27; firstborn, 41; *kashrut* and, 28–31, 33; lungs of, 72; male, 49; respect for (*tza'ar ba'alei chai'im*), 121, 127; slaughter of, 30–31, 44, 71; snake, 17, 34

Anorexia, 24, 141

Anti-Semitism, 3, 71, 205, 324

Aristotle, 301

Asceticism, 102, 103

Asham (guilt offering), 49–50

Assyrian invasion, 32, 279

Atomic bomb, 111

Auschwitz, 6

Baal Shem Tov, 118

Babylonia (Babylonians), 21, 149, 161, 190, 356, 362; exile from, 10, 23, 32, 41, 60, 91, 361; first temple and, 31, 94, 99; rabbis in, 269, 274, 275

Bal taschit (don't destroy), 121–123, 127. *See also* Environmentalism

Bar Kokhba revolt, 54, 80, 279, 291

Bar (Bat) Mitzvah, 318, 319, 333–334

Bathsheba, 258–259, 267

Battles: Bar Kokhba revolt, 54, 80; against philistines, 21–22; against Samarians, 23

Beit chesed (house of nurturing love), 223, 331–332, 339

Beit seichel (house of prudence), 223, 332

ben Eleazar, Rabbi Simeon, 95

ben Gamaliel, Rabban Simon, 84

Berman, Phyllis, 329, 331

Biblical era, 8–9, 52–53, 160, 165; agriculture in, 5, 20–21, 27, 46, 147, 148, 149, 364; economic issues in, 147–165, 174–175, 212–213; fasting during, 90–92; festivals during, 19–20, 33, 44–48, 51; food in, 8–9, 16, 18, 21–25, 26–29, 30, 31–36, 38–39, 40–41, 43–44, 48–51, 57, 59, 61, 71, 91, 107–108; gluttony and, 89–92; hunger during, 89; land ownership in, 149–150, 360; marriage in, 246–251, 253, 254, 258, 260; money in, 147–165, 182–183; poverty in, 162–165, 360; sexuality in, 243–268, 321; shabbat and, 19–20, 46, 354–364, 375; taxation in, 154–162; women in, 155–157, 243–268

Bikkurim (first fruits), 40

Bilhah (*pilegesh* to Jacob), 252

Birds, 28
Blessings, 11, 23, 122, 136–137, 231; over bread, 79; for festivals/occasions, 67; food and, 61–64, 65–68, 132, 133, 139, 387; over fruit trees, 62–63; over human excrement (Asher Yatzar), 104–105, 106, 140; Jewish renewal and, 125, 139–140; Kabbalah and, 100–101; for lovers, 340; for marriage, 281, 283; meaning of, 67–68; money and, 231, 238; for shabbat, 66–67; for weekday, 66; women and, 85–86
B'nai Jeshurun, Temple, 121
Boaz (husband to Ruth), 260–261
Body: breathing, 124–125; sacredness of, 31–32; sh'mirat haguf (protection of one's), 122, 127
Boycott, 120, 225
Bread, 79. See also Matzah; challah, 79–80, 85, 138
Brooklyn, N.Y., Jewish community in, 110
Buber, Martin, 198, 202, 335
Buddhism, 110
Bulimia, 22, 141
Bundism (Yiddishe Arbeiters Bund), 113, 196–197
Burnt offering (olah), 50
Business, 173–175, 372, 388

Calendar, Jewish, 37
Cannibalism, 22
Capitalism, 209; in the United States, 204–205
Cardin, Rabbi Nina Beth, 5
Carnal Israel (Daniel Boyarin), 285
Celibacy, 266, 272, 317, 323
Chattat (sin-offering), 49–50
Chicken. See Poultry
Chief Rabbinate (Israel), 81
Childbirth, 3, 259, 261, 265–266, 291–293
Children, 18, 87, 255–256, 259, 260, 261, 268, 271, 318, 319. See also Family
Children of Light, 54
Chosen people, 8
Christianity, 53, 110, 185, 196, 269, 270, 282, 295, 324
Circumcision, 18–19, 41, 67, 255, 256–257, 302, 356
Class issues, 32
Clothes, 91, 92, 95, 96, 124, 163
Cohen, Jeremy, 291
Commerce. See also Marketplace relations; Money; business and, 173–175, 372, 388; ethical behavior and, 178–180; talmudic rabbis and, 177–184; weights and measures, 178
Communalism, 18, 198, 219
Communism, 197–198
Community, 2, 4, 16, 24, 65; individualism and, 65, 120, 310; intellectual resources on, 385

Conception, 314, 339
Conservative Jewry, 109, 113; eco-kosher practice and, 130; kashrut and, 70, 72, 77, 79, 81; marriage/divorce and, 326, 329; sexuality and, 316, 318, 321; Temple B'nai Jeshurun, 121
Consumerism, 121, 126, 236, 237–238
Contraception, 260, 292–293, 328, 348
Cooperatives, 132
Cost-sharing, 219–221
Creation story, 34–36, 38, 354–356, 363, 369

Dairy products: and kashrut (milchig), 70, 75–78; milk, as prepared by Jews (chalav Yisrael), 77
Daniel, Prophet, 94
David, King, 250, 251, 253, 258–261, 267, 271, 361
Dead Sea sects, 54, 109, 272
Death, 3
Democracy, 110, 310, 347
Deuteronomy, authorship of, 32
Diaspora Jewry, 60, 79, 80, 114, 115, 190, 225, 269
Divorce, 172, 251, 281, 329–331; civil law and, 330; egalitarian, 330–331, 345; get (bill of divorce), 293–294, 330; talmudic rabbis and, 293–294
Douglas, Mary, 34
Down-to-Earth Judaism. See also ALEPH; Eco-Judaism; Eco-kosher; Jewish renewal; festivals and, 372; food and, 107–143; intellectual resources for, 383–391; kashrut and, 121–126; money and, 212–239; sex and, 310–350; shabbat (rest) and, 371–381; work and, 372
Drought, 21, 92–93, 124

Earth cycles, 45, 318, 319–320, 358–359
Eastern European Jews, 86, 112, 113, 194–195, 196–199, 200–202, 204, 387; emigration to United States, 198–199, 200–202, 204
Eating disorders, 22, 24, 141
Ecclesiastes (Kohelet), 278–279, 319
Eco-Judaism, 96
Eco-kosher, 87–88, 107–143, 221, 225. See also Down-to-Earth Judaism; Eco-Judaism; Jewish renewal; God and, 131–132; kashrut and, 88, 117–118, 128, 135–137; practice of, 135–137
Eco-kosher project, 126–129
Eggs, 74. See also Dairy products
Egypt(ians), 149; food and, 33; Jews in, 60; liberation from, 19, 22, 29, 66, 154, 217, 257–258, 334, 355, 363

Eilberg-Schwartz, Howard, 34–35, 38, 256
Einstein, Albert, 98
Eleazar, Rabbi, 293
Eliezer, Rabbi, 84, 179, 284
Elimelekh, Rabbi of Lizensk, 105–106
Elisha, Prophet, 22
Elon, Ari, 275
Energy (heat/light/power), 124
Enoch, Book of, 94
Environmentalism, 47–48, 89, 94–96, 106, 118,
    121, 210, 316, 388. *See also* Bal taschit; Eco-
    Judaism; Pollution; as a Jewish issue, 6, 88,
    94–96, 125, 214–217, 226–227, 372,
    387–388; modernism and, 119–125; as a
    spiritual crisis, 216; Talmud and, 94–96,
    125; women and, 229–230
Epstein, Isidore, 288
Esau, 19, 27, 253
Esther, 253, 275
Ethical behavior, 121–123, 179, 325
Eve. *See* Garden of Eden
Ezekiel, Prophet, 23, 37, 248, 360, 361

Falk, Marcia, 135
False messiah, 305, 306
Family: childrearing, 18, 48, 87–88, 255–256, 260,
    261, 268, 271, 318, 319; extended, 88;
    food and, 23, 24; homosexuals and, 322;
    Kibbutz and, 203, 334; levirate marriage
    and, 260, 261; modern era, 228–229; in
    rabbinical era, 228–229; sexual relations
    and, 260; work and, 173
Famine, 21, 23, 89, 90, 92, 94
Farming, 43
Fasting, 22, 90–93, 94; biblical era and, 90–92;
    rabbinical era and, 92–94; sexual abstinence
    and, 60, 91, 92; Tisha B'Av and, 141;
    Yom Kippur and, 60, 90–91, 92, 141, 362
Feminism, 110, 118, 137–138, 142, 208, 220,
    229, 329. *See also* Women; and God,
    perception of, 230
Festivals (Celebrations), 3, 33, 67, 180, 234, 312,
    386. *See also* Shabbat; *specific holidays*; in
    America, 44–45, 47–48, 79; in biblical era,
    19–20, 33, 44–48, 51; Down-to-Earth
    Judaism and, 372; earth (life) cycles and,
    45, 318, 319–320, 325, 347, 358–359; in
    Israel, 202; in modern era, 51, 312; in
    other cultures, 34
Fig trees, 19
First born, 41, 42, 93
Fish, 27, 34
Fishermen, 27
Flood, 17

Food (Diet, Eating, Meals), 1, 10, 15–16, 19, 36.
    See also Eco-kosher; *Kashrut*; in biblical era,
    16, 18, 21–25, 26–29, 30, 31–36, 38–39,
    40–41, 43–44, 48–51, 57, 59, 61, 71, 91,
    107–108; blessings and, 61–64, 65–68,
    132, 133, 139; boycotts of, 120; family
    and, 23–24; festivals and, 58–59, 79; God
    and, 18, 40–41; Hassidim and, 72, 77,
    102–103; intellectual resources on, 386–
    387; manna as, 19–21, 29, 64, 355; in
    modern era, 15–16, 26, 38, 41, 81, 107–
    116; organically grown, 26, 137; rabbinical
    era and, 38, 57–64, 69–82, 107–108;
    sacredness of, 24, 40–43, 50; tithes and, 85;
    Torah and, 38, 65, 132, 134; unhealthy,
    122; women and, 18–19, 79, 108–111;
    words as, 23, 55, 87–88, 139
Food preparation, cooking, 74, 133, 134; men/
    women and, 18–19, 84, 87–88, 133, 171–
    172
Freud, Sigmund, 98
Fromm, Erich, 371
Fruit (trees), 41, 46, 62–63, 100

Gamaliel, Rabban, 278
Gandhism, 118
Garden of Eden (Garden of Delight), 17–20, 21,
    100, 119, 136, 186, 246–247, 268, 315,
    363, 374–375
Gates of Mitzvah, 113
Gay rights, 208
Gemara, 62, 366
Gender issues, 4–5, 133–134, 171–172, 374–375.
    See also Men; Women
Gershom, Rabbenu, 282, 293, 327
Ghetto, 110
Glatt kosher, 72–73
Gluttony, 89, 91
God, 28, 73; and eco-kosher practice, 130–131;
    economic issues and, 161–162, 186–187;
    feminism and, 230; food and, 18, 40–41;
    gender of, 142; hassidim and, 230;
    kabbalists and, 99–101, 368–371; manna
    and, 20
Goddess worship, 130
Gold, Rabbi Shefa, 139
Goldman, Emma, 198
Gordon, Aaron David, 114
Grace. *See* Blessings
Grains, 27, 41, 47
Grape(vines), 19, 27. *See also* Wine
Greco-Roman culture, 53
Greeks, 53–54, 58, 296, 301–302. *See also*
    Hellenism

Guide of the Perplexed (Maimonides), 97–98, 301–302

Guilt: offering (*asham*), 49–50; and sex, 340

Halakha (legal code), 122–123, 310, 325
HaLevi, Yehudah, 299
HaNagid, Samuel, 296–298
Hanina bar Pappa, Rabbi, 62
Hanukkah, 3, 45, 138
Hassidim, 102–103, 109, 202, 230; human waste and, 105–106; Jewish renewal and, 142; *kashrut* and, 72, 77, 102–103; Lubavitcher, 118; rabbis, 141; sexual relations and, 305, 317; Torah and, 131
Havurot, 88, 193, 218, 318, 319, 320
Health insurance, 174–175
Hekhsher (certificate for *kashrut*), 80–81, 115–116
Hellenism, 8–9, 53–54, 322; rabbinical era and, 58, 108, 109, 269; science and, 28; sex and, 270–273
Heschel, Rabbi Abraham Joshua, 77, 371
Heschel, Rabbi Abraham Joshua (Hassidic rabbi of Apt), 141
Heschel, Susannah, 137
Hezekiah, King, 95
Hillel, 183
Hiroshima, 6
History, use of, 2, 6, 10, 36–37
Holidays, 44–45. *See also* Festivals/Celebrations; in the United States, 45
Holiness Code, 149
Holocaust, 3, 8, 56, 108, 111, 113, 115, 199, 204
Holocaust museum (Washington, D.C.), 207
Homosexuality, 248, 250, 252, 260, 272, 313, 320–325, 348, 389–390; family and, 322, 325; marriage (commitment) and, 343, 344, 348; Spanish Jewry and, 297–300
Honey bees, 70
Hosea, Prophet, 248–249, 253, 271, 306, 344
Hunger, 22–23, 94. *See also* Famine
Hunters, 27, 30
Hydroponics, 81

Ibn Ezra, Moses, 298–299
Ibn Gabirol, Solomon, 299
Iggeret HaKodesh ("The Holy Letter"), 303–304
Illness, 48
Incest, 249–250
Individualism, 2; and community, 63, 120, 310
Industrialism, 119, 196
Insects, and *kashrut*, 28, 70
Intermarriage, 78, 343

Investments, 127, 218; divestment, 225; socially responsible, 125–126, 225, 227, 237–238, 388
Isaac, 18, 21, 27, 86, 251, 255, 256
Isaiah, 60, 91; Second Isaiah, 362
Ishmael, 27, 255
Ishmael, Rabbi, 94
Israel (State of), 3, 80, 81, 114–115, 210. *See also* Zionism; agricultural exports of, 80; *kashrut* and, 69, 74, 80–81, 115; kibbutzim in, 81, 115, 202–204; modern Jewry and, 109, 205, 207, 208; philanthropy and, 209–210, 234; socialism in, 114, 197, 199, 202; women and, 69, 74, 80–81, 115, 203
I-Thou relationship, 336, 375

Jacob, 19, 21, 27, 73, 251, 255
Jacob, Rabbi Walter, 113
Jacobson, Rabbi Burt, 139
Jeremiah, Prophet, 41, 152, 248, 361
Jerusalem, 10, 25, 41, 90, 108
Jewish Agency, 209
Jewish Federations, 209
Jewish Fund for Justice, 135, 219
Jewish National Fund, 7, 209
Jewish renewal, 3, 142–143, 205–208, 210–211. *See also* ALEPH; Down-to-Earth Judaism; food and, 132–144; intellectual rersources on, 385; justice and, 212–214; *kashrut* and, 121–123, 124–126; marriage/divorce and, 326, 330; spirituality and, 142, 385
Jews. *See also* American Jewry; affluence of, 205–207, 389; African Americans and, 208; as chosen people, 8; claustrophobia among, 7; distinctiveness of, 31–36, 38, 78; Eastern Europe, 86, 112, 113, 194–195, 196–199, 200–202, 204, 387; farmers as, 5, 27; in the Middle Ages, 9; and non-Jews, 27, 78, 188, 189, 190, 262–265; past, use of the, 37; time, perception of, 36–37; victimization and, 208
Jews, Money and Social Responsibility (Shefa Fund), 238
Joel, Book of, 90
Jonah, Book of, citations from, 91
Jonathan (son of King Saul), 21–22, 259, 267
Jubilee (*yovel*) year, 149–152, 164, 227–228, 232, 359–360, 361–362, 364, 371, 388
Judaism, contemporary. *See* Down-to-Earth Judaism
Jungian psychology, 118, 130
Justice. *See also* Tzedakah; economic justice and, 178, 179, 180–181, 195, 227–228; Jewish renewal and, 212–214; Jewish tradition and, 91, 151, 163, 174, 178, 179, 180–181, 325, 358–359, 360–364; modern era and, 363; politics and, 194–204; social responsibility and, 41

Kabbalah, 387; consumerism and, 236–237; fasting and, 94; God and, 99–101, 368–371; human waste, 105–106; Jewish renewal and, 142; *kashrut* and, 98–103; sexual issues and, 296, 305, 306, 311; shabbat and, 368–371

Kaplan, Mordecai, 385

Kashrut, 3, 7, 15, 28–31, 33, 121, 386–387. *See also* Eco-kosher; amphibians and, 28, 34; animals and, 27, 28–29, 30–31, 41, 44, 70, 71–72, 74; birds and, 70; commercial success of, 115–116; conservative Jewry and, 70, 72, 77, 79, 81; dairy products and, 70, 75–78; distinctions among Jews, 72–73; domesticated animals and, 27; Down-to-Earth Judaism and, 121–126; ethics and, 123, 124–125; fish and, 70, 76; fowl (poultry) and, 71, 75–76; glatt, 72–73; hassidim, 72, 77, 102–103; *Hekhsher* (certification of), 80–81, 115–116; insects and, 70; in Israel, 69, 74, 80–81, 115, 203; kabbalah and, 98–103; kitchens and, 83–88; mammals and, 27, 70; meat and, 29–31, 33, 38, 71, 73–74, 75–78, 81; medical justification for, 97–98; *milchig/fleishig,* 75–78, 97–98, 107; in modern era, 81, 82, 111–113, 115–116; non-Jews and, 115–116; opposition to, 120; origin of, 27–28; orthodox Jewry and, 70, 72, 77, 81, 115; ovens and, 77; *pareve,* 76, 81; plants and, 78–81; preparation for, 71–74; purpose of, 38–39, 69–70, 97–103; questions about, 82; reform Jewry and, 112–113; salt, 74; sciatic nerve, and 73; talmudic rabbis and, 69–70, 71, 83, 97–98; time restrictions and, 77; *treyf* (unkosher), 72, 107, 126–127; utensils and, 76; wine and, 78–79; women and, 83–88

Kibbutz, 81, 115, 202–204, 210, 334, 387

Kiddish, 64, 79, 370

King, Martin Luther, Jr., 118

Kings, Book of, 22

Kohanim, 31, 263, 306. *See also* Priests

Kosher. *See Kashrut*

Labor relations: in biblical era, 174–175; labor unions (guilds), 175, 195–197, 199, 204; strikes, 175; talmudic rabbis and, 174–176

Labor Zionism, 197, 199, 203; Histadrut and, 203

Lamentations, Book of, 23

Land, 21, 147–148; ownership of, 149–150, 360

Landauer, Gustav, 198

Landsmannschaften, 200–202, 204, 209, 210, 218

Leah, 253

Lemlich, Clara, 198

Levites (tribe), 41–42, 80, 159–162, 263, 306

Leviticus, 31–32

Life cycle, 45, 151, 318, 319–320, 325, 347, 358–359; ceremonies for, 333, 334; contemporary Judaism and, 325

Life phases, 337–340

Lilith, 292, 305

Liturgy, 124

Livelihood (occupations), 1, 48, 166, 167. *See also* Work; affluence and, 205–206; business and, 173–175, 372, 388; economic justice and, 195, 227–228; entrepreneurship, 173; professions and, 205; right to a job, 227; talmudic rabbis and, 168–170, 173–174

Locke, John, 98

Love, hunger for, 89

Luria, Isaac, 99–101

Luxemburg, Rosa, 198

macrbiotic diet, 120

Maimonides (Rambam), 97–98, 187, 188, 234, 289, 296, 301–302, 303, 306

Mammals, and *kashrut,* 27, 70

Mamzerim ("illegitimate" child), 294, 330

Manasseh, King, 149

Manna, 19–21, 29, 64; story of, 20, 355

Marketplace relations, talmudic rabbis and, 177–181

Marriage, 313–314, 319, 326–329. *See also* Divorce; Sexual Relationships; Wedding; Zug; agreements (*ketubah*), 344–345; betrothal (*shiddukhin*), 280; in biblical era, 246–251, 253, 254, 258, 260; commitment ceremonies, 326; economic issues in, 171–172, 344–345, 349; equality in, 326, 343–344, 345–347; homosexuals and, 325, 343–344; intermarriage, 244–245, 262–265; in Mishnah, 280; polycentric, 328; polygamy and, 260, 282, 317; sexual relations and, 281–282, 283–287, 316–318; talmudic rabbis and, 273, 276–278, 280–287, 291–293, 316–317, 329–330

Matalon, Rabbi Rolando, 121

Matzah, 79

Mazon, 135, 210

Meat, 15–16; blood of, 74; broiling, 74; butcher shops and, 81; dairy (*fleishig*) and, 75–78; diet and, 137; *kashrut* and, 29–31, 33, 38, 71, 73–74, 75–78, 81; organs (heart/liver), 74; porging and, 73–74; salting of, 74; sheep, 27, 41; slaughter of, 28, 30–31, 71–72

Medieval period, 8

Meir, Golda, 199

Melchitzedek, 18

Men: circumcision and, 18–19, 41, 67, 255, 256–257; and homemaking, 84, 87–88, 133; and *mikveh*, 344; Mishnah and role of, 84–85; misogyny of, 54, 248; Modern era and, 87–88, 110; as rulemakers, 83; seminal emissions and, 48, 244, 265–266, 292, 305; sex and, 249–250, 292; Torah, study of, 85; and women, dominance over, 243–254, 257, 264, 271–274, 294, 306, 312, 323; and women, equality with, 305–306, 312–314, 323, 374

Menstruation, 7, 48, 79, 244, 261; menarche ceremony and, 334; *niddah* (taboo) and, 287–291, 329, 331, 345; talmudic rabbis and, 265–266, 273, 287–291

Merton, Thomas, 118

Mesopotamia, 161

Messiah, 21, 53, 66, 94, 279, 292, 305–306, 367, 378

Meyer, Marshall, 107

Michae (wife of King David), 258, 267

Mid-life, 347

Mikveh (ritual bath), 266, 276, 290, 344

Milder, Rabbi Laurence K., 224

Miriam, 257

Mishkan, 154–155, 357, 366, 367

Mishnah, 55, 57, 62–63, 288. *See also* Talmud; blessings and, 139; dairy and meat, 75; gender issues in, 84–85, 290–291; marriage and, 280; shabbat and, 364–365; taxation and, 157

Misogyny, 54, 248. *See also* Men

Moab, 261

Modern era, 8, 9, 56, 108–116, 123, 143, 363; defined, 6; economy in, 152, 172–173, 185–186, 213, 215; family in, 228–229; festivals/celebrations in, 51, 58, 59–60, 88, 128, 137, 312, 345; food and, 15–16, 26, 38, 41, 81, 107–116; gender issues in, 87–88, 111, 228–230; *kashrut* and, 81, 82, 110, 111–113, 115–116, 121–123

Modernism, 110–114, 142, 143, 270, 308–309. *See also* Postmodernism; doubts about, 111; environmentalism and, 119–125; Jews and, 195–196, 199, 306

Money, 10, 211; biblical era and, 147–165; Christianity, Jews and, 185; debts, 151, 364; Down-to-Earth Judaism and, 223–230, 231–239; ethical questions about, 221–222, 231–239; intellectual resources on, 387–389; interest, 184–185; investments, 125–126, 127, 218, 225, 227, 237–238; loans (borrowing), 150, 182–185; modern era and, 185–186; openness about (cost sharing), 219–221; pensions and, 175; profiteering (*hafka'at sh'arim*), 170, 179; saving, 237; sharing of (*tzedakah*), 186–189, 231, 234–235; Torah and, 232–235, 237–238; wealth 151–152, 185, 205–207, 389

Moon: full, 58; new (Rosh Chodesh), 45, 47, 57, 93, 329

Moses, 32, 186, 257, 262, 355; Sinai and, 20, 55, 94, 102, 147, 217, 266, 356, 357–358

Motherhood. *See also* Children; breastfeeding and, 87

Mourning (*shiva*), 67, 95–96

Movement for a New Society, 220

Muslims, 116, 137, 269, 295, 296, 327

Mysticism, 94, 98–103, 118. *See also* Kabbalah

Nachmanides (Rabbi Moshe ben Nachman), 307

Naomi, 21, 260

Native Americans, 130

Nazarite, 49

Nehemiah, 362

Neo-conservatives, 208

New Israel Fund, 210, 234

Newton, Isaac, 98

Nile River, 21

Nixon, Richard M., 132

Noah, 291

Non-Jews, 115–116, 188, 189, 190. *See also* Intermarriage

Nuclear energy, 118, 131

Nuclear weapons, 111, 224–225

Offerings, 386. *See also* Sacrifice; Temple offerings; individual, 48–51; at the Temple, 40–41, 43–44, 48–51, 53, 57, 58, 61, 64, 71, 124, 138

Oil (cooking), 41

Olah (burnt offering), 50

Onan, 292

Organically grown food, 26, 137

Oriental Jews, 70, 102, 199

Orthodox Jewry, 109, 113; agriculture and, 81; eco-kosher and, 126, 130, 137; *kashrut* and, 70, 72, 77, 81, 115; marriage/divorce and, 326, 329; sexuality and, 317, 321

Packaging, 16, 26

Palestine, 202. *See also* Israel

Pareve, 76, 81

Patriarchs, 57

Peace offering (*shlamim*), 50

Pesach (Passover), 3, 28, 39, 45, 46, 50, 83, 157;
 fasting and, 93; food and 58–59; *Haggadah*,
 58; matzah and, 79; meaning of, 59–60; in
 modern era, 59–60, 88, 128, 137;
 rabbinical teachings and, 58–60; seder, 58–
 59, 100, 136, 137–138, 194, 306

Philanthropy, 135, 209–210, 219, 234

Philistines, battle against, 21–22

Philo of Alexandria, 60, 109, 273

Philosophy, Jewish, 286, 301

Piercy, Marge, 140

Plato's *Symposium*, 58

P'nai Or Religious Fellowship, 117

Poetry, Jewish, 336; erotic, 296–300, 341, 390

Political (social) activism, 132, 142. *See also*
 Socialism; in biblical era, 160; Jews and,
 225–228; intellectual resources on, 385; in
 the United States, 197–198, 207–208;
 women and, 229

Pollution, 109, 125. *See also* Environmentalism

Population pressure, 310

Postmodernism, 118–119. *See also* Modernism

Poultry (chicken), 15, 27, 71, 75–76, 137

Poverty (poor people), 132, 134; in biblical era,
 162–165, 360; talmudic rabbis and, 180,
 188; Torah and, 91, 164–165, 183

Prayer, 57–58, 65, 85–86, 325. *See also* Blessings

Priests, 31, 34–35, 41, 176. *See also Kohanim*;
 Levites; rabbinical era and, 53, 169;
 sexuality and, 245–246, 262–263, 266;
 temple offerings and, 44, 57, 71, 80

Pri Eytz Hadar [*Fruit of the Beautiful Tree*] (Luria),
 100–102

Privacy, 203

Property, 48, 91; marriage and, 172

Prophets (*see also* by name), 19, 160, 361; and
 sexual issues, 248, 259, 262–263

Prophets, The, 66

Prostitution, 251, 263

Psalms, The, 66, 67

Psychotherapy, 51, 142

Puberty. *See* Youth

Punishment, 50; death as, 358; offering as, 48

Purchases, 121, 126, 127, 236, 237–238

Purim, 45, 138, 157

Rabbinate, Chief (Israel), 81

Rabbinical Assembly, 321

Rabbinical courts: *beit chesed* (love), 331–332, 339;
 beit din (judgment), 222, 331

Rabbinical era, 8–9, 53–68, 109. *See also* Talmudic
 rabbis

Rachel, 253

Rape, 251

Rationality, 113; and *kashrut*, 97–98

Rebekah, 19, 21, 253, 255

Reconstructionist movement, 69, 70, 109, 387;
 issues of sexuality and, 320, 326, 330

Reform Jewry, 69, 109; eco-kosher practice and,
 126, 130; *kashrut* and, 112–113, 387;
 marriage/divorce and, 316, 330; and
 nuclear weapons, 224–225; sexuality, issues
 of, 320, 326, 330; and traditional Judaism,
 112–113

Reich, Steven, 143

Reincarnation, 103

Religion, evolution of, 37

Reptiles, 17, 28, 34

Rest. *See also* Shabbat; intellectual resources on,
 391

Restaurants, 81

Reuben, 252

Roman Catholic Church, 225, 348

Roman Empire (Romans), 9, 54, 60, 129, 190,
 225, 364; defeat by, 80, 99

Rosh Chodesh (new moon), 45, 47, 57, 93, 329

Rosh Hashanah, 3, 45, 47, 138, 359; in modern
 era, 88, 345

Russia (Russians), 196, 206. *See also* Soviet Union

Ruth, 91, 138, 260–261, 262, 265

Sabbatai Zevi (Sabbatian messianists), 305–306,
 307

Sabbath. *See* Shabbat

Sabbatical (*shmitah*) year, 149–151, 164, 227–228,
 358–359, 360, 364, 371–372, 388

Sacrifice (offering), 30–31, 41, 43–44; during
 Pesach, 46; during Shavuot, 46; during
 Yom Kippur, 47

Samaria, 22–23

Samuel, Prophet, 159

Sanhedrin, 278–279

Sarah, 18, 21, 253, 255

Sartre, Jean Paul, 98

Saul, King, 21–22, 250–251

Schachter-Shalomi, Rabbi Zalman, 117–118, 126

Scholem, Gershom, 306

Science, and modern Judaism, 110, 112

Seasons of Our Joy (Waskow), 1

Second Isaiah, 362

Secular Jews, 69, 112, 113–114, 118, 130

Senior citizens, 175

Seventh-Day Adventists, 116

Sex (sexuality), 3, 10, 18, 323, 340, 389. *See also* Sexual relationships; in biblical era, 243–268; bisexuality, 325; celibacy, 266, 272, 317, 323; contraception and, 260, 292–293, 328, 348; counselors, 342, 348; and disease, 314, 319; and family life, 243–244; fasting and, 60, 91, 92; Hellenism, influence of, 270–273; holiness of, 340; homosexuality, 248, 250, 252, 260, 272, 313, 320–325, 348; intellectual resources on, 387–390; intercourse, 303–304; masturbation and, 260, 292, 330, 335; in midlife, 347; pleasure of, 260, 261, 267, 279, 285–287, 315–316, 322; and power relationships, 300, 321; and procreation, 18, 255–256, 260, 261, 268, 271, 279, 287, 291–293, 294, 310, 316; prohibitions of, 249–250, 260, 288; promiscuity, 262–263; prostitution, 251, 313; rape, 251, 313; as sin, 323; and Spanish Jews, 296–300, 301; talmudic rabbis and, 168, 170–171, 178, 269–274, 278–279, 311, 316–317, 321

Sex education, 335–337

Sexual relationships, 243, 337–339, 341–347, 348–349. *See also* Divorce; Marriage; Zug; adultery, 247–248, 249, 251, 277–278, 326–328, 330; ceremonies and, 325, 326, 334, 341, 343–344, 345; Down-to-Earth Judaism and, 310–350; ethics and, 310–332, 348–349; equality of, 305–306, 310, 312–315, 323, 326, 343–347; jealousy and, 247, 253, 277; in marriage, and, 281–282, 283–287, 316–318; monogamy and, 314, 317, 319, 326–328, 345; with non-Jews, 244–245, 262–265, 343; nonmarital, 307–308, 315, 316, 318, 340; *pilegesh* (concubines), 251–252, 254, 307–308, 318, 325; virginity and, 248, 249–250

Shabbat (Sabbath), 3, 33, 41, 45, 83, 93, 138, 157, 391; in biblical era, 19–20, 46, 354–364, 375; blessings during, 66–67, 345; Down-to-Earth Judaism and, 371–381; justice, and issues of, 358–359, 360–364; Kabbalists and, 368–371; Kiddush during, 64, 79; meaning of, 214, 217–218, 353–372; in rabbinical era, 57, 364–367; women and, 79, 85–86, 290, 373–375; work and, 364–367, 372, 373

Shalom bayit, 325

Shavuot, 45, 46, 88, 115, 138, 157

Shechita (slaughter), 71–72, 75, 98

Shefa Fund, 210, 234, 238

Shekhinah (divine feminine), 304–305, 311, 368–371

Shepherds, 5, 27, 43, 46

Shlamim (peace offering), 50

Sh'ma, 57

Sh'mini Atzeret, 47, 359

Shochet (ritual slaughterer), 71, 74, 137

Shofar (Ram's horn), 27, 232, 362

Shulchan Aruch (code of Jewish law), 289–290

Siegel, Hanna Tiferet, 139

Sin, 48, 323

Sinai, Mt., 260; revelation at, 20, 55, 94, 102, 147, 217, 266, 355–356

Sin-offering (*chattat*), 49–50

Slavery, 152, 163, 194, 217, 358, 360, 361, 363

Socialism, 194–200, 203; Israel and, 114, 197, 199; Jews and, 112, 113, 118, 204, 207, 210; and rabbinical law, 198–199; United States and, 197–199; women and, 198–199

Sodom and Gomorrah, 261

Solomon, King, 159, 250, 258–259

Song of Songs, 19, 253–254, 267–268, 271, 278–279, 306, 311, 323; sexual ethic in, 315–316, 322, 344

Soviet Union, 199, 202, 204; Jews from, 69, 206

Spain, Jews in, 295–300, 301

Spices, 125

Spirituality, intellectual resources on, 385

Sufism, 118, 130

Sukkot, 47, 93, 115, 128, 157, 359

Swados, Elizabeth, 143

Synagogues, 193, 209, 320–321

Syphilis, 314

Talmud, 68. *See also* Gemara; *Halakha*; Mishnah; Talmudic rabbis; Torah; Babylonian influence on, 270; *B'rakhot*, 61, 62, 63; characteristics of, 61, 63; drought and, 21, 92–93, 124; environmentalism, 94–96, 125; human excrement and, 105; Israelite influence on, 270; marriage and, 283–287; meals and, 139; origin of, 55–56, 57; sex and, 270, 285–287, 307–308; *tzedakah* and, 186–187, 232

Talmudic rabbis: commerce and, 177–184; economic issues and, 169–176, 179, 180–181, 183–185, 186–189, 189–192; emergence of, 53–54; fasting and, 92–94; food and, 38, 57–64, 69–82, 107–108; gender issues and, 170–172, 292–293; Hellenism's influence on, 270–273; *kashrut* and, 69–70, 71, 83, 97–98; livelihood and, 166–167, 169–170 173–174; marriage/divorce and, 273, 276–278, 280–287, 291–293, 329–330; Messiah and, 259, 378; Pesach and, 58–60; political

issues and, 225; prayer and, 57–58;
sexuality issues and, 168, 170–171, 178,
269–274, 311, 316–317, 321, 389–390;
shabbat and, 57, 364–367; Song of Songs
and, 278–279; Torah and, 55–56, 168–
169, 272–275, 276–278, 311; *tzedakah* and,
186–189, 232, 235; women, attitude
toward, 84–86, 271–274, 306; work,
teachings about, 169–176; Yom Kippur
and, 60
Tamar, 258, 261, 262, 265
Taxation. *See also* Temple offerings; Tithes; in
biblical era, 154–157, 158–162; internal
(for Jewish institutions), 190; in modern
era, 191–192; progressive, 191; in
rabbinical era, 189–192
Technology, 119, 213, 215, 372, 373
Television, 3
Temple, 10, 25, 47, 109, 157, 266, 288; destruction
of, 53, 80, 85, 90–91, 99, 250, 275, 361;
first (Babylonia), 31, 157; Pesach and, 58;
second (Jerusalem), 60, 80, 91, 156; shabbat
and, 364; Yom Kippur and, 60
Temple offerings, 40–41, 43–44, 53, 124. *See also*
Sacrifice; food and, 57, 61, 71; holy days
and, 58, 64, 138; as income taxation, 158–
162; by individuals, 48–51; *korbanot* (food
offerings), 43–44; *Tenufah* (physical
elevations), 40–41; *Terumah* (uplifting
dedication), 40–41, 57
T'fillin, 27
Thanksgiving (American), 45, 47
Thurman, Howard, 118
Ticktin, Rabbi Max, 151, 331
Tikkun olam (healing the world), 139, 218, 345
Time, understanding of, 37
Tisha B'Av, 90, 91, 92, 141
Tithes, 41, 43, 80, 85, 150, 189. *See also* Taxation
Torah: agriculture and, 80–81; and eco-kosher,
128; economic issues and, 150, 153, 155,
213–214, 232–235, 237–238; food and,
38, 65, 132, 134; as Goddess, 275–276;
hassidim and, 131; justice issues in, 91,
151, 163; meat slaughter in, 28, 33;
poverty and, 91, 164–165, 183; priesthood
and, 42; rabbis, and study of, 55–56, 85,
168–170, 272–273, 275–278, 311;
rationality of, 98; sexual issues and, 246–
254, 267–268; Song of Songs, 267–268;
strangers, treatment of, 324, 358; tales of,
3; talk and, 139; tithing and, 159; war and,
155; women, and study of, 87, 133, 277–
278; work and, 166–176
Tradition, importance of, 2, 6, 16

Trees, 19, 41, 46, 47, 100; blessing over, 62–63;
protection of, 94–96
T'shuvah (turning life around), 377–378
Tu B'Shvat, 45, 100–102, 136, 138
Tzedakah (moral responsibility/sharing), 388;
contemporary Jews and, 187–188, 218–
221, 231, 232–235, 325, 342; talmudic
rabbis and, 186–187, 232
Tzipporah, 257
Tzitzit (fringes), 27, 372

Union of Orthodox Jewish Congregations, 81, 115
United Jewish Appeal (UJA), 117, 219
United States: economics of, 204–205; holidays in,
44–45, 47–48, 79; Jews in the, 113, 194–
195, 200–202, 204–205, 207, 311–312;
pluralism of, 348; political activism in,
197–198, 207–208
Universalism, 110, 118

Vegetables, 27, 137
Vegetarianism, 15, 26, 100, 120, 135–136, 387

Washing ritual, 62, 346; fast days and, 91, 92
Waskow, Arthur, as youth in Baltimore, 83
Wedding, 3, 67, 93, 281–282, 313, 343
Whole-earth Judaism. *See* Down-to-Earth Judaism
Wine, 41; alcoholism and, 180–181; blessing over,
62; *kashrut* and, 78–79; Pesach and, 58
Women, 4–5, 7; abuse (harassment) of, 313; in
biblical era, 155–157, 243–268; blessings
and, 85–86; commandments for, 79; in
Eastern Europe, 86; economic issues and,
155–157, 227; environmentalism and,
229–230; equality of, 305–306, 310–315,
323, 374–375; food and, 18–19, 79, 84,
87–88, 108–111, 171–172; girls, in Jewish
culture, 86; as homemakers, 84–86, 171–
172; isolation of, 56; *kashrut* and, 83–88;
kibbutz and, 203; lesbianism, 250, 252;
liberation of, 59, 142, 312; marriage/
divorce, 258, 293–294; men and, 4–5,
133–134, 171–172, 243–254, 257, 264,
271–274, 294, 305–306, 312–314, 323,
374–375; menopause and, 347;
menstruation and, 7, 48, 79, 244, 261,
265–266, 271–274, 287–291, 294, 306,
312, 323, 329, 331, 334, 345; and *Mikveh*
(ritual bath), 266, 276, 290; in Mishnah,
role of, 84–85, 290–291, 387; in modern
era, 87–88, 111, 228–230; motherhood
and, 87; non-Jewish, 262, 264; politics and
198–199, 229; power of, in biblical

Women (*continued*)
253–254; prayers (*tekhinnes*) for, 85–86;
protection of, 277; rabbinical era and, 84–
86; sexual issues, 243–268, 273, 285–286;
shabbat and, 79, 85–86, 290, 373–375;
Song of Songs, 267–268; Talmud, attitude
toward, in, 84–86, 271–274, 306; Torah
and, 87, 133, 277–278; virginity of, 248,
249–250; work and, 170–172
Women Strike for Peace, 229
Words, food as, 23, 55, 87–88, 139
Work, 2, 10; Down-to-Earth Judaism and, 372;
environmentalism and, 125; ethical issues
and, 166–167, 169–170; family and, 173;
in modern era, 172–173, 215, 349; in
rabbinical era, 166–176; shabbat and, 364–
367, 372, 373; Torah and, 166–176;
women and, 170–172
Workers: in biblical era, 158; labor relations
and, 174–176, 195–197, 199, 204;
oppression of, and food, 26; *oshek*
(nonoppression of), 123; political activism
and, 196–200

Workmen's Circle (Arbeiter Ring), 113
World War I, 111, 198

Yehudah, 258, 261
Yemenite Jews, 70
Yeskel, Felice, 220
Yiddish, 109, 112, 196
Yochanan, Rabbi (the Beautiful), 276
Yochanan, Rabbi ben Zakkai, 277–278
Yogi, 118
Yom Kippur, 3, 45, 47, 58, 60, 290, 345, 359;
fasting and, 90–91, 92, 141, 362
You Shall Be as Gods (Fromm), 371
Youth (puberty), 333, 335; sex education for,
335–337

Zealots, 53
Zen, 130
Zionism, 112, 113–114, 197, 199, 207, 309
Zohar (Book of Splendor), 98, 100, 296, 304–
305, 368–370
Zug (unmarried couple), 319, 328, 337–340, 341–
343, 346; commitment ceremonies for, 343

Arthur Ocean Waskow and his wife, Phyllis Ocean Berman, decided to share a new middle name when they got married. They live in a lively integrated Philadelphia neighborhood, Mount Airy, among trees, streams, and a Toonerville Trolley. In his own down-to-earth life, Waskow worries about food and money, enjoys sex, and oscillates between overwork and laziness. He has two grown children of his own and is "associate parent" for three others. He is a Pathfinder of ALEPH: Alliance for Jewish Renewal, an international network with headquarters in Philadelphia.

Since 1969, Waskow has been one of the leading creators of theory, practice, and institutions for Jewish renewal. He founded the journal *New Menorah*, and wrote such classics of Jewish renewal as *The Freedom Seder; Godwrestling, Round Two;* and *Seasons of Our Joy.* He helped found the National Havurah Committee and taught at the Reconstructionist Rabbinical College, Swarthmore College, and Temple University.

Waskow has often worked closely with other members of his family. When his children, David and Shoshana, were young, they wrote together a book of tales of the Creation, *Before There Was a Before.* With his brother Howard he wrote *Becoming Brothers*, a "wrestle in two voices" about their process of conflict and reconciliation. He and Phyllis, who is also a leader of Jewish renewal and is the founding director of a unique school for adult immigrants and refugees from all around the world, often join to speak, teach new forms of prayer, tell stories from their book *Tales of Tikkun*, and lead retreats and workshops in many Jewish, interreligious, and college settings.

Waskow was born in Baltimore in 1933. He studied United States history at Johns Hopkins University and the University of Wisconsin. He worked as a legislative assistant for a U. S. congressman, and through the 1960s, as one of the founding Fellows of the Institute for Policy Studies, he wrote several books on military strategy, nonviolence, and social change, and was active in opposing the Vietnam War.

Judith Hankin, the printmaker and graphic artist whose works illustrate this book, lives in Eugene, Oregon. These prints are based on papercuts—a traditional form of Jewish art in Eastern Europe. Hankin brings to them a new freshness and boldness of imagery. Her work, inspired by the Jewish life cycle, festival calendar, liturgy, and spiritual practices, brings new life and spirit to the holidays, rituals, and traditions. Hankin is a member of the American Guild of Judaic Art and the Accredited Synagogue Artists of the Union of American Hebrew Congregations. She has exhibited for more than twenty years in numerous solo and group shows across the country, and her papercut designs can be found in galleries, museum shops, synagogues, and publications.